£48.95

SPORT
AND
PUBLIC POLICY

Social, Political, and Economic Perspectives

Charles A. Santo, PhD
University of Memphis

Gerard C.S. Mildner, PhD
Portland State University

Human Kinetics

Library of Congress Cataloging-in-Publication Data

Sport and public policy : social, political, and economic perspectives / Charles A. Santo,
Gerard C.S. Mildner, editors.
   p. cm.
 Includes bibliographical references and index.
 ISBN-13: 978-0-7360-5871-1 (hard cover)
 ISBN-10: 0-7360-5871-0 (hard cover)
 1. Sports--Economic aspects. 2. Sports--Social aspects. I. Santo, Charles Andrew
II. Mildner, Gerard C. S.
 GV716.S584 2010
 338.4'779604--dc22

2009039156

ISBN-10: 0-7360-5871-0 (print)
ISBN-13: 978-0-7360-5871-1 (print)

The Web addresses cited in this text were current as of July 2009, unless otherwise noted.

Acquisitions Editor: Myles Schrag; **Developmental Editor:** Kathleen Bernard; **Managing Editor:**
Melissa J. Zavala; **Assistant Editor:** Casey A. Gentis; **Copyeditor:** Robert Replinger; **Indexer:**
Andrea Hepner; **Permission Manager:** Dalene Reeder; **Graphic Designer:** Bob Reuther; **Graphic
Artist:** Tara Welsch; **Cover Designer:** Keith Blomberg; **Photographer (cover):** © Human Kinet-
ics; **Photographer (interior):** © Human Kinetics, unless otherwise noted; **Photo Asset Manager:**
Laura Fitch; **Photo Production Manager:** Jason Allen; **Art Manager:** Kelly Hendren; **Associate
Art Manager:** Alan L. Wilborn; **Illustrator:** Alan L. Wilborn; **Printer:** Sheridan Books

Printed in the United States of America   10 9 8 7 6 5 4 3 2 1

The paper in this book is certified under a sustainable forestry program.

Human Kinetics
Web site: www.HumanKinetics.com

United States: Human Kinetics
P.O. Box 5076
Champaign, IL 61825-5076
800-747-4457
e-mail: humank@hkusa.com

Canada: Human Kinetics
475 Devonshire Road Unit 100
Windsor, ON N8Y 2L5
800-465-7301 (in Canada only)
e-mail: info@hkcanada.com

Europe: Human Kinetics
107 Bradford Road
Stanningley
Leeds LS28 6AT, United Kingdom
+44 (0) 113 255 5665
e-mail: hk@hkeurope.com

Australia: Human Kinetics
57A Price Avenue
Lower Mitcham, South Australia 5062
08 8372 0999
e-mail: info@hkaustralia.com

New Zealand: Human Kinetics
P.O. Box 80
Torrens Park, South Australia 5062
0800 222 062
e-mail: info@hknewzealand.com

E3430

Contents

PART IV   Sport and Globalization

Contributors

John Amis
University of Memphis

Greg Andranovich
California State University

Matt T. Brown
University of South Carolina

Matthew J. Burbank
University of Utah

Bryan E. Denham
Clemson University

Jennifer Dill
Portland State University

Charles H. Heying
Portland State University

Chad D. McEvoy
Illinois State University

Gerard C.S. Mildner
Portland State University

Mark S. Nagel
University of South Carolina

Dorothy Norris-Tirrell
University of Memphis

David C. Ogden
University of Nebraska, Omaha

Dan A. Rascher
University of San Francisco

Nathaniel Sampson
Portland State University

Charles A. Santo
University of Memphis

Susan Tomlinson Schmidt
University of Memphis

Crystal Southall
University of Northern Colorado

Richard M. Southall
University of North Carolina

Lynn Weigand
Portland State University

Zenon X. Zygmont
Western Oregon University

Preface

In the summer of 2005 Americans found themselves wrapped up an unlikely passion. An international bicycling road race was drawing 1.6 million viewers a day to the otherwise unknown Outdoor Living Network and receiving coverage in media outlets ranging from *Time* magazine to the *Daily Show With Jon Stewart*. Rapt attention to sport contests is not unusual in the United States, but cycling is far from a national pastime. But there were good reasons for the buzz. Texan Lance Armstrong was vying for his seventh straight victory in cycling's premier event, the Tour de France. Sport fans, whether cycling enthusiasts or not, were captivated by the drama of the moment: a single man attempting to overcome 188 competitors over a period of 23 days and more than 2,000 miles (3,200 km) for the seventh time in a row. But at the time Lance Armstrong was more than an athlete, and the realm of interest in his story spread far beyond sport fans.

Armstrong was an inspirational figure of mythic proportions and a human interest story, having overcome a grueling battle with cancer in 1996 just a few years before his first Tour win in 1999. He was also a charity giant. The Lance Armstrong Foundation had raised millions of dollars to support people affected by cancer, most notably through the sale of yellow silicone bracelets embossed with the word *LIVESTRONG*, which had become ubiquitous from high school hallways to the halls of the highest chambers of government.

The feel-good story of Lance Armstrong was tinged, however, by controversy and ethical conflict, fueled by doping allegations levied against the American rider. Alongside athletes from more prominent sports, like all-time home run leader Barry Bonds, Armstrong had become a lead character in a growing and troubling public discourse on performance-enhancing drugs in professional sports. The source of the main accusations against Armstrong, French journalists, led some to discredit the reports as deceit motivated by jealousy, and discussion ensued about the role of the media in framing the issue. The controversy also came to symbolize an undercurrent of tension between French and American culture that was, in part, wrapped up in conflicting national policies toward military action in Iraq.

Back in the States, a separate (and much smaller) controversy brewed over the United States Postal Service's sponsorship of Armstrong's racing team. The federal agency incurred over $40 million in expenses to serve as the team's primary sponsor from 1996 through 2004. During the same period the price of a first-class stamp increased four times, from $0.32 to $0.37.

Whether hero or villain, cheater or testament to hard work (or maybe freak of nature), in 2005 Lance Armstrong was a lightning rod—a sport figure who drew attention from a disparate and diverse audience for a wide variety of reasons. His story is an example of the vast and varied ways in which sport organizations, events, and figures become intertwined with our lives.

eBook available at HumanKinetics.com

These connections between sport and life are sometimes obvious, especially for athletes or sport fans, but are often subtle or unexpected. Beyond the drama of Armstrong's athletic quest—indeed, contributing to the theater of the event—were story lines that connected sport to culture and social causes. They involved legal challenges, anchored public debate about ethics and drug use, called into question the use of taxpayer money, and underscored tension in international relations.

As the chapters of this book will illustrate, these less obvious effects of sport often relate to public policy decisions or have important social, economic, or political implications. Let us explore where some of these policy linkages and implications occur.

■ **Congress and the courts**. Such relationships are perhaps most apparent when sport issues appear on the agenda of our nation's highest courts or legislative bodies. Recent examples include the congressional probe into steroid use in Major League Baseball and former Ohio State running back Maurice Clarett's challenge of National Football League draft rules as illegal restraint of trade.

■ **Local public finance**. In recent decades, high-level sports have also had clear public finance implications as cities have competed with one another to host sport teams or events, offering sport facility subsidies as bargaining chips. Stadiums and arenas have also become common elements of downtown revitalization efforts.

■ **Urban development and public health**. The implications of local policy decisions extend beyond the world of spectator sports. Public health issues reflect our ability to be active where we live and are linked to development policies and public investment decisions that hinder or encourage healthy lifestyles. Public officials make decisions that determine whether neighborhoods will be walkable, whether road networks will accommodate cyclists, and whether community residents will have access to parks and recreation facilities. Community sport programs can provide a vehicle for hands-on attempts at social change, such as the First-Tee program, which focuses on teaching life skills and values while exposing disadvantaged kids to the sport of golf.

■ **Political and social messages**. Sport often hosts transformative social or political messages. Consider the statement made by Jesse Owens' symbolic Olympic triumph amidst the hostile propaganda of Hitler's Berlin in 1936, Tommie Smith's black power salute at the 1968 Games, or Billie Jean King's victory over former Wimbledon champ Bobby Riggs in the "Battle of the Sexes" tennis match in 1973. Reflect on the subtle war protest of a handful of Major League Baseball players who sit in the dugout while others stand during the singing of "Star-Spangled Banner" to the perceived role of baseball in the nation's recovery from September 11, 2001.

■ **Globalization and international diplomacy**. Sport can also reflect the state of international diplomacy, beyond the Pollyanna symbolism of the Olympic Games, and represent the changing impacts of globalization. Advances in communications technology have made it easy to find international sporting events on American television. Meanwhile, American sport leagues have developed a clear and explicit business agenda of global expansion by staging exhibitions, broadcasting events, and scouting for talent across the world. The factors behind this agenda are similar to those that have driven the global expansion of many other American industries: maturing or stagnating demand in home markets, the related desire to create overseas markets for consumption, and the allure of less expensive labor.

The purpose of this book, then, is to share and explore some of the vast, varied, and sometimes unexpected ways in which sport affects our society and to illustrate the social, political, and economic implications of sport and the relationship of sport to public policy.

Such a task could not be completed without considering a diversity of viewpoints, so exposure to a variety of disciplinary perspectives on sport and public policy is a second objective of this book. As the Lance Armstrong story illustrates, anyone from any background can care about sport for any number of reasons. Indeed, researchers from a broad spectrum of disciplines have found sport a subject worthy of attention. The chapters to follow bring together perspectives from disciplinary backgrounds as diverse as economics, history, urban planning, nonprofit administration, public health, communications, political science, and philosophy.

Just as sport affects our lives in unexpected ways, we too affect sport. Our final objective is to the help the readers of this book consider their role as participants in sports, whether as active participants in a recreational sense, as employees in an industry, as parents of Little Leaguers, as members of a nonprofit organization that uses sport to improve lives, or as actors who influence markets and policy through decisions and behaviors. Even in the chapters that describe the economic structure of professional sports, the approach of this book is to stress the relationship between individual choices, public policy decisions, and the status quo. For example, how do individual preferences and behaviors contribute to players' salaries? How does public policy allow leagues to operate as cartels, and what are the implications? What are the political and economic factors that influence public investment decisions regarding sport stadiums?

This book is organized into four parts, each of which provides a useful base of understanding regarding a specific range of topics. Together, the four parts allow the reader opportunities to access insights from multiple disciplines and to develop new perspectives, while building a broader understanding of the relationship between sport and public policy. The four parts are as follows:

- Part I Structure of Professional Sports
- Part II Professional Sports, Cities, and Public Finance
- Part III Amateur Athletics, Participation, and Public Health
- Part IV Sport and Globalization

To understand the social, political, and economic implications of sport and see the relationship of sport to public policy, we need to look beyond the simple conception of sport as entertainment and recreation. Part I lays a foundation by exploring the unique nature of the professional sport industry. For example, sport teams are at once competitors and partners in a business venture. The level of cooperation that exists between team owners goes beyond what would be allowed by competing companies in other industries, leading to collusive behavior that affects players, fans, and cities. The chapters in part I explain the public policy decisions and precedents that permit this behavior, prepare the reader to understand the implications, and compare the organization of American sport leagues to alternative international structures.

Part II builds on this foundation to explore how some of these implications, combined with our appetite for sports, affect cities, whose residents are affected not necessarily as fans but as taxpayers and voters. The chapters focus on policy decisions regarding public investment in sport facilities and events, exploring related economic impacts and examining the mix of economic circumstances, political influence, and private power that influence such decisions.

Part III expands our scope beyond the realm of professional and spectator sports to consider amateur athletics, participation, and public health issues. The chapters in part III examine how development decisions and policy priorities can hinder or encourage active lifestyles, and create or remove barrier to participation in organized sports. In addition, these chapters explore the link between policy and ethics as related to amateur athletics and performance-enhancing drugs.

Finally, part IV expands the scope once more to look beyond local and national borders and consider perspectives on sport and globalization. If the world is flat (as Thomas Friedman proclaims in his best-selling 2005 book), so too is the playing field. The chapters in part IV focus on how sport affects and is affected by international relations and the phenomenon of globalization.

The chapters to follow cover a wide range of concepts as they apply to sport and public policy: from marginal revenue product to semiotic analysis, from new urbanism to urban regime theory. Enjoyment of the book, however, does not require prior knowledge of any such concepts or a background in any particular field. The book has been prepared to appeal to a broad audience; we hope that the discussions included will be useful to inform policy decisions of public officials and sport organizers, but we also hope to accomplish a simpler goal of contributing to a critical awareness among sport consumers and others affected by the many connections between sport and society. And by using the lens of sport as a filter, we hope to generate new interest in and awareness of public policy issues.

PART I

Structure
of Professional Sports

Although most people think of sport as entertainment—as a recreational pastime—the evidence of sport as business, with wider implications, is all around us. On a daily basis, the sports section of any major newspaper is likely to include several stories that are unrelated to the outcome of the previous night's games.

- Will the players and owners reach an agreement in time to avoid a strike?
- Should the city commit public funds to build a new stadium?
- Can a professional league exclude players younger than 19 years of age from its draft?
- How big is the star quarterback's new contract?

The first three chapters of this volume provide an important foundation for understanding the social, political, and economic implications of sport by helping the reader to look beyond the simple conception of sport as entertainment and to explore the organizational structure of the sport industry.

In chapter 1, Nat Sampson and Gerard Mildner explore the unique nature of American sport leagues, focusing on the unusual degree of cooperation that exists among team owners, who run otherwise competing business interests. Although this cooperation helps to ensure a compelling product, it also enables the kind of collusive behavior that is expressly prohibited in other industries and would typically be considered a violation of antitrust law. Mildner and Sampson examine the history of judicial interpretations, congressional actions, and public policy precedents that have permitted this behavior among sport leagues.

Chapter 2 builds on this foundation by looking beyond the major American sports to provide a comparative perspective. Gerard Mildner offers lessons from alternative approaches to organizing sport leagues and events, using examples from international team sports. The chapter discusses the organization of several sports that tend to be more popular outside the United States than inside: soccer, cricket, and rugby

In chapter 3, Zenon Zygmont asks why professional athletes are paid so much money, especially in comparison with salaries received in professions like nursing and education. Zygmont introduces economic concepts that are essential in understanding the link between individual preferences, market behavior, and player salaries. These concepts equip the reader to consider the ways in which athletes' salaries reflect our social values. The chapter also examines the sources of conflict between team owners and players that lead to strikes and lockouts. These sources of conflict are artifacts of the unique structure of the professional sport industry, enabled by the policy precedents described in chapter 1.

CHAPTER 1

Cooperation Amidst Competition

The Nature of Sport Leagues

Nathaniel Sampson and Gerard C.S. Mildner

Although many consider professional sports to be mere entertainment, the business aspects of the industry—including escalating salaries, frequent labor conflicts and strikes, and public investment in stadiums and arenas—can captivate and infuriate fans and nonfans alike. To understand these business matters, one must first recognize the distinctive nature of sport leagues and the public policy decisions that have enabled their behavior.

Sport leagues are unique entities by which the owners of teams that compete on the field cooperate with one another off the field as business partners. This apparent contradiction of cooperation amidst competition serves to maximize the collective benefit of those involved. Team owners cooperate to ensure an attractive product by establishing rules and governance structures and developing systems to ensure balanced competition. Although these elements of cooperation are benign and beneficial, the league structure also allows owners to collude with one another to control the terms of trade between teams and players, squeeze out competition from rival entities, and control supply to increase the price paid by both fans and cities that compete to host a limited number of teams. Through this collusion leagues essentially act as cartels, exhibiting the kind of monopolistic behavior that would typically be considered in violation of antitrust law.

Marginal in their legality and embodying an inherent contradiction between the necessity and the potential problems of cooperation among league members, sport cartels raise various public policy concerns. Since the early 20th century, policy makers have weighed the need and appropriateness of government intervention in professional sports against a laissez faire inclination to leave it to owners and players to define the powers and policies of sport leagues. Starting with baseball, this chapter examines the evolution of American professional sport leagues and the effect of their behavior on competition, athletes, fans, and cities. The chapter explores how the monopoly power of professional sport leagues has been both challenged and institutionalized by policy decisions of the courts and Congress, and by private agreements between players and team owners.

Why League Cooperation Is Necessary

From the beginning, competitors in organized sports have cooperated with one another to ensure order and provide a marketable product. A natural outgrowth of associations between individual franchises, leagues have enhanced the viability and stability of their professional sports by providing structure and ensuring an even field for competition.

Setting Rules and Schedules

The early years of British soccer and American college football were often played under "house rules" determined by the host team, which sometimes led to chaotic disputes and violent outcomes. Concerned by some of the extreme events, college presidents unified the rules of college football and instituted a number of measures to ensure the safety of players. The colleges hired impartial third-party referees to allow each team to participate under conditions of fair play.

As professional sports developed, league organizations established common rules of play so that fans could understand the game and teams could prepare for the next game without worrying that the rules would be tailored to help the home team.

A second reason for sport leagues to organize is the need to arrange a schedule among participating teams. Unlike other fields of commerce, each sport team needs to meet its rivals, so some coordinating authority must arrange a schedule of games. Moreover, fans find interest in the determination of the best team in that sport through a league table or league championship. For such a champion to be determined in a fair way, each participating team should play the other teams in their league in an equal or near equal number of circumstances.

Competitive Balance

Sport fans draw interest from seeing sporting events in which the outcome is uncertain and the strength of each team is more or less balanced. In practice, the intervention required for a league to ensure that the teams within the league have a competitive balance is extensive. For most of the 20th century, however, sport leagues did not make a great effort to ensure competitive balance. Dynasties thus emerged, such as the New York Yankees in baseball (winners of 6 American League titles between 1921 and 1928 and 8 World Series titles between 1947 and 1958) and the Boston Celtics in basketball (winners of 10 NBA championships between 1959 and 1969).

One can argue that competitive balance within a league is not necessary to draw fan interest to a sport, as evidenced by the attendance figures in baseball and basketball during the era of the Yankees' and Celtics' dominance. Dynasties create familiar players and story lines for fans to follow. More recently, the emergence of fantasy sport leagues has allowed fans to follow a game focused on the statistical performance of players whom they "own" rather than the outcome of the game itself.

Nevertheless, a number of innovations to improve league competitive balance have been created in recent decades. For example, consider the following:

■ **Order of the draft.** One of the first innovations was the creation of the reverse-order-of-finish player draft, which allows the previous year's worst team to have the first choice among new players entering the league. To some extent, this system promotes equality of teams over time.

■ **Unequal schedules.** The National Football League (NFL) has implemented a policy of unequal schedules (challenging one of the foundations for league organization described earlier) to create greater uncertainty in league outcomes. Schedules are drawn so that the division-winning teams of the previous year play other division winners more often, and last-place teams play each other more often as well. This policy enhances the likelihood that weaker teams will have better win–loss records and helps the league schedule a greater number of compelling matchups than would be generated by a random schedule.

■ **Revenue sharing.** Dominance and dynasties emerge in part because teams in larger cities have access to more revenue than do teams in smaller cities; they can sell more tickets at higher prices and charge higher prices to television networks that want to broadcast their games. To mitigate this potential imbalance, some leagues have established procedures to redistribute revenue from rich teams to poor teams or to provide equal shares of revenue that is generated at a leaguewide level. For example, current league agreements in Major League Baseball require that each team contribute 31 percent of its local revenue (which includes revenue from broadcast contracts and ticket sales) to a common pool that is then redistributed evenly to all teams in the league. The largest source of revenue for NFL teams is television broadcast rights. In the NFL, contracts for broadcast rights are negotiated directly between the league as whole and national networks, rather than between individual teams and their local networks. This policy allows the league to distribute the revenue evenly to all teams regardless of their market size.

■ **Salary caps.** Several leagues also implement salary caps, which limit the amount of money that each team can spend on player payroll, to ensure that teams in larger markets (or with wealthier owners) cannot simply buy up all the best talent by outspending smaller-market teams. Luxury taxes, which are levied as a financial penalty on teams with payrolls above a certain threshold, are designed to serve a similar purpose.

Many critics of professional sport leagues view their obsession with competitive balance in recent years as more of an attempt to increase firm profitability by gaining an economic advantage over players in labor negotiations or by gaining advantage over broadcasting companies in the market for broadcasting rights. In addition, revenue-sharing agreements can often create perverse incentives for teams to lose. A team owner with a low payroll often stands to gain more in profit from revenue-sharing redistribution than he or she might by making the kind of payroll increases necessary to field a winning team.

Downside of Cooperation

At some level, leagues play a benign and beneficial role as a convener of events and guarantor of fair play. Although we accept that the home team has the advantage of its partisan crowd and its familiarity with the home stadium, no one would accept today having the home team hire the referees, pick which ball should be used, or establish the penalties for fouls. But sport leagues also present a troubling set of contradictions. Although leagues allow owners to work together to promote fair play and balanced competition between member teams, they simultaneously allow competing business people to collude with one another to gain control over individual players, squash any competition that might emerge from rival leagues, and exert influence over fans and city finances through market power. Such collusion among entities who are otherwise competitors is a hallmark characteristic of a cartel. Therefore, sport leagues also represent a contradiction in American public policy because their monopolistic operations are aberrations in the face of antitrust law. This contradiction has been enabled by a series of judicial and congressional precedents, which are summarized in table 1.1 and are discussed in detail throughout the remainder of this chapter.

TABLE 1.1

Major Public Policy Precedents Regarding Professional Sports

Court case or congressional action	Year	Issues involved	Impetus	Outcome or effect
Federal Baseball Club of Baltimore v. National League of Professional Baseball Clubs	1922	Alleged antitrust activities of Organized Baseball	The Baltimore franchise of the Federal League sued the American and National Leagues when the Federal League failed, leaving Baltimore without a professional team.	The Supreme Court ruled that Organized Baseball did not qualify as an illegal monopoly, declaring that baseball was inherently neither interstate nor commerce. Baseball seemed to have been given an exemption from antitrust law.
Congressional Subcommittee on the Study of Monopoly Power Hearings	1951	Alleged antitrust activities of Major League Baseball	Congress considered granting a blanket exemption to Major League Baseball to protect it from pending antitrust lawsuits.	Not willing to support the "baseball monopoly," Congress refused to take any action, leaving it to the courts to decide the legality of baseball's actions. Congress' inaction, however, was seen as an endorsement of baseball's antitrust exemption.
Toolson v. New York Yankees	1953	Baseball's reserve clause and antitrust activities	A player in the New York Yankees franchise opposed a demotion and sued the team and the league, charging that their monopolistic practices were an illegal restraint of trade.	The Supreme Court reaffirmed baseball's antitrust exemption, citing the exemption given the sport in the *Federal* case and Congress' inaction in 1951.

Court case or congressional action	Year	Issues involved	Impetus	Outcome or effect
United States v. International Boxing Club of New York	1955	Alleged antitrust activities of a professional boxing club	The federal government charged the International Boxing club of New York with being an illegal monopoly on the grounds that it controlled boxing exhibitions and broadcasts in various states.	The Supreme Court ruled the International Boxing Club an illegal monopoly and declared that baseball's antitrust exemption did not apply to other sports.
Radovich v. National Football League	1957	Football's reserve clause and alleged antitrust activities	William Radovich, a former NFL player, sued the league when he was blacklisted after leaving the NFL to play for a team in a rival league.	The Supreme Court declared the NFL's reserve clause illegal under antitrust laws. Baseball's exemption did not apply to other sports leagues.
Sports Broadcasting Act	1961	Congressional protection for sports' leagues controls over broadcasting	Sports leagues sought special protection from antitrust laws so that they could negotiate broadcast contracts for their member teams.	Congress began setting parameters on acceptable monopolistic activities, proving willing to grant exemptions for favorable reasons.
NFL–AFL Merger	1966	Congressional protection for football leagues to merge and set up a football cartel	The National Football League and American Football League sought approval to merge into one league, eliminating competition in professional football.	Congress approved the merger, largely because of popular interest for a unified league championship (the Super Bowl). Congress, however, later rejected a proposed merger between the National Basketball Association and the American Basketball Association in 1971.
Mackey v. National Football League	1976	The legality of the "Rozelle Rule," a football policy designed to restrict free agency	A policy requiring a team to give up players if it signs a free agent from another team was challenged as an illegal restraint on trade.	A district court ruled the "Rozelle Rule" illegal, supporting free agency in football and other professional sports. Courts proved willing to support players' challenges to sport cartels' powers.
Smith v. Pro Football	1976	The legality of football's player draft	The college player draft was challenged as an illegal restraint on trade.	A district court ruled the draft system an illegal limitation on an athlete's opportunities and salaries, but the draft was preserved as part of a collective bargaining agreement.
L.A. Memorial Coliseum v. National Football League	1984	The right of an owner to move his franchise	Unhappy with his stadium deal, Oakland Raiders owner Al Davis sued the NFL for the right to move his franchise to Los Angeles.	A district court ruled it illegal for a sports league to prevent one of its member owners from moving his franchise, asserting some power for owners and paving the way for franchises to move freely at their owners' desires.

American legal codes outlaw monopolistic organizations and monopolistic practices. This position dates back to the early days of the republic and America's legal traditions that opposed monopolies as antithetical to the values of free enterprise and open competition. American lawmakers codified this opposition to monopolies in 1890 when Congress passed the Sherman Antitrust Act, forbidding any "contract, combination in the form of trust or otherwise, or conspiracy in restraint of trade or commerce," forbidding any person or combination that attempted to monopolize commerce between the states, and empowering the federal circuit courts to prosecute any entity that violated these restrictions ("Sherman Anti-Trust Act," 1890).

By the time that Congress passed this first antitrust law, the first sport cartel had already emerged. Although baseball was the first sport with national popularity and the first to become professional, the developments of the baseball cartel were largely repeated by the other sport leagues, and therefore the monopolistic issues and antitrust concerns that arose in baseball have largely applied to all sports.

Organized Baseball: Evolution of a Cartel

Baseball emerged in the mid-19th century and quickly realized widespread popular appeal and commercial viability. The sport's origins in men's social organizations provide a nostalgic image of a simple game imbued in pastoral ideals of camaraderie and healthy competition. But from its fraternal origins, the sport quickly developed into a serious form of competition that could bring pride and profit to successful teams. Professionalization and organized leagues soon followed, transforming the nature of the game and giving baseball more of a business character.

The origins of the sport in local social clubs also resulted in variations within the game played by different teams. For the general purpose of creating common rules and trying to preserve the character of the game, many of the leading amateur teams came together in 1857 in an arrangement called the National Association of Base Ball Players (NABBP). Although this development brought together many of the leading baseball teams throughout the country into a loose confederation, the composition, organization, and policies of the association fluctuated over the next couple of decades and the league suffered from problems of instability and financial distress. Maintaining their right to act independently, owners often pursued their own best interest, sometimes to the detriment of the overall health of the league. Because several teams often existed in the same city, owners frequently lowered ticket prices in an effort to undercut their rivals and outdraw the competition. Owners also tried to lure leading players from other clubs by offering them more lucrative contracts. These actions led to instability and the frequent disbanding of teams that could not find financial success (Rader, 2002; Voigt, 1983).

The Rise of the Senior Circuit

Under the auspice of resolving the problems within the NABBP, owners of some of the more successful teams met in 1876 and adopted a constitution establishing a new league, the National League of Professional Base Ball Clubs. The constitution of the National League created a stronger organizational structure and strict regulatory policies designed to control member teams and players. Most of the restrictive elements of the new league stemmed from the National League owners' desires to eliminate competition from rival leagues and keep players from breaking their contracts. Owners sought to increase stability and eliminate internal competition by restricting membership to select cities in the Northeast and Midwest, limiting membership in the league to only one franchise per town, and setting strict conditions governing admission of new teams into the league. These controls enabled owners to coalesce power and monopolistic control over professional baseball into the hands of a few owners (Seymour, 1960).

A lack of serious competition from rival leagues or teams enabled owners to extend control over their players and pass restrictive regulations that the players otherwise might not have accepted. The National League represented the highest level of professional baseball, and to achieve such distinction players subjected themselves to restricted terms of employment. Under these conditions, owners became able to define terms of contracts, management instituted disciplinary codes that regulated player behavior on and off the field, and players were required to pay some of the operating costs for teams. Having entered into the agreement voluntarily and lacking other suitable options for playing professional baseball, players possessed no way to air their grievances. When players did voice discontent over such arrangements, the league responded harshly (Voigt, 1991; Reiss, 1995).

Apart from the disciplinary controls that the league exercised over the players, team owners also subjugated players through the creation of the reserve clause. Enacted in 1880, this provision tied players to their teams and gave owners complete control over their players' services. Under the reserve clause, the team that first signed a player had control over that player for the duration of his career or until the owner decided to trade him. If an employed player refused to sign a new contract, the team still had the option of reserving that player's services for the upcoming season. Furthermore, team owners agreed to respect the contracts and reserves held by each other and to work collectively to outlaw any player who "jumped" his contract or his reserve clause to play in a different league, instituting a blacklist against such players. As the league progressed, owners extended their powers by enacting greater controls over player salaries and more comprehensive restrictions on player behavior (Seymour, 1960; Ross, 1991).

Although league owners sought control over individual players and teams as a way to prevent potential instability, they also continued to take action against any serious threat from competitor leagues. A profitable enterprise, professional baseball spurred the creation of various leagues in the late 19th century, but the National League exercised its power and employed a variety of tactics to defeat these rivals and maintain control over the sport. Through expansion into rival cities, the purchase of players and teams from competing leagues, changes to game rules and league policies, and collusive deals with opposing owners, the National League eliminated most of its competitors within a few years and held firm control of professional baseball at the end of the 19th century (Szymanski and Zimbalist, 2005).

A Rival Worthy of Merger

A new and more vigorous rival appeared in 1900, forcing the National League to pursue new tactics to eliminate its competition. The new American League presented the old circuit with similar problems as previous competitors did, challenging the established league for players, franchise territory, fan support, and financial backers.

Unable to eliminate the competition quickly and easily and realizing that a prolonged fight could take years and extract serious losses, the National League acted to end the rivalry by offering to make the junior circuit a second major league, joining the two leagues together in a system of shared control that followed the policies and practices of the older association. Through this combination, the baseball cartel grew stronger with the creation of the National Committee, a regulatory panel that constituted a new governing structure with the duties of legislating the rules of the game and regulating disputes between teams and players, simultaneously giving an air of legitimacy and presenting an impression that baseball could take care of any problems in the game by itself (Rader, 2002).

By the first decade of the 20th century, Organized Baseball, the term used for the conglomeration of major and minor leagues, existed as a monolithic system that almost completely controlled professional baseball in America. The major leagues enjoyed stability and security, and Organized Baseball possessed the power to divert any competitive threats.

Antitrust Law Interpretations and Baseball

Despite Organized Baseball's monopolistic characteristics and practices, including its controls over players, teams, and the marketplace, no legal challenges to it had emerged by 1910. The Sherman Antitrust Act specified that the behavior of an alleged monopoly could be classified as illegal only if it met two conditions: First, it had to demonstrate a restraint of trade, and second, that trade had to occur across state lines. Debate about the extent to which sport cartels and their operations met those criteria have shaped the determinations of the legality and appropriateness of sport leagues and specific policies, and as the views of legislators and judges on these points have varied over time, sports' positions under antitrust law have also varied. Under the Constitution, Congress had the power to regulate commerce between states, so the antitrust law passed by Congress could therefore apply only to interstate commerce. In establishing what constituted interstate commerce, lawmakers and judges could look upon many Supreme Court rulings from the 19th century that addressed this issue in which the Court held a relatively limited view of commerce. By the end of the 19th century, the prevailing interpretation held that the antitrust laws applied only to the distribution or exchange of goods across state lines (Freyer, 1989).

Under this restrictive interpretation of the regulatory powers of Congress, little antitrust action occurred in the first decade after passage of the act. Throughout the first decades of the 20th century, however, the federal government increasingly prosecuted trusts as the Supreme Court broadened the government's power to control trusts by expanding the prevailing interpretation of interstate commerce, holding that even solely intrastate activities could affect interstate commerce and that organizations conducting solely local affairs could fall within the jurisdiction of the antitrust laws (Letwin, 1965).

Considering the prevailing interpretation of antitrust law in the early 20th century, the legality of the baseball cartel seemed questionable. Although no direct antitrust charges had been filed against the sport, the issue of Organized Baseball's exercise of monopolistic control over the game had actually arisen many times in court, but usually as a peripheral point in other cases involving the sport. During the period when it faced rival league competition, the National League owners actually turned to the courts for injunctions to prevent players from jumping to teams in other leagues. In many of these instances, the courts upheld the restrictive injunctions, or at least significant elements of them, despite the fact that the involved players argued against the reserve clause as an unfair labor practice reflective of a repressive and monopolistic system (Rossi, 2001).

The Federal League Challenge and the Court's Interpretation

In the 1910s a more serious threat to the baseball monopoly emerged from a new rival league. Seeking to capitalize on the popularity of baseball and emulate the American League's success in elevating itself to major-league status, the Federal League presented itself as a challenge to the established majors in 1914. As the Federal League challenged Organized Baseball for players and markets, the leaders of the American and National Leagues responded in typical fashion, turning to the familiar tactics of propaganda, coercion, and collusion to undermine and eliminate the rival. The Federal League reacted by filing lawsuits that accused Organized Baseball of being a combination and an illegal monopoly engaging in conspiracy and antitrust practices, leading to the first test of the baseball monopoly.

With the federal government increasingly taking a hard stance against monopolistic organizations, the legal contest between the major leagues and the Federal League presented a serious threat to the structure and practices of Organized Baseball. While the lawsuit sat in the courts, the Federal League managed to finish two seasons as a major league, but it struggled to attract the crowds, financial support, and quality players of the American and National Leagues. So when the leaders of Organized Baseball proposed a settlement, most of the Federal League owners approved of the plan. In the deal, the heads of the established majors agreed to buy out some of the teams and stadiums of the rival circuit and allowed some Federal owners to buy control of some of the American and National League teams in return for the Federal League owners' agreeing to drop their antitrust suits (Spink, 1974). But the settlement did not satisfy all members of the Federal League. The owners of the Baltimore Federal League club desired a major-league team in their city. Not receiving a team or adequate attention or compensation from Organized Baseball, the Baltimore franchise refused to drop its antitrust charges (Duquette, 1999; Spink, 1974).

Initially, the courts ruled against Organized Baseball, finding its operations and policies monopolistic. On appeal, however, the decision was reversed, and the case progressed to the Supreme Court for a final ruling on the legality of baseball's operations. In the case of *Federal Baseball Club of Baltimore, Inc. v. National League of Professional Baseball Clubs* (1922), the justices unanimously agreed that baseball did not fall under the terms of the Sherman Act and that Organized Baseball, therefore, did not constitute an illegal monopoly. In his written opinion for the court, Judge Oliver Wendell Holmes suggested that professional baseball did not represent either a business or interstate commerce. Baseball games, the judge claimed, occurred as exhibitions and these exhibitions were "purely state affairs," and therefore "not interstate commerce within the meaning of the Anti-Trust Acts." The transport of players and equipment across state line and the paying of players to do so was "a mere incident, not the essential thing." Furthermore, Holmes argued that the restrictive contracts preventing players from jumping to another team, and thereby limiting the talent available to competitors, "were not an interference with commerce among the states." Having examined both the issues of the leagues' structure and player contracts, the Court found that the activities of Organized Baseball did not represent a restraint or interference on commerce between the states and therefore remained outside the scope of the antitrust laws. More broadly, the Court's decision suggested not only that did baseball not constitute interstate commerce but also, because of its status as an exhibition, that it did not even constitute commerce and therefore could not become subject to antitrust regulation (*Federal Baseball Club of Baltimore, Inc. v. National League*, 1922). The baseball monopoly had survived its first test in the courts and received an antitrust exemption that would go unchallenged for nearly three decades.

Congress' Interpretation

By the late 1940s the character of professional sports had changed. Football, basketball, and hockey had by then become meaningful professional sports, and each had a monopolistic league that controlled the game in a fashion similar to Organized Baseball. Additionally, the advent of broadcasting and the increase in attendance and players' salaries made sport more clearly a business, one that through the broadcasting of games across state lines now clearly had an interstate component. Broadcasting brought the question of the legality of the sport monopolies back into debate, and baseball was again the center of attention. Through arrangements that granted private companies the rights to play-by-play broadcasting and defined the geographic parameters for programming, Organized Baseball exercised extensive control of broadcasting. Accusations of monopolistic practices arose from smaller local radio stations, leading to lawsuits that charged the heads of professional baseball with illegally trying to eliminate competitive outlets and controlling the business of broadcasting baseball games (U.S. Congress, *Organized Baseball, hearings*, 1951).

The threat of another legal investigation of the baseball monopoly and possible disruptions that could occur from a ruling against the sport frightened many supporters of Organized Baseball and drew the attention of Capitol Hill. To protect the national pastime from possible antitrust lawsuits, Representatives Wilbur Mills (D-AR), Albert S. Herlong, Jr. (D-FL), and Melvin Price (D-IL) introduced legislation in May 1951 to exempt baseball from antitrust laws. These proposals prompted the first congressional investigation into sports when the House Subcommittee on the Study of Monopoly Power took up the matter and held hearings on Organized Baseball in the summer of 1951. Chaired by Brooklyn Democrat

Emanuel Celler, a leading antimonopolist of the period, the hearings examined baseball's operations and allegedly monopolistic aspects, which included the reserve clause, the power of the commissioner, controls over franchises, problems with the draft, the geographical distribution of teams, and the more recent issues related to broadcasting and televising baseball games (U.S. Congress, *Organized Baseball, hearings*, 1951).

At stake in these hearings was whether Congress should place baseball within the parameters of antitrust laws, produce legislation favoring an antitrust exemption for the sport, or leave it to the courts to determine the acceptability of baseball's practices. Rejecting the grounds on which the *Federal* decision rested, the committee intended to take a serious look at the policies and practices of Organized Baseball. The panel sought the testimony of numerous current and former players, owners, league officials, and members of the media, believing that those witnesses would provide a fair representation of all relevant views, reflect the sentiments of most baseball fans, and serve as a good indicator of public interest (U.S. Congress, *Organized Baseball, hearings*, 1951). Although most of the witnesses delivered testimony supporting the existing structures and practices of the sport, committee members remained reluctant to grant Organized Baseball a complete exemption. The panel favored a limited exemption that might protect aspects of Organized Baseball considered essential to the preservation of stability and order in this cherished American institution. But the members of Congress did not consider the legislature the best place for defining the legal parameters of the baseball monopoly. The courts, the committee reasoned, could better determine the legality of Organized Baseball's operations. As questions of the legality of baseball's controls over players and broadcasting continued to circle, the committee thought the courts would soon have the opportunity to assess the appropriateness and reasonableness of baseball's structures and practices and effectively set parameters on the baseball monopoly. The panel, therefore, opted against taking any action either extending or revoking baseball's antitrust exemption (U.S. Congress, *Organized Baseball, report*, 1952).

The Supreme Court's Review

As congressional committee members had anticipated, it did not take long before the courts had the opportunity to rule on the legality of the baseball monopoly and its policies and practices. During the hearings, the reserve clause had emerged as a central issue. Many witnesses claimed that the ability to protect players served an integral role in preserving fairness, equality, and stability in the professional game; the contractual element, meanwhile, also provoked some of the strongest attacks from opponents of the baseball monopoly. This disagreement about the legality and appropriateness of this restrictive contractual element laid at the heart of a case that came before the Supreme Court in 1953. In the case of *Toolson v. New York Yankees*, George Toolson, a player in the New York Yankees' system, filed an antitrust suit against the team when it assigned him to the minor leagues. Believing that he should have the right to offer his services to another organization willing to give him the opportunity to play at the major-league level, Toolson refused to report to his assignment. The commissioner's office responded by blacklisting Toolson, prompting the former player to file antitrust charges attacking the reserve clause and the monopolistic control that teams possessed over players (Quirk and Fort, 1992).

In deciding on this case, the Court again focused on whether baseball games constituted "trade or commerce" within the meaning of antitrust laws and whether Organized Baseball itself was engaged in such trade or commerce. Developments in the previous decades seemed to suggest that the sport had cause for concern because of recent shifts in the position of the Court on labor matters and the accepted definition of interstate commerce. The justices increasingly supported workers' rights and opposed restrictive labor contracts and other unfair labor practices. The Court had also broadened its definition of interstate commerce, adopting a position that even local commercial activity was connected to commercial endeavors elsewhere, making it relevant to interstate commerce and thereby subject to regulation by the federal government (Leuchtenburg, 1995).

When the Court ruled on *Toolson* in 1953, however, it defied expectations by reaffirming Organized Baseball's antitrust exemption. In a 7-2 decision, the justices ruled in favor of Organized Baseball, citing the exemption given the sport by the *Federal* case over three decades previously and the recent decision of Congress not to take any action to end the exemption. In the majority opinion, Chief Justice Earl Warren argued that in the *Federal* case the Court had decided that baseball did not fall within the scope of existing federal antitrust laws and that Congress had "had the ruling under consideration but had not seen fit to bring such business under these laws by legislation." Stating that "if there are evils in this field which now warrant application to it of the antitrust laws it should be by legislation," Warren expressed the Court's belief that any efforts to end the exemption needed to come from Capitol Hill. With Congress seemingly endorsing the baseball monopoly and with the *Federal* ruling having stood for over 30 years, the Court decided against overruling the prior decision without even reexamining the underlying issues (*Toolson v. New York Yankees*, 1953). The baseball monopoly had passed another important test.

Antitrust and Other Leagues: Are All Sports Equal?

The decisions of the courts and Congress regarding baseball allowed the cartels that ran other sports to feel secure in their policies and procedures, assuming that they possessed an equal position in antitrust matters. This assumption was tested in the 1955 Supreme Court case of *United States v. International Boxing Club of New York, Inc.*, in which the federal government attacked a professional boxing organization as an illegal monopoly on the basis that it controlled boxing exhibitions in various states and sold the rights to broadcast and film matches for interstate distribution. The heads of the International Boxing Club cited the exemption granted Organized Baseball in the *Federal* case and reiterated in the *Toolson* suit, suggesting that these rulings gave an exemption to all professional sports. The Court, however, disagreed. In a 6-2 decision, the justices declared that International Boxing fell within the parameters of the Sherman Antitrust Act and did not have any special protections from the Court or Congress. Writing the majority decision for the Court, Chief Justice Warren explained that because the Court had never before considered the antitrust status of boxing it could approach the issue without having to consider previous rulings. The broadcasting and distribution of filmed recordings of the matches meant that boxing was interstate commerce and was therefore subject to federal regulation. Because the Supreme Court had not previously issued a ruling granting boxing an antitrust exemption, Warren argued, the issue confronting the Court was not "whether a previously granted exemption should continue, but whether an exemption should be granted in the first instance." That matter, the chief justice concluded, was

Soccer's Open Competition Alternative: Promotion and Relegation

As described in this chapter, most American sport leagues exist as joint ventures; business decisions are made jointly by franchise owners seeking to maximize overall profits. These leagues can be considered closed systems. An enterprising fantasy baseball aficionado cannot start up her own real major-league team by simply ordering some uniforms and hiring a roster of players; she must be admitted into the exclusive club by the existing franchise owners.

The closed system of joint venture entities is not the only way to organize professional sport teams into an optimally sized league. Soccer, cricket, and rugby leagues throughout the world have open structures, in which membership is contingent on success. (The organization of these world sports is described in detail in chapter 2 of this book.) League membership changes each season based on a system of promotion and relegation. Perhaps the most famous promotion and relegation system exists in British soccer, in which the highest level of competition is the English Premier League. At the end of each season, the three worst teams are booted from the Premiership and replaced with three teams from a lower-tier league.

Open competition leagues do not have the same monopolistic characteristics of closed system leagues, in part because they do not designate exclusive rights to territories and they do not control the location of teams. Anyone with the money and desire can start a team anywhere they choose, starting, of course in the lowest tier. Under such a system, all locations that can financially support a team are likely to have one.

Promotion and relegation increases meaningful competition and obviates the need for elaborate revenue-sharing mechanisms designed to ensure competitive balance. The system removes the potential for perennial cellar dwellers and eliminates the problem of teams that tank to secure a higher draft pick or owners who are content to pad their profits by collecting from revenue sharing rather than spending the money required to field a competitive roster. Such teams would simply be replaced by teams with owners who are motivated by winning rather than by profit alone.

In a somewhat tongue-in-cheek piece written for the online news magazine *Slate*, Nate DiMeo (2007) proposed promotion and relegation as a strategy to save the financially distressed National Hockey League (NHL). Suggesting that part of the NHL's problem is that it has grown beyond its optimal size, DiMeo offered relegation as a means to cut the league down to a more appropriate size while at the same time prodding fan interest by increasing the number of meaningful games. "While pro basketball's worst team lose on purpose to secure a better position in the draft lottery, the dregs of your league will leave their blood in the ice. Picture it: 'Tonight on Versus, it all comes down to one game for the Atlanta Thrashers. Beat the Colorado Avalanche or say goodbye to the NHL.'"

"for Congress to resolve, not this court" (*United States v. International Boxing Club of New York, Inc.*, 1955).

The tenuous legality of the professional sport cartels was further muddied in 1957 as a result of *Radovich v. National Football League*, which tested the legality of the National Football League's version of the reserve clause. William Radovich, a player for the Detroit Loins, decided to leave the team to play for the Los Angeles Dons of the new rival All-America Conference, an action that violated the condition in players' contracts that prevented them from signing with any other team without the consent of their present club. When Radovich decided to return to organized football by becoming a player–coach for a franchise in a lesser, affiliated league, the heads of the parent league issued a blacklist to prevent any associated team from employing him. Radovich accused the professional football organization of conspiracy and monopoly practices, including restraint of trade, and argued that radio and television broadcasts of the sport made the game a business constituting interstate commerce. The league's defense cited the *Federal* case and the *Toolson* decision in suggesting that the sport had protection from antitrust regulation. In a 6-3 verdict, however, the Supreme Court sided with Radovich, declaring that the association's activities fell within the coverage of the antitrust laws and that the baseball rulings did not apply to professional football (*Radovich v. National Football League, et al.*, 1957).

Acknowledging that the ruling presented a contradiction of sorts, Justice Tom Clark used the opportunity to explain the *Toolson* doctrine and the Court's stance on the legality of professional sports. The Court, Clark explained in the majority opinion, believed that *Toolson* applied only to baseball, accepting an exemption for that sport only because Congress had examined the issue a few years earlier and "chosen to make no change." To delineate the Court's position further, clarify apparent inconsistencies, and place responsibility to act back on Congress, Clark declared that "were we considering the question of baseball for the first time upon a clean slate we would have no doubts," but because Congress had not acted to overturn the exemption enjoyed by Organized Baseball, the Courts did not consider it appropriate to reverse the decision. Calling congressional processes "more accommodative" to the process of defining the sport's legality and less immediately disruptive and detrimental to the industry and the public in the event that a reversal of policy should occur, Clark declared that any action would have to come from Congress. "As long as Congress continues to acquiesce," the opinion concluded, the Court would "adhere to—but not extend" to other sports, the antitrust exemption (*Radovich v. National Football League, et al.*, 1957).

The rulings regarding boxing and football clearly established different conditions for baseball and the other sports, and set the foundation for future regulations that would either focus on broad efforts to equalize the sports or concentrate on limited efforts to address specific sports or specific aspects of sports.

Beginning in the late 1950s, a series of hearings occurred in both branches of Congress to examine proposals to extend a blanket exemption to all professional sports. Unease about the appropriateness of the existing exemption for baseball and disagreements between politicians over specific legislative details blocked these equalizing efforts. Congress investigated this issue in numerous hearings during the late 1950s, the 1960s, and thereafter, but never passed any action to extend the exemption. Lacking baseball's legal protection, the fate of the other sport cartels rested in the hands of the legislative and judicial branches. They would have to petition Congress to exempt specific practices, and any unprotected activities could be subject to the courts' assessments of their appropriateness and legality under antitrust laws.

Congress initially showed itself willing to protect certain monopolistic activities of professional sports if they appeared to serve the public interest. Primarily through the lobbying of the National Football League, Congress in 1961 passed the Sports Broadcasting Act, which enabled sport leagues to negotiate broadcasting contracts that would apply to all member franchises. Opponents of the league-coordinated broadcasting deals claimed that these contracts violated the rights of individual teams to arrange their own, and perhaps more lucrative, contracts. But largely though the argument that leaguewide arrangements would benefit smaller-market clubs and thereby promote league stability and competitive balance, Congress supported the measure. Apart from baseball, where teams retained the right to arrange their own broadcasting plans, the act applied to all the professional sports. To protect college football from competition from the NFL, the legislation generally prohibited the NFL from broadcasting games on Saturday afternoons (Lowe, 1995).

A few years later professional football again petitioned Congress for an exemption when the National Football League (NFL) and the American Football League (AFL) sought to merge. Formed in 1959, the AFL had quickly proven itself a worthy competitor to the older league, rivaling the NFL in quality of play and challenging the senior league for players, fans, and financial backers. Recognizing the benefits that bringing the two leagues together under a single legal and competitive structure would have for his own league, NFL commissioner Pete Rozelle proposed a merger in 1966. Because the combination eliminated competition in favor of one powerful cartel, it raised the specter of antitrust litigation. The heads of professional football turned to Congress for support. Some ardent antitrusters in the House of Representatives opposed the move as an endorsement of an illegal monopoly, but the growing interest in professional football among the public and members of Congress and the hope of seeing a unified professional championship facilitated the easy passage of the bill (Lowe, 1995).

Congress had proved itself willing to grant antitrust exemptions to professional sports, but this support varied depending on the sport, the attitudes of the current members of Congress, and prevailing public sentiment about the sport and the matter at hand. The uncertainty of Congressional support, and therefore the difficulty of having to rely on the political process for protection, became apparent when the leaders of professional basketball sought a merger between the National Basketball Association and the American Basketball Association in the early 1970s. The ABA formed in 1966 and mounted a serious challenge to the NBA, drawing players and fan support from the NBA and setting off a rivalry in which player salaries rapidly escalated. By 1971 the older association decided to end the contest and proposed the joining of the two leagues into a system of shared control. Whereas football's merger had merely raised the specter of antitrust charges against the enlarged league, basketball's proposal produced a lawsuit as the NBA Players Association charged that the combination would enable the leagues to retract player salaries and otherwise strip the athletes of their recent gains (Lowe, 1995).

Congress took up the issue of the proposed merger in hearings beginning in 1971. Although the merger plan mirrored football's in many ways and therefore seemed to warrant a similar exemption, basketball had a harder time convincing Congress. The heads of both leagues testified on the need for a merger to end the rivalry and rein in financial costs. The commissioners warned of the financial ruin of one or both leagues and the downfall of professional basketball because of the escalating financial costs stemming from the interleague competition for players. Strong opposition to the planned merger, however, appeared from both players and members of Congress. Critics of the merger pointed out that the league owners had brought financial strain upon themselves through the large salaries that they offered players, and opponents claimed that the leagues could alleviate some of their fiduciary struggles by restructuring their economic policies, especially their procedures governing profit sharing and the distribution of gate receipts (Lowe, 1995). The merger of the two leagues was not approved until 1976, after the antitrust suit filed by the Players Association was settled out of court.

Effect of Public Policy on the Balance of Power

In general, the courts have taken a more prominent role than Congress in setting parameters on sport leagues' practices and procedures, showing a preference for granting more power to players and individual teams. In recent decades, the courts have provided many key rulings that have aided players in their efforts to assert their rights against the power and control of team owners and the league hierarchy. In the *Radovich* case, the Supreme Court freed football, basketball, and hockey players from the restrictions of the reserve clause, and subsequent cases further reduced the influence that sport leagues exercised over athletes. In 1976 a district court ruling in the case of *Mackey v. National Football League* invalidated the "Rozelle Rule," a replacement to the reserve clause that similarly discouraged teams from signing free agents from other teams. Passed in 1963, this restrictive condition stated that any team signing a free agent from a different club in the league would have to surrender at least one player to the free agent's former team. Ruling this another form of conspiracy designed to prevent players from switching teams and to block any disruptive escalations in player salary associated with free agency, the court declared the Rozelle Rule an unreasonable restraint of trade (Yasser et al., 2000).

That same year, in a ruling in the case of *Smith v. Pro-Football, Inc.* (1976), another court found that the college player draft system was an illegal conspiracy because it deprived players of individual bargaining rights. The justices of the federal district court in Washington, DC, declared that the system, in which teams draft college players and then retain the rights to that player, was an illegal limitation on the athlete's opportunities and salary. The decision had primary significance for the plaintiff, Yazoo Smith, but it also revealed the court's perception of illegality and undue influence in the way that football, basketball, and hockey treated prospective employees and limited the rights of those athletes. The draft system

Municipalities Confronting the Cartels: Hamilton County Board of Commissioners v. National Football League

In efforts to secure public financing for new stadiums, many professional sport teams have argued that their current facilities do not generate enough revenue to allow them to compete in terms of payroll. The control that leagues exert over the supply and location of member franchises empowers teams in their demands for new facilities, but contests over new stadiums have also created a new antitrust battleground focusing on cartel behavior and oversight of team financial records.

In 1995 the owners of the Cincinnati Bengals declared that their team could not compete financially with the other teams in the National Football League because of the limited revenue that Riverfront Stadium provided them. The Bengals argued that without a new stadium deal they might have to relocate. In response, Hamilton County voters passed a measure to help finance a new football-only stadium the following year. The county and the team finalized the deal in 1997, and the new stadium opened in 2000. The year after the stadium opened, the *Los Angeles Times* disclosed information showing that of the 31 teams in the NFL, the Bengals collected the 8th highest profit in 1996 and the 9th highest profit in 1997. Following this discovery, the Hamilton County Board of Commissioners sued the National Football League, arguing that the league had colluded to withhold information to help the Bengals mislead county residents and policy makers. The plaintiffs also argued that the league violates antitrust law by restricting public ownership and using relocation threats to coerce public spending on stadiums.

The courts refused to intervene, and the U.S. Court of Appeals for the 6th Circuit in 2007 upheld a lower-court ruling that dismissed the complaint on the grounds that the statute of limitation had expired before the filing of the case. According to the courts, the limitation period expired four years after the signing of the new lease—in the same year that the league released its records, in 2001. The courts also cited a similar charge against the NFL filed by the St. Louis Rams in 1995 and claimed that any concerns regarding antitrust practices and the NFL would have existed when the county signed the deal in 1997, justifying that as the starting date for the limitation period. The courts further argued that the disclosure of teams' profits had not changed the leagues' antitrust standing.

As Stanford economist Roger Noll put it, "Making a bad decision is not the same thing as being defrauded" (quoted in Horn, 2004).

remained largely unaffected by this ruling because players and owners had agreed on the arrangement as part of a collective bargaining deal. Subsequent collective bargaining contracts refined only certain elements of the draft and teams' controls over drafted players. Nevertheless, the court's decision represented another ruling against the restrictive practices of a sport league (Yasser et al., 2000; Roberts, 1991). The *Mackey* and *Smith* cases together revealed a judicial inclination to support players in their challenges to the power of the sport monopolies.

The limited effect of the *Smith* decision also reflected the growing importance of collective bargaining in determining the policies and operations of professional sport leagues. Although the courts delivered some rulings that helped empower athletes, the players themselves have played an important role in reducing the power of the owners' cartels by forming powerful organized unions. Strikes, lock-outs, and other work stoppages resulting from conflicts between players' unions and franchise owners have at times had negative effects on fans and the game but have played an important role in reducing the power of the sport cartels and establishing more balanced agreements between owners and players. These issues are addressed in depth by Zenon Zygmont in chapter 3 of this book.

Apart from the reduction in leagues' and owners' controls over players, individual teams and owners have also challenged league powers, having the effect of further decreasing the authority of the sport cartels. A key ruling that limited the power of sport leagues and empowered individual teams came in the case of *Los Angeles Memorial Coliseum Commission v. National Football League* (1984), which arose when the NFL attempted to block Oakland Raiders' owner Al Davis from moving his franchise to a larger stadium and larger market in Los Angeles. The court ruled it an illegal conspiracy effort of the league to interfere with the transfer of one franchise to a different location and essentially declared it illegal for a professional sport league to block individual teams or owners from pursuing their own course of action. The decision not only paved the way for the Raiders' move to Los Angeles but also set off a wave of franchise relocations in football, basketball, and hockey during the 1980s and 1990s (Roberts, 1991). Because leagues still limit the overall supply of franchises, cities that desire to host a team must compete with one another. This circumstance gives leverage to team owners, and publicly financed stadiums often become the bargaining chip with which cities negotiate. Many teams have parlayed relocation threats into new facilities. (The issue of stadium subsidies is addressed in detail by Charles Santo in chapter 5.)

Future Trends

Congress and the courts remain active monitors and advisors on the organization and actions of professional sport leagues, but neither entity seems to have a strong direct influence over the cartels. In the decades since Congress first examined Organized Baseball in the 1950s, the government has held numerous hearings and committees investigating myriad aspects of sport leagues and their operations. Perhaps most notably, the hearings into the use of performance-enhancing drugs in professional baseball and the subsequent report by commission chair George Mitchell in 2007 (as discussed in chapter 10) shook the sport world and brought the national pastime under close examination of Congress. The Mitchell Report led some members of Congress and some journalists to suggest that the government watch professional sports more vigilantly, and it spurred talk of possible governmental intervention or regulation of sports. Even so, no direct congressional action resulted. Although Major League Baseball did enact stricter drug-testing policies at the urging of policy makers, the congressional inquiry served mainly to pressure the league to make changes.

The courts have served a more important role in helping delineate the powers and limitations of sport leagues, but even the judiciary has played only a marginal role in checking league controls in recent decades. The courts have often shown a reticence to intervene, and when they have, their rulings have at times had little practical effect. More important has been the greater influence of players unions and collective bargaining. In the *Mackey* case, for example, the courts repudiated the college player draft, but the practice remains because owners and players have agreed to allow it to continue under the terms of their collective bargaining agreements. Most policies in the major professional sports now seem contingent on agreements between the parties directly involved, and this system seems preferred by the players, the courts, and Congress. So while the legislature and judiciary will surely continue to monitor and advise the sport leagues, practical decisions on the policies and powers of the sport leagues now seem most likely to come from the owners and players themselves.

Conclusion

The need to establish schedules, rules, standards for player behavior, and other elements of the games compelled the formation of leagues and their related monopoly powers in the first place. These roles still have importance in modern sports because they provide structure and competitive balance in the professional game. Legislators, the courts, and the players have all played a role in challenging the extent to which sport leagues can control the terms of trade between team owners and players, react to competition from rival leagues, and exert influence over fans and city finances through market power. In some cases the cartels' monopoly powers have been limited, whereas in others they have been institutionalized by policy decisions.

Team owners and players, through collective bargaining, legal action, and appeals to policy makers, will continue to search for the balance of power that suits both sides while preserving the market appeal of their products. Fans will continue to express their acceptance or disdain for league behavior with their actions and spending behavior, but the ability of consumers to influence the market is limited without checks on the collusive business practices of cartels.

CHAPTER 2

Beyond the Major Leagues

Lessons from the Organization of International Sports

Gerard C.S. Mildner

The range of organized sports is much wider than the four major professional team sports that are dominant in the United States: football, baseball, basketball, and hockey. Many sports, such as golf, tennis, and track and field, are individual competitions in which an organized tour highlights the individual talents of the players. Other sports, particularly women's sports, are much more popular at the collegiate level than they are at a professional level. Often, the so-called minor sports are organized in novel formats that emphasize the survival of the league over the survival of an individual team. And sports that are more prevalent outside the United States often have organizations that differ significantly from the American model that emphasizes private ownership of individual professional teams and team control of professional leagues. In many cases, these alternative structures reduce the monopoly power of sport teams and leagues, creating greater benefits for fans and communities.

This chapter looks beyond the major American sports to provide a comparative perspective and offer lessons from alternative approaches to organizing sport leagues and events. We will discuss the organization of several team sports that tend to be more popular outside the United States than inside: soccer, cricket, and rugby. In each case, tension is present between the demand for national competition and club competition that rarely exists within traditional American sports, which often accentuates the public's enjoyment of these sports. Also, the organization of soccer leagues—including the emphasis on multiple levels, the mixture of professionalism and amateurism, and the dynamic of the promotion and relegation system—is different from anything seen in the United States. Because soccer is the world's most popular sport, succeeding on both a financial and cultural level, an American audience may have something to learn from it. We will also consider the decision by some of the minor sports to organize in a single-entity format that promotes survival and success of that league, sometimes for the public's benefit and sometimes at its expense.

Organization of Soccer, the World Sport

Soccer leagues are found in almost every country in the world. The popularity of soccer is derived from its relatively simple rules and the low cost of sporting equipment. The game was formalized in England and was introduced to the world during the years of the British Empire.

The dominant leagues of soccer developed in a much different manner from the professional sport leagues in the United States. Teams participate in leagues that are sanctioned by the national associations, such as the Football Association, which governs soccer in England. In fact, the term *soccer* is thought to be derived from an abbreviation of *association*, and it gained popularity in usage as a way to differentiate between *association* football games and *rubgy* football games.

National Associations and the Relegation System

The Football Association and its counterparts in other countries have created an open system of competition that promotes the development of new teams and clubs throughout the country. The open system reduces the monopoly power of teams relative to cities and arguably increases participation and enjoyment. Each club is assigned a league based on its performance during the previous season. The leagues are then ranked in a hierarchy, leading up to a top national league, whether it is the Premier League in England, Serie A in Italy, the Bundesliga in Germany, or the Primera Liga in Spain.

Following the end of the season, the best teams in each league are promoted to the next higher-level league. The worst-performing teams are relegated to the league immediately below. The exact number of promoted and relegated teams differs depending on the country and its national association.

Promotion and relegation creates an open system of competition. Newly formed clubs are permitted to compete in the lowest level league within that country and, year by year, are able to advance to the highest level of the game. Fans pay great attention at the end of the season, not just to see who wins the league competition or table but also to see who ranks at the bottom of the table and thus is relegated to the lower league.

Competition at the bottom and top of each league is intensified by the difference in economic returns associated with participating in leagues at different levels. Because lower leagues produce little broadcasting revenue, teams facing relegation face a dramatic loss of revenue-earning potential, leading those teams to unload player talent, which they can no longer afford. On the other hand, teams experiencing promotion face a windfall of higher broadcasting revenue and attendance and are able to hire players that are more skilled. Indeed, the teams being promoted to a higher division must hire players that are more skilled to compete and stay within that league. The financial benefit to clubs of promotion appears to be quite long lasting, even if the team lasts only a few seasons at the higher level (Noll, 2002).

Many observers have noted that the relegation system creates a form of hypercompetition among soccer teams because the rewards for success and the penalties for failure are large. But the presence of both rewards and penalties for teams at both the top and bottom of the league competition encourages teams to remain competitive throughout the season. By comparison, teams in the traditional American sports have been accused of giving up and trading away their best players to save costs after they have lost the opportunity of a playoff season (as discussed in chapter 1, especially in the first sidebar).

National Teams and Club Teams

A second feature of soccer that distinguishes it from the traditional American sports is the level of competition between national teams, sponsored by their respective national associations. These international competitions, whether in the form of continent-wide championships like the European or Latin American championships or the World Cup, held every four years, bring massive fan interest to the game and produce enormous revenues for national sport organizations.

Players from the top soccer-playing countries, who otherwise play on different club teams, often in different national leagues, are united in international play. These national teams become all-star teams, each with a distinctive character and an intense national following. Under long-standing rules established by the Football Association and other national federations, the national team has a first claim on talent and clubs are expected to release their top players to the national team during important matches. From this perspective, the club teams are subservient to the national association and the national team. Revenue from the international competitions is then used to help fund sport development programs within each country, at little or no expense to taxpayers.

This relationship between clubs and national associations is not entirely one-sided. Success on the international stage is an effective way for players to develop reputations that spill over to their careers as club players. A strong performance by a player for his national team builds fan interest in the subsequent matches of his club.

Labor Market and the Bosman Case

The sport of soccer has traditionally been characterized by limitations on player movements, both to support national team competitions and to support clubs' efforts to train players. As described earlier, the national association can call on a club to release a player for an international competition. In addition, until a legal case known as the Bosman ruling, most associations allowed teams to prevent their players from signing with other teams, even in other leagues. Teams could extract a transfer fee from an acquiring club, ostensibly to compensate them for training that player. In practice, transfer fees are a form of economic rent that allows clubs to extract part of the economic value of the player's labor. The system of transfer fees allowed clubs to keep their players' salaries well below their economic value. To cite a well-known example, the English soccer league was able to enforce a maximum wage policy of 20 pounds per week up to the year 1961 (Disney, 2006).

The Bosman case is named after a Belgian player, Jean-Marc Bosman, who was prevented from moving to another club in 1990 after his contract expired. Bosman objected, and the case reached the European Court of Justice in Luxembourg, which ruled that the transfer restrictions constituted a restriction on the freedom of movement for labor. The Bosman case also had the effect of prohibiting quotas within leagues for a certain percentage of home country players. The combination of these two aspects of the case has greatly increased the competition for player talent among European teams, increased player mobility, and directed more of the economic returns of the game into player salaries, which, given their critical contribution to the fans' enjoyment, seems more equitable than greater profits for owners.

On balance, the sport of soccer developed an organizational pattern far different from that of the traditional American team sports. National associations govern soccer, in cooperation with regional and world federations. National associations operate national teams as a source of income for player development. Clubs also earn income through leagues that are sanctioned by the national association, and they must conform to the rules of national association (or face the ultimate penalty of banishment). Because of the Bosman ruling and the rivalry among leagues, players have effectively won free agency rights and earn high salaries. Unlike in America, player unions do not have much of a role.

Women's Soccer: The Trial of a Single-Entity League

Many of the minor sports in the United States are structured as single-entity leagues rather than associations of separately owned clubs. Teams are organized under collective ownership to reduce ruinous competition between franchises, which leads to lower player salaries and a better bargaining position with broadcasters and cities. Franchises are operated more like divisions or branches of a single firm than as separate companies competing with each other. For sports with a relatively small fan base, organization as a single entity may be the only way for the sport to survive. From that perspective, both fans and league owners benefit from the creation of this kind of monopoly.

Following the success of the U.S. women's national soccer team in the World Cup of 1999, a group of investors organized the Women's United Soccer Association (WUSA) as a single-entity league. Following the model of European soccer, the league was sanctioned by the United States Soccer Federation, which laid out several stringent guidelines that the league would have to satisfy:

- The presence of teams in three of the four U.S. time zones, with a minimum of eight teams
- At least 20 games per team
- A minimum operating budget of $1,000,000 per team
- The requirement that the league release players for national team competitions (Southall et al., 2005)

The intent of these restrictions was to ensure that the U.S. women's soccer league would become the premier women's professional soccer league and attract the best players from across the world.

The league operated for three seasons before folding when investors declined to continue subsidizing its operations. In their analysis, Southall et al. (2005) found that the league's organizers and the soccer federation had overambitious plans for launching a major league from scratch. The league failed to control costs within its potential revenue. By beginning with a large number of teams located all across the country, the league forced high travel and operating costs on its teams, thereby reducing money that could have been spent on marketing.

Comparison with other minor leagues and single-entity leagues is instructive. Arena football slowly built from a small number of teams as demand warranted. Its initial four teams were placed within close proximity of one another to reduce costs. Baseball's minor leagues are often located in a single state or region. Even the National Football League and the National Basketball Association were located in single regions in their formative years (Southall, 2005). Women's soccer could have followed the model of rugby by forming a small number of clubs and using revenue from national team matches to subsidize their operations.

Rugby: The Contest over Professionalism, Nations, and Clubs

The sport of rugby offers many contrasts to the pattern of how other sports developed. Brought to the rest of the world from England, Scotland, Ireland, and Wales by the British Empire, rugby has a number of unique organizational features.

Foremost among those differences is that rugby developed two different rules, or codes: rugby union and rugby league. The two codes differ in terms of the field, the ball, and the rules of tackling and ball possession, as well as issues such as whether the game should be played on Sunday. But the core of the schism between rugby league and rugby union came in the differences regarding professionalism and amateurism. Until 1995 rugby union was an amateur sport, popular in southern England, Scotland, and Wales, whereas rugby league was a professionalized sport that was particularly popular in northern England and among working-class supporters (Dunning and Sheard, 1976).

Between the two games, rugby union has tended to become more dominant internationally, headed by the International Rugby Board (IRB) in Dublin, Ireland. But the Board resisted the idea of professionalism and the idea of a world championship for many years. Rugby was one of the last major sports to remain amateur (Morgan, 2002). Competition was dominated by matches among northern hemisphere teams, known as the Five Nations Championship (later, the Six Nations Championship) and by teams in the southern hemisphere (the Tri-Nations Championship). In 1987 the IRB agreed to host the first Rugby World Cup. Proceeds from these events accrued to the national rugby bodies, which then distributed the proceeds to local clubs for the development of players.

As these sporting competitions became more popular and broadcasters and advertisers paid more to the national governing bodies for televising these events, players agitated for a greater share of the proceeds (Morgan, 2002). Following its success in the first World Cup, the New Zealand All Blacks team lost several of its key players to play in rugby leagues on a professional basis (Hope, 2002). As the 1995 World Cup approached, the IRB agreed to allow professional players to participate in rugby union and the various national associations followed suit.

As players became professional, management of individual clubs became more tenuous, because player salaries overwhelmed profits and required greater subsidies from national organizations. In the southern hemisphere, a proposal by a broadcaster to establish his own professional league led the national governing bodies of Australia, New Zealand, and South Africa to establish the so-called Super-12 League, providing full-time professional play for elite players who would play for the national team when called on. In this model, the national association preempted the formation of an owner-dominated professional league. The formation of the Super-12 League is often credited with the dominance of the sport by the southern teams in subsequent years.

In England and Wales, pressure mounted to establish a similar system of a club league to support the national teams. A professional league with more skilled, full-time players would create a better national team. But the traditional amateur club teams already had established commercial brands, and several clubs switched from member-supported organizations to private commercial entities, building on the pressure to maintain profitability. After years of debate, the clubs and the national association established an agreement to coordinate schedules, share player talent between international competitions and club competitions, and use some of the profits of the international competitions to subsidize operation of the clubs (Morgan, 2002).

These changes in the organization of rugby show how club teams and national teams depend on one another. Unlike soccer, in which broadcast revenue is sufficient for clubs and national teams to be financially independent of each other, in rugby only the national teams are able to generate income above costs. Yet a truly successful national team needs to have its athletes playing each week on a full-time basis, a schedule that only a club league can provide.

Cricket: The Broadcasters' Leagues

The third great English sport, cricket, has been among the most traditional of sports, long characterized by adherence to amateurism and the dominance of the sporting organizations. Until 1993 a private membership club, the Marylebone Cricket Club in London, was the organization that determined the rules of cricket and governed the game internationally. Yet this traditional sport has seen dramatic changes, led by private entrepreneurs seeking a more modern game.

In the late 1970s the Australian Cricket Board faced a challenge by the Australian broadcaster Nine Network, which sponsored a new cricket competition—World Series Cricket. Nine Network's owner, Kerry Packer, formed the new league in response to not receiving the broadcasting rights to the Australian national team test matches from the Australian Cricket Board.

World Series Cricket (WSC) featured several innovations including a one-day format to make the game more viewer friendly, rather than the staid, multiday format of test matches. WSC hired star players from around the world, offering them considerably more than national teams would offer (*World Series Cricket*, 2008).

More recently, factors similar to those behind the formation of World Series Cricket have influenced the creation of a new professional cricket league in India. As in Packer's case, broadcaster Subhash Chandra formed a new Indian Cricket League (ICL), after his network was denied broadcasting rights to test cricket by the Board of Control of Cricket in India (BCCI) (David, 2007). The league uses the increasingly popular Twenty20 format that reduces the duration of a cricket match to three hours, roughly equivalent to the length of a football match. The ICL has found a steady line of advertising sponsors (*Economic Times*, 2007). At this date, the BCCI has banned players who are participating in the ICL, whereas the ICL is willing to release its players for national team competitions (*Indian Cricket League*, 2008). At the same time, the BCCI has sponsored its own professional league, the Indian Premier League (IPL), to compete with the ICL. The jury is still out on this competition among the leagues.

The examples of World Series Cricket and the Indian Cricket League suggest the important role played by advertisers and broadcasters in the growth of professional sports. Television networks need sport programming to attract viewers and advertising dollars. When sport leagues and sporting associations block their access, advertisers and broadcasters have the option of sponsoring their own leagues as entertainment. And when the traditional leagues and associations fail to distribute the growing revenues back to the players or favor an unpopular competition format like multiday test cricket, they risk a revolt involving a much greater challenge than a single entrepreneur.

The most successful rival league in American sports, the American Football League, was established in part through the sponsorship of the ABC television network, which wanted to establish its legitimacy as a major network. More recently, the NBC network formed a rival league, the XFL, after its bid to broadcast NFL games was denied. Combined with the natural desire of players to earn better salaries, these new leagues can radically change the organization of team sports.

Lessons for American Sports

Seen from a global perspective, it is hard to dismiss how differently American team sports are organized relative to other major international sports. Beginning with baseball in the early 1900s, American sport leagues quickly became cartels of competing owners of profit-making teams, which hired professional players. The private owners established the rules of the game as well as the rules of the business, limiting the pay of players, blackballing teams outside their league, sharing revenue, and in later years developing mechanisms for promoting competitive balance among teams. And although the teams colluded to keep player salaries low, American team sports never had any confusion over the merits of amateurism versus professionalism, leaving that issue for colleges and universities to wrestle with.

As sports moved from the spectator era to the broadcasting era, American sport leagues bargained collectively with television networks, rewarding themselves handsomely and, to a lesser extent, the players. Much of the dispute in professional sports has been about how to divide the income.

Moreover, in American baseball, football, basketball, and hockey, league competition is the apex of the sport. International competition, even after the Olympics became professionalized, remains a sideshow, which the leagues accommodate (or not) according to their commercial interest. In no case has a national governing body (or legislature) intervened or sanctioned the professional league for not allowing its players to participate in international competitions.

Although national team competitions are a minor factor in the American sports, it is not correct to describe those sports as insular or provincial or interesting only to Americans. Following the lifting of the restrictions on black players in American sports in the 1950s, professional leagues in the United States have welcomed talent from wherever they can find it. Players from overseas play an important role in American sports—hockey players from Europe, baseball players from Latin America, and basketball players from Europe, Asia, Africa, and Latin America. Only football can be described as a sport dominated by Americans, perhaps because of the level of violence or the cost of the equipment and training. Rarely has anything like the pre-Bosman rules in European soccer leagues been used to establish quotas for domestic players. Factoring in the global marketing power of American professional leagues, they are arguably world sports at the caliber of men's soccer and are certainly much more significant than rugby, tennis, golf, women's soccer, or cricket.

Future Trends

Most observers expect the development of worldwide sporting leagues to continue as the cost of communication and transportation continues to fall. Traditional American sports may find themselves in greater competition from sports that have held dominance in other countries. How will sport leagues adapt to the new level of competition? Should we view the models in other countries as ways to reform U.S. sport leagues, with their problems of monopoly power and restriction of entry?

Noll (2002) and Ross (2001) have explored the idea of converting American professional sport leagues from a closed system into an open multileague system with promotion and relegation. Such a system might be used to reduce the size of the top league and increase the total number of professional teams that have an opportunity to reach the top of the sport. By having a smaller number of teams in the top league, the top players would play each other more frequently. Teams would still have monopoly power over broadcasting rights, but lower-performing teams would need to exert greater effort (i.e., pay higher salaries) to retain their share of league profits in the next season.

Unfortunately, such a proposal would prove risky for owners of franchises that might be relegated. Their sport franchises would lose value if they were placed in a lower league. Moreover, teams in major metropolitan areas might find another franchise from their local area joining the higher league and dividing their monopoly rent. Conversely, the league would face the risk of not having a major metropolitan area market covered following relegation. These issues do not matter to soccer leagues with relegation because teams do not have territorial exclusivity guaranteed in the first place, and the major cities often have several teams, commensurate with their population size. London, for example, has six soccer teams in the Premier League.

Ultimately, it is hard to see how such a change might occur. The leagues themselves are unlikely to be agents of change. For them, accepting a relegation system would greatly endanger their franchise values and would mean forgoing fee income from new franchise owners. National sporting associations are not a threat. No national sporting body has sufficient power to force the U.S. professional leagues to compromise. The only authorities with more power than the professional leagues are Congress and the Supreme Court. Both of these bodies have deferred to the current balance of power between players and owners on issues of labor market competitiveness. And Congress appears to have little interest in forcing the leagues to loosen their monopoly relative to upstart teams and leagues or in reducing the teams' bargaining power with respect to local government.

Conclusion

This chapter has built on the foundation laid in chapter 1, which outlined the conflicts created by league organizations, by looking beyond the major American sports to provide a comparative perspective. The range of organized sport is much wider than what most Americans recognize as the four major professional team sports. Sports that are more prevalent outside the United States, like soccer, cricket, and rugby, operate within structures that differ significantly from the American model, which emphasizes private ownership of individual professional teams and team control of professional leagues. These alternative structures come with their own sources of conflict, but they tend to reduce the monopoly power of sport teams and leagues, creating greater benefits for fans and communities.

CHAPTER 3

Why Professional Athletes Make So Much Money

Zenon X. Zygmont

During the 2009 baseball season, New York Yankees infielders Derek Jeter and Alex Rodriguez earned annual salaries of $21.6 million and $33 million, respectively. Jeter and Rodriguez are superstar players, and both are likely to be inducted into baseball's Hall of Fame after they retire. Although their salaries are among the highest in baseball, other MLB players and athletes in the other major professional sport leagues also tend to be well paid. The median player salary is about $1 million in MLB, $1.2 million in the NHL, $3 million in the NBA, and $0.9 million in the NFL. Those figures are very different from the median annual salaries for nurses (roughly $56,700) and those employed in education, training, and library occupations (about $40,800).

Why are professional athletes paid so much money, especially in comparison to the salaries received in professions like nursing and education? And which profession is more important to society: athletics, or nursing and teaching? Suppose that the government passed a law that limited player salaries to a maximum of $500,000. How many players would quit sports and take up an alternative occupation? Even if many players refused to play, would the outcome be undesirable if we employed fewer athletes and more nurses and teachers? Would lower player salaries result in lower ticket prices, lower fees for cable and on-demand broadcasts of games, and reduced demand by team owners for public subsidies of sport facilities?

The author thanks David Ashby for his comments on an earlier version of this chapter. This chapter is dedicated to the memory of Carl Stevens.

This chapter explores many of the controversies surrounding the labor market for professional athletes and relates those issues to larger questions of public policy. In keeping with the other chapters in this book, and with the tradition of good public policy analysis, this chapter emphasizes the positive rather than the normative. After you have a good grasp of how the labor market operates, you may then evaluate other possibilities and determine whether changes in labor policies in professional sports are desirable or necessary.

The NHL's Missing Season

In February 2005 an unprecedented event occurred in professional sports: The entire 2004–2005 National Hockey League season was suspended because of labor strife between owners and players. The disagreement, not surprisingly, was based on money. One year earlier the National Hockey League (NHL) published the *Independent Review of the Combined Financial Results of the National Hockey League 2002–2003 Season*. The report documented losses of $273 million for the 2002–2003 season (an average of $9 million per team). NHL team owners warned that unless the NHL Players Association (NHLPA) made significant concessions, contraction of the league was inevitable. Yet as Edge (2004, p. 105) noted, "the players' association viewed the [report] with caution"; they assumed that it was no coincidence that the report was published shortly before the expiration of the collective bargaining agreement (CBA) in September 2004. The NHLPA was also aware of the accounting tricks that teams sometimes used to inflate their financial losses, such as understating revenues or overstating expenses. The players did not reject the report entirely, however, and they offered to reduce their salaries, reportedly by as much as 24 percent. Despite this concession, the NHL imposed a lockout on the players in February 2005. A new CBA was not signed until July 2005.

Although the loss of the entire NHL season was an extraordinary event, strikes and lockouts in the four major professional sports are more common than one might expect. (A strike refers to a situation in which employees refuse to work; a lockout occurs when an employer refuses to allow employees to work.) Table 3.1 shows the number of labor disruptions in professional sports since 1970. During the period from 1981 to 2004 professional athletes were approximately 25 times more likely to be involved in a strike or lockout than nonathletes were (Berri, Schmidt, and Brook, 2006). The frequency of these labor disruptions is unusual given overall trends in labor relations in the United States. According to the Bureau of Labor Statistics, work stoppages are becoming less frequent, and a significant decline in such events has occurred since the 1970s (BLS, n.d.).

The occurrence of a labor dispute in professional sports also seems odd given that the salaries and working conditions for athletes are superior to those experienced by workers in other industries. Why would leagues and franchise owners risk canceling games that generate millions of dollars in revenues and potentially taint long-term fan interest? Similarly, why would athletes with million-dollar salaries and relatively pampered lifestyles want to strike? And why do professional athletes make so much money to begin with?

Understanding the source of the friction between owners and players requires some familiarity with player salaries and the labor market for professional ath-

TABLE 3.1

Labor Disruptions in Professional Sports Since 1970

Sport	Date	Event	Duration
NFL	1971	Lockout and strike during training camp	20 days
NFL	1974	Strike during training camp	42 days
NFL	1982	Strike during regular season	57 days
NFL	1987	Strike during regular season	24 days
MLB	1972	Strike during regular season	13 days
MLB	1973	Lockout during spring training	12 days
MLB	1976	Lockout during spring training	24 days
MLB	1980	Strike during spring training	8 days
MLB	1981	Strike during regular season	50 days
MLB	1985	Strike during regular season	2 days
MLB	1990	Lockout during spring training	32 days
MLB	1994-1995	Strike at end of 1994 season and beginning of 1995 season	232 days total including offseason (52 days in 1994, 25 days in 1995)
NBA	1995	Lockout before season	74 days
NBA	1998-1999	Lockout during regular season	191 days
NHL	1992	Strike before playoffs	10 days
NHL	1994-1995	Lockout during regular season	103 days
NHL	2004-2005	Lockout	Entire season

From http://en.wikipedia.org/wiki/Category:Sports_labor_disputes;
http://projects.ldc.upenn.edu/TDT3/topic.research/topic3006.html;
http://www.usatoday.com/sports/football/nfl/2006-03-08-labor-deal-reaction_x.htm

letes. The next section introduces that labor market and shows how salaries are determined. Subsequent discussion looks at the effect of free agency, player productivity, and other salary-related issues.

Wage Determination in Professional Sports

A labor market occurs when sellers of labor interact with buyers of labor. People in the workforce sell labor services to prospective employers in return for a payment. In a competitive labor market, buyers and sellers are numerous. Consider the labor market for accountants. In most cities, many firms employ accountants and many people are trained to work as accountants. A firm will hire an accountant only if the wage that it has to pay the accountant is exceeded by the value generated by the accountant. That value is known as the marginal revenue product

(MRP), the value that an employee produces after all other input costs are taken into consideration. For example, suppose Andrea produces $1,500 in accounting services each week for her employer, firm A, and the cost of the inputs that she needs to do her job (e.g., a computer and an office) is $300 per week. Under these circumstances, firm A should be willing to pay her up to $1,200 every week. It would prefer to pay her less, of course, but it must take into consideration the other accounting firms that are competing for Andrea's services. If firm B offers Andrea a higher wage than she currently receives, she may switch jobs. Similarly, although Andrea prefers to earn the highest possible wage, she realizes that many other trained accountants are in the market. If other equally skilled accountants are willing to work for less than Andrea's MRP of $1,200, she may find herself unemployed if she insists on a wage of $1,200. The competition on both sides of the market is what determines the prevailing wage or salary and the number of people employed.

MRP is defined as the product of marginal product and marginal revenue (MRP = MP × MR). MP is a measure of how productive a worker is in terms of output, and MR is a measure of the additional revenue generated by each new unit of output. For a bakery, MP might be measured as the number of additional cakes produced when an additional baker is hired. MR reflects the additional revenue created when an extra cake is sold. The new baker's value to the bakery is equal to the number of cakes he contributes multiplied by the revenue created by each new cake.

An athlete's value, or MRP, can be thought of as the number of wins that he generates for his team multiplied by the value of each victory.

In a perfectly competitive market, in which athletes' wages are equal to their marginal revenue products, only two factors can explain increasing player salaries: (1) an increase in marginal product or (2) an increase in marginal revenue. The first factor is straightforward; a player who improves and contributes more to the team receives a higher wage when the time comes to renew his contract. The second factor reflects demand, and it is driven by willingness to pay—the willingness of fans to pay for tickets, of networks to pay for broadcasting rights, and of advertisers to pay for slots during those broadcasts. To a large extent, athletes' salaries are high because willingness to pay is high. In other words, fan interest in professional sports causes salaries to be large.

In professional sports, athletes tend to be paid according to their MRP. But several key factors distinguish the labor market for accountants or bakers from the market for athletes. First, athletes create enormous MRP for their employers. The New York Yankees pay third baseman Alex Rodriguez over $20 million each year because he generates at least that amount in ticket sales, television broadcasting rights, and other revenues. It is doubtful that any accountant can produce an MRP of a similar magnitude.

Second, there are far fewer athletes than accountants. The scarcity of athletes compared with accountants is another reason why salaries for the former exceed those of the latter. Simply put, many more men and women are qualified to be accountants than professional athletes. As an example, what percentage of the nation's population is tall enough to play in the NBA?

Third, the labor market for athletes is not perfectly competitive; rather, it has characteristics of a bilateral monopoly. A bilateral monopoly consists of a single

Are Player Salaries Responsible for Higher Ticket Prices?

Many sport fans believe that ticket prices will rise if a team pays a player a higher salary. To understand why this belief is false, consider the following scenario. Suppose that Shaquille O'Neal decides that he wishes to return to Los Angeles to finish off-season his career playing for the Lakers. The Lakers sign him to a multimillion dollar contract. Shortly thereafter, the Lakers announce an across-the-board increase in ticket prices of 15 percent. Lakers fans, while happy that the "Big Aristotle" has returned to town, are nevertheless upset by the price increase—an increase that they might believe was caused by Shaq's large contract.

Let us change this story slightly. Suppose that Shaq announces, "I am willing to play in Los Angeles for free." Will the Lakers still increase ticket prices by 15 percent? Yes. From the perspective of the Lakers, the value of Shaq's contract is irrelevant in determining whether or not to increase ticket prices. The Lakers know that Shaq's return to Los Angeles creates an increase in demand for tickets. As we know from basic economic principles, when demand increases relative to supply, prices rise. (The supply of tickets is limited by the capacity of the arena.) There are many possible explanations for why demand will increase, but the most likely one is that people will expect the Lakers to win more games with Shaq.

We can also answer this ticket price question by reminding ourselves of how the Lakers (or any team) go about maximizing their profits from ticket sales. For simplicity, let us assume that all tickets sell at the same price. Like any profit-maximizing monopolist, the Lakers' ticket price is determined by marginal cost (MC) and marginal revenue (MR). Ticket prices will increase if MC rises, if MR rises, or if both rise. Shaq's contract will not cause MC to increase because MC is unaffected by changes in fixed costs, and player contracts are a fixed cost for a team. As just suggested, however, demand will increase. If demand increases so does MR. Any increase in MR will cause ticket prices to go up.

buyer (a monopsonist) and a single seller (a monopolist). Although the sport labor market is made up of many teams and many players, teams organize into a single league, which exercises monoposonistic power, and players organize into a single labor union, which exercises monopolistic power. Labor (players' unions) and management (league officials) meet every few years to negotiate a new CBA; these negotiations can become contentious, and strikes and lockouts often result from an inability to reach a mutual agreement on the terms and conditions of the CBA. In some respects these negotiations are like the periodic bargaining that goes on between a teachers' union and the school district, between city hall and the firefighters' association, or between the autoworkers and the car companies. The group that has greater bargaining power tends to get their desired result. The same applies to a great extent in professional sports. The bargaining process is a battle in which players try to pull wages up to levels at or above their MRPs, and team owners try to push wages below MRP.

Fourth, unlike teachers, firefighters, or autoworkers, athletes' salaries are only partly determined through negotiation of the CBA between the league and the union. With some exceptions (noted later), the player unions do not establish pay scales or bargain for specific wages for individuals. Rather, the unions establish guidelines that allow each player to bargain for a salary approximating his MRP (later we will see that the crux of the bargaining process is an accurate evaluation of productivity). Economists are generally skeptical of any distortions in the market, including monopolization. Professional sports provide an interesting exception. The introduction of a players union in a market dominated by a single buyer tends to result in players earning something closer to a competitive salary. As described in the next section, before the introduction of unions, players were at the mercy of team owners and earned far below their productivity.

Fifth, price controls are present in the labor market for athletes. Rookies are typically paid a minimum salary. In 2007 a first-year MLB player earned $380,000 and a rookie NBA player made $427,163. CBAs commonly include a pay scale for the years before free agency, but some leagues extend the pay scale even farther; for example, an NBA player with at least 10 years' experience earned a minimum of $1,262,275 during the 2006–2007 season. The NBA and the NHL also have maximum salaries. If salary determination is beginning to sound complicated, it is. The best way to learn about specific salary policies and the myriad loopholes that exist is to read the specific CBAs for each sport (these are available online) and books like Edge's (2004) or Yost's (2006). But let us not lose sight of the main issue: Players want to be paid their MRP.

The NHL's New Collective Bargaining Agreement

We began this chapter discussing the NHL lockout. After the debacle of 2004–2005 a new CBA was signed in July 2005. The new agreement is described as owner friendly because it features a $39 million salary cap per team (although, as mentioned earlier, there is also a salary floor of $21.5 million), limits the top salary earned by any player to 20 percent of the salary cap, establishes a maximum for rookie contracts at $850,000 per year, and cuts signing bonuses. Some notable concessions by management to the players include an escalation of the salary cap if revenues increase (players are guaranteed a minimum of 54 percent of hockey-related revenues), an increase in the minimum player salary from $180,000 to $450,000, a reduction in age for qualification as a free agent, and increased contributions to the pension fund. The NHLPA sought, unsuccessfully, for the imposition of a luxury tax, but players may still benefit from a revenue-sharing program in which the 10 richest franchises subsidize the 15 poorest. The new CBA expires on September 15, 2011.

Limits on total player payroll, commonly known as salary caps, are in place to ensure competitive balance and financial stability. As you learned in chapter 1, leagues strive to keep the talent level as equal as possible across teams. A limit on payroll expenses is also designed to achieve financial stability across franchises by reducing the probability that individual teams will overpay talent (wage > MRP) and become subject to the winner's curse (discussed later).

Sixth, we know that MRP is determined by the combination of a worker's productivity and the price of the good or service that her labor is used to produce. The price of a product produced for sale by a monopoly will be higher than the price of a product produced by a firm in a competitive market. Therefore, if an accountant works for a firm that is a monopoly, the value of her MRP will be greater than it would be if she worked for a firm in a competitive market. This fact is relevant to professional sports because sport leagues are monopolies (more precisely, cartels). Therefore, teams can sell tickets and other products to sport fans at higher prices than they could if the league were in a more competitive market (e.g., if more than one league was present). Because of the monopoly both teams and players capture more revenues.

Free Agency

The watershed event in the history of player–owner labor relations was the introduction of free agency. Free agency simply means that at some specific point in a player's career (usually after four to six years of professional experience), a player is free to sign a contract with any team of his choosing. When a player achieves free agency he is free to sell his services to the highest bidder.

Before the introduction of free agency, players were bound to their teams by a clause in their contracts. In professional baseball this was called the reserve clause. When a player's contract was about to expire, the clause gave his team the option of re-signing him for his previous salary. The clause could be used indefinitely. The effect of such a stipulation was to force a player to stay with a team for as long as the team wished to employ his services, at a wage that did not increase if the player performed better. Because MLB teams agreed not to compete with one another for talent (they colluded), a baseball player could either accept the team's offer or be unemployed; those were his two choices. The other three sport leagues had similar restrictions on players. The result was that players had little bargaining power. Even superstar athletes were paid much less than their MRP.

Players unions formed in the 1950s, but not until two decades later did a combination of union bargaining tactics and litigation bring about the first widespread erosion of the reserve clause. In 1975 MLB was the first league to achieve widespread free agency. The NBA followed in 1981, the NHL in 1993, and the NFL in 1994. Although there is a great deal of commonality across the four leagues, each has slightly different rules about free agency. Leagues differentiate between restricted and unrestricted free agents; the former have fewer years of experience. A team that a restricted free agent belongs to has a right of first refusal if the player receives an offer from another team. This right allows the player's current team to match the salary offer from the new team. If the team does not exercise this right and the player signs with the new team, the original team receives compensation; in the NHL this is a future draft pick. If the player has more years of experience and is considered an unrestricted free agent, he may sign with any team that he chooses, including his current team. In the case of MLB the former club is compensated with one or more draft choices even if the free agent whom they lose is unrestricted.

Economic research documents the importance that free agency has had on player salaries. In baseball, in which MRP estimates are considered the most reliable, the seminal study is by Scully (1974). Scully compared actual salaries to estimates of player productivity, and his results suggest that players bound by the reserve clause were paid only 15 to 20 percent of their MRP. The gap between a player's MRP and his salary (wage < MRP) reflects monopsonistic exploitation. Subsequent research by, among others, Zimbalist (1992), MacDonald and Reynolds (1994), and Krautmann (1999), refined and extended Scully's approach. Although this research remains far from conclusive, the studies tend to confirm the following: A gap between salary and MRP remains in the years before free agency and a pronounced jump in salaries occurs after free agency. Table 3.2 shows average player salaries in each league for the five-season period before and after the introduction of free agency; note that the averages rose substantially after free agency was introduced in each of the leagues.

Note that the compensation system for players is markedly different before and after free agency. Although salary determination is not as one-sided as it used to be, teams continue to have significant monopsonistic power in the early years of a player's career. This stems, in part, from the way that teams initially acquire players—through a draft. The draft is the mechanism through which leagues allocate new talent (e.g., high school and college players) to teams. The first league to use a draft was the NFL in 1936. The NBA followed in 1949, the NHL in 1963, and MLB in 1965. Drafts are structured according to reverse order of finish; the team with the worst record in the previous season usually picks first. But regardless of the round in which a player is drafted or which team drafts him, he remains bound to that team at the team's discretion until he achieves free agency.

The emergence of rival leagues occasionally weakens the monopsonistic power of teams. The appearance of new leagues was especially frequent in the period from 1960 until the early 1980s when the upstart American Basketball Association (ABA), American Football League (AFL), and World Hockey Association (WHA) competed against the incumbent leagues. This increased competition in the labor market clearly benefited players. For example, the entry of the WHA in 1972 promoted competition in the product market—more franchises were added

TABLE 3.2

Average Salary Before and After Free Agency (in 2008 $)

League (first year of free agency)	Five-season period before free agency	Five-season period after free agency	Percentage increase
MLB (1976)	$175,612	$350,512	100%
NBA (1982)	$487,281	$769,436	58%
NHL (1994)	$576,474	$1,466,204	154%
NFL (1995)	$878,103	$1,059,998	21%

Adjusted to current dollars to account for inflation.

Data from http://www.rodneyfort.com/SportsData/BizFrame.htm

in North America—and in the labor market. The WHA, in an effort to produce a quality product, bid talent away from the NHL. Average salaries rose more than 100 percent, and restructured labor contracts favored the players (Edge, 2004; Kahn, 2000). Unfortunately for the players, rival leagues tend to be short lived because they face formidable financial problems, especially in securing television broadcasting contracts as lucrative as those of the incumbent leagues. As financial problems develop, the incumbent league offers to absorb some of the rival's franchises, usually those on the firmest financial footing or located in cities where the incumbent league does not have a presence. The demise of the rival league follows (as was the case for the ABA, AFL, and WHA). But players have another alternative: They can play in leagues outside the United States. These alternatives include, among others, the Canadian Football League, professional basketball leagues in Europe (salaries in the Spanish and Italian leagues are often competitive for journeyman players), and hockey leagues in Russia and Scandinavia.

Free agency aside, the other significant modification in player–owner labor relations concerns dispute resolution over salary, especially in the years before free agency. Even before they reach free agency, players gain bargaining power as they gain experience (Navin and Sullivan, 2002). Third-party dispute resolution is common, mostly in the form of arbitration. Under a system of arbitration the player and the team (or their designated representatives) present a salary offer to the arbitrator. The arbitrator may choose one offer, the other, or make a compromise offer that usually splits the difference. This third possibility creates an incentive for teams to make extremely low offers and the player to make unreasonably high demands. And arbitrators may have the incentive to split the difference to keep both sides happy (Marburger, 2004). The NHL uses the standard arbitration procedure, but in certain cases, if the team disagrees with the arbitrator's salary ruling, the team can exercise its "walk-away rights" and the player becomes an unrestricted free agent. MLB uses a final-offer arbitration system first developed by Stevens (1966). The arbitrator must choose one offer or the other; no splitting the difference or other bargaining takes place. This method encourages each side to make a reasonable offer.

Player Productivity

One of the most interesting labor market issues in professional sports is evaluation of player productivity. As discussed previously, a monetary estimate of productivity (MRP) is the primary determinant of a person's wages or salary. Given the plethora of player performance statistics in baseball, basketball, football, and hockey (e.g., batting average, free throw shooting, yards rushed, goals scored), evaluation of a player's productivity should be straightforward. If quarterback A and quarterback B are similar in every respect except that quarterback A throws more touchdown passes than quarterback B, A should earn a higher salary than B. As we shall see in a moment, this is not always the case.

Salaries, with some of the exceptions noted previously, are negotiated on a case-by-case basis. Players retain agents to negotiate salary, bonuses, and other contractual terms with teams on their behalf. Economists recognize that information is asymmetric and that the advantage in bargaining goes to the side who has better information. For example, a player might know more about his productivity, whereas the team may better understand the financial contribution (the marginal revenue) generated by the player. In any event, determination of MRP is the heart of the process; players want to earn a salary close to their MRP, and owners want to pay less. But as economic research demonstrates, there are many reasons why player productivity is hard to assess.

To begin with, information may be lacking, especially when estimating the MRP of young players. Assessing the skills of a player when he files for free agency is easier than when he is a rookie, simply because more information is available. Many players selected early in the draft turned out to be complete flops in the pros, notably former quarterback Ryan Leaf (once described as "the biggest bust in the history of professional sports"). Conversely, some players, like baseball player Mike Piazza, enjoyed long and productive professional careers but were picked late in the draft or not drafted at all. Teams typically invest considerable resources scouting players before they are drafted to gather as much information as possible. Teams are constantly looking for better ways to assess a young player's potential for a successful career. Not all these assessment tools are based on physical skills or player performance; teams now routinely administer IQ tests and psychological tests to assess intelligence and character. For example, the NFL administers the Wonderlic test (see Merron, n.d.).

Teams recognize that the average player's productivity is nonlinear. It does not continue to increase over time; rather, it rises until a player is at his peak and then begins to decline. Given this, one strategy a team might use is a human capital approach to salary determination. They may pay players less than their MRP early in their careers and more than their MRP later; this possibility was studied by Richardson (2000) for the NHL.

A second issue is the fact that many professional athletes play as part of a team, not as individuals; this element introduces additional complexity to evaluating performance. A professional golfer or tennis player who plays badly has no one else to blame. But in a team sport the performance of a player, say a running back, depends not only on his productivity but also on that of his teammates, especially the offensive line. Economists realize that estimates of MRP must consider the performance of both the player and his teammates. An example of this kind of research is the work of Idson and Kahane (2000). They addressed the issue of the effect of coworker productivity on NHL player salaries. Their hypothesis is that a player's salary is determined directly (through individual and team performance) and indirectly (depending on the extent to which that player is considered a complement or substitute for his teammates). They show that a player's salary may increase or decrease depending on whether the coach and general manager believe that the player's skill is complementary or substitutable in relation to his teammates. If the latter, the team may derive little value from having him on the roster and will not reward this skill as much as will teams who view him as more of a complement.

The third point is that MRP will be influenced by the size of the market in which a player plays. If two MLB players have identical skill levels but one player is on a team that plays in a large market like New York City while the other plays

Is the Labor Market for Athletes Efficient?

In economics and finance an efficient market refers to a market in which buyers use all available and relevant information to determine the value of an asset, such as a stock, bond, or futures contract. A recent publication that illustrates the importance of finding better information in assessing player performance and using it more efficiently is *Moneyball* by Michael Lewis (2003). *Moneyball* describes the player valuation approach used by Oakland A's general manager Billy Beane in determining which players to acquire for the team. In a nutshell, Beane and his staff act like investors in financial markets. They attempt to identify assets that are currently underpriced and undervalued. To accomplish this, Beane uses a set of quantitative tools that incorporate information that other teams ignore or discount, like on-base percentage. Because other teams ignore this information, Beane is able to buy players at a price that is a relative bargain. Does this efficient markets approach work? The A's often have one of the best records in baseball even though they are in one of the smallest markets and have one of the lowest budgets. *Moneyball* also demonstrates that imitation is the sincerest form of flattery. Many MLB teams have jettisoned their old ways of assessing player talent and adopted Beane's asset valuation approach.

Moneyball makes a convincing case that Beane's approach is superior to the conventional wisdom that the status quo player valuation methods are the best. What is lacking in *Moneyball* is a description of the statistical techniques that Beane and the A's use to ferret out the underpriced talent. Berri, Schmidt, and Brook's *The Wages of Wins* (2006; hereafter *WoW*) begins to fill this gap by describing more sophisticated methods of explaining and predicting player productivity. *WoW* touches on MLB and the NFL, but its focus is on the NBA. One of its contributions is to debunk the belief that the most productive players, those that contribute the most to a team's winning percentage, are those that score the most often. This belief is promulgated in part by the NBA itself. The authors of *WoW* argue, "People in the NBA are mistaken about the relative value of scoring and other aspects of player performance" (2006, p. 200). In other words, although scoring is an important element in winning games, it is overrated when other performance metrics, like field goal percentage, are taken into consideration. Nevertheless, the NBA, team owners, general managers, and coaches continue to make scoring the centerpiece in their evaluation of talent. (Some other useful presentations of the *Moneyball* hypothesis include Hakes and Sauer, 2006, and Bradbury, 2007, in particular pp. 176–198).

in Milwaukee, the first player's MRP will be greater than the second's will. Consequently, the first player will earn a higher salary. Simply put, greater revenue will be generated in markets with larger populations, more businesses, and more media exposure. This relationship, noted by Scully (1989), has support elsewhere in the literature (e.g., Burger and Walters, 2003, and Gustafson and Hadley, 2007).

Fourth is the question of incentives. Team owners want to structure contracts with players to elicit the maximum performance possible. Players, however, may choose a lower level of effort or ignore other provisions in the contracts. This circumstance creates a moral hazard problem. One area in which this is problematic is with multiyear contracts. From the player's perspective a multiyear contract is better than a year-to-year contract. A team may also benefit from the certainty of having a player on its roster for an extended period rather than for only a season or two. But a drawback from the team's perspective is the difficulty of ensuring that the player will perform at the level of his MRP for the duration of the contract. To borrow a phrase from the financial markets, "Past performance is no guarantee of future returns" (Berri, Schmidt, and Brook, 2006, p. 166; hereafter Berri et al.). In other words, what is the probability the player will shirk? Economic research provides mixed evidence that shirking occurs (see Lehn, 1990, and Berri and Krautmann, 2006). Still, to counter the potential for shirking, teams typically do two things: They offer shorter contracts or insist on performance-based incentives in the player's contract (e.g., part of a basketball player's salary is determined by the number of assists that he makes over the course of the season). Note that empirical work suggests that players increase their level of effort in the last year of a contract, especially if in the subsequent year they are eligible for free agency (e.g., Stiroh, 2007).

Finally, as discussed in the next section, teams may systematically overpay for talent (pay salaries greater than MRP), especially for free agents.

Is It Possible to Pay Too Much?

Before the 2007 season the San Francisco Giants acquired 29-year-old free agent Barry Zito from the Oakland A's (Zito was one of the underpriced players originally acquired by Billy Beane). At the time that he was signed by the Giants, few doubted that this three-time all-star was one of the premier pitchers in MLB. Yet a question remained: At $126 million (for seven years) did the Giants pay too much for Zito's services?

When teams bid on free agents they are participating in an auction. Economists recognize that an auction mechanism can lead to an unintended consequence known as the winner's curse, in which the winning bidder pays more than the item for sale is worth. The curse occurs in a variety of settings including the labor market for professional athletes (see Cassing and Douglas, 1980, and Burger and Walters, 2008).

The competitive process in which a free agent is hired is essentially an auction; numerous bidders (the teams) vie against each other, and no one wants to lose. Why might a winning bid for a free agent exceed a player's true value? Three factors come to mind. First, there is uncertainty because teams have imperfect information. No team has a crystal ball that can accurately predict the effect that the player will have and the MRP stream that he will generate. Their bids thus become no more than guesses, not informed choices. The team that guesses the most will be the high bidder. A paradoxical logic may be at work: Informational uncertainty can cause some teams to over- or undervalue a player's productivity, but overvaluation increases the team's probability of having the winning bid! Second, research in psychology and behavioral economics suggests that people tend to be overconfident in their decision-making abilities; team owners (and other front-office staff) may think they are better at evaluating talent than they really are. Therefore, if an owner believes that scoring is the most important attribute of a basketball player, convincing him otherwise may be difficult even if the facts suggest that his belief is incorrect. And third, nobody likes to lose. Auctions often cause people to become caught up in the heat of moment and make bids that are too high just so that they can come out on top.

Another possible explanation for overpayment is risk aversion. Teams pay "too much" for talent because owners and general managers view players as a kind of insurance policy in case the team has a losing season or is viewed to have underperformed. Imagine that you are the general manager of the San Francisco Giants. In 2006 the team's disappointing 76-85 record did not qualify it for the playoffs. In the off-season, to help the team compete in 2007, you want to sign a free agent left-handed starting pitcher. Zito is available, but so are several other pitchers including Odalis Perez. Perez does not have the same career credentials as Zito, but he is a seasoned veteran about the same age as Zito and he can be acquired at a lower salary.

If you hire Zito, his salary is $18 million; if you choose Perez, his is $7 million. If Zito wins 18 games, he costs you $1 million per win. But if Perez happens to win 18 games, you are paying him only $389,000 per win. Which player do you choose? You probably pick Zito. Although he is far more expensive, by hiring him you have purchased insurance. If the Giants have a poor season, you have a ready response for the team owner, the fans, and the media: "But we signed Barry Zito. If Zito can't help us to the playoffs, then no one can." But if the Giants tank after you sign Perez, you would likely be subject to more criticism from fans and the media. Your job could be in jeopardy. As Berri et al. pointed out (2006, p. 213), "Millions of people watch and pay attention to sports. When coaches and general managers make mistakes in sports, not only do they lose their jobs, but they are also open to ridicule from a very large group of people." If the conventional wisdom says that Zito should be selected before Perez, regardless of Zito's salary, a team is likely to choose Zito.

Future Trends

The bilateral monopoly nature of the labor market and the fact that professional sport leagues create billions of dollars in revenues suggest that lockouts and strikes will continue to occur in the future. Do these labor conflicts have potential public policy implications? For example, could a strike or lockout have a negative financial effect on both a franchise and the local community? Let us consider the second possibility first. As you will learn in chapter 4, substantial economic research indicates that the economic effect of a professional sport franchise on the economy of a city is negligible. If a franchise contributes little to the economy of a metropolitan area during the season, then it makes sense that a labor dispute that causes games to be lost will not broadly cause economic harm (see Coates and Humphreys, 2001, and Berri et al., 2006). Cancellation of games may have a narrow economic effect in the form of lost jobs at the stadium or arena (e.g., ticket sales and concession sales) and less traffic at bars and restaurants near the facility, but on net a negative macroeconomic shock to the city will not happen.

A larger issue concerns the financial viability of a franchise. Player salaries are both a fixed cost and the largest cost item to a team. Thus, they may contribute to a franchise's lack of profitability, which in turn can create an incentive for the team to move to another city (or seek public subsidies). Three of the four leagues have a salary cap, and the fourth, the MLB, uses a luxury tax to attempt to curb excessive spending by teams on athletes, spending that may imperil the financial viability of the franchise. But again, in a worst-case scenario, the loss of a franchise, for financial or other reasons, will not jeopardize the local economy; it will have only the narrow effects previously mentioned. Fans, and perhaps local politicians, will be disappointed, but the city will be fine.

Conclusion

Recall that strikes and lockouts are part of an ongoing battle in which players try to pull wages to levels at or above their MRP, whereas team owners try to push wages below MRP. In a competitive labor market, employees such as accountants tend to be paid their MRP. Although the labor market for professional athletes in not perfectly competitive, players' salaries do tend to reflect MRP, in part because of the strength of players' unions and the establishment of free agency. Individual salaries often increase because of improvements in athletes' performance (increasing MP), but to a large extent, rising salaries in sports are driven by increasing marginal revenue. Fans, television executives, and advertisers have a high demand for the products of professional sports and are willing to pay high prices for them. So the next time that you gawk in disbelief at the big money offered by your favorite team to sign a journeyman middle relief pitcher, remember that players' salaries reflect our demand for professional sports. Yet our passionate interest in sports does not mean that we consider other occupations, like nursing and teaching, to be unimportant. Consider the following information from the *Statistical Abstract of the United States*: In 2006 personal consumption expenditure on all spectator sports was an estimated $17.2 billion, whereas expenditure on K–12 education was approximately $521 billion. Yes, we enjoy professional sports, but we also recognize where our priorities lie.

PART II

Professional Sports, Cities, and Public Finance

© Jim Cowsert/Icon SMI

In the introduction to part I, we illustrated that sophisticated sport fans are receiving a crash course in public policy and economics as they read the sports section of their local newspaper. But certain aspects of the sport industry affect a much wider segment of the population, extending beyond the exclusive range of sport fans.

Elected officials and other city leaders see professional sports as big business with mass appeal, and view sport teams, venues, and events as potential elements of economic development policies or plans designed to recast city image. Because of the limited number of teams and big-time events available, cities that pursue such strategies must compete with one another. As a result, hosting a team or event often comes at great public expense.

To evaluate the merit of economic development and planning strategies that include sport subsidies, one must develop an understanding of related economic theory, other social and political factors that can influence such decisions, and potential workable alternatives to the status quo.

In chapter 4, Charles Santo opens the discussion of public investment in sport by exploring the relative magnitude of professional sports as an element of the local economy and examining how related economic impacts are predicted and whether they are real.

Santo continues this discussion in chapter 5, which helps the reader understand recent trends in stadium and arena construction. The chapter considers some possible explanations for the continued support of sport facility subsidies, focusing on the mix of economic circumstances, political influence, and private power that sways public investment decisions. Santo also considers the relative importance of the intangible and consumption benefits generated by sport teams and facilities.

Community ownership is often proposed as an alternative approach that could limit the threat of franchise relocation and reduce related stadium subsidies. In chapter 6, Dorothy Norris-Tirrell and Susan Tomlinson Schmidt present a unique model of nonprofit community ownership in action and introduce the role and effect of social entrepreneurship. Their chapter uses the minor-league baseball Memphis Redbirds as a case study.

CHAPTER 4

Economic Impact of Sport Stadiums, Teams, and Events

Charles A. Santo

From the X-Games to the Olympic Games, from bush league ballparks to state-of-the-art major-league stadiums, governments spend large amounts of public money to lure sporting events or host teams. This chapter begins an exploration of public policy decisions regarding investment in sport by laying a foundation that focuses on the economic impacts of stadiums, teams, and events. This focus provides an essential grounding for the evaluation of public investment decisions that are often framed in the context of economic development policy. Building on that foundation, chapter 5 considers other reasons that officials and residents might support public investment in sport, and illustrates how such decisions are swayed by a mix of economic circumstances, political influence, and private power.

The contents of the current chapter will

- examine the role that professional sports play in a local economy;
- explain the process used to project the economic impacts of sport stadiums, teams, and events, and describe the main sources of error (or abuse) that lead to exaggerated projections of economic impacts; and
- review some empirical studies that cast doubt on the ability of stadiums, teams, and sporting events to serve as economic catalysts.

Public Cost of Big-Time Sports

The expenditure of public money on sport facilities and events is an international phenomenon that occurs at every level of government. The government of Portugal spent $732 million to host Euro 2004, the European soccer championship tournament (Smale, 2004, June 2). Public money paid for the construction of seven new stadiums in a country about the size of the state of Indiana. Portugal's spending paled in comparison with the cost associated with the 2002 World Cup, cohosted by South Korea and Japan. To prepare for the event, various Japanese localities built 7 new stadiums and renovated 3 others at a cost of $4.5 billion. South Korea spent $2 billion on 10 new facilities (Struck, 2002).

Olympic spending dwarfs even these figures. The Greek government spent $12.8 billion to hold the 2004 Summer Olympics in Athens, and the Chinese government invested over $43 billion for the Beijing Games in 2008 (Gross, 2008). This type of spending is often speculative in nature; cities take on construction projects long before they are awarded host status. Public spending on the 2002 Salt Lake City Games began in 1990 when a portion of state and local sales tax revenue was diverted to fund construction of bobsled, luge, speed skating, and ski jump facilities. Salt Lake City was not awarded the 2002 Games until 1995 (Burbank et al., 2001). The Los Angeles Coliseum (built in 1923), Chicago's Soldier Field (1924), and Cleveland's Municipal Stadium (1931) were all built with public money in failed bids to host the Olympic Games. (Los Angeles did successfully attract the 1932 Games.) These facilities all eventually played host to professional baseball or football teams.

Recent spending on stadiums for top-level professional teams has generated a great deal of attention. Between 2000 and 2009, 31 major-league stadiums and arenas opened across urban America at a public cost of approximately $8 billion. A few were built to attract new teams, but most replaced existing facilities for incumbent teams. Cincinnati's Cynergy Field (formerly called Riverfront Stadium), former home of the NFL Bengals and MLB Reds, was replaced by two new stadiums built with over $600 million in subsidies from Hamilton County. Multiple facilities were also built to replace Three Rivers Stadium in Pittsburgh and Veterans Stadium in Philadelphia. The average cost of a football or baseball stadium built since 2000 is $528 million. The average cost of a basketball or hockey arena built during this period is $276 million. Public money has typically covered about two-thirds of these costs. (Chapter 5 provides a detailed assessment of recent stadium construction trends.)

Economic Magnitude of Sport in Perspective

The significant investment by local governments suggests that the economic returns of sport must be quite large. Indeed economic benefits are often proffered as the justification for sport subsidies. Teams, stadiums, and events are commonly promoted as economic catalysts. For example, in 1997 a group campaigning for a new publicly funded football stadium for the San Francisco 49ers used the slogan "Build the Stadium—Create the Jobs!" (Epstein, 1997). The Oregon Stadium Campaign, a group working to bring major-league baseball to Portland, ran an ad in the local newspaper that read, "$150 million company seeks move to Oregon. Will bring jobs, development, snappy new uniforms."

If you have read the previous chapters of this book, we hope that you are now convinced that talking about sport as big business is legitimate. Sport leagues cater to ever-expanding global markets. Wealthy individuals and powerful conglomerates buy and sell teams for hundreds of millions of dollars. Unions struggle with owners for their share of revenue, and salaries climb increasingly higher, in part because of escalating television contracts. Big business indeed, but how big is big? By many indicators, sport teams as individual firms play only minor roles within complex urban economies.

Many professional sport teams have annual revenues that exceed $100 million. Average annual revenues are approximately $155 million in the NFL, $130 million in MLB, $95 million in the NBA, and $70 million in the NHL (Zimbalist, 2003). These numbers may seem large, but some comparisons can provide perspective. If you are enrolled in a state university, chances are that your school takes in more revenue and spends more than the closest professional sport team. For example, Portland State University has a budget of nearly $200 million, more than twice that of the Portland Trailblazers. For another comparison, consider this: In 2003 the average Costco wholesale store had annual sales of $113 million, exceeding the revenues of most sport teams (Heylar, 2003). Few would expect a big-box warehouse store to be a major player in an urban economy, yet they are typically bigger businesses than sport teams. Of course, the local warehouse store does not have devoted fans who wear Costco hats, paint their faces in Costco blue and red, and follow the successes and failures of the store on the nightly news. We will discuss those benefits (consumption benefits) in the next chapter, but for now let us focus on the role of sport teams in the local economy.

Another way to put the economic magnitude of sport teams in perspective is by examining the share of total payroll and employment that they represent within their local economies. We can use Portland as a case study to explore the current significance of the Trailblazers and the potential significance of adding a professional baseball team.

Table 4.1 shows total private-sector employment and payroll for Multnomah County and Portland's six-county primary metropolitan statistical area in 2001. The table also shows employment and payroll figures for the spectator sport industry, as defined by the North American Industry Classification System (NAICS). This industry category (NAICS 71121) includes all professional and semiprofessional sport teams; athletes involved in individual professional sports; and businesses associated with automobile, horse, and dog racing. For the Portland metropolitan

TABLE 4.1

Employment and Payroll in Portland's Spectator Sport Industry

	EMPLOYEES			PAYROLL ($100,000s)		
	Total	Spectator sports	Spectator sports as % of total	Total	Spectator sports	Spectator sports as % of total
Multnomah County	380,379	762	0.20%	14,130,922	116,550	0.82%
Portland Metropolitan Area	836,996	762	0.09%	31,086,682	116,550	0.37%

Data from Bureau of Labor Statistics.

area, the Trailblazers make up the bulk of this category, but it also includes payroll and employment related to a minor-league baseball team, Portland International Raceway, Portland Meadows horse-racing track, Multnomah Greyhound Park, and other small spectator sport ventures. Still, the industry accounts for less than 1 percent of Multnomah County's private sector payroll and only 0.2 percent of the county's jobs. At the metropolitan area level, the contributions of spectator sports are even more diminutive.

Using this approach, we can examine how things would look if the Oregon Stadium Campaign were successful in adding a major-league baseball team to Portland's sport landscape. Remember the newspaper ad "$150 million company seeks move to Oregon. Will bring jobs, development, snappy new uniforms"? For starters, the $150 million figure seems too high. According to figures furnished by Major League Baseball in 2001, average team revenue was $118 million. *Forbes* estimates average team revenues for 2003 to be about $130 million. Although a few teams have revenues that exceed $150 million, a team willing to relocate to Portland would likely be on the low end of the revenue spectrum (at or below $100 million).

Let us make the generous assumption that a Portland baseball team would have a payroll of about $80 million, near the league average. Again, the teams most likely to move are low-payroll franchises. For example, in 2004 the Oregon Stadium Campaign worked diligently to lure the Montreal Expos, whose payroll at the time was $44 million. The opening day 2009 payroll of the Florida Marlins was approximately $36 million. As shown in table 4.2, a firm with an $80 million payroll would account for about 0.5 percent of Multnomah County's payroll and 0.25 percent of the metropolitan area payroll. Table 4.2 also revises table 4.1 by adding this $80 million to the overall payroll figure for the spectator sport industry. Even with the addition of a baseball team, the spectator sport industry would account for just slightly more than 1 percent of the county's total private sector payroll and less than 1 percent at the metropolitan area level. (For the record, we do not doubt the part about the snappy new uniforms!)

TABLE 4.2

Portland's Spectator Sport Industry With an MLB Team

	PAYROLL ($100,000s)		
	Total	New MLB team	MLB team as % of total
Multnomah County	14,210,922	80,000	0.56%
Portland Metropolitan Area	31,166,682	80,000	0.26%
	PAYROLL ($100,000s)		
	Total	Revised spectator sports	Revised spectator sports as % of total
Multnomah County	14,210,922	196,550	1.38%
Portland Metropolitan Area	31,166,682	196,550	0.63%

Data from Bureau of Labor Statistics.

Promoting Sport Investment Through Economic Impact Analysis

Based on the preceding analyses, it would seem difficult to argue that stadiums and sporting events can serve as economic engines. But promoters of public investment in sport usually present impressive numbers to back up their campaign slogans. They assert that the economic benefits of sport are bigger than team revenues or contributions to local payroll. You have likely heard of or seen reports that tout the projected economic impact of sport investments. For example, a study regarding the construction of a stadium to host the MLB Arizona Diamondbacks predicted annual economic impacts of $162 million for the City of Phoenix and $230 million for the state of Arizona (Deloitte & Touche, 1993). The St. Louis Regional Chamber and Growth Association (2004) asserted that the Cardinals baseball team generated an annual regional economic impact of $163 million. Similar predictions are made for one-time mega sporting events like Super Bowls and all-star games as well. Predicted economic impacts of the 2010 Olympic Games to be held in Vancouver are as high as $10.7 billion (InterVISTAS, 2002; Shaffer et al., 2003).

These figures come from studies called economic impact analyses—predictive tools that are the dominant marketing device used by sport investment campaigns. These studies provide projections of the economic impact that a team or event will generate. Almost every new stadium proposal is accompanied by an economic impact analysis. Proponents use these studies to argue that sport investments are justified because the predicted benefits exceed the costs.

Explaining Economic Impact Analysis

The term *economic impact* refers to a measure of the spending, income, or employment associated with a sector of the economy or a specific project (such as the construction of a new facility). The economic impact of a team can be bigger than its revenue or payroll because the impact is not limited to immediate spending at the ballpark. The expenditures of an individual firm are not self-contained. Each firm interacts with other parts of the economy when it purchases goods and services or when its employees spend part of their income. These secondary transactions are elements of the firm's overall economic impact. Looking beyond the revenue and payroll of a team to define its economic impact is perfectly legitimate, but for a variety of reasons, promotional studies have tended to overstate the economic impacts of sport teams and events. Before examining the sources of such errors, let us look at how economic impact analysis works.

At the center of economic impact analysis is the concept of the multiplier. The multiplier accounts for the fact that an injection of spending in one sector of the economy can set off waves of activity in related sectors. As the initial spending circulates and recirculates through the economy, its impact is multiplied. To project the overall economic impact on the local economy, the initial local spending is weighted by a factor called the multiplier.

To illustrate the multiplier concept, let us examine how these waves of economic activity occur with a hypothetical sporting event. Figure 4.1 illustrates the process. By following the money from initial injection to final economic impact, we will

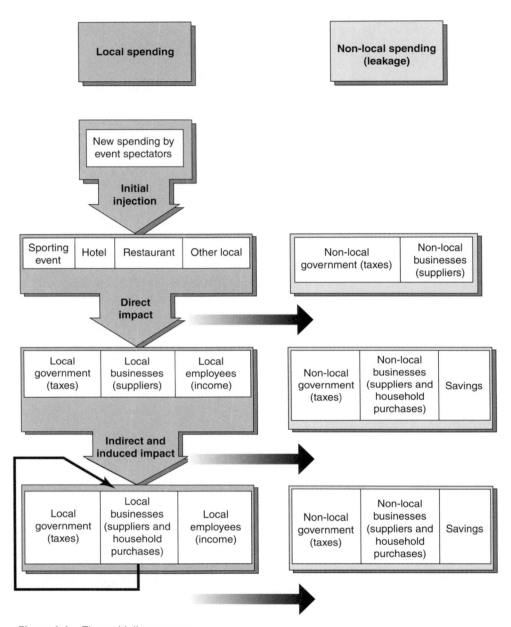

Figure 4.1 The multiplier process.

work backward to calculate the multiplier. (We must work backward because in reality the final economic impact is not known. Analysts use an estimate of the initial local spending and a predetermined multiplier to project the final impact.)

Suppose that your city hosts a tournament and that all the spectators who attend the event are visitors from outside the metropolitan area. Further, suppose that the sole purpose of each of spectator's visit is to attend the tournament. If these spectators spend $200,000 in the metropolitan area over a long weekend, that $200,000 represents the initial injection of money into the local economy. The initial spending will flow to the organization that puts on the tournament, as well as to the hotels, restaurants, and other local establishments where spectators spend their money.

These firms will spend some of this money within the local economy, buying goods and services from local suppliers, paying employees who live in the metropolitan area, and paying taxes to the local government. This first round of additional spending is called the direct impact. Direct impacts accrue to local firms that directly support the tournament or supply the local hotels or restaurants that are affected. Not all of the $200,000 initial injection will be circulated within the local economy; some of it will escape. The firms might import some of their supplies from nonlocal businesses or pay some employees who do not reside in the metropolitan area, and they will almost certainly pay state and federal taxes. The process by which money escapes the local economy is referred to as leakage. Only the money that remains in the local economy can be considered an economic gain to the city. Let us say that $100,000 of spending remains in the metropolitan area.

The money that remains in the local economy is subsequently spent again, just like the initial injection. The businesses that received a share of the direct impact in the first round of spending now circulate the money to *their* suppliers and employees and pay taxes. Of course, more leakage occurs as some of the money escapes to nonlocal sources. This second wave of spending is the beginning of a chain reaction of future waves called indirect impacts. Besides the money exchanged by local firms, the wages paid to employees along the way further the economic ripple effects. The portion of these earnings that workers spend on local goods and services is called the induced impact. For example, if an employee of the local firm that provides marketing services for the tournament spends some of his earnings to remodel his home, additional induced impacts would occur. Earnings spent on nonlocal purchases or put into savings do not contribute to economic gains for the city, because they are removed from local circulation.

These additional waves of spending continue to occur. Some money escapes in each round into savings or nonlocal spending until the initial injection diminishes to an insignificant amount. Figure 4.1 depicts the various waves of economic activity as a chain, but the process could also been shown as a loop, because local businesses and residents recirculate the initial injection by transferring it other local business and employees, who then spend it with local business again, and so on. The total economic impact is the sum of the direct, indirect, and induced impacts. Figure 4.2 provides a simplified example of how total economic impacts accrue over several rounds of spending.

In this example, a direct impact of $100,000 generates a total impact of about $167,000 in sales. The multiplier is simply a ratio of the final impact to the direct impact, which can be expressed as

Multiplier = (Direct + Indirect + Induced Impacts) / Direct Impact

From our example:

Multiplier = $166,557 / $100,000 = 1.67

A sales multiplier of 1.67 indicates that every dollar spent by tournament visitors creates $1.67 worth of total local sales.

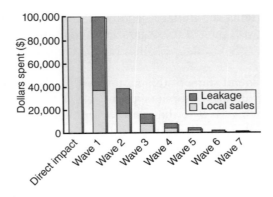

Initial injection	$200,000	
Direct impact	Local sales: $100,000	Leakage: $100,000
Indirect and induced impact		
Wave 1	$40,000	$60,000
Wave 2	$16,000	$24,000
Wave 3	$6,400	$9,600
Wave 4	$2,560	$3,840
Wave 5	$1,024	$1,536
Wave 6	$410	$614
Wave 7	$164	$246
Total impact	$166,557	

Figure 4.2 A simplified example of the multiplier.

Remember, in this example we have worked backward, calculating the sales multiplier from initial and total spending. In practice, economic impact analysis is used to predict the total spending. Analysts begin with an estimate of the direct impact and apply a predetermined multiplier to project the total spending. Rearranging the preceding formula, we get

(Direct + Indirect + Induced Impacts) = Direct Impact × Multiplier

or

Projected Total Impact = Direct Impact × Multiplier

Because analysts cannot calculate individual multipliers with primary data for each economic impact analysis, they apply predetermined multipliers. The Bureau of Economic Analysis (BEA) provides a set of standard multipliers, or analysts can develop customized figures using IMPLAN (IMpact analysis for PLANning) software and data. These multipliers vary by industry and region. They are determined by examining the inputs and outputs of an industry to gauge its interactions with other industries. For example, to determine the overall impact of increased demand in the timber industry, the BEA needs to know which other industries supply inputs to the timber industry and how much of those inputs are needed. They also need information about how those industries are linked to others, and so on. An industry that imports few of its inputs will have a larger multiplier than one that uses many imports. Industries in larger, more diverse regions will likely import fewer inputs than those in smaller or rural regions. A multiplier for a state will be larger than the multiplier for one of its counties because less spending escapes the larger area through leakage.

Identifying Types of Multipliers

Economic impacts can be measured in three different ways by applying different types of multipliers. The preceding example illustrated the sales multiplier, which projects the total change in local sales, or output, resulting from an initial increase in local spending. (The sales multiplier is sometimes referred to as the output multiplier or transaction multiplier.) Analysts might also wish to predict the number of jobs that will be generated by a certain event, project, or sector of the economy. The employment multiplier is a factor applied to the initial increase in local spending to project the total number of jobs created. Local residents might be most concerned with the effect that a project or event will have on their household income. Remember that wages paid to local employees are part of the waves of spending described earlier. The overall impact on local household income is projected by applying an income multiplier to the initial increase in local spending (Archer, 1982; Crompton, 1995).

Sources of Exaggeration in Economic Impact Analysis

Although the multiplier is a valid economic concept and economic impact analysis is a legitimate technique, it is not an exact science. The projection process requires the analyst to make numerous assumptions, including defining the local area, estimating the direct impact, and choosing the multiplier. These assumptions leave the process open to error or manipulation and allow the exaggeration of impacts. Because these studies are often commissioned by team owners or groups trying to justify a public investment, the potential for bias is high. Unchecked partiality can contribute to deleterious policy decisions. Public officials considering the worthiness of public investment in sport should be cautious about relying on promotional economic impact analyses as the main criteria for decision making. And citizens should be wary of policymakers who blindly accept and tout the results of such analyses. (See chapter 5 for a discussion of the potential for private power to influence political decision making.) Next, we will explore some of the main sources of error (or abuse) that lead to overstated economic impacts.

Inclusion of Substitution Spending

Economic impact analyses often fail to account for substitution spending and incorrectly assume that all money spent at stadiums or sporting events is "new money," rather than spending that is redirected from elsewhere in the local economy. A stadium or sport event creates economic impact by prompting local spending that would not have otherwise occurred. Recall that in our hypothetical tournament example, all the spectators who attended the event were visitors from outside the area; thus, all their spending represented new money. In reality, most of the fans in stadiums or arenas are residents of the local metropolitan area. Sources show that between 70 and 95 percent of sport spectators are local (Crompton, 1995; Noll and Zimbalist, 1997). (This figure depends on how the local area is defined—an issue that will be discussed in a later section.) Sporting events provide additional entertainment options for metropolitan area residents but do not increase their leisure budget. When residents spend at the ballpark or neighborhood restaurants before the game, they are merely shifting their leisure spending from elsewhere in the local economy, perhaps decreasing spending at local bowling alleys or movie theaters. This spending is substitution spending—spending that would have occurred anyway—rather than new spending. Substitution spending should not be included in the direct impact of the stadium. Analysts should concentrate on the spending of visitors from outside the defined local area. Including the spending of local residents leads to substantially inflated impact projections.

The inclusion of "casuals" and "time switchers" also contributes to inflated impact projections (Crompton, 1995). Recall that in our hypothetical example, the sole purpose of each spectator's visit was to attend the local sport tournament. In contrast, casuals are visitors in town for business or other reasons who elect to attend a sporting event. In the absence of the event, they would likely spend their money on some other form of entertainment in the city. Time switchers are spectators who may have been planning a trip to the area for some time but change the timing of their visit to coincide with the event. Again, their spending within the local economy would have occurred without the event. Spending by casuals or time switchers should be considered substitution spending and, like spending by local residents, should be excluded from the impact projection.

Hudson (2001) reviewed 13 economic impact analyses related to professional sport teams and found that 11 of the studies included spending from locals or casuals. Crompton (1999) argued that "the widespread admonition from economists to disregard locals' spending is frequently ignored because when expenditures by local residents are excluded, the economic impact numbers become too small to be politically useful" (p. 18). Crompton used an economic impact analysis that he conducted to illustrate the difference that excluding substitution spending can make. The study projected the impact of a 10-day festival that incorporated over 60 sport and cultural events. When he included the spending of locals, casuals, and time switchers, Crompton projected a total impact of $322 million in sales and $137 million in household income. After these sources of spending were excluded, the impacts dropped to $25 million in sales and $16 million in household income.

There is one exception to the rule that the spending of local residents should be ignored. A team or event might cause some local residents to spend money inside the local economy that they would have otherwise spent outside the area. For example, a family might forgo their annual summer trip to Las Vegas to attend a ballgame at home. This effect is referred to as import substitution and can be considered new local spending rather than substitution spending.

Understating Leakage

Aside from overstating the new local spending generated by sport teams and events, some projections exaggerate the total economic impact by using inappropriately large multipliers. These studies often understate the leakage associated with professional sport teams. Recall that leakage is the process by which money escapes the local economy. The greater the amount of money that escapes, the lower the multiplier should be.

Most of the money spent at a stadium goes to player salaries. Player payrolls account for between 55 and 75 percent of team revenues in the NFL, NBA, NHL, and MLB (Spiros, 2004). The bulk of the remaining money goes to well-paid owners and executives. The total impact of this spending depends on how much of it is respent in the local economy (Siegfried and Zimbalist, 2000; Spiros, 2004).

Owners and players generally face a high federal tax rate and have high savings rates, so a large portion of their earnings does not go into local circulation. In addition, players and owners often do not live in their host city year round. For example, Siegfried and Zimbalist (2002) found that only 29 percent of NBA players permanently resided in the city of their team during the 1999–2000 season. Players who live elsewhere spend their money elsewhere. Thus, a large percentage of the money spent at local games escapes the local economy through leakage, which serves to dampen the multiplier effect. If this is not accounted for in the choice of the multiplier that is applied, the indirect impacts will be overstated.

Inconsistent Local Area Definition

To determine which spectators are locals and which are visitors, analysts must define the boundaries of the local area. The area can be defined as the city, the surrounding metropolitan area, the entire state, or in some other manner, but after the definition is determined, it should be consistently applied. Defining the local area with a small radius increases the percentage of spectators who can be counted as visitors (and whose spending can therefore be counted as new money), but a larger geographical area allows the use of a larger multiplier because leakage decreases as area size expands. Using different definitions of the local area for different parts of the analysis is a serious flaw that can lead to substantially inflated projections. A study of the impact of the Commonwealth Games in Victoria, British Columbia, considered all spectators from outside the city to be visitors but projected the economic impacts for the entire province (Crompton, 1995; Hudson, 2001).

A similar problem arises if an analyst defines the local area as the city or county and then applies a standard regional multiplier. Such a multiplier would be inappropriately large because more leakage occurs at the city or county level than at the larger regional level.

Misleading Employment Projections

Economic impact analyses create projections of total employment that can be misleading. These studies often fail to distinguish between full-time and part-time jobs created, leaving readers to draw their own conclusions. In addition, the projection process assumes that all existing employees in the local economy are fully utilized before the event in question, so that an increase in visitor spending will necessarily lead to an increase in employment. This assumption is especially problematic in estimating the impact of tournaments or other events of short duration. Local employers are not likely to hire new workers to meet the increased demand associated with a weekend event. Servers that attend to 15 tables an hour might simply be asked to serve 25. Any jobs that are created are likely to be only temporary. Even in the case of a new sport team coming to town, affected businesses might simply require employees to work harder rather than increase their staff. In addition, there is no reason to believe that all jobs created will be filled by residents of the defined local area.

Ex Post Facto Empirical Evaluations

Because of the shortcomings just described, economists have been wary of the findings of economic impact analyses. In response, researchers have conducted numerous independent empirical studies that serve as ex post facto evaluations, or "after-the-fact audits" (Baade and Dye, 1990), of the effect of sport investments on local economic indicators. Unlike predictive economic impact analyses, these studies examine what has already happened. Evidence from this research casts further doubt on the ability of stadiums, teams, and sporting events to serve as economic development engines (see Austrian and Rosentraub, 1997; Baade, 1996; Baade and Dye, 1990; Coates and Humphreys, 1999; Porter, 1999; Rosentraub, 1997; Siegfried and Zimbalist, 2000).

Empirical Evaluations of Stadiums and Teams

Siegfried and Zimbalist (2000) summarize the findings of ex post facto studies regarding teams and stadiums as follows:

> Few fields of empirical economic research offer virtual unanimity of findings. Yet, independent work on the economic impact of stadiums and arenas has uniformly found that there is no statistically significant positive correlation between sport facility construction and economic development. (p. 98)

Leakage and substitution spending are the main reasons that stadiums tend to have little impact on economic growth. Much of the money spent at a sport stadium escapes the local economy through various forms of leakage. In addition, stadiums do not create much new spending; they simply cause a reallocation of leisure spending. Because of this effect, a stadium could lead to a reallocation of economic activity from one part of a metropolitan area to another. For example, metropolitan area residents might spend their leisure dollars at the new downtown ballpark rather than at a suburban movie theater. This effect might be appealing to officials in the central city, but it does not represent a net economic gain to the metropolitan area.

Several empirical studies have used a cross-section or time-series approach to evaluate the relationship between sport and local economies. These studies compare the economic characteristics of localities with teams or new stadiums to those without (cross-section), or examine the economic performance of localities before and after they gain a team or build a new stadium (time series). To isolate the effect of the sport team or stadium, these studies also control for other variables that might affect local economic characteristics.

For example, Baade (1996) examined per capita income growth in 48 cities between 1958 and 1987 and found no significant difference in cities with teams or new stadiums and those without. Baade and Sanderson (1997) found no significant increases in employment or output in 10 metropolitan areas that gained a new team between 1958 and 1993. Coates and Humphreys (1999) studied the economies of all 37 U.S. metropolitan area that hosted a top-level sport team between 1969 and 1994. After controlling for other factors that affect economic performance, the authors found that some sport franchises actually had a negative impact on per capita income. These findings are consistent with the effects of substitution spending and leakage. The authors speculate that the results "might indicate a substitution of consumer spending away from goods with relatively high local multipliers, such as trips to bowling alleys and local movie theaters, to goods like stadium events with relatively low local multipliers" (p. 615).

Empirical Evaluations of Mega Sporting Events

One-time mega sporting events, such as the Super Bowl, World Cup, or Olympic Games, can attract more out-of-town visitors than sport leagues do, but empirical studies indicate that their economic effects are limited as well. The ability of such an event to stimulate the local economy is hindered by an effect referred to as crowding out. First, event visitors might simply displace, or crowd out, tourists who would have otherwise visited the host city. These potential tourists might stay away to avoid event-related congestion and inflated prices (at hotels, restaurants, parking lots, and so on). In addition, local residents are also likely to alter their routines and leisure spending patterns if they are averse to event-related crowds.

Porter (1999) examined monthly sales data from three counties that hosted six Super Bowls between 1979 and 1996. After accounting for other factors that might have affected sales, he found no measurable impact on spending associated with any of the games. Porter attributes the lack of impact largely to crowding out. An in-depth look at three of the events revealed that local hotel room prices had increased significantly from the same time the previous year whereas occupancy rates had not significantly changed. Anticipating higher demand, hotels charged higher rates, but non–Super Bowl tourists stayed away. Porter suggested that the booking policies of some hotels created additional crowding out.

International sporting events can also displace significant spending through crowding out. One study conducted for the 1984 Los Angeles Olympics reported that 6,000 to 8,000 hotel rooms in the area remained unoccupied during the Games (Standeven and Knop, 1999). Another estimated that the event displaced $163 million of visitor expenditures (*Community impact of the 1984 Olympic Games in Los Angeles*, 1986).

Although international events attract many out-of-town visitors, the effect of substitution spending cannot be ignored. When the public investment for a sporting event is made at the national level, restricting an evaluation of economic effects to the individual host city is not appropriate. A boom in tourism for one city could mean a slump for another. Hotel occupancy in Australia during the 2000 Summer Olympics illustrates this point. The Games took place in Sydney from September 16 through September 30. During this period Sydney hotels neared 100 percent occupancy, but hotels in other markets experienced significant demand shortfalls relative to the first half of the month and to the same period the previous year. Hotel occupancy in Adelaide, Melbourne, and Brisbane dropped by between 10 and 20 percent during the two-week Olympic period, and hoteliers reported that "domestic leisure travel traditionally taking place during the September school holiday period was displaced to Sydney for the Olympics" (Arthur Andersen, 2000).

Economic Impact Versus Cost–Benefit: Vancouver 2010

In 2002 the provincial government of British Columbia released a study that projected that the economic impact of the Vancouver 2020 Olympic Games would be $10.7 billion (InterVISTAS). Concerned with the limitations of the information that had been made available to the public, including those described in this chapter, the Canadian Centre for Policy Alternatives (CCPA) prepared a more comprehensive cost–benefit analysis.

The CCPA described the difference between economic impact analysis and cost–benefit evaluation in the following way:

> Economic impact analyses consider all spending as having a positive impact; they do not differentiate between the money spent to build a new hospital, a sport facility or money spent to dig a hole in the ground. These analyses do not consider costs, they overstate the benefits, and they fail to consider what might have been accomplished had the same resources been directed toward other activities. A cost–benefit evaluation, in contrast, looks at the broader questions of what society gains and loses as a result of undertaking a major capital project (Shaffer, Greer, and Mauboules, 2003, p. 4).

The CCPA study attempted to move toward broader understanding of the net impacts of hosting the Olympic Games by considering costs and benefits in multiple accounts. These included economic development, government financial, environmental, social, and resident/consumer.

In line with one of the themes of this chapter, the study argued that the economic impacts predicted by the InterVISTAS report were grossly exaggerated because of several questionable assumptions. For example, the CCPA authors pointed out that the economic impact estimates included benefits related to an expanded convention center that was not planned as part of the Olympic bid and would be built regardless of the Games. Under the government financial account heading, the cost–benefit analysis estimated the net cost to the province of hosting the Games to be $1.2 billion, after considering event-generated revenue and contributions from the federal government.

Besides the more tangible costs and benefits, the CCPA study also addressed potential environmental and social impacts and considered the existence of consumption benefits (which do not show up in economic impact analyses), such as pride in hosting the Games, the opportunity to attend events, and the long-term use of new facilities and transportation infrastructure.

Although the CCPA study broadened the discussion of net Olympic impacts beyond the mere consideration of spending, it was ultimately inconclusive because it did not place a monetary value on the intangible costs and benefits described earlier; it simply identified them as issues that should be part of any dialogue regarding costs and benefits. But without empirical measure, these issues cannot be understood and weighed by the public as fungible accounting entries in the same way that predicted economic impacts can be evaluated, regardless of the accuracy of such predictions.

In the executive summary of the study, the authors concluded, "The Games will carry substantial net financial and other costs or risks, but will also bring benefits. Whether these benefits outweigh the costs is a matter of individual opinion" (p. 6). As will be discussed in chapter 5, within the political reality of sport subsidies, some individual opinions matter more than others do.

Policy Implications of Relying on Predicted Economic Impacts

Despite a growing body of academic research that casts doubt on the ability of sport teams, stadiums, and events to serve as economic catalysts, reliance on predictive economic impact analyses remains common. This circumstance poses potential dangers for public policy, for reasons described earlier.

Besides the pitfalls associated with sources of error and abuse in economic impact analyses, one other caveat should be noted regarding their use. These studies simply do not account for costs. We have already discussed costs associated with facility construction and event bidding and preparation, but stadiums and sport events also create other less obvious costs that should be considered. These include the negative impacts of increased traffic congestion and pollution created by crowds and well as the costs of increased police protection. In addition, the spending displaced by crowding out should also be considered a cost.

The need for continuing maintenance of new stadiums and infrastructure can also impose a significant and enduring cost. Saitama prefecture in Japan spent $667 million to build a stadium for the World Cup. The prefecture expects to spend $6 million a year to maintain the facility, which the local professional soccer team cannot fill (Struck, 2002). Demick (2009) described the long-term fate of Beijing's hugely expensive Olympic facilities:

> The National Stadium, known as the Bird's Nest, has only one event scheduled for 2009: a performance of the opera *Turandot* on August 8, the one-year anniversary of the Olympic opening ceremony. China's leading soccer club backed out of a deal to play there, saying it would be an embarrassment to use a 91,000-seat stadium for games that ordinarily attract only 10,000 spectators. The venue, which costs $9 million a year to maintain, is expected to be turned into a shopping mall after several years.

Perhaps the most important cost that is commonly overlooked is the opportunity cost of the public money invested in sport facilities and events. The opportunity cost represents the value of the best alternative use of that public money—the projects or programs that otherwise could have been funded. Using taxes to subsidize sports creates opportunity costs because it reduces private consumption that otherwise would have occurred. Public investment in a stadium or sporting event would not be appropriate if an alternative use of that public money would yield greater returns.

An evaluation that includes costs as well as benefits would be considered a cost–benefit analysis rather than an economic impact analysis. (This chapter's sidebar discusses the differences in these two types of analyses and illustrates the complexities of understanding the true net impacts of the Vancouver 2010 Olympic Games.) Of course, some less tangible benefits associated with rooting for the home team do not appear in an economic impact analysis. These would need to be considered in a proper cost–benefit analysis. We will explore those types of benefits in the next chapter, which provides a detailed assessment of the recent stadium construction boom, as we examine why policy makers and elected officials are willing to spend so much public money if the conventional economic returns to investment are so small.

Conclusion

This chapter has shown that cities and other governments often spend large amounts of public money to host sporting events or teams. Although stadiums are often promoted as economic development tools, professional sports play only a minor role in their local economies. Economic theory and evidence from independent empirical studies indicate that sport stadiums, teams, and events have little or no positive effect on local employment, income, or output. The projections of economic impact analyses conducted to justify public investment in sport stadiums or events are open to error and abuse and should be treated with caution.

CHAPTER 5

Cities, Stadiums, and Subsidies

Why Cities Spend So Much on Sports

Charles A. Santo

Americans have a fascination with stadiums that transcends the interest in the games that they host. They are the physical embodiments of a part of our culture and are widely recognized architectural symbols of our cities. At any souvenir shop in St. Louis, tourists can find Busch Stadium postcards and snow globes right next to those displaying the Gateway Arch. In his book *Sports in America*, the late American novelist and Pulitzer Prize winner James Michener suggested that sport stadiums are the pyramids of our time (1976).

In the summer of 2004 Jim and Andrea Siscel completed a pilgrimage to every major-league and minor-league baseball stadium in the United States and Canada (Brooks, 2004). "It was to see baseball, but mostly it was to see America," explained Mr. Sicscel. Sport road trips have become so popular that Fodor's now publishes a "baseball vacations" travel guide for stadium tourists (Adams and Engel, 2002) and ESPN hosts the Sports Travel Web page (http://sports.espn.go/travel).

For sport fans, nothing sparks feelings of nostalgia quite like the old stadium. Philadelphia's Veterans Stadium—maligned for its leaky ceilings, rat infestation, and general lack of charm—was widely considered one of the worst facilities in major-league sports during its tenure as home of the NFL Eagles and MLB Phillies. Yet just before it was imploded in 2004, people came in throngs to buy up patches of turf and bottles of infield dirt at the "Final Pieces" charity auction. An outfield seat where Bobby Abreu's September 13, 1998, home run landed sold for $1,900 (Kenny, 2004). (You don't remember Bobby Abreu's September 13, 1998, home run? It wasn't exactly the shot heard 'round the world.)

The recent boom in sport facility construction means new ballparks to tour and a growing list of erstwhile stadiums to feel nostalgic about. The majority of major-league teams now play in stadiums less than 15 years old. A great deal of recent interest in sport facilities has focused on the massive amount of public money that has supported this boom. Since 1990, 79 major-league sport facilities have been built at a public cost of over $15 billion. Of the 50 metropolitan areas that host a major-league team, an astonishing 41 have spent public money on stadium or arena construction since 1990.

This chapter continues our exploration of public investment in sport with a focus on the recent trend in stadium and arena construction and some possible explanations for the continued support of sport facility subsidies. This chapter will

- examine the evolution of major league sport facility development and explain the rise of public investment in such facilities;
- discuss the magnitude and extent of the recent boom in sport facility construction and describe the factors that have contributed to it;
- illustrate how public investment decisions are affected by a mix of economic circumstances, political influence, and private power;
- consider why public officials and residents might support public investment in sport facilities despite their inability to generate economic development; and
- explore the importance of the intangible and consumption benefits generated by sport teams and facilities.

Evolution of Major-League Sport Facility Development

To understand the factors that drive sport facility construction today, it is helpful to explore the context from which current stadiums and arenas have evolved. The recent surge in stadium and arena construction represents the latest turn in a sport facility development cycle that dates back to the early 1900s. Stadium and arena construction has occurred in stages as leagues have expanded and waves of new facilities have been built to replace older ones. Sport venues have evolved over time, and changes have occurred in design, purpose, ability to generate revenue, and reliance on public investment. Using these changes as markers, the sport facility development cycle can be divided four distinct eras, as follows.

■ **Dawn of the Modern Professional Sport Facility (1909–1942):** The prewar years saw an early boom in the construction of baseball parks followed by a surge in arena construction as teams moved into more permanent facilities. Private financing was the norm during this era.

■ **Rise of the Modern Sport Facility Subsidy (1945–1959):** During this era, a number of cities successfully used publicly built stadiums to lure teams from other cities. It served as a period of transition from private to public financing of sport facilities

■ **Era of Subsidies Writ Large (1960–1989):** All the major sport leagues expanded significantly during this era, and public investment became the norm for cities hoping to attract or keep a team. Many of the classic ballparks of the prewar era were replaced. Although many of the stadiums built during this era were multiuse, utilitarian structures, construction costs escalated dramatically.

■ **Era of Escalation and Extravagance (1990–present):** The current era, the most prolific in the history of sport facility development, has been marked by an escalation in the number of facilities built and the cost of such facilities. Public–private partnerships have become more common during this era. Many of the cookie-cutter multiuse stadiums of the previous era have been replaced with single-use retro venues designed to maximize in-stadium revenue streams.

The remainder of this section explores these four eras in more depth. Table 5.1 summarizes each of the eras in terms of facility construction activity, expenditures, and level of public investment.

Table 5.1 shows both nominal and real costs. Nominal costs represent the cost at the time of construction, whereas real costs account for inflation to provide a value equivalent to today's dollars. The median is used instead of the mean to describe the typical sport facility investment of each era because the mean is skewed by extreme high or low outliers. For example, the mean real cost of stadium development for the 1960–1989 era is $300 million, but when the anomalously expensive Olympic Stadium is excluded the mean drops to $209 million.

Dawn of the Modern Professional Sport Facility: 1909–1942

At the turn of the 20th century, major-league baseball was the only American sport league organized in its current format. Teams played in wooden ballparks that were simple, small, and privately funded. The facilities were built quickly and inexpensively, giving owners the flexibility to move their teams and follow expanding and shifting populations. Hilltop Park in New York was constructed in six weeks at a cost of $75,000 in 1903 (Danielson, 1997; Sullivan, 2001). The impermanence of these parks, however, was not always the result of owners' desires. Fires destroyed or damaged a third of the stadiums in the National League in 1884 alone (Danielson, 1997). Several players helped fans escape a blaze that erupted at Chicago's West Side Grounds by breaking through a fence with their bats (Leventhal, 2000). In other cities shoddy grandstands packed with fans collapsed during games. By 1909 the increasing popularity of professional baseball convinced several owners that larger ballparks would be economically beneficial. By virtue of stricter building and fire codes that required the use of safer and costlier material, these ballparks would also be more permanent. These changes ushered in the first era of modern sport facility construction.

In 1909 Philadelphia's Shibe Park became the first ballpark constructed of steel and reinforced concrete. Forbes Field in Pittsburgh opened the same year, kicking off what can be considered America's first stadium building boom. By 1915, 11 steel-and-concrete ballparks had been erected, including Comiskey Park, Tiger Stadium, Ebbets Field, and the enduring classics, Wrigley Field and Fenway Park.

Because the more substantial structures required expensive building materials, team owners looked to control costs by building on inexpensive land. As a result some stadiums were put up on the outskirts of town, whereas others were crammed into existing urban grids. A tight fit accounts for Fenway's asymmetrical

TABLE 5.1

Eras of Major-League Sport Facility Development

	Number of stadiums opened	NOMINAL COST			REAL COST (IN 2009 DOLLARS)		Number of arenas opened	NOMINAL COST			REAL COST (IN 2009 DOLLARS)	
		Total	Public	Public share	Total	Public		Total	Public	Public share	Total	Public
1909-1942												
Total	18	$24.24	$14.86	61%	$375.43	$199.12	8	$25.65	$0.00	0%	$331.75	$0.00
Median		*$0.60*	*$0.00*		*$11.60*	*$0.00*		*$2.15*	*$0.00*		*$30.28*	*$0.00*
1945-1959												
Total	6	$19.22	$18.97	99%	$153.61	$151.38	1	$5.90	$5.90	100%	$43.70	$43.70
Median		*$2.75*	*$2.75*		*$21.59*	*$21.59*		*$5.90*	*$5.90*		*$43.70*	*$43.70*
1960-1989												
Total	30	$2,418.89	$2,091.19	86%	$9,283.07	$8,399.03	30	$1,025.00	$672.00	66%	$3,606.14	$2,232.88
Median		*$32.00*	*$27.75*		*$198.14*	*$172.66*		*$22.00*	*$17.00*		*$88.00*	*$72.00*
1990-2009												
Total	41	$15,296.80	$8,751.20	57%	$18,201.62	$10,812.44	38	$7,061.90	$3,611.50	51%	$9,276.16	$4,659.53
Median		*$306.00*	*$200.00*		*$394.53*	*$237.29*		*$170.00*	*$87.25*		*$226.07*	*$124.11*

Costs are millions of dollars.

From Leventhal 2000; Keating 1999; Rafool 1998; Rappaport & Wilkerson 2001; *Sports Facility Reports 2009*; www.ballparks.com; www.msfc.com/nextgen.cfm

layout with its shallow left field and imposing Green Monster wall. In Griffith Park the center-field fence jagged in to circumvent five houses and a tree just beyond the outfield. The *Pittsburgh Press* labeled Forbes Field "Dreyfuss' Folly," ridiculing the decision of Pirates' owner Barney Dreyfus to build the stadium in an area three miles from downtown (Leventhal, 2000). Of course, as these cities grew, ballparks that were once on the outskirts of town became surrounded by dense urban neighborhoods and were typically accessible by streetcars.

Despite some less-than-prime locations, the 11 new facilities built between 1909 and 1915 were considerably more expensive than their wooden predecessors; the average construction cost was over $500,000. Barney Dreyfuss spent $1 million to build the elaborate Forbes Field. By contrast New York's Hilltop Park cost $75,000 to build in 1903, and the construction of Columbia Park in Philadelphia cost a mere $7,500 in 1901 (Leventhal, 2000; Sullivan, 2001). Fortunately for team owners, the new stadiums also generated more revenue than past ballparks because larger seating capacities and more comfortable accommodations helped attract a wider audience. The old wooden parks typically held fewer than 10,000 fans, but the new concrete and steel structures all had more than 20,000 seats. Yankee Stadium set a new standard when it opened in 1923 with a capacity of 58,000.

Ballpark construction cooled after Yankee Stadium was built, but arena construction took off as the NHL began to take shape. Beginning with the Montreal Forum and ending with Toronto's Maple Leaf Gardens, each of the original six NHL teams built new indoor arenas with ice-making capability between 1924 and 1931. During this era most NFL teams played in baseball stadiums. The NBA was not organized until 1949, and pro teams in the league's predecessors often played in college or high school gymnasiums (Quirk and Fort, 1992).

Private financing was the rule for major-league facilities built before World War II, and the few exceptions exhibited unique circumstances. Three stadiums were built with public money in attempts to land the Olympics Games. The Los Angeles Coliseum was completed in 1923 as part of a failed bid for the 1924 games. Chicago's Soldier Field (built in 1924) and Cleveland's Municipal Stadium (1931) were both built to attract the 1932 Olympics (Danielson, 1997; R. Keating, 1999; Rosentraub, 1999; Siegfried and Zimbalist, 2000). Those games were instead awarded to Los Angeles. The MLB Cleveland Indians began to play some of their home games in Municipal Stadium (sometimes called Cleveland Stadium) in 1932, but the Los Angeles Coliseum and Soldier Field would not host major-league teams until after World War II.

Sport facility construction tapered off in the 1930s under the weight of the Great Depression. Between the opening of Cleveland's Municipal Stadium and the end of World War II, only two more facilities that would eventually host major-league teams were built. The privately financed Sick's Stadium in Seattle opened in 1938 as the home of the Pacific Coast League (baseball) Rainiers. The facility would later host the MLB Pilots for one season in 1969. Buffalo's War Memorial Stadium opened in 1937 as a project of the federal Works Progress Administration (WPA)—a New Deal job creation program implemented by Franklin Roosevelt. The stadium was used mostly for parades and civic events until the Buffalo Bills of the All-America Football Conference began play in 1947. The American Football League version of the Bills moved into the stadium in 1960 (the AFL would later merge with the NFL) (http://rockpile.buffalonet.org/home.html). The WPA built numerous smaller parks across the county, but Buffalo's was the only facility that would go on to host a major-league team. No major-league facilities were built during the U.S. involvement in World War II.

In all, 26 top-level sport facilities opened between 1909 and 1942, including 10 baseball stadiums between 1909 and 1915, and 7 hockey arenas between 1924 and 1931. During this first era of modern sport facility construction, every stadium or arena built with the explicit purpose of hosting a major-league team was privately financed. These facilities represented large sunk costs for franchise owners, and as a result none of the teams that played in them relocated during the era. Both circumstances would change shortly after World War II.

Rise of the Modern Sport Facility Subsidy: 1945–1959

The postwar era began with the construction of Denver's Mile High Stadium (called Bears Stadium at the time), a privately financed facility that opened in 1948 as a minor-league baseball park but would later host the NFL Broncos. The course of stadium building then shifted in 1953 when the Boston Braves moved to Milwaukee, becoming the first baseball team to relocate since 1903. The Braves had become unprofitable in Boston, where they were far less popular than the Red Sox, and team owner Louis Perini was attracted by Milwaukee's publicly funded County Stadium (Danielson, 1997). As the lone team in a smaller market, the Braves found renewed financial success.

What followed was a series of moves among baseball teams, each involving publicly built stadiums. In 1954 the St. Louis Browns became the Orioles when the team moved into Baltimore's publicly funded Memorial Stadium. The Philadelphia Athletics moved to Kansas City in 1955 after the city spent $2.5 million to renovate Municipal Stadium. Like the Braves, both of those teams had received second billing in their old homes cities, where the Cardinals and Phillies were favored. The publicly built Metropolitan Stadium in Bloomington, Minnesota, opened in 1956 and hosted a minor-league team until the first incarnation of the Washington Senators moved in and became the Twins in 1961. The willingness of local governments to absorb the large sunk cost associated with stadium construction removed what had been the biggest impediment to franchise relocation. As indicated in table 5.2, these teams all draw much larger crowds in their new locations.

The biggest relocation news of the era occurred in 1958, when both the New York Giants and Brooklyn Dodgers moved west. The Giants' move to San Francisco was similar to those described earlier. The team had become less successful than its local rivals, the Yankees and Dodgers, and the appeal of a new market was sweetened by the promise of a publicly built stadium. Walter O'Malley's Dodgers, on the other hand, were one the most successful teams in the National League, and their move to Los Angeles was not contingent on a public stadium. Dodger Stadium was privately financed, although Los Angeles provided a 300-acre site and the necessary infrastructure improvements (R. Keating, 1999). The relocation was a risk that paid off financially, but Walter O'Malley is vilified to this day for his decision to uproot the Dodgers (this chapter's first sidebar provides a discussion of whether O'Malley's bad rap is justified). Although the Giants and Dodgers moved in 1958, their new stadiums would not open until 1960 and 1962 respectively.

TABLE 5.2

Average Annual Attendance Before and After Relocations, 1953–1960

	Last three seasons in old city		First three seasons in new city		Pct. increase
Braves	Boston	698,735	Milwaukee	2,002,488	187%
Browns/Orioles	St. Louis	339,239	Baltimore	960,933	183%
Athletics	Philadelphia	439,837	Kansas City	1,058,591	141%
Giants	New York	815,570	San Francisco	1,470,198	80%
Dodgers	Brooklyn	1,073,985	Los Angeles	1,993,685	86%
Senators/Twins	Washington, D.C.	572,786	Minnesota	1,326,001	132%

Data for attendance records from http://businessofbaseball.com/data.htm

The desire for a new stadium was not the sole motivating factor behind any of these moves; the nation's changing demographics also played a large role. But the promise of a state-of-art facility at no cost to the team certainly added to the appeal of relocation and quickly became standard practice. The sport subsidies of the era were not restricted to baseball. The Los Angeles Sports Arena, built with public money in 1959, helped attract the NBA Lakers from Minneapolis in 1960. The NFL Green Bay Packers moved into Lambeau Field, a city-funded stadium, in 1957. Baltimore's Memorial Stadium, which hosted the relocated Orioles, was also home to the new NFL Colts.

Seven major-league sport facilities were built between 1945 and 1959. The only one that was not publicly funded was Mile High Stadium. The successful use of public stadium development in the 1950s to attract footloose teams established a precedent that would quickly be expanded.

Era of Subsidies Writ Large: 1960–1989

Relocation slowed in the 1960s, but public stadium development continued on an even larger scale, driven by a variety of factors. If cities could use stadiums to lure teams, then localities with incumbent teams would have to use similar strategies to keep them. In addition, cities hoping to land an expansion team were now expected to play the stadium game as well.

Each of the major sport leagues expanded significantly in the 1960s and 1970s, generating demand for new facilities that was typically met by local governments. Major League Baseball grew from 16 teams in 1960 to 26 by 1977. The NHL doubled in size from 6 teams to 12 in 1966. The NBA grew from 8 teams to 22 between 1960 and 1976, and added 5 more franchises during the 1980s. Professional football also became more prominent during this period. After merging with the American Football League in 1966, the NFL grew to 28 teams by 1976.

Besides the new stadiums built to accommodate expansion, many of the original concrete and steel stadiums that were privately built during the prewar

Walter O'Malley: Villain or Scapegoat?

Walter O'Malley is often blamed for starting the trend of publicly built stadiums and is sometimes spoken of as the personification of all things greed-related in professional sports. The truth is more subtle. Folklore holds that O'Malley took the Dodgers west because his demands for a publicly funded facility went unmet in Brooklyn. In fact, O'Malley wanted to build a ballpark with his own money at the intersection of Atlantic and Flatbush Avenues, but Robert Moses, New York's most powerful bureaucrat, would not allow it (Sullivan, 2001). Moses wanted to move the team into a new public stadium in Queens. (That stadium would later be built for the expansion Mets.) O'Malley was not interested in a municipal stadium, saying, "That would mean a political landlord, which isn't desirable" (Danielson, 1997).

By the time the Dodgers moved to Los Angeles in 1958, three other team owners had been lured to other cities (Milwaukee, Baltimore, and Kansas City). As described in this chapter, those moves were motivated largely by the fiscal strain each team faced in their original market coupled with the promise of a publicly owned stadium in their new market. But the Dodgers were among the most financially successful teams in baseball, and there was no promise of a publicly financed stadium awaiting the team in Los Angeles. O'Malley's move was predicated by impending demographic change, both in Brooklyn and out west. While the West Coast was experiencing a population boom, Brooklyn was growing poorer. In Neil Sullivan's *A Diamond in the Bronx* (2001), Buzzie Bavasi, the Dodgers' general manager at the time of the move, recalls an encounter with O'Malley regarding this matter:

> As Bavasi relates, O'Malley had summoned him to his office, pointed out the window, and said, "Look down there. What do you see?"
>
> "Across from our office was the welfare office. I looked out the window and the problem was apparent."
>
> "I see a long, long line of Puerto Rican people getting their welfare checks," I said.
>
> "The Puerto Rican part did not bother Walter. What did bother him was the word *poor*. By looking out the window, he could see the future. And the future involved too many people without enough money to adequately support the Dodgers" (quoted in Sullivan, 2001, p. 111).

Despite the growing poverty, O'Malley set out a plan to build a new stadium in Brooklyn with his own money, although he did request that the city use its condemnation powers to assemble the land around Atlantic and Flatbush, which he would then purchase from the city as a single plot. That request was denied, partly in light of the interests of Robert Moses.

Although O'Malley's move was the not the first of the era, it did set a tone. If the successful, profitable, and beloved Dodgers could pick up roots and move, any team could.

era were replaced at public expense. For example, Shibe Park, Forbes Field, and Crosley Field (in Cincinnati) all closed their turnstiles in 1970 and 1971. Most of these aged facilities were much smaller than their newer counterparts, and their locations were not convenient for fans who were increasingly traveling to games in private automobiles. Other prewar facilities underwent costly renovations. According to some estimates, New York City, which purchased Yankee Stadium from private owners in 1971, spent over $100 million to renovate the facility in 1975 (Leventhal, 2000; *Sports facility reports*, 2003; Sullivan, 2001).

Several common location and design elements defined the stadiums of this era. In response to the desires of a suburbanizing population, they were usually built away from the city center, adjacent to freeways, and on large parcels that provided acres of parking. In addition, local governments typically built multi-use facilities that accommodated both football and baseball teams. Previously, professional football teams rented game time in stadiums designed for baseball, but as the sport grew in popularity, the typical baseball stadium was no longer large enough to accommodate growing football crowds. Kansas City's Kauffman Stadium (formerly called Royals Stadium), which opened in 1973, was the sole baseball-only facility built between 1962 and 1991.

Although they contained more amenities for fans, the stadiums of this era were generally utilitarian, without elaborate or memorable architectural features. The wide-open parcels on which they were built allowed for field configurations that were perfectly symmetrical and, well, boring. In fact, many of the stadiums built during this period looked remarkably similar, as if a fleet of flying saucers had descended on the interstate highway system throughout metropolitan America. Former major leaguer Richie Hebner remarked, "I stand at the plate at the Vet and I don't honestly know whether I'm in Pittsburgh, Cincinnati, St. Louis or Philly. They all look alike" (quoted in Leventhal, 2000).

As indicated in table 5.1, stadium construction costs rose substantially during this era. Much of this increase can be attributed to the grand scale of these new facilities, both in terms of structure size and acreage. Building away from down-town might have helped local governments control costs to some extent, but the desire to accommodate massive parking lots drove up the amount of land required, significantly counteracting any savings. Likewise, building one stadium might be cheaper than building two, but stadiums built to accommodate both baseball and football take up more space than do single-use facilities. Their larger size is due in part to their larger seating capacity, but they also require a larger field area to allow the transformation from one use to another. In addition, the facilities of this era were built without the steel grandstand supports that obstructed the view of spectators in previous-generation stadiums. To accommodate this change, the upper levels of these stadiums were pushed farther back from the field, again increasing the size of the structures and the amount of land required. Philadelphia's multiuse Veterans Stadium opened in 1971 on a 74-acre (30 ha) site. In compari-son, Shibe Park, the stadium that the Vet replaced, was built within a city block that measured 521 feet by 480 feet (159 by 146 m) (Munsey and Suppes, n.d.).

This era also introduced the domed stadium and its companion, artificial turf. (Artificial turf was not just for indoor facilities. Multiuse outdoor stadiums like Veterans Stadium in Philadelphia and Three Rivers Stadium in Pittsburgh also rolled out the carpet because of its increased durability.) In Montreal, what was to be the first sport facility with a retractable roof instead became one of the greatest stadium building debacles of all time. Olympic Stadium was built to host the 1976 Olympics and the MLB Expos, who had been playing in a "temporary" facility since their inception in 1969. Because of a construction workers' strike, the roof was not ready in time for the opening ceremonies of the Games, but the stadium was used anyway as an open-air facility. The Expos moved in the following season and began play without a roof. Cost overruns and engineering problems further delayed the completion of the elaborate roof system, which was not put in place until 1988. The stadium's Kevlar covering was designed to be raised and lowered by a set of cables attached to a 550-foot (168 m) tower looming over that stadium at a 45-degree angle, but the system never really worked. The retractable roof remained in the closed position until it was removed and replaced with a permanent non-retractable covering in 1999 (Leventhal, 2000; Munsey and Suppes, n.d.). Olympic Stadium remains one of the most expensive North American sport facility ever built; its total construction costs were estimated at $770 million (Canadian dollars) (R. Keating, 1999; *Sports facility reports*, 2003). Toronto's Rogers Centre (formerly called SkyDome) became the first fully functional retractable roof stadium when it opened in 1989.

Of the 30 stadiums built during this era, only 5 were privately financed and owned. Only 6 of 30 arenas were privately developed. For the most part, the 49 government-owned facilities of the era were financed without any private contributions. Only the RCA Dome (formerly called the Hoosier Dome) in Indianapolis and the Rogers Centre in Toronto involved significant contributions from private sources. Public–private partnerships would become more common in the 1990s.

Era of Escalation and Extravagance: 1990–Present

The current era represents the most prolific sport facility construction period in history. As indicated in table 5.1, the public share of stadium and arena construction expenditures has actually decreased since 1990, but the number of facilities built and the cost of these facilities has escalated dramatically compared with the previous era. To illustrate the magnitude of building that has occurred during the current period, consider the following statistics:

- In the 19 years between 1990 and 2009, 79 new major-league sport venues opened, compared with 60 in the previous 30-year era.
- Of the 50 metropolitan areas that currently host a major-league sport franchise, 41 have spent public money on stadium or arena construction since 1990; 21 have subsidized more than one facility during this period.
- Of the 49 arenas currently used by NBA and NHL teams, 37 have been built since 1990; another 6 have been renovated during this period. Of the 61 stadiums currently used by MLB and NFL teams, 41 have been built and 4 have been renovated since 1990.

Governments have spent over $15 billion on sport facilities since 1990, up from a total public expenditure of $11 billion in the previous 30-year era. The emergence of public–private partnerships in the 1990s has blurred the line between privately developed and publicly developed facilities. Team owners have increasingly contributed to the financing of publicly owned stadiums and arenas, and governments have shared in the development costs of facilities that are privately owned. As a result, the public share of construction costs has decreased to 55 percent in the current era, compared with 80 percent in the previous era. Despite this drop, the size of the median public investment in stadiums and arenas has risen in the current era (in both nominal and real dollars), as indicated in table 5.1. So although localities have paid a smaller share of construction costs, they have typically spent more per facility, a function of a substantial increase in facility development costs. The remainder of this section examines the factors that have driven the escalation in both construction activity and costs that characterize this era.

Expansion, Relocation, and (Mostly) Replacement As in the previous era, expansion has played a role in the recent sport facility construction boom. Since 1990 the four major sport leagues have added 20 new teams: 9 in the NHL, 4 in the NFL, 4 in MLB, and 3 in the NBA. The 16 facilities built to accommodate these new teams, however, account for only a small fraction of the 79 stadiums and arenas developed since 1990. Another 7 facilities have been built for teams that relocated during the era, but the majority have opened as replacement facilities for teams already in place. Although prewar classics like Comiskey Park, Tiger Stadium, and the Montreal Forum are among those that have been replaced in the current era, most of the stadiums and arenas built since 1990 have taken the place of facilities that opened in the 1960s and 1970s. As a result of this replacement cycle and the building for expansion and relocation, the median age of facilities in use dropped from 21 years in 1989 to 13 years in 2009 (see table 5.3).

Return of the Single-Use Stadium Table 5.3 shows that although the number of major-league teams increased by 20 between 1989 and 2009, the number of facilities in use increased by 33. This discrepancy stems from the demise of the multiuse stadium and a return to the construction of facilities designed exclusively for one sport. Although the multiuse facilities of the previous era were able to accommodate both baseball and football, they did not provide an ideal venue for either sport. From the fans' perspective, the large circular or square structures put too many seats in the outfield for baseball games and too many seats behind the end zone for football games. In addition, the behemoth venues were less intimate than their single-use counterparts, pushing the prime seats along the baselines and sidelines far away from the field of play. Because the multiuse facilities were built to handle the larger crowds associated with football, thousands of seats often remained empty during baseball games. (Baseball teams typically have lower attendance than football teams because they hold 81 home games each season compared with 8.) At covered facilities like Seattle's Kingdome, the emptiness created a disturbing cavernous atmosphere. Finally, the artificial turf that was so appealing to the designers of multiuse facilities for its durability and flexibility was almost universally despised among athletes and fans. (Perhaps team physicians

TABLE 5.3

Major-League Teams and Facilities in 1989 Compared With 2009

	1989	2009	Difference
Number of teams	103	123	+20
Number of facilities in use	77	110	+33
Median age of facilities	21 years	13 years	-8 years

and trainers liked the stuff; its inability to give when players are tackled or make quick cuts has been blamed for numerous knee injuries.)

No multiuse facilities have been built since Toronto's Roger Centre (SkyDome) opened in 1989 (which hosts an MLB team and a Canadian Football League team). The return to single-use stadiums has meant an increase in the number of facilities built and a related increase in public spending, even though governments typically cover a smaller share of total construction costs. Multiuse facilities have been replaced with multiple single-use stadiums in Atlanta, Cincinnati, Philadelphia, Pittsburgh, and Seattle. In each of these cities, public money covered a smaller share of the construction costs associated with the new stadiums, but in each case the total amount of public spending increased. Table 5.4 compares multiuse public spending with single-use public spending. For example, Philadelphia's multiuse Veterans Stadium was entirely publicly funded at a cost equivalent to $225 million (real dollars). Public funds covered less than half of the cost of two new facilities that replaced the Vet in 2003 and 2004, but the total public spending on these facilities exceeded $370 million.

Shared facilities remain more common in the NBA and NHL because the shapes of the playing surfaces are similar, but some teams have moved into separate facilities. In 1998 and 1999 public funds helped build two new arenas in the Miami metropolitan area—one for the NHL Panthers and one for the NBA Heat. In the Phoenix area the NBA Suns play in the America West Arena, which opened in 1992, and the NHL Coyotes moved into Jobing.com Arena (formerly called Glendale Arena) in 2004 (both are publicly owned). Currently, Phoenix and Detroit are the only metropolitan areas with four major-league teams that play in four separate facilities. (Miami's football and baseball teams share a facility, although the Marlins are building a ballpark of their own.)

Revenue Streams and Franchise Values   Aesthetics and spectator sight lines were not the only factors behind the desertion of multiuse facilities; they were also unpopular among team owners because of their associated revenue implications. Lease terms and shared revenue streams became a source of contention between teams that shared facilities. League revenue-sharing plans in baseball and football have increased the importance of stadium-related revenue streams. Although teams in these leagues share revenue associated with ticket sales, they are allowed to keep all nonticket revenue generated by the stadium, which includes income associated with concession rights, naming rights, advertising, parking, club seats, and luxury suite rentals. (Club seats and luxury suite revenues are not shared in the same way that gate receipts are because when spectators buy these premium seats they are paying for an array of amenities beyond admission to the game, such as access to private lounges, concierge service, and private parking lots. Only the fraction of the cost associated with admission to the stadium is counted for revenue-sharing purposes.)

Although the facilities of the previous era had not become physically obsolete, they quickly became economically inferior to the new single-use facilities of the 1990s, which were designed with these built-in revenue streams in mind. New stadiums and arenas are typically packed with revenue-generating features like themed restaurants, museums, and shops. Club seats and luxury suites, which often rent for over $100,000 per season, have become key elements of current-era

TABLE 5.4

Comparison of Multiuse Public Spending to Single-Use Public Spending

	PREVIOUS MULTIUSE STADIUM			NEW SINGLE-USE STADIUMS COMBINED		NEW BASEBALL STADIUM			NEW FOOTBALL STADIUM		
	Year opened	Public spending	Public share of total cost	Public spending	Public share of total cost	Year opened	Public spending	Public share of total cost	Year opened	Public spending	Public share of total cost
Atlanta	1965	$110	100%	$275	51%	1997	$0	0%	1992	$275	100%
Cincinnati	1970	$258	100%	$651	90%	2003	$224	75%	2000	$427	100%
Philadelphia	1971	$225	100%	$371	43%	2004	$174	50%	2003	$197	38%
Pittsburgh	1970	$261	100%	$333	63%	2001	$169	71%	2001	$164	38%
Seattle	1976	$217	100%	$741	73%	1999	$434	76%	2002	$307	56%
Total		$1,071	100%	$2,371	65%		$1,001	58%		$1,370	70%

Figures represent real costs (2003 dollars) in millions.

From Keating 1999; Rappaport & Wilkerson 2001; *Sports Facility Reports* 2009; http://www.ballparks.com;
http://www.msfc.com/nextgen.cfm

facilities. In addition, new stadiums and arenas tend to draw larger crowds, the financial impact of which is compounded by the existence of built-in revenue generators. This financial advantage has driven the demand for facility construction, because team owners claim that they cannot field a competitive team without their own new arena or stadium.

In their final season at the old Memorial Stadium, the Baltimore Orioles took in $5 million in stadium-related revenue. In their first season at Orioles Park at Camden Yards, which opened in 1992, that figure jumped to $21.5 million, a dramatic 330 percent increase. Although part of that increase can be attributed to larger crowds, attendance increased by only 40 percent. Clearly, the new stadium is able to generate revenue in ways that the old facility could not. The stadium's 72 luxury suites and 3,800 club seats are prime contributors. Similarly, the Cleveland Indians saw their stadium-related revenue surge from $3 million in their last season at Municipal Stadium to $11 million in their first full season at Progressive Field (formerly called Jacobs Field), which boasts 122 luxury suites and 2,064 club seats. In 1995, when the NFL Rams moved from Anaheim to a brand new stadium with 124 luxury suites and 6,500 club seats in St. Louis, their stadium-related revenue soared from $4 million to $13 million. The NFL Washington Redskins are among the highest revenue-generating teams in all sports. Their stadium includes 280 luxury suites and 15,000 club seats (Ozanian, 2003). Fans benefit from this increased revenue if owners use it to sign players that are more exciting or put together winning teams. This chapter's second sidebar explores the relationship between new baseball stadiums, payroll, and team performance.

Because playing in a new stadium or arena bolsters revenue, it also increases the value of a team. For example, the Jacobs brothers paid $35 million for the Cleveland Indians in 1986 and sold the team for $323 million in 2000. A group of investors, including George W. Bush, bought the Texas Rangers baseball team in 1989 for $80 million. In 1998, four years after moving into a ballpark financed by Arlington taxpayers, the club was sold for $250 million (Zimbalist, 2003).

The many bells and whistles incorporated to create revenue streams in current-era stadiums and arenas have contributed to the escalating expense of such facilities. To deal with these growing construction costs, and mounting resistance to tax increases, localities have turned to more creative public funding sources and sought significant private contributions from team owners. Team owners, in turn, have been willing to make larger contributions to ensure access to the revenue-generating potential of current-era facilities. In fact, 22 of the facilities built since 1990 are privately owned, compared with just 10 in the previous era. Many of these privately owned facilities, however, have been financed with substantial public assistance. Private ownership is more common with arenas because such facilities can host events like concerts and exhibitions during nongame days and can generate revenue year round. Fifteen of the 22 privately owned current-era facilities are arenas.

Favorable Lease Terms Team owners willing to share in the costs of publicly owned facilities have often taken steps to ensure that their investments pay off by negotiating favorable lease arrangements with their host localities. Of course, owners who privately finance and own their facilities do not have to pay rent, but they do generally carry heavy debts. Making a small contribution to the cost of a public facility and leveraging that investment into a sweetheart lease can be a more lucrative strategy for team owners.

The owners of the NHL Phoenix Coyotes contributed just $40 million toward the $220 million cost of Jobing.com Arena (formerly called Glendale Arena), which opened in 2004. The City of Glendale collects just $500,000 a year in rent and gives the team all the revenue generated by arena advertising, club seats, and luxury suites (Heath, 2004). Seahawks owner Paul Allen contributed $130 million to the $430 million construction cost of Qwest Field in Seattle. The team pays about $1 million a year in rent but collects all sponsorship and premium-seating revenue generated by the facility, an amount estimated at $25 million for 2003 (Ozanian, 2003).

Cleveland's Progressive Field and Quicken Loans Arena (formerly called Gund Arena), both of which opened in 1994, were financed by a combination of public and private funds but are publicly owned. The Indians' annual rent is based on attendance; payments start after 1.85 million tickets are sold. The team keeps all parking, sponsorship, concessions, luxury suite, and club seat revenue. The lease for the NBA Cavaliers' Quicken Loans Arena was arranged at the same time as that of Progressive Field, and rental payments are tied to the same ticket sales thresholds (payments start after 1.85 million tickets are sold) (Noll and Zimbalist, 1997a). The arena, however, has half as many seats as Progressive Field does and hosts half as many games per season. Even if the Cavaliers sold out every one of

New Ballparks and On-Field Success

Table 5.5 summarizes payroll changes for the 11 nonexpansion MLB teams that moved into new stadiums between 1990 and 2001. The table shows each team's average payroll for the four-year period before and after moving into their new facilities, and compares those payrolls to the leaguewide average. (A four-year average is used rather than a single-season payroll figure because teams are likely to see significant attendance spikes and related revenue increases during the first year in a new facility. Averaging payroll over a four-year period provides a better measure of the lasting effect of a new stadium.) All but one of the teams increased their average payroll by over 50 percent, and many of the teams more than doubled their old payrolls after moving into their new facilities. The Cleveland Indians, for example, increased their four-year average payroll by 225 percent during a period in which the leaguewide four-year average grew by only 34 percent. The White Sox, Orioles, Rangers, Indians, and Giants all went from below average to above average in terms of payroll. The payroll of the Detroit Tigers and Pittsburgh Pirates remained below average, but the teams did reduce the gap between themselves and the rest of the league. The Houston Astros and Milwaukee Brewers, on the other hand, fell further below the average payroll after opening new facilities.

The team that had the largest increase in its four-year average payroll, the Cleveland Indians, also saw the largest improvement in performance. The Indians made the playoffs in each of their first four seasons at Progressive Field (Jacobs Field) and posted a winning percentage of .598 during that period. The only teams from table 5.5 that did not make the playoffs at least once in the four years after beginning play in a new stadium were the Tigers, Brewers, and Pirates.

(continued)

TABLE 5.5

Payroll in Old Stadium Versus Payroll in New Stadium

	LAST FOUR SEASONS IN OLD STADIUM				FIRST FOUR SEASONS IN NEW STADIUM			
	Average payroll	MLB average	Deviation from MLB average	Year opened	Average payroll	MLB average	Deviation from MLB average	Pct. increase in avg. payroll
White Sox	$10,291,461	$13,013,997	-$2,722,536	1991	$32,633,468	$29,419,757	$3,213,711	217%
Orioles	$11,421,069	$16,397,884	-$4,976,815	1992	$35,166,977	$31,471,833	$3,695,144	208%
Rangers	$24,469,135	$25,410,952	-$941,817	1994	$38,489,716	$34,045,138	$4,444,578	57%
Indians	$13,706,141	$25,410,952	-$11,704,812	1994	$44,609,595	$34,045,138	$10,564,457	225%
Braves	$48,031,958	$32,126,626	$15,905,332	1997	$72,304,647	$46,099,150	$26,205,496	51%
Mariners	$43,068,649	$36,392,995	$6,675,654	2000	$77,868,528	$64,568,776	$13,299,752	81%
Tigers	$24,803,662	$40,332,471	-$15,528,810	2000	$53,496,743	$64,568,776	-$11,072,033	116%
Astros	$38,020,500	$40,332,471	-$2,311,971	2000	$62,093,034	$64,568,776	-$2,475,742	63%
Giants	$38,396,099	$40,332,471	-$1,936,372	2000	$69,430,624	$64,568,776	$4,861,848	81%
Pirates	$18,387,417	$46,099,150	-$27,711,734	2001	$45,447,990	$67,789,422	-$22,341,432	147%
Brewers	$32,928,610	$46,099,150	-$13,170,540	2001	$40,380,542	$67,789,422	-$27,408,880	23%

Data from http://businessofbaseball.com/data.htm

New Ballparks and On-Field Success *(continued)*

A closer look at those teams reveals a variety of reasons that a new stadium does not automatically translate to improved on-field performance. The Tigers, Brewers, and Pirates each had payrolls that remained below the average in the years after their new stadiums opened. Although a new stadium increases revenue, it is not an economic panacea. Regardless of how much revenue their stadiums generate, small-market teams like the Pirates and Brewers remain at a financial disadvantage to teams in larger cities that can generate enormous local media revenues.

In addition, those teams came in on the back end of a stadium building cycle. Teams like the Orioles and Indians, who were among the first teams to occupy new ballparks early in the current era of facility construction, received a revenue boost that put them out in front of the pack. With so many teams now in new facilities, the revenue boost of a new stadium simply allows teams to keep pace (Zimbalist, 2003).

Finally, a new stadium will have little effect if team owners are not willing to spend some of the revenue that it generates. The plight of the Brewers illustrates what happens when ownership expects a new stadium to generate revenue windfalls without improving team quality. After moving into Miller Park in 2001, the Brewers, who were owned at the time by the Selig family, drew nearly twice as many fans as they had the previous season, but no corresponding increase occurred in team payroll, which remained well below the league average. For Brewers fans, the novelty of a new stadium with the same old bad team wore off quickly, and by 2003 attendance had dropped back to pre-Miller Park levels. In 2004 the Brewers actually cut their payroll from $40 million to $27 million, giving them the lowest payroll in baseball at the time. (Lower even than the collectively owned Montreal Expos.) This move prompted anger among fans, taxpayers, and public officials alike. State Representative Steve Foti, who was involved in crafting the public funding package that financed Miller Park, offered this response to the cuts: "We should have let them go. I think the Brewers have deceived the public" (Shook, January 4, 2004).

In 2005 the Selig family sold the Brewers franchise for $220 million; the family paid only $11 million for the team in 1970. By 2008 the Brewers payroll was up to $81 million, putting them in the middle of the pack. The team finished only two games back in the National League Central Division in 2007 and made the 2008 playoffs as a wild-card team.

their 41 home games they would draw only 843,042 fans per season, more than a million below the payment threshold. To be fair, tickets sold for nonbasketball events at the arena also count toward the threshold and the team pays some rent based on a percentage of suite and club seat revenue. However, reports indicate that the Cavaliers have not been required to pay a dime in rent based on standard ticket sales since the arena opened (Bartimole, 2003).

Ironically, federal legislation that was designed, in part, to curb the subsidization of sport facilities has encouraged governments to arrange such concessionary leases. Governments that finance sport facilities generally raise the capital needed by selling bonds. They prefer to issue bonds that are tax exempt because such bonds have lower interest rates, and therefore allow the locality to make smaller payments to entities that purchase the bonds. Before the Tax Reform Act of 1986, bonds for stadiums were issued as private activity bonds but were among the few exceptions for which such bonds remained tax exempt. The 1986 act removed this exemption for stadiums and stated that a bond issue would be deemed a private activity bond and taxable if more than 10 percent of the bond proceeds were used by a nongovernmental agency and more than 10 percent of the debt service was secured by property used directly or indirectly in a private business. The act affected all bonds issues after 1990 (Zimmerman, 1997). The intent was to limit the use of tax-exempt bond financing for privately used sport facilities. In practice, however, localities instead began to issue tax-exempt bonds called governmental bonds for stadiums. Because they could not collect more than 10 percent of the debt service in the form of rent payments, they necessarily had to offer extremely favorable leases. The persistence of concessionary lease arrangements has made publicly owned stadiums and arenas all the more attractive and has contributed to the increased demand for such facilities.

Cartel Power   As described in chapter 1, the members of a sport league act as a cartel, cooperating to ensure the greatest collective profit. Along with a desire for more revenue, the flexing of cartel power has been a constant during the last three eras of sport facility development. Because leagues control the location and limit the overall supply of franchises, cities that desire to host a team are forced into competition with one another. This circumstance gives leverage to team owners, as stadiums become the bargaining chips with which cities negotiate.

Many teams have parlayed relocation threats into new facilities. Since the highly successful and profitable Dodgers abandoned Brooklyn for Los Angeles in 1958, cities have had to consider all such threats as valid. During the 1990s, eight NHL and NFL teams moved to new cities. After losing the NFL Cardinals to Phoenix in 1988, St. Louis successfully lured the Rams from Los Angeles in 1995 by building a domed football stadium. (Because NFL teams share a large portion of their gate receipts and media revenue, a new stadium is particularly attractive bait, even in a smaller market.) Baltimore and Nashville used similar strategies to attract teams from Cleveland and Houston, respectively. Cleveland and Houston both later publicly financed new stadiums to land expansion football teams.

When MLB promised to relocate the struggling Montreal Expos, the league opened a bidding war among a number of cities hoping to host the team. Baseball commissioner Bud Selig made it clear that the winning city would be one that was willing to provide a new stadium fully funded by the public. The Expos became the Washington Nationals in 2006, after the DC city council agreed to approve over $600 million in bond financing for a new ballpark (*Sports facility reports*, 2007).

In 2001 Selig wrote a letter to the Florida legislature warning that the future of the Marlins hinged on the development of a new stadium. "Bluntly, the Marlins cannot and will not survive in south Florida without a new stadium" (quoted in Fainaru, 2004). During a visit to Oakland in 2004, Selig told city officials that the Athletics needed a new stadium if they were to continue playing in Oakland (Crowley, 2004).

In 2004 Hamilton County joined a federal lawsuit originally filed by an individual taxpayer, alleging that the Cincinnati Bengals and the NFL abused monopoly power by coercing the county into building a new stadium and arranging a lease that was highly favorable to the team. The lawsuit claimed that the NFL was in violation antitrust laws because it misled communities about the economic condition of its franchises and used relocation threats to win huge concessions from localities (Andrews and Horn, 2004). (This case is discussed in detail in the sidebar on page 19 in chapter 1).

Downtown Location and Retro Design   Although teams have been able exert a great deal of leverage over cities, localities that have chosen to invest in stadiums and arenas have at least been able to control the location of such facilities. Cities have increasingly opted to incorporate stadium and arena construction into downtown development plans. (The motivating factors behind this trend and its implications will be discussed in the next section of this chapter.) This location choice has contributed to the escalating cost of facility development. Building downtown often requires the consolidation of expensive parcels of real estate.

Oriole Park at Camden Yards set a new standard for baseball stadium development when it opened in 1992. Situated near Baltimore's Inner Harbor, a redeveloping downtown tourist district, the stadium's design recalls the architectural elements of classic ballparks. Other downtown ballparks with retro influences soon followed, including Progressive Field in Cleveland, Coors Field in Denver, Comerica Park in Detroit, and AT&T Park (formerly called SBC Park and Pac Bell Park) in San Francisco. These facilities incorporate design elements ranging from brick facades and exposed steel support beams to asymmetrical field layouts (which are often artificially imposed). Seattle's Safeco Field and Houston's Minute Maid Park combine retro styling with the modern convenience of a retractable roof. These elaborate design elements add to the appeal of current-era facilities, but they also significantly drive up their cost.

With this background in place, we turn to the question of why public officials and metropolitan area residents have been so willing to support public investment in sport facilities over the years. As illustrated in the previous chapter, economic theory and a host of empirical studies indicate that conventional economic indicators cannot justify such spending. The evidence suggests that stadiums and arenas have little or no impact on metropolitan area employment or income. A growing number of economists and policy analysts have been sounding this caution since the 1970s (Noll, 1974; Okner, 1974). In light of this evidence, the continued proliferation of public investment in sport facilities might seem to reflect a collective irrationality among policy makers, but alternative explanations are plausible. One such explanation has to do with the political economy of stadium development; another is related to the notion that stadiums and teams generate tangible and intangible consumption benefits that could justify some level of public investment. We explore these concepts in the remainder of this chapter.

Political Economy of Sport Facility Development

The decisions that public officials make regarding urban development are conditioned by a combination of economic circumstances, political influence, and private power. For policy makers in declining cities, sport facility investment might represent a desperate desire to spur badly needed downtown revitalization. Public officials in emerging cities might turn to sport development in attempts to establish a big-league image for their locality. Decision making in this context is often affected by the interests and influence of the local business community and other elites who benefit from certain types of development.

Downtown Revitalization

Many older U.S. cities have struggled with the effects of economic and spatial changes that emerged in the latter half of the 20th century. The suburbanization of both population and jobs and a decline in the importance of manufacturing have contributed to the deterioration of many once-vibrant city centers. In response, city governments have sponsored downtown revitalization efforts, often focusing on entertainment and tourism. As key elements of these strategies, downtown stadiums and arenas have taken on a much broader purpose than the utilitarian facilities of the previous era. Policy makers have looked toward sport development strategies to spark urban renaissance, reestablish the cultural importance of downtown, and stem the outward flow of population and employment. Although sport facilities are unlikely to generate large economic impacts, they could possibly contribute to the redevelopment of a particular area.

Austrian and Rosentraub (2002) have examined the ability of stadium investments to facilitate urban revitalization. The authors make an important distinction between such impacts and impacts on overall economic activity:

> If the justification for using public resources to build downtown sports facilities is that these structures will shift economic activity to an area that that needs redevelopment, then the issue is not whether overall economic activity increased or decreased, but whether the vitality or centrality of the downtown area was enhanced or sustained. (p. 551)

Austrian and Rosentraub (2002) studied development patterns in four metropolitan areas: Cincinnati, Cleveland, Columbus, and Indianapolis. These Midwestern cities have each faced similar struggles related to the migration of population and economic activity to suburban localities. Cleveland and Indianapolis both employed sport development strategies to revive struggling downtown areas, whereas Cincinnati and Columbus did not invest in such facilities until more recently. Austrian and Rosentraub present evidence that Cleveland and Indianapolis benefited from their early investment in downtown sport facilities but that Cincinnati and Columbus have continued to struggle. During their study period, both Cleveland and Indianapolis saw an increase in the number of downtown jobs. The number of jobs in downtown Cleveland increased despite continued population loss and a slow regional growth rate. In contrast, the number of downtown jobs in Cincinnati steadily decreased during the study period, and Columbus lost downtown jobs despite a growth rate in regional jobs that exceeded the national growth rate. Austrian and Rosentraub concluded, "Sports and a hospitality concentration did help focus economic attention and political support for the maintenance of a downtown presence for employers in both Cleveland and Indianapolis" (p. 560).

Recall from the discussion of substitution spending in chapter 4 that these benefits do not stem from the creation of new spending but are rather the result of a redistribution of economic activity. This means, for example, that job growth in downtown Cleveland occurred at the expense of other nearby localities or even other parts of the city. Although this job growth might serve the goals of politicians, it does not represent a net increase in economic activity. It also raises equity concerns, because part of the financing burden for Cleveland's sport facilities fell on taxpayers throughout Cuyahoga County. Sport-related revitalization strategies are also open to questions regarding efficiency and opportunity costs. Nearly $500 million of public funds were spent on downtown sport facilities in Cleveland during the 1990s. As Austrian and Rosentraub pointed out, "It is relatively easy to make the case that an expenditure of this magnitude for any number of other investments in downtown Cleveland could have had the potential to bring similar if not greater economic returns" (p. 561).

Growth Coalitions and Urban Regime Theory

Public decisions regarding urban development are often influenced by powerful businesses, landowners, and other private interests that benefit from growth and intensification of land use. When these entities band together, either formally or informally, to pursue their common goals more effectively, they are referred to as a growth coalition (Logan and Molotch, 1987; Molotch, 1976). Regardless of whether downtown sport facilities generate a net increase in economic activity, numerous interests benefit from their development. These interests often act together to exert growth coalition influence and push for facility construction.

Sport facility development means jobs for local construction unions and increased business for local utilities. Downtown landowners and real estate interests profit from increased property values associated with facility construction, especially when such development represents redevelopment of underutilized land. Facility financing requires the sale of bonds and other lending activity, which means business for financial institutions and lawyers. Downtown business owners see increased activity and exposure. Finally, the local media, who devote a significant percentage of their news coverage to sports, clearly benefit from the presence of professional sports. These entities are commonly vocal proponents of downtown sport development strategies.

Analysts point out that local elected officials are also inclined to advocate growth-related development policies for a number of interrelated reasons. Growth creates a strong political legacy and is therefore vital to the political longevity of elected officials. In addition, growth is imperative to a city's fiscal well-being. Finally, elected officials rely on the support of the powerful private interests who have made growth their priority. These private interests can exert influence and direct resources, but they cannot dictate local development decisions. On the other hand, local officials can develop growth-minded policies, but they do not necessarily have access to the economic resources needed to carry out development plans. Urban regime theory recognizes that local officials and growth coalitions often work in partnership with one another to overcome their individual limitations and effectively carry out urban development (Elkin, 1987; Stone, 1989). This occurs through both informal interactions and formal arrangements, such as public–private partnerships.

Public Choice Theory

Public choice theory provides similar insights into the incentives for public investment in sport facilities. Whereas urban regime concepts stem from the field of political theory, public choice theory is a branch of economics that developed from the study of taxation and public spending. Classical and neoclassical economists assume that people are motivated mainly by self-interest. Public choice economists apply this notion to the actions of public officials, arguing that politicians are not driven by an altruistic desire to serve the public interest but rather by a desire to promote their own self-interest. In other words, politicians seek actions that maximize their chances of being reelected or gaining higher office.

Because politicians attempt to respond to the desires of the electorate, their actions will often reflect the public interest. The problem is that politicians are more likely to be aware of, and responsive to, the desires of well-organized and vocal group interests. Groups that would directly benefit from the development of downtown sport facilities, such as those described earlier, have a powerful incentive to organize and make their interests known. They might also attempt to exert influence with political contributions. In addition, the fans of a team that is seeking a new stadium are motivated to support public spending. Those without a direct stake in the outcome do not have the same incentive to invest the time and effort required to influence decision making. Opposition efforts, therefore, tend to be poorly funded and disorganized. As a result, a small collection of motivated interests can gain an important degree of influence over decision making.

Officials seeking to advance their political careers might find stadium projects especially attractive because of their high profile. In addition, although the political benefits of such a project accrue in the short term, the costs of public investment are invariably spread into the distant future. According to public theory, self-interested elected officials are likely to be more concerned about the next election than the long-term fiscal health of their locality.

Cleveland's downtown sport investments of the 1990s provide an example of urban regime influence and public choice theory concepts in action. During the 1980s downtown redevelopment had become a priority among city officials and organized business interests. The Jacobs brothers, property developers who had significant real estate interests in downtown Cleveland, purchased the Indians in 1986 and soon began lobbying for a new downtown stadium. Michael White, who was elected mayor in 1989 with the support of Cleveland's business community, became the most visible political advocate of a sport development strategy known as the Central Market Gateway Project (often referred to simply as Gateway). Besides the proposed baseball stadium, the project would also include a new arena to lure the basketball Cavaliers back to downtown; the team had been playing in Richfield, a suburb between Cleveland and Akron, since 1974. Cleveland Tomorrow, a council of the chief executives of the region's largest corporations, offered a contribution to construction costs, and local business interests helped develop a $1 million campaign to support a tax referendum to fund the project (D.W. Keating, 1997; Rosentraub, 1997). The Gateway project was approved in 1990, and both facilities opened in 1994. After considerable cost overruns, public sources contributed far more to the total construction cost than the 50 percent originally anticipated.

The most vocal proponents of the Gateway project were those who knew that they would benefit from its development. Team owners gained increased revenue from the new facilities, and the Indians were eventually sold for a large profit. Downtown business interests and landowners saw renewed activity and increased property values. Mayor Michael White gained a political landmark and was credited with transforming downtown Cleveland. White was the longest-serving mayor in Cleveland's history when he stepped down in 2001.

These benefits are quite concentrated, and the favorable lease terms negotiated with the teams have limited the direct fiscal benefit of the project to the public. For reasons described in chapter 4, the overall economic impact of the Gateway project is likely to be small.

Considering all this, making a legitimate case for public investment might seem difficult, but other potential benefits to area residents must be taken into account. For example, if the renewed vitality of downtown Cleveland served to enhance civic pride or quality of life among residents, then the benefits of this revitalization extend beyond the improvement in employment centrality documented by Austrian and Rosentraub. The magnitude and scope of these kinds of intangible benefits are more difficult to determine, but they are likely to be important to local residents. The remainder of this chapter focuses on the role of these consumption benefits.

Importance of Consumption Benefits

Sport facilities and teams create a variety of benefits that are completely unrelated to their ability to generate jobs or income. The cultural importance and psychological benefits associated with professional sport teams likely outweigh their economic impacts, providing residents a common ground, a topic of conversation, and sometimes a source of pride. An entire region can benefit from an enhanced central city image, and many believe that professional sport teams simply improve quality of life. Residents need never purchase a ticket to derive utility from a sport team. These benefits exist regardless of any contribution of the team or facility to the local economy.

Recall our Costco example from chapter 4. Although the typical Costco wholesale store generates more annual revenue than most major-league sport teams do, a sport team almost certainly has a greater cultural influence on its community. Sport fans derive utility from following their favorite team that they could never get from any other type of local investment or enterprise. Euchner (1993) provides the following analogy to illustrate the unique nature of the professional sport industry:

> It is hard to imagine Baltimoreans rooting for the Esskay meat company, a local firm, over a rival cold-cuts firm like Oscar Meyer of Madison, Wisconsin. The two firms do not carry the city's name and do not confront each other as symbols of their communities they way sports teams do.

Consumption benefits help explain why cities are more likely to offer subsidies to sport teams than to big-box warehouse stores or producers of deli meat.

To understand the importance of consumption benefits, it is helpful to categorize them as either private or public consumption benefits. Private consumption benefits accrue to fans who attend games. In this context, consumer surplus arises when the amount that a person is willing to pay for a ticket to a sporting event is greater than the actual cost of the ticket. The difference represents a benefit to the consumer. For example, if a fan is willing to pay $40 to attend a game, but can get a ticket for $20, that fan receives a consumer surplus of $20. A net consumer surplus generated by a sport team represents a welfare gain to its locality.

Public consumption benefits encompass the intangible rewards associated with hosting a major-league sport team and are related to rooting for the home team more generally, independent of attending games. These benefits accrue to fans who derive utility from watching games on television, discussing the home team with friends, or reading about the team in the local newspaper. A hockey fan in Toronto can derive substantial pleasure from the Maple Leafs and identify with them as "his team" without ever buying a ticket. Nonfans who consider the team a contributor to enhanced city image also benefit from its existence.

Public consumption benefits are related to the economic concepts of positive externalities and public goods—two types of market failure. A variety of government interventions are justified on the grounds that the marketplace does not efficiently provide public goods or properly account for externalities on its own.

Externalities and Public Goods

Externalities can be thought of as economic side effects, or spillovers. They are costs or benefits that stem from an economic activity but that affect people other than those directly involved in a market transaction. The private market essentially ignores these external costs or benefits, leading to inefficient levels of production.

For example, if a factory emits pollution, it imposes a cost, or a negative externality, on nearby residents. Because the cost of pollution is not born by the factory owner, it does not signal him or her to reduce production. If I pay for a flu shot, my neighbors and coworkers benefit from a positive externality; they do not have to worry about getting the flu from me. Because I do not consider the health of my neighbors and coworkers in my decision-making process, I might not find it worth my while to get a flu shot. In general, if goods or activities create negative externalities, the market will tend to produce more than the socially optimal amount. If goods or activities create positive externalities, the market will tend to produce less than the socially optimal amount.

Government intervention is commonly used to address these inefficiencies. In the case of goods or activities that produce negative externalities, governments impose regulations or levy taxes designed to be equivalent to the incidental costs created. To stimulate the production of goods that create positive externalities, governments provide subsidies. This action is equivalent to paying producers for the incidental benefits of their activities. Taxes and subsidies are designed to internalize the external costs and benefits of production.

Because residents can derive a variety of benefits from local sport teams without ever attending a game, teams can be said to generate positive externalities. For example, newspapers, television news programs, and talk radio shows devote a great deal of their attention to local sport teams. Sport fans consume this coverage with no compensation to team owners. Water cooler conversations about the upcoming pennant race may create pleasure for local sport fans, but they cost fans nothing and have no effect on team revenue. Because of the presence of these externalities, the direct demand experienced by a team understates the total benefit of that team to local residents.

Public goods have two defining characteristics: nonrivalrous consumption and nonexcludability. A good or service that exhibits nonrivalrous consumption can be used by one person without detracting from the ability of others to use the good or service as well. For example, a levee protects my house along the river without limiting the ability of the levee to protect my neighbor's house. Nonexcludability means that excluding some people from enjoying the benefits of a good or service is impossible or impractical, even if they are unwilling to pay for them. After that levee is built, it will protect my house along the river regardless of who paid for it. I cannot be excluded from that protection even if my neighbor built the levee him- or herself.

In contrast, private goods exhibit rivalrous consumption and excludability. After you consume a bottle of beer, no one else at the bar with you can enjoy that drink. If you are unwilling to pay for a beer, the barkeeper will exclude you from consuming one by refusing to serve you.

Because nonpaying users cannot be excluded from enjoying the benefits of a public good after it is supplied, producers of such goods and services have a hard time collecting fees equal to the benefits that they create. This circumstance is referred to as the free-rider problem. If a resident can receive all the benefits of the community's levee regardless of his or her contribution, the person has no incentive to pay. Because of the free-rider problem, the private market cannot efficiently provide public goods. Because of this inefficiency, the production of public goods is generally left to governments, who coerce payment for their benefits through taxation.

Sport teams produce both private and public goods. Tickets to games and subscriptions to cable sport packages certainly exhibit rivalrous consumption and excludability, but sport teams also create certain benefits that are jointly consumed and from which no one can be excluded. These might include things like civic pride, greater community cohesion, and the image benefits of status as big-league city. Such benefits accrue to fans as well as nonfans.

In a survey of 1,536 Indianapolis residents, Rosentraub and Swindell (1998) found significant evidence of "social spillover benefits" associated with local sport teams. Respondents ranked auto racing, the NFL Colts, and the NBA Pacers as Indianapolis' top three contributors to civic pride and national reputation. These results demonstrate that sport teams can produce positive externalities or public goods that are valued by local residents.

Suggesting that these kinds of benefits can justify the enormous public subsidies that cities offer for sport facilities might seem absurd, but Noll and Zimbalist (1997b) offer a hypothetical investment situation that provides an important perspective. They put forth a stadium, receiving a subsidy of $250 million in a metropolitan area of 5 million residents. The annual cost of servicing the debt to finance such a stadium would be equivalent to approximately $5 per resident.

> It does not vastly stretch credulity to suppose that, say, a quarter of the population of a metropolitan area derives $20 per person in consumption benefits annually from following a local sport team. If so, the consumption benefits of acquiring and keeping a team exceed the costs. (Noll and Zimbalist, 1997b)

For this hypothetical investment to be truly justified, the cost would need to be spread across the entire metropolitan area. Often, stadium financing plans affect only a particular city or county of a metropolitan area, whereas potential consumption benefits extend to a much wider area. For the 2.5 million residents of Cleveland and Cuyahoga County, the estimated per capita cost of the Gateway complex is equivalent to approximately $10 per year (Rosentraub, 1997). It is not beyond reason to suppose that the average Clevelander would willingly pay $10 a year for the opportunity to enjoy the Cavaliers and Indians, and the intangible benefits created by those teams and their downtown facilities.

If a stadium creates no significant benefits in terms of jobs or income, then the sum of the private and public consumption benefits that it creates must exceed the public cost of the facility if it is to pass a simple cost–benefit test. Although many economists acknowledge the existence of consumption benefits associated with sport facilities, research devoted to their empirical measurement has been scarce. However, a variety of analytical tools can be used to assess the magnitude of such benefits, and a handful of studies provide a foundation for further research.

Estimating Private Consumption Benefits

A measure of consumer surplus can be generated by estimating a demand curve and comparing demand to price. Recall that consumer surplus is generated when the price that a consumer is willing to pay for a good is higher than the actual price of that good. The size of consumer surplus is represented graphically as the area above the price and below the demand curve. In the case of sporting events, data regarding ticket prices and quantities demanded (attendance) can be gathered from various sources and used to estimate a demand schedule.

Irani (1997) developed an empirical estimate of the annual consumer surplus associated with MLB teams by generating a demand curve for baseball games (assumed to be linear). Using data collected from all MLB cities, he calculated the total consumer surplus generated by each team in 1985. The resulting estimates ranged from $2.2 million (Cleveland Indians) to $54.1 million (Los Angeles Dodgers). The average across all stadiums was $18.4 million. Given these findings, Irani asserted that baseball teams generate "nontrivial consumer surplus" and concluded, "Even though a stadium might not provide direct economic benefits to the locality, it does provide a positive amount of welfare gain" (p. 249). In fact, over the life of a 30-year bond, assuming a discount rate of 6 percent, an annual consumer surplus of $18.4 million translates to a net present value of $253 million—a figure that surpasses the public investment level of many recent stadium developments.

These findings illustrate that ticket sales can create benefits beyond generating profits for team owners, but because Irani's methodology was unable to account for price discrimination practices, these estimates represent upper-bound estimates of consumer surplus. Monopolistic team owners use price discrimination to eliminate, or capture, some of the consumer surplus created. They do this by charging different prices to different buyers rather than charging a single price to all buyers. This practice helps ensure that individual buyers pay a price that closely resembles the maximum price that they are willing to pay. The closer the actual price is to the buyer's willingness to pay, the smaller the consumer surplus—and the greater the profit to the monopolistic team owner. Examples of price discrimination include charging different rates for different seats, selling personal seat licenses, and selling ticket packages that bundle the best games with those least in demand.

Estimating Public Consumption Benefits

The consumer surplus measurement accounts only for the extra benefits that accrue to persons who attend games. It does not account for public consumption benefits—the external benefits received by residents who derive utility from the existence of a team without ever purchasing a ticket.

Compensating Differentials Rappaport and Wilkerson (2001) refer to these public consumption benefits as "quality-of-life contributions" and suggest that their relative magnitude can be understood by considering the valuations of other attributes that also contribute to quality of life.

> For instance, the quality-of-life net present value associated with one extra day per year of pleasant weather for 30 years turns out to be similar in magnitude to many of the recent outlays on stadium projects. So if the contribution to quality-of-life from hosting a major league team is at least as great as the contribution from one extra day per year of pleasant weather, then the public outlays on sports stadiums and arenas may be justified. (p. 73)

The value of quality-of-life attributes that differ across region can be measured by variations in wages and housing costs, when all other variables are held constant. Regional amenities, such as a pleasant climate or world-class theaters, attract residents. All else being equal, this circumstance drives up housing costs and drives down wages. Economists refer to these effects on wages and housing costs as compensating differentials. Lower wages and higher housing costs serve as negative compensation for the existence of quality-of-life attributes. The compensating differential can be thought of as the implicit price that people are willing to pay to live in a locality that provides a certain amenity.

Because all else is not equal, some amenity-rich cities have above average wages as well as high housing costs. Wage levels and housing costs are influenced by a vast variety of factors beyond the existence of regional amenities and disamenities. For example, firms generally pay higher wages in larger cities because they can be more productive in such locations. Economists attempt to isolate the effect of amenities on wages or rents by holding these other variables constant.

Imagine that after graduating from college, you are faced with the choice of accepting a job in city A with a salary of $50,000 or taking the same job in city B for $49,000 a year. The two cities are identical in every way except that city B is home to a major-league baseball team. If you would be willing to take the lower pay in city B, that difference of $1,000 reflects the implicit annual price that you would be willing to pay for the amenities associated with the presence of a baseball team. Recall from chapter 4 that a study conducted by Coates and Humphreys (1999) found that the presence of a professional sport team actually had a negative effect on per capita income in some metropolitan areas. Although the authors offer substitution spending as a possible explanation, they also consider that this could reflect a compensating differential effect.

Economists use a technique called hedonic pricing to measure the effects of certain amenities or disamenities on wages and housing costs. The basic premise of hedonic pricing is that the price of a good reflects the total value of the bundle of characteristics that make up that good. For example, the price of a house reflects the number of bedrooms in the house, its lot size, age, location, and so on. We can value the individual characteristics of a good by examining how the price people are willing to pay for that good changes when its characteristics change.

Carlino and Coulson (2002) used hedonic analysis to measure the compensating differentials that exist in National Football League (NFL) cities. After controlling for other factors, the authors found that the presence of an NFL team raises annual rents by approximately 8 percent. With an average rent of $500 in the sample cities, an 8 percent premium equates to $40 per month, or $480 per year, per household. Carlino and Coulson also offer a lower-bound premium estimate of 2.9 percent, which equates to an annual price of $174. When multiplied by the approximately 290,000 households in the average sample city, this lower-bound estimate implies an aggregate NFL amenity value of about $50 million per year, on average. Over the life of a stadium, this figure far exceeds the cost of a typical subsidy.

This study represented the first attempt to measure the external benefits of professional sport teams using hedonic pricing, and the results have been subject to some skepticism. It is not clear whether the technique employed by Carlino and Coulson was able to account for all other city-specific variables that could confound the relationship between NFL teams and rents. The combinations of attractive attributes that could exist in coincidence with the existence of an NFL franchise are limitless. The authors acknowledged this point in their explanation of the wage results.

> It might be thought that the NFL dummy variable did not represent the effect of NFL teams, per se, but some unobserved characteristic correlated with overall growth of economic climate—this despite our careful attempts to control for such unobservables. If this were the case, one might expect such a force to have a positive effect on wages, since the growth probably raises the cost of living. (p. 18)

Contingent Valuation   Suppose that to attract a professional baseball team, public officials in Portland and Multnomah County, Oregon, spent $250 million of public money to build a stadium. The annual per capita cost of the debt service on a 30-year bond (with a 6 percent interest rate) to finance the facility would be equivalent to approximately $27. An analytical technique called contingent valuation (CV), which directly elicits individuals' willingness to pay, allows the most direct comparison of per capita consumption benefits and per capita costs. Using CV would therefore allow a locality to determine the level of per capita investment justified by per capita consumption benefits.

CV methodology is commonly used to measure the value of environmental amenities. It can also be employed to determine the magnitude of consumption benefits associated with sport teams and facilities. CV is a nonmarket valuation method that elicits respondents' willingness to pay for the protection or provision of public goods through the use of surveys that present hypothetical opportunities to "buy" the public good in question. Respondents to CV surveys express their willingness to pay, contingent on a specified hypothetical payment vehicle and provision of the good. Measurements of willingness to pay include both use and existence values (sometimes referred to as nonuse or passive-use values). The existence benefits of a stadium comprise the benefits that the facility and team provide to those who do not participate as buyers or sellers of tickets. These are the external benefits, or public consumption benefits, described earlier.

A study conducted by Johnson and Whitehead (2000) demonstrated how CV methodology can be used to measure the external benefits generated by a sport facility. The authors examined two facilities proposed to be built in Fayette County, Kentucky—a new basketball arena for the University of Kentucky (UK) and a minor-league baseball facility. The UK arena would be built with private money, but its construction would represent a cost to Fayette County because it would decrease the rent received at Rupp Arena, the county-owned facility where UK basketball games are currently played. The minor-league baseball park would cost the county approximately $10 million and would be built to host a AA Southern League team. Johnson and Whitehead surveyed 230 county residents to determine their attitudes toward UK basketball and minor-league baseball, and elicit their willingness to pay for the proposed facilities.

The results showed that "the production of UK basketball games generates substantial nonrivalrous and nonexcludable public goods" (p. 51). Although 60 percent of respondents did not attend any UK basketball games, 56 percent reported watching at least 11 games on television, 72 percent reported reading about UK basketball regularly, and 71 percent reported that they regularly discuss UK basketball with others.

Respondents were asked, "What is the most you would be willing to pay out of your own household budget per year to make a new arena possible?" The mean annual willingness to pay for a new basketball facility was $6.36, which Johnson and Whitehead estimated would support capital costs in the range of $3.71 to $7.28 million. The projected cost of the new arena was $100 million. Using statistical analysis, the willingness-to-pay estimate was disaggregated into use and existence value. The estimated existence value would support between $1.12 and $2.20 million in capital costs. For the baseball stadium, the mean annual willingness to pay was $6.17, which would support capital costs between $3.60 and $7.06 million. The existence value would only support between $361,000 and $709,000 in capital costs.

This analysis indicates that the proposed facilities would not generate enough public consumption benefit to justify any significant public investment. These results are a reflection of the preferences and attitudes of local residents regarding the proposed investment. Johnson and Whitehead suggested that Fayette County residents, even those who described themselves as fans, had little incentive to support an investment in a new UK arena. This circumstance is partly because the UK basketball team is place bound by nature and would remain in Fayette County regardless of whether a new arena was constructed. "The public goods produced by the team would continue to be produced" (p. 57). The same cannot be said of professional sport franchises. A locality facing threats of relocation or the possibility of acquiring a new team would have to consider different factors in constructing their willingness to pay. The public consumption benefits associated with a major-league baseball team are likely to be greater than those associated with a minor-league team, as measured in this case. In this sense, the nature of the specific cases examined by Johnson and Whitehead limits the applicability of their findings to more typical stadium investment decisions. This conclusion does not, however, limit the applicability of the methodology.

Santo (2007) used a similar technique to quantify the potential consumption benefits that would be associated with attracting a major league baseball team to Portland, Oregon. The study found that consumption benefits would support a capital investment of approximately $74 million; a figure far smaller than the typical stadium subsidy, but not wholly insignificant. The majority of projected benefits was associated with expected public goods and externalities, rather than anticipated attendance, indicating that an equitable financing plan would need to employ nonuser revenue sources. The willingness of residents to pay for stadium construction was tempered by a concern about other pressing social needs in the Portland area and a reaction to the existing tax climate.

Because of their contrasting results, these studies do not clearly reveal whether consumption benefits can justify large public investments in professional sport facilities, but they do illustrate the potential importance of such benefits. The efficiency and opportunity cost warning comes into play again here. Sport development projects should be measured against other public investments that have similar ability to generate community consumption benefits. Unlike public art museums or parks, most of the financial benefits created by new ballparks are privately appropriated (Zimbalist, 2003). If teams can afford to pay for their own facilities, public subsidies may be inefficient regardless of the magnitude of consumption benefits.

Future Trends

Because so many major-league stadiums and arenas have been built during the past 20 years, one might expect the pace of development to begin to slow, but the pipeline of pending facilities remains full. Among others, plans are in place for a baseball-only stadium in Miami to host the Florida Marlins (who currently play in Landshark Stadium), a new hockey arena in Pittsburgh, and a new basketball arena in Orlando to replace a 20-year-old facility. (The majority of funding for each of those facilities will come from public sources.) Stadium subsidy debates rage on in places like Minneapolis, where construction of a baseball stadium for the Twins (heavily subsidized by a county sales tax) is underway, while the Vikings continue to seek state support for a new football stadium. And teams like the San Francisco 49ers and Oakland Athletics are openly exploring the possibility of moving to other localities within the bay area to satisfy their desire for new facilities.

The five most recently opened facilities—Nationals Park in Washington, DC, Lucas Oil Stadium in Indianapolis, Citi Field and Yankee Stadium in New York, and Cowboys Stadium in Arlington, Texas—are remarkably expensive, ranging in cost from $600 million to $1.3 billion. The new Meadowlands Stadium, being built to replace Giants Stadium in New Jersey, is also expected to cost in excess of $1 billion. Following a general trend of the current era, the share of private investment in most of these facilities has been significant, but because of their massive price tags, even a small public contribution in terms of share represents a large public investment. For example, the City of Arlington's contribution to the new Cowboys stadiums represents just a third of the overall cost but totals a hefty 325 million (generated from sales, hotel, and car rental tax revenue).

A potentially promising trend in sport facility development is the growing use of community benefits agreements (CBA). A CBA is a legally enforceable contract between a developer and a community coalition designed to ensure equity and address community concerns by outlining specific benefits that developers agree to provide to affected residents and institutions. Benefits often include provision of affordable housing, living wage jobs for local residents, and contributions to neighborhood parks and schools. In exchange for the promise of these benefits, the community coalitions agree to show support as the developers navigate the process of requesting political and administrative approvals.

In 2001 a coalition of Los Angeles community groups, motivated by their concerns about a proposed retail, residential, and entertainment development associated with the Staples Center arena, negotiated what has become a model CBA. Ultimately, the developers agreed to ensure that 20 percent of new housing units were affordable to low-income residents, to provide funding to nonprofit housing developers for the creation of additional affordable housing, to give hiring priority for new jobs to displaced and low-income neighborhood residents, and to provide $1 million for community parks and recreation programs (Crowell, 2005).

Other CBAs related to sport facility development have recently been enacted or are currently being negotiated in San Diego, Pittsburgh, and New York (associated with both Yankee Stadium in the Bronx and the proposed Atlantic Yards arena in Brooklyn).

Well-formed CBAs can mitigate some of the negative social impacts of sport facility construction and help ensure more equitable distribution of benefits, but CBAs are not entirely immune to the political influence and private power that otherwise affect stadium development decisions. Furthermore, the successful implementation of a CBA requires that the community groups involved have some legitimate leverage (i.e., a real ability to influence subsidy or land use decisions). The CBA that was prepared to ease concerns about the construction of the new Yankee Stadium in the Bronx, which eliminated 20 acres of parks, has drawn heavy criticism (Williams, 2006). In fact, some argue that the term *community benefits agreement* is inappropriate in this case because the agreement was negotiated between the Yankees and elected officials (the Bronx Borough president and the Bronx Delegation of the New York City Council), without the involvement or signature of any community groups. The agreement includes the creation of a $28 million fund to be distributed to community interests over a 40-year period, but because the administrator of the fund will be appointed by the same elected officials responsible for the CBA, critics are wary of how the money will ultimately be used (Williams, 2006; Schuerman, 2006). Williams (2008) pointed out that although the CBA is enforceable by courts, "Officials who normally ensure that the terms of a contract are carried out—such as the city comptroller—have no oversight because municipal money is not involved."

Conclusion

This chapter has illustrated that although the current stadium and arena construction boom is unique, especially in terms of magnitude and scope, it is just the most recent stage in a cycle of sport facility development. Because of their many revenue-generating features, current-era facilities are extremely valuable to the teams that they host. The value of these facilities to their host communities is more difficult to assess. Despite their inability to generate net economic impacts, public officials might rationally pursue sport development strategies to spur microlevel redevelopment or to advance their political careers. In addition, sport facilities and teams create a variety of consumption benefits that exist regardless of any contribution of the team or facility to the local economy. The value of such benefits, which are often intangible externalities, could conceivably exceed the cost of subsidies and justify public investment.

Techniques that allow consideration of consumption benefits clearly provide an opportunity to improve the evaluation process and enhance the debate regarding stadium subsidies. The current framework for discussion and analysis relies too heavily on fallible claims of economic development. In the face of contrary evidence, this remains the case likely because the economic catalyst argument is easier to sell to nonfans and because economic development benefits are easier to quantify, however arbitrary they might be. An understanding of the distribution of public and private consumption benefits can also contribute to the development of an equitable stadium financing plan.

Community Ownership of Professional Sport Teams and the Role of Social Entrepreneurship

Dorothy Norris-Tirrell and Susan Tomlinson Schmidt

With a legacy dating back 20 years, San Diego sport fans were shocked when Major League Baseball denied McDonald's heiress Joan Kroc's attempt to give the Padres franchise to the city of San Diego in 1990. The Padres had been plagued with weak seasons during their early years, prompting their owner, C. Arnholt Smith, to arrange a deal to sell the team and move them to Washington, DC, for the summer of 1974. The move was so expected that the club was packed and ready to go, and baseball card companies had printed the cards for the new season with the word *Washington* instead of *Padres* for the team name. In a characteristically bold move, McDonald's Corporation founder Ray Kroc stepped in and bought the team to keep it in San Diego. Kroc brought his unorthodox management style to the franchise, creating controversy but also improving the team's record and financial stability. In January 1984 Kroc died, leaving the Padres and his massive fortune to his wife. Uninterested in baseball but deeply committed to helping players with drug problems, Joan Kroc decided to sell the team and focus on her philanthropic pursuits, but she wanted to make sure that the team stayed in San Diego. In 1990 Kroc offered to donate the Padres franchise, along with a $100 million trust to ensure the organization's continued operation, to the City of San Diego. Under pressure from a faction of National League franchise owners, Major League Baseball prevented her from giving the team to a municipal owner. Later that year Kroc sold the team for $75 million to a group of local businessmen. Although she was not successful in her bid for community ownership, the model conceived by Joan Kroc was visionary.

The current era of professional sport team ownership has become renowned for conflict, including lockouts, strikes, steroid scandals, and debates about public subsidies for new stadiums and arenas. Heated standoffs that pit city and civic leaders, die-hard fans, and owner conglomerates against each other are common headlines. But cities continue to see professional sport teams as important to their public image.

With little opportunity remaining for expansion within leagues, the most likely way for a city to gain a professional sport team is through the relocation of an existing franchise. Because of the limited supply of teams and the cartel nature of sport leagues (as discussed in chapters 1 and 5), cities seeking to host teams are forced into competition with one another. Competing cities often seek to lure teams by offering to build new sport facilities at significant public cost. For their investment, governments hope to gain intangibles in the form of residents' increased perceptions of quality of life and tangibles such as downtown revitalization (Kennedy and Rosentraub, 2000). Complicating the use of incentives is the understanding that loyalty to one location is a thing of the past. Footloose teams leave cities for a number of reasons—weak fan support, insurmountable debt combined with the need for a larger population to raise revenue, or the lure of a new stadium or arena deal elsewhere. After cities invest in a team, losing the benefits that the team brings can be devastating and the resulting psychological effect can create distrust among the team's once loyal fan base.

In response to the recurring frequency of relocation for professional sport teams, municipal and civic leaders have turned to alternative community ownership strategies. The two most obvious benefits of a community ownership structure, like the model proposed by Joan Kroc in San Diego, relate to increased stability and opportunity for new revenue streams. Teams owned by a community entity (e.g., a local government, a community-based nonprofit, or a nonprofit common stock corporation) are place-based instead of footloose. Creating permanent ties to place eliminates the type of reactionary spending that a private owner might demand when threatening to relocate. These benefits of community ownership alternatives are discussed by Kraker (2000), Kraker and Morris (1998), and Meder and Leckrone (2002). This chapter presents a framework for nonprofit community ownership alternatives and examines related benefits that have thus far received less attention. The Memphis Redbirds Baseball Foundation, a tax-exempt nonprofit organization, is presented as an example of a unique community ownership structure that introduces the role and effect of social entrepreneurship.

Identifying Community Ownership Alternatives

Ownership of both professional teams and the stadiums in which they play can take many forms. Three types of ownership are currently in practice: private, joint, and community. Private, for-profit ownership is a clearly identifiable form that may involve a single owner (e.g., Jerry Jones' Dallas Cowboys), a group of owners (e.g., Memphis Grizzlies), or a publicly traded corporation (e.g., Cablevision's New York Rangers). This form of ownership is the predominant model of ownership among major-league sport teams. Community ownership is a more complex category. Community-owner entities are nonprofit or local government structures that allow access to community-based resources, ranging from taxpayer (public) funding to individual and corporate donations. Joint ownership indicates some form of shared ownership among any of these types of structure, in which ownership is proportionate to construction cost and revenue split (e.g., Milwaukee Brewers' Miller Stadium: 64 percent Southeast Wisconsin Professional Baseball Park District, 36 percent Brewers).

The least studied of the ownership types is community ownership, which can be classified into four models: local government, nonprofit–fan owned, nonprofit–government backed, and nonprofit–charitable purpose (see table 6.1). These models promote place-bound teams, eliminating the harmful side effects of cartel leagues and offering new prospects for financial and community support. In the examples listed in table 6.1, all teams are minor-league baseball affiliates. Under Major League Baseball rules, players and coaches of minor-league teams are employees of the pro team that they support. This unusual situation creates an opportunity for community ownership, which is outlawed informally by Major League Baseball and is prohibited by current regulations for other major leagues.

Local government ownership can be through a municipality or county. These entities are often interested in bringing professional sports to their area because of the potential effect on image and perception. Civic leaders may also want to use a professional team and its stadium as an anchor institution or community asset to initiate or bolster revitalization. The question of when and how to use taxpayer dollars in this way is controversial. Governments may create special bodies or authorities of appointed citizens to oversee the publicly owned facilities or teams.

TABLE 6.1

Community Ownership Models

Model	Ownership entity	Funding distinction	IRS standing	Governance structure	Example
Local government	Municipality or county	Part of local government budget	Nonregulated body	Unit within government entity (e.g., stadium authority, parks and recreation)	Scranton–Wilkes-Barre (PA) Yankees
Nonprofit–fan owned	Nonprofit corporation	Common stock offering	Not recognized (taxpaying)	Board of directors, elected by shareholders	Appleton (WI) Timber Rattlers
Nonprofit–government backed	Nonprofit corporation	Local government	Charitable recognition (tax exempt)	Volunteer board appointed by local government leadership (e.g., mayor, county commissioners)	Toledo (OH) Mud Hens
Nonprofit–charitable purpose	Nonprofit corporation	Private donors	Charitable recognition (tax exempt)	Volunteer board of directors, self-electing	Memphis (TN) Redbirds

The Scranton–Wilkes-Barre Yankees (formerly Red Barons) are an example of this form of community ownership (Kraker and Morris, 1998). The Lackawanna County (PA) Commission built the PNC stadium after a local attorney mounted a campaign to bring professional baseball to the Scranton–Wilkes-Barre area. The civic entrepreneur launched a campaign to create a nonprofit, Northeastern Baseball Inc., to purchase the team and then sell it to the Stadium Authority for $1.

One of the more unusual and often misunderstood structures among community ownership options is the nonprofit professional sport team. The sidebar on this page lists sport-related nonprofit organizations. Although many of these organizations are familiar to those who follow sports, the idea of a nonprofit team may not be. Nonprofit tax-exempt organizations must have a public or collective good as their ultimate mission. Chartered by state governments and recognized as tax exempt by the U.S. Internal Revenue Service, nonprofit organizations are prohibited from disbursing net earnings to owners or shareholders, as private organizations do; rather, nonprofit organizations use net revenue to further their mission. A special class of nonprofits recognized under IRS code 501(c)(3) also allows donations to be tax deductible to the giving individual or corporation. Nonprofits are governed by a volunteer board of directors, who act as the owners group in a nonprofit professional sport team.

Nonprofit ownership in minor-league baseball takes on three forms: fan owned, government backed, and nonprofit–charitable purpose. Fan-owned teams are nonprofit corporations that have some form of common stock offering to fans.

Nonprofit Status and Sport Organizations

A number of sport-related groups are organized as nonprofits. Here are a few:

- Amateur sport leagues
- Booster clubs for school sport teams
- Community recreational sport leagues
- Competitive youth sport leagues
- Sport-specific interest groups
- Fan clubs
- Wheelchair sport leagues
- Special Olympics
- Olympic committees
- Professional leagues
- Professional sport team-affiliated foundations
- Health promotion organizations

Although incorporated as nonprofits through their home states, these organizations are not recognized as tax exempt by the Internal Revenue Service (IRS) because of shareholder ownership. Shareholder benefits vary slightly among teams and range from priority access to season tickets and seating preference to voting privileges only. An example of the nonprofit fan-owned structure is the Appleton Timber Rattlers. The Appleton Baseball Club, Inc. is a Wisconsin nonprofit that owns the Timber Rattlers, a class A affiliate of the Seattle Mariners. Formed in 1994 to finance a new stadium, the Appleton organization has 240 share-holding members who elect a board of directors to oversee the stadium and baseball operations.

Government-backed teams are another form of nonprofit ownership. This structure pairs a nonprofit corporation with local government funding to purchase a team, build a stadium, and maintain operations of both. The nonprofit is recognized as tax exempt because of the team's effect on overall community vitality. These organizations are governed by a volunteer board of directors that is appointed by the local leadership and typically includes elected and appointed officials. An example of this community ownership structure is the Toledo Mud Hens. Frustrated by several moves back and forth from Toledo, Ohio, a group of

Football's Famous Fan-Owned Team: The Only Major-League Example

First incorporated in 1923, the Green Bay Packers Football franchise is the only nonprofit National Football League (NFL) team. Although this unique structure has provided long-term stability for one of the NFL's most successful teams, nonprofit ownership is now prohibited in the league. The Packers remain the one exception because the organization predates the NFL ruling.

The Green Bay Packers boast the oldest team name still in use today and an impressive legacy of on-field success. Although Green Bay is the smallest media market of any North American major professional sport team, the organization enjoys a strong regional fan base and ends annually in the black, in large part because of its unusual structure. The Packers enterprise includes a nonprofit stock corporation that operates the football franchise, a trust that holds the dividends from stock sales, and a charitable nonprofit that awards grants to local organizations.

Shareholders of the stock corporation have voting rights, but share redemption price is minimal, no dividends are ever paid, and stock cannot appreciate in value. The franchise operates with a board of directors that is elected by the corporation's shareholders. This board elects a seven-member executive committee to serve as the decision-making body for the Packers organization. The president of the executive committee represents the organization at NFL owners meetings and is the only person on the executive committee to draw a salary. The Packers corporation is exempt from local and state taxes but must pay federal tax because the IRS does not recognize the organization as tax exempt. The Packers trust, funded from stock sales proceeds, is retained for stadium renovation and maintenance.

The Green Bay Packers Football Foundation is a 501(c)(3) nonprofit affiliated with the team corporation. This operating foundation makes small grants to sport and recreation charitable organizations in the region.

civic leaders formed the Toledo Mud Hens Baseball Club in 1965 as a nonprofit organization to purchase the triple-A minor-league baseball franchise so that the team would remain permanently in Toledo. The purchase of the team was backed financially by the Lucas County (OH) government.

Nonprofit charitable purpose is a newer entry into the community ownership category. This structure uses the nonprofit corporation in its more traditional form. For the nonprofit–charitable purpose sport team, the sport endeavor becomes an elaborate social enterprise opportunity, providing a sustainable revenue stream to fund mission-based programs. These programs are typically sport related and are either direct services (e.g., youth sport leagues) or grant making (e.g., small operational grants to existing sport-related charities). Although on the surface this structure may make little sense in the usual professional sport team context, nonprofit–charitable purpose community ownership is an ideal way to ensure that a team remains place bound and does not relocate on the whim of a single owner. In addition, this model of team and stadium ownership opens the door to a broadened mix of traditional and innovative revenue streams.

To illustrate this form of community ownership, the next section takes an in-depth look at minor league baseball's only nonprofit–charitable purpose team, the Memphis Redbirds. The case introduces the concept of social entrepreneurship and its role in local sport team ownership.

Using the Nonprofit–Charitable Purpose Structure: The Memphis Redbirds Baseball Foundation

The Memphis Redbirds Baseball Foundation is a 501(c)(3) nonprofit organization, operating a minor-league triple-A team for the St. Louis Cardinals and sport stadium (AutoZone Park). With a mission that states, "Baseball is our business, but the community is our bottom line," the Redbirds Foundation uses the net revenue from its operation to fund sport programs for inner-city youth.

The story of the Memphis Redbirds Baseball Foundation began in 1992, when several events occurred that led to the eventual creation of this unique organization. The St. Louis Cardinals player development contract with the Louisville, Kentucky, triple-A minor-league team expired. At the same time, Memphis resident Dean Jernigan, chairman of Storage USA, began pursuing the possibility of bringing a professional baseball team to Memphis. Frustrated by a history of failed professional sport teams in Memphis, Jernigan wanted to configure the team so that threatening to leave town could not be used as a bargaining chip. Shelby County mayor Jim Rout suggested the innovative idea of combining the operation of a triple-A baseball team with a nonprofit 501(c)(3) structure to accomplish this goal. Jernigan and another successful Memphis entrepreneur, Willard Sparks, proposed that the Cardinals bring a triple-A team to Memphis as a nonprofit foundation that would fund educational and youth sport programs through the revenue generated by baseball games and other activities at a state-of-the-art stadium. The Cardinals were enthusiastic about the idea of having a triple-A team in Memphis because of its proximity to St. Louis and the existing Cardinals support in Memphis, and they supported the idea of a nonprofit operation.

Jernigan and Sparks began garnering local support for the idea that included a 14,230-seat stadium funded by tax-exempt bonds to be paid off by income contractually obligated from the park itself. A group of local banks brokered the deal with over $80 million in variable-rate and fixed-rate series bonds, all intended to be tax exempt.

Upfront commitments from a number of individuals and corporations also made the deal viable:

- The Jernigans provided the funds for the demolition and excavation of the park site and a bridge loan.
- AutoZone agreed to pay $250,000 a year for 15 years for naming rights of the stadium.
- Coca-Cola pledged $250,000 a year for 15 years for pouring rights.
- FedEx guaranteed the sale of 750 club seats a year.
- Ovations Food Services guaranteed $750,000 in income from concessions.
- The Redbirds Foundation contracted 44 luxury suites at two price levels, $38,000 and $45,000 a year, in long-term leases.

The Redbirds Foundation was recognized as a 501(c)(3) tax-exempt organization in 1998, with a mission focused on sports, education, and inner-city youth. With the financing in place, the remaining obstacle was the Internal Revenue Service's resistance to allowing the Redbirds Foundation to construct the stadium with the 501(c)(3) tax-exempt bonds.

The IRS questioned the request under the private-use test, an IRS standard that requires any project being financed by 501(c)(3) debt to have no more than a 5 percent private benefit or use. Because the players and field staff of the Memphis Redbirds are employees of the St. Louis Cardinals, not the Redbirds Foundation, private use appeared to be predominant (Kinnander, 2001). According to attorneys representing the Redbirds Foundation and lawyers for Memphis Center City Revenue Finance Corporation, the entity that ultimately issued the bonds, "The bond analysis, provided by Chicago law firm Chapman & Cutler, counters that the Cardinals don't control the stadium, the foundation does," making the bonds tax free (Clubb and Johnson, 1999, p. A1). The decision to maintain the tax-exempt status of the bonds occurred in 2001 after the Redbirds Foundation paid the IRS a one-time $1.6 million payment to cover a portion of the interest on the initial $28 million bond, which was issued before the tax-exempt discrepancy was resolved (Kinnander, 2001). The stadium, designed as a centerpiece to downtown revitalization, opened on April 14, 2000, to record minor-league baseball crowds.

Structure and Programs

The Memphis Redbirds baseball team is one of six St. Louis Cardinals minor-league teams. The team is a part of the triple-A Pacific Coast League. The field staff and players for the Memphis Redbirds are employees of the St. Louis Cardinals. A private management company runs the day-to-day operations of the team and the stadium for a fee of $1 per year. The 25-person board of directors of the Redbirds Foundation is responsible for all decisions about sustaining the organization's mission and purpose, raising revenue, paying the bond debt, and the hiring and firing of the management company. See figure 6.1 for an organizational chart that shows the relationship among these entities.

Redbirds Foundation revenue from the 15-year stadium suite contracts, as well naming rights, pouring rights, and club level season ticket sales, is applied directly to the bond debt. Other revenue, such as annual Redbirds Foundation memberships, silent auctions, online auction sales, golf tournament, and other fundraiser revenues goes into foundation operational funds to support RBI and STRIPES.

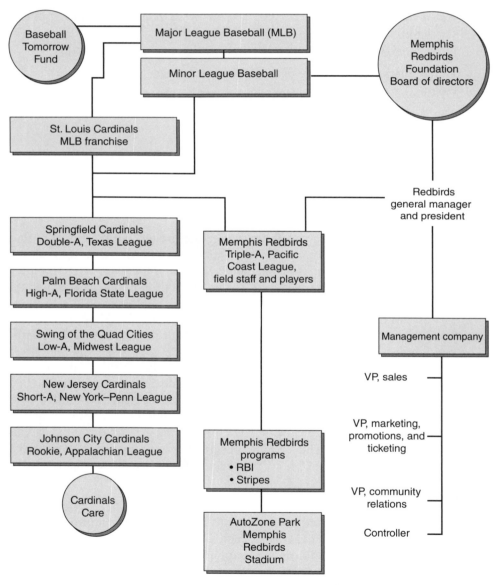

Note: Organizations represented with circles indicate a nonprofit structure

Figure 6.1 Memphis Redbirds Foundation organizational chart.

Game revenues (including ticket sales, gift shop, and concessions) pay the fees for the Pacific Coast League affiliation for the triple-A Memphis Redbirds team.

Net revenues to the Memphis Redbirds Baseball Foundation fund two programs that serve over 2,000 inner-city youth annually: RBI (Returning Baseball to the Inner City) and STRIPES (Sports Teams Returning in the Public Education System). RBI is an eight-week summer program offered free to children ages 6 through 15. The program provides uniforms, equipment, daily lunches, and Memphis Redbirds game tickets (Memphis Redbirds Foundation, 2004). The STRIPES program was designed to return baseball to the public school systems in grade levels 6 through 9.

The cost of these two outreach programs is approximately $600,000 per year. Operations have been subsidized by personal loans or loan guarantees from the Redbirds Foundation founders to balance the budget, ensure that the team's needs are met, and continue the RBI and STRIPES programs.

Markers of Success

For all organizations, identifying markers of success is an important exercise. For nonprofit organizations, success can be measured in many different ways including revenue-to-expenditure ratios, quality markers, and outcome indicators. For the Redbirds Foundation, the outcome indicators are varied and complex. Highlighting the important role that the Redbirds Foundation has played in the revitalization of downtown Memphis, Dave Chase, formal general manager and president of the Memphis Redbirds Baseball Foundation, said, "Memphis is a safer place when our stadium lights are on" (personal communication, April 16, 2007). Since AutoZone Park opened the FedEx Forum (home to the NBA Grizzlies), and Peabody Place, a shopping and entertainment venue, have been built a few blocks away, providing evidence of the role of the ballpark as a catalyst for commercial development. The Redbirds Foundation is one of many players in the quest for economic development in downtown Memphis, but its influence is often noted as coming early in the game and spurring much of the subsequent positive change.

Another important measurement of success for the Redbirds Foundation is defined by stories of RBI and STRIPES program participants. Although efforts to track early participants in these programs has not been a priority, stories of successful participants going on to college and of one alum being drafted by a professional team (the Seattle Mariners) are important indicators of program performance. Additionally, the Redbirds Foundation was a key force in initiating the Civil Rights Game, a Major League Baseball national event played at AutoZone Park in its inaugural years. In summing up the role of the Redbirds Foundation in community development, Chase argued, "Historically, major league baseball thought doing good meant letting Little Leaguers come to games for free. The Memphis model has changed this" (personal communication, April 16, 2007).

Lessons from the Redbirds Foundation

The creation of the Memphis Redbirds Baseball Foundation and the ongoing presence of the Memphis Redbirds team has been important to the continuing redevelopment of downtown Memphis and created new programs for inner-city youth to develop life skills through playing baseball. Understanding how the

Redbirds Foundation was created and its usefulness to other localities is the focus of this section. The concept of social entrepreneurship is used as a theoretical lens for examining the organization's structure and the stakeholder relationships important to the Redbirds Foundation origination and ongoing viability.

As a topic of research, social entrepreneurship is a rapidly growing entry, building on traditional entrepreneurship research. Rooted in a literature of broad scope and depth, the typical entrepreneur is seen as an individual that begins a business, creating some form of value (Dees, 1998), capitalizing on innovation and change (Dees, 1998; Guo, 2006), taking risks (Peredo and McLean, 2006; McClearly, Rivers, and Schneller, 2006), exploiting opportunities (Dees, 1998; Guo, 2006) and exhibiting resourcefulness (Peredo and McLean, 2006; Guo, 2006). A social entrepreneur introduces these traits to community issues. Social entrepreneurs are change agents (Dees, 1998; Sharir and Lerner, 2006) and collaborative leaders (Agranoff and McGuire, 2003). They identify opportunities and resources where others see only problems (Bornstein, 1998; Sharir and Lerner, 2006; Peredo and McLean, 2006). Social entrepreneurs seek practical, sustainable, and innovative approaches (Schwab Foundation, n.d.), while accepting that risk taking is necessary to achieve aggressive goals (Peredo and McLean, 2006).

The Redbirds Foundation case suggests a typology that differentiates social entrepreneurial behavior by individuals and at the organization level, social enterprise strategies, and social purpose partnerships involving for-profit corporations, governments, and local nonprofit organizations. Table 6.2 summarizes indicators found in the literature on this topic and examples from the Redbirds Foundation case.

Social Entrepreneurial Activity

The existing literature on social entrepreneurship focuses on individual attitudes, approaches, and actions. Although this individual focus reflects the traditional view of entrepreneurship, many of these characteristics are also evidenced at the organizational level. The Memphis Redbirds case illustrates this dual understanding of an evolving concept.

Individual Focus   The Redbirds Foundation case has many strong examples of individual social entrepreneurial activity, particularly in the role and insight of the founders. These successful business entrepreneurs took their idea, their connections, and their personal wealth to invest in the creation of a unique nonprofit organization. Dean Jernigan, a former amateur baseball player, wanted to restore inner-city youth access to sports. The creation of the Redbirds Foundation was a culmination of his interest in baseball, youth participation in sports, and community revitalization. His enthusiasm attracted other local entrepreneurs to the table. Since this initial commitment, this group has also contributed personal money and loan guarantees to balance the budget and assure the implementation of the RBI and STRIPES inner-city youth programs.

The founders also displayed determination and resourcefulness in working with the IRS to allow the foundation to exist as a 501(c)(3) organization and retain the $80 million bonds as tax exempt. Without the individual social entrepreneurs

TABLE 6.2

Typology of Social Entrepreneurship Activity

Indicators from literature	Redbirds Foundation examples
DIMENSION: SOCIAL ENTREPRENEURIAL ACTIVITY	

Individual:
 	
• Risk taking (Peredo and McLean, 2006; McClearly et al., 2006)
• Resourceful (Peredo and McLean, 2006; Guo, 2006)
• Opportunistic (Dees, 1998; Guo, 2006)
• Change agents (Dees, 1998; Sharir and Lerner, 2006)
• Collaborative leaders (Agranoff and McGuire, 2003)
• Starting point for change (Light, 2006)
• Creative and critical thinker
	• Successful business entrepreneur founders with a passion for
	  – Baseball
	  – Youth participation in sports
	  – Downtown revitalization
	• Creative nonprofit structure sold to St. Louis Cardinals, IRS, and Memphis
	• Local capital raised from individuals and Memphis-based corporations

Organization: • Includes innovative programming that creates social value (Dees and Anderson, 2006)	• Nonprofit organization owns and operates the baseball stadium and the team, and offers two programs for inner-city youth
DIMENSION: SOCIAL ENTERPRISE STRATEGIES	

• Blend "social motivations/business methods" (Dees and Anderson, 2006)
• Market-based solutions for social problems (Dees and Anderson, 2006)
• Business opportunities that may incorporate job training and employment for constituents (Massarsky, 2006)
• Venture that generates revenue (Massarsky, 2006)
• Types of ventures include (Massarsky, 2006):
  – Program-related product or service
  – Real estate property
  – Licensing and intellectual property rights
  – Cause marketing
	• Memphis Redbirds ticket sales
	• Stadium naming rights
	• Stadium pouring rights
	• Stadium concessions
	• Stadium suite contracts
	• Stadium rental
	• Billboard advertising at the stadium

SOCIAL PURPOSE PARTNERSHIPS	
Corporate: • Companies that proactively engage in social progress by the manner in which they do business (Kramer and Kania, 2006) • Bring resources to the table, such as products and services, skilled employees, industry expertise, global infrastructure, network of connections, credibility, and influence (Kramer and Kania, 2006)	• Federal Express prepaid a 15-year contract for multiple suites; revenue is applied to the bond debt • AutoZone bought the naming rights to the stadium in a 20-year contract; revenue is applied to the bond debt • Coca-Cola purchased pouring rights for AutoZone Park; revenue is applied to the bond debt

(continued)

TABLE 6.2 *(continued)*

Indicators from literature	Redbirds Foundation examples
DIMENSION: SOCIAL ENTREPRENEURIAL ACTIVITY	
Government: • Bring awareness to an issue or cause; speak out, organize forums (Korosec and Berman, 2006) • Assist in acquiring resources, especially from municipality to use as leverage (Korosec and Berman, 2006) • Provide access to elected officials and data, and navigates processes (Korosec and Berman, 2006) • Add legitimacy to cause (Korosec and Berman, 2006) • May help in coordination and implementation (Korosec and Berman, 2006)	• AutoZone Park was financed by $80 million in tax-exempt bonds issued by Memphis' Center City Revenue Finance Corporation • The city and county contributed $8 million in site preparation and utility work • The bonds are being paid off by stadium income, and Memphis taxpayers have no responsibility for them
Nonprofit: • Can be teams of organizations (Light, 2006) • Have a shared vision (Winer and Ray, 1994) • Coordinate joint action (Winer and Ray, 1994) • Increase scope and depth of service • Serve shared target populations • Combine resources	• Many nonprofit organizations use AutoZone Park for events • Nonprofits' volunteers serve as concession stand workers to earn funds for their organizations • Partnership with local nonprofits to build sport leagues • Future: Use revenues to provide grants to local nonprofit programs focused on youth, sports, and education

and their commitment to community ownership, the Memphis Redbirds and AutoZone Park would not exist.

Organization Focus   The conception of a minor-league baseball team and stadium owned by a nonprofit organization in which the revenues generated by these entities could fund community programs focused on youth, sports, and education is a classic example of social entrepreneurial activity. Although the IRS initially questioned the tax-exempt status of the organization and the use of tax-free bonds, the strategy was unquestionably innovative, beginning a tradition that continues in the other activities of the organization.

Social Enterprise Strategies

Social enterprise strategies offer "market-based solutions to social problems," helping organizations "align economic and social value creation" (Dees and Anderson, 2006, p. 44). Recently, researchers and practitioners have used the term *venture* for such efforts, which implies a new undertaking that involves risk (Massarsky, 2006). Social enterprise activity may be categorized by type of venture: a program-related product or service, a service that uses staff and client resources, real estate–related property income, soft property income, licensing and cause-related marketing, and cause marketing (Massarsky, 2006).

Social enterprise is a "sector-bending activity" (Dees and Anderson, 2006, p. 44) that is not appropriate for all nonprofit organizations. Massarsky described social enterprise as a social movement at its "tipping point," the plateau of an idea, when a "critical mass of people or institutions participate in an event that dramatically alters the landscape in which the movement operates" (Massarsky, 2006, p. 68). Despite its current popularity, some researchers have noted negative implications associated with the massive growth of enterprise activities. Eikenberry and Kluver (2004) warned that a growing focus on the bottom line may risk the traditional nonprofit activity of developing social capital to accomplish goals and lead non-profit organizations to rely less on typical stakeholder groups and networks (i.e., donors, members, partner organizations). Additionally, focus on social enterprise may displace board member recruitment priorities from those connected to the community to those with business expertise (Kerlin, 2006).

The Redbirds Foundation's success results from its social enterprise strategy of using the minor-league baseball team and the stadium as revenue generators to create and fund nonprofit programs related to youth, sports, and education. The specific revenue generation strategies include Memphis Redbirds ticket sales, stadium naming rights, stadium pouring rights, stadium concessions, stadium suite contracts, stadium rental, and billboard advertising at the stadium.

Social Purpose Partnerships

Finally, social purpose partnerships describe organizational relationships that are often cross-sector, involving nonprofit, business, and government entities. This type of arrangement focuses on social goals, realigning traditional stereotypes of "noble nonprofits and malevolent businesses" (Kramer and Kania, 2006, p. 25), and allowing each partner to concentrate on what it does best. Innovative cross-sector partnerships require nonprofits to approach these organizations as business partners rather than in their more traditional role as funding sources (Kramer and Kania, 2006).

Corporate Corporate philanthropy and social responsibility both describe a mind-set in which large companies are changing their roles in solving community problems. Doing business as usual continues to load the burden of solving social problems on the nonprofit sector, thereby limiting corporate ability to intervene directly in social problems and actively engage in social progress (Kramer and Kania, 2006). Rethinking these roles and purposefully making decisions that attend to social goals result in a sense of corporate social responsibility. When corporations take a proactive approach to social problems, they bring a number of resources to the table, such as products and services, skilled employees, industry expertise, global infrastructure, a network of connections, credibility, and influence (Kramer and Kania, 2006). Partnerships with corporations including FedEx, AutoZone, Coca-Cola, and Ovation were essential for the success of the Redbirds Foundation from the very beginning.

Government Government agencies can be similarly influential on social goals but by different means. These organizations bring awareness to an issue or cause by creating a public agenda, organizing forums, and speaking out. Government officials can assist in acquiring resources, especially directly from the municipality to use as leverage. Government partnerships provide social actors with access to elected officials, data, and knowledge of navigating regulatory processes that may be necessary for social change, and such partnerships may help in coordination and implementation of outcomes. Government partnerships also add legitimacy to the entrepreneur and the cause (Korosec and Berman, 2006).

Government played an important role in recognizing the nonprofit structure and in funding the stadium. AutoZone Park was financed by $80 million in tax-exempt bonds issued by Memphis' Center City Revenue Finance Corporation. The City of Memphis and Shelby County Government invested $8 million for site preparation and utility work. The bonds are being paid off by stadium income, and Memphis taxpayers have no responsibility for them. Without these creative solutions and cooperative relationships, financing a stadium for the team would have been a high hurdle.

Nonprofit   Partnerships among nonprofit organizations are also a useful strategy for social entrepreneurship. Often described as collaboratives or cooperatives, these partnerships create teams of organizations (Light, 2006) that work toward a collective purpose. Although participant motivators for creating a collaboration are varied, Winer and Ray (1994) suggested that these organizations share a vision that will most likely be realized through coordinated, joint action. Working in collaboration allows nonprofits to increase the scope and depth of services, to serve shared target populations, and to create efficiencies by combining resources.

The Redbirds Foundation has a diverse range of existing partnerships with local nonprofit organizations including concession stand operations that allow agency volunteers to raise money for their causes and the Redbirds Foundation. Many nonprofit organizations including the American Heart Association, St. Jude Childrens' Research Hospital, and the Alzheimer's Association use the stadium as a location for events (Sheffield, 2003). In addition to its own RBI and STRIPES programs, the Redbirds Foundation is currently building partnerships with local nonprofit agencies to implement baseball leagues with broader youth participation.

The most important nonprofit partnership, however, is planned for the future after the bond debt has been paid off. At that point, the Redbirds Foundation will become a grant maker for local nonprofit organizations that share their mission focus on education and youth. Redbirds staffers project that as much as $7 million a year could be used to meet local needs (Clubb, 1999, p. A1).

Future Trends

The big questions related to the future of the Redbirds Foundation, particularly at the point when the bonds are paid off and organization leaders have the opportunity to put their dreams into action, remain unanswered. Long-term financial stability is a major issue. The Redbirds Foundation is responsible for guaranteeing the bond payment until the debt is resolved in approximately 2018. At that point, the vision of supporting community-based sport and education programs can truly become a reality. In the meantime, the organization must struggle with how to sell baseball tickets and maintain its multiple corporate, government, and

Is the Nonprofit–Charitable Purpose Model Replicable?

The community ownership model appears to be blackballed at the major-league level, formally in the NFL and informally among other sports. Major-league owners are largely entrepreneurs who thrive on the cartel model, leaving little room for the concept of a volunteer board of directors and the demands for accountability that accompany the nonprofit organization structure.

Rationale for discouraging community ownership at the major-league level varies. Although the ideal of fan ownership seems appropriate, public and nonprofit ownership is problematic and runs the risk of political interference that is not as great a threat when ownership is private. Additionally, public owners are not prepared to take the heat for losing seasons, soaring salaries, bad trades, and poor attendance (Danielson, 1997, p. 299). Private major-league owners may feel threatened by the community owned teams' access to innovative funding sources.

But government-backed nonprofit examples do exist, and nonprofit–charitable purpose ownership may still find a place at the table in the minor leagues. With an emphasis on community investment, a nonprofit structure could accommodate the IRS tax-exempt ruling and fund operations through the typical sport business. Following proper procedure to establish the organization and fulfill exemption requirements before beginning operations and building an organization that emphasizes the community orientation mission is key.

nonprofit partnerships, all while marketing its nonprofit status to garner needed donations to support the inner-city youth programs. Success in the latter role, the one of most interest to the IRS, has thus far has been limited.

The social entrepreneur role was pivotal to the creation of the Redbirds Foundation. As with every organization, internal and external factors are forcing the Redbirds to evolve. The organization continues to be an example of social entrepreneurship that now must learn to balance competing needs, including the requirements of nonprofit status and the vision of the Redbirds Foundation, to realize long-term success. Finding balance requires having the right people at the table. The composition of this group may change throughout the growth of the organization. In the Redbird Foundation example, a mix of business people, community residents, and social issue experts have given the initiative a solid start. This mix brings the opportunities for organization legitimacy, public awareness, and access to needed resources.

Conclusion

The Memphis Redbirds Baseball Foundation pairs a tax-exempt charitable nonprofit with an auxiliary for-profit organization that is responsible for daily management of the baseball team. The nonprofit itself is exempt from most taxes, can utilize tax-free bonds to fund stadium construction, and because of its IRS 501(c)(3) status can solicit private donations and foundation grants that are available only to nonprofits. At the same time, this novel use of the nonprofit structure presents challenges for the organization. Communicating the unusual structure and dual purpose to key stakeholders (e.g., IRS, national sport league affiliates, players, and potential donors) can be difficult. Managing both a competitive sport endeavor and nonprofit programming requires a wide range of skill sets among limited staff. Identifying the right volunteer and paid leadership to sell the larger vision of the strategy while managing the innovative organization is crucial to successful operation.

The Redbirds Foundation story includes struggles with the Cardinals and the IRS to understand the foundation's long-term vision of providing large-scale funding of education and youth sport programs after the retiring of the stadium bonds. With a complex governance and operating structure, the foundation has met all its financial obligations to date and has funded two programs for inner-city youth that reach thousands of participants each year. The foundation brings together the vision of socially minded individuals, a creative organization structure, the overwhelming needs of a community, and favorable timing that made downtown redevelopment a good investment.

The case is also useful for exploring social entrepreneurship. According to Weerawardena and Mort (2006), "Social entrepreneurship is a bounded multidimensional construct that is deeply rooted in an organization's social mission, its drive for sustainability and highly influenced and shaped by the environmental dynamics." This is certainly true in the case of the Memphis Redbirds, in which the identified dimensions of social entrepreneurial activity, social enterprise, and social purpose partnerships are easily documented. Although many questions related to their future remain, the Redbirds Foundation has expanded the potential role of a professional sport team in community development beyond sponsoring sport camps for youth and individual player charity work.

The Redbirds Foundation case suggests that the nonprofit–charitable purpose structure is a viable strategy with the potential for significant long-term benefits to host localities. The broader implications offer insight into replicating and expanding the use of these approaches. This fuller understanding of the application of social entrepreneurship concepts facilitated by the nonprofit structure opens the door for future ventures in other traditionally for-profit arenas. But government regulators, particularly the IRS, play a key role in determining how nonprofits can legitimately use these strategies to further their missions. What is certain is that innovative, boundary-pushing endeavors using a nonprofit structure provide rich opportunity for further research and application.

PART III

Amateur Athletics, Participation, and Public Health

© Eric Bretagnon/DPPI/Icon SMI

The first two parts of this book have focused on public policy connections to professional sports. In this regard, we have considered the role of the typical reader (who is unlikely to be a professional athlete) only as that of an individual actor who influences markets and policy through decisions and behaviors, rather than as an active participant in sports. That focus changes in part III, where we expand our scope beyond professional sports to focus on policy issues related to amateur athletics, participation, and public health.

In chapter 7, Jennifer Dill and Lynn Weigand discuss the role of local governments in providing access to opportunities for exercise and active recreation. The chapter explores the link between healthy, active lifestyles and the physical elements of cities and neighborhoods, as influenced by the development policies and public investment decisions of local governments. The chapter focuses on urban form and infrastructure, including how we design and build our cities, transportation systems, and parks.

In chapter 8, David Ogden considers how policy priorities and programs can create or remove barriers to participation in organized sports (amateur, and by extension, professional). Ogden focuses on the dwindling levels of African-American participation in baseball at the youth and professional level, and examines the message and effectiveness of specific policy and programmatic responses sponsored by Major League Baseball and implemented by local non-profit organizations.

Chapter 9 explores the link between policy and ethics in the context of amateur athletics. Richard Southall, Mark Nagel, John Amis, and Crystal Southall discuss the workings of one of the most prominent organizations in amateur sports, the National Collegiate Athletic Association (NCAA). Each year nearly 400,000 young men and women participate in amateur athletics under the sanction of the NCAA. Big-time college sports present a unique set of contradictions as an amateur venture that generates significant revenue through ticket sales and corporate sponsorship. This chapter considers the messages sent by the National Collegiate Athletic Association and whether the organization's actions are in line with its stated principles and values.

Perhaps the issue that encompasses sport, public health, policy, and ethics most prominently in the current public discourse is that of performance-enhancing drugs. In chapter 10, Bryan Denham identifies the individuals and organizations with a stake in the use and regulation of performance-enhancing drugs. The chapter offers a chronology of public policy initiatives related to doping, and considers the role of media representations and the problems that those representations can cause.

CHAPTER 7

Influences of Urban Form on Physical Activity

Jennifer Dill and Lynn Weigand

Does where you live make you fat? Certainly, Americans are getting fatter, just as metropolitan areas become more spread out. But is one thing causing the other? Although the premise is hard to prove, it is safe to say that the sprawling, autocentric cities are not helping to reduce waistlines or increase physical activity. Economic costs result from these health problems, and economic benefits may accrue to communities that promote more physical activity.

The health effects of being overweight or obese are well documented, including hypertension, type 2 diabetes, stroke, heart disease, and some cancers. Regular physical activity can help control weight and reduce the risk of these same health problems, as well as enhance psychological well-being (U.S. Department of Health and Human Services, 2003). The direct medical costs associated with Americans being overweight accounted for about 9 percent of medical expenditures in 1998 (Finkelstein, Fiebelkorn, and Wang, 2003). The total costs, including the indirect costs related to morbidity and mortality (such as lost income), were estimated to be $117 billion in 2000 (CDC, July 2005).

Despite these costs, the problem has been escalating. The share of adults who are obese (a body mass index greater than or equal to 30.0) more than doubled from 15 percent to 33 percent between 1976 and 2004 (Centers for Disease Control, National Center for Health Statistics, 2007). During the same period, the share of children who were overweight tripled among most age groups, reaching 14 percent of 2- through 5-year-olds, 19 percent of 6- through 11-year-olds, and 17 percent of 12- through 19-year-olds. Declining physical activity levels have contributed to the obesity problem.

As waistlines have been expanding, so have metropolitan areas, which have been growing faster "around" (in area) than in population. In the 38 largest urban areas in the United States, land area grew an average of 478 percent from 1950 to 2000, while population grew by 338 percent (calculated from U.S. census data). For most of these urban areas, land area grew more than twice as much as population did.

This chapter focuses on how the design of cities, including urban form, transportation, and parks, influences physical activity. It starts with some background information on the amount and types of physical activity, and on how urban areas, infrastructure, and parks have developed. The next section discusses strategies that public agencies can apply to increase physical activity, including examples from the United States, and evaluates how effective these policies might be. The chapter concludes with some final thoughts and a look to the future.

Importance and Decline of Physical Activity in the United States

The Centers for Disease Control and Prevention (CDC) recommends that adults engage in at least 30 minutes of moderate-intensity activity five days per week or 20 minutes of vigorous activity three days a week (CDC, 2007). Moderate activity increases breathing and heart rates and includes such activities as walking briskly or bicycling on flat terrain. This activity can be accumulated through short sessions of 10 minutes or more, such as two brisk 15-minute walks per day to and from a train station or around a local park (Haskell et al., 2007).

Persuading inactive people to be more active could have greater health benefits than increasing activity levels of people who are already active. Medical research has shown that the marginal health benefits of having a sedentary person increase his or her activity by one unit (e.g., 20 more minutes per day) may be greater than having an active person increase his or her activity by the same amount (Pate et al., 1995). These medical findings and recommendations indicate that inducing more people to walk and bike regularly for transportation and recreation in their own neighborhoods could have significant health benefits and therefore economic benefits.

More than half of American adults do not achieve the recommended level of daily physical activity (CDC, December 2005). That daily physical activity could occur during leisure time, such as going to the gym, playing basketball, or swimming, or during everyday activities, such as walking to school, gardening in the backyard, or work-related activity. Americans have 35 to 40 hours of free time per week, but they spend only a small part of that time on active pursuits. When we do choose an active form of leisure, walking is the top choice among American adults (Godbey et al., 2005). Public health officials promote walking for physical activity and health primarily because it is easy, accessible, and inexpensive.

Americans are also not physically active during nonleisure time. According to the 2001 National Household Travel Survey (NHTS), less than 9 percent of all trips people made for daily travel were on foot and less than 1 percent of trips were on a bicycle. In terms of total distance of travel, these shares are much lower. Moreover, over one-third of all adults (35 percent) did not make any walking trips in the previous week, and only 30 percent made five or more walking trips in the previous week. The numbers are far lower for bicycling; only 7 percent of adults made a bicycling trip during the previous week. Children are not walking much either. In 1969, 48 percent of children walked to school, compared with 15 percent in 2001 (Transportation Research Board, 2005).

Why are we driving more? There is no single answer. Increasing wealth and decreasing costs of car ownership and driving have contributed. Demographic trends, such as the increasing share of women in the workforce, have also generated more demand for travel. The change in our urban landscape has contributed as well. Destinations are farther apart, reducing the feasibility of walking and bicycling. Homes in post–World War II neighborhoods are less likely to be within walking distance of a grocery store, high school, offices, or other destinations. In lower-density cities, transit service is not cost effective and must be heavily subsidized, resulting in less service and, hence, lower ridership. But despite greater distances between destinations, many of the trips that we make are still within a reasonable walking or biking distance. Over 60 percent of all trips that people make on a daily basis are 5 miles (8 km) or less (a reasonable biking distance), and 27 percent are 1 mile (1.6 km) or less (a reasonable walking distance) (calculated from 2001 National Household Travel Survey data). Except for trips of 0.25 mile (0.4 km) or less, however, a majority of these short trips are not made on foot or bike (see figure 7.1).

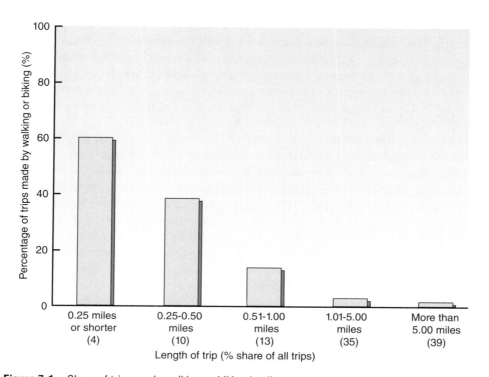

Figure 7.1 Share of trips made walking or biking by distance.

Data from *2001 National Household Travel Survey* (NHTS), U.S. Department of Transportation.

How Urban Growth Has Made Us Less Active

Urban areas can provide many opportunities for daily physical activity. Transportation-related activity (such as walking to the store, bicycling to work, or walking to a train station) depends on the availability of infrastructure such as streets, sidewalks, and trails, as well as on having certain land uses (destinations) within reasonable distance. Recreational activity (such as walking or jogging) can also take place on streets and sidewalks, as well as in public parks. How we design this infrastructure helps determine whether people use it.

Transportation and Land Use Planning

Since the rise of the automobile in the early 1900s, and particularly after World War II, a primary objective of our transportation infrastructure has been to provide a safe and efficient way for motor vehicles to get from point A to point B. Transportation engineers and planners have focused on reducing travel time, which has an economic cost. This focus on mobility has led to hierarchical street systems, in which local neighborhood cul-de-sacs and streets funnel into collector streets, up to faster-moving arterials or boulevards, and then to freeways. The system may work well for moving lots of vehicles efficiently, but it can make walking and bicycling less direct, less pleasant (particularly along higher-speed arterials), and often less safe.

Land use patterns have also evolved over time, often in response to transportation technology. Before 1900 most travel was by foot, horse, or horse-powered vehicles. The slowness of these modes required destinations to be close together. The electric streetcar, which became common in cities around 1900, allowed cities to expand along new transit lines to suburbs, providing lower-density housing, compared with tenements and apartments near downtowns. Still, these streetcar suburbs included shops and other businesses along the line, allowing people to get off, shop for groceries, and continue home, for example.

During this time, employment in many cities was concentrated in industries that emitted foul odors and other pollution. Therefore, planners and developers wanted to separate industry and jobs from housing. Starting in the 1920s, and particularly after World War II, auto ownership became more common and residential suburbs started filling in the areas between the streetcar lines and beyond. Buses were used more often for transit, and streetcar lines were removed from most cities. Most cities were planned to separate land uses to reduce nuisances that occur when, for example, houses are near a factory or commercial district. Other factors, such as financial incentives for home ownership, also contributed to this growing and sprawling suburbanization.

Some of these trends in transportation and land use are beginning to change. In recent decades, more transportation professionals have embraced the concept of improving not just mobility but also accessibility. To understand the difference between accessibility and mobility, we need to consider why we travel. Generally, we travel because there is something that we want to do, see, or obtain at a different location, not because we want to drive our cars (with some exceptions, of course!). We can improve our means of getting to the things that we want to do, see, or obtain by speeding up traffic (mobility), or we can improve the accessibility of things by locating them closer together or by providing electronic access to work or shopping, for example.

This increasing focus on accessibility, in addition to mobility, has coincided with other shifts in thinking. In the late 1960s and 1970s attention focused on energy consumption and air pollution. Over the next decades, concerns over sprawl, traffic congestion, and now climate change and obesity have also motivated a different approach. On top of this, our transportation funding system has not kept up with demand, adding to the difficulty of expanding roads to improve mobility. Approaches to improving accessibility include changing land use patterns to reduce automobile dependence and providing infrastructure for all modes of transportation (walking, biking, transit, cars, and freight).

Park Planning

Most people think of parks as places where people are physically active. But in reality, many parks are not designed for activity and recreation. Today's parks serve a number of functions, including environmental protection, storm water retention, visual amenity for new developments, spaces that confer civic identity, gathering places for neighbors, and places for passive activities, such as picnicking, bird watching, or just sitting. Even when parks contain features for active uses, many park users, especially adults, tend to be sedentary.

Early American parks, such as Central Park in New York, were intended to improve the health of urban residents by providing fresh air, access to nature, settings for active recreation, and places for social interaction. Most people still obtained plenty of physical activity through daily activities, so providing settings for additional activity was not a priority. This concern changed in the early part of the 20th century when the playground reform movement, focused on the benefits of vigorous physical activity for youth, set the precedent for park playground designs for organized play (Cranz, 1989). Many features of park and playground design from this era are still evident in contemporary neighborhood park plans.

By the mid-20th century, Americans were spending fewer hours at the workplace and had more time for other pursuits. The growth in leisure time led to a demand for increased recreation opportunities, and most park agencies responded by providing sport facilities and other settings for recreational activities.

But this emphasis on recreational services was short lived because the environmental movement and growth of cities after World War II fueled yet another vision for parks. Environmental protection in the form of open space and habitat preservation became important as cities spread outward and consumed more land. By the 1970s use of parks had moved from active to more passive uses in most cases, concurrent with a move from providing recreation facilities to providing recreation experiences (Cranz, 1989). Today, physical activity is just one of many roles that public parks fulfill. Besides providing recreation opportunities, parks function as settings for passive uses and communing with nature, gathering spaces that bring people together and generate social capital, areas that provide green vistas and enhance property values, and sites that provide environmental benefits and protection.

Despite the perception that parks encourage physical activity, that is often not the case in American communities today. In fact, recent studies of park use and users show that most adults are sedentary in parks. They tend to sit, eat, or watch children play, resulting in little or no physical activity (Cohen et al., 2007; Floyd et al., 2007; Frumkin et al., 2005; Weigand, 2007). Parks that provide places to walk have the greatest potential for adult physical activity (Floyd et al., 2007; Weigand, 2007), but many parks do not contain walking trails, often because of their small size (Weigand, 2007).

The Economics of Our Decision Making

The decision to walk or bike to reach a destination, rather than drive, depends on many factors. Most research indicates that the primary factor is cost, in both time and money. For example, if walking takes 20 minutes longer than driving does, but driving will cost $2 in gas and $3 to park, a person will weigh those costs to make a decision. In this example, if the person's time is worth more than $15 per hour ($5 for 20 minutes), she or he is more likely to drive, all else being equal. That last phrase, *all else being equal*, is important. Travel decisions are not that simple. In our example, some people may decide to walk, even if their time is worth more than $15 per hour, because they want to reduce their impact on the environment or improve their health. In a sense, they are placing a value on those "goods" by spending their time.

Alternatively, another traveler might be concerned about personal safety, related either to crime or to being hit by a car, and decide to drive, even if doing so is more expensive in terms of time and money. The person is placing a value on personal safety and paying for it through the gas and parking costs. Sociodemographic factors, such as age, income, and sex, can influence how people value these trade-offs. Note that this discussion assumes that the person has options. People who do not have access to private vehicles or who cannot physically drive, walk, or bicycle do not have as many choices for these tradeoffs.

As with any economic decision, information plays a role. For example, some people may not know how long it would take to walk or bike between two places. That lack of knowledge leads to another factor—habit. As with many daily behaviors, people are creatures of habit. If you have been driving to work every day, changing that behavior is difficult. Moreover, driving to other places is often easier as well, because you know the roads, the route, and the time required to get there. If a person does not have experience walking or bicycling in an area, how will she or he know how long a trip would take or what a safe route might be?

Public Policies to Increase Physical Activity

This discussion has pointed out how our land use patterns, infrastructure, and parks encourage or hinder people from being physically active in their travel or leisure time activities. Public policy directly influences all these factors. Public agencies at all levels in the United States, but particularly cities and counties, directly influence land use and urban design, the transportation system, and parks through either regulation or direct provision. Therefore, governments can adopt many strategies that could change our cities, towns, and suburbs to make them more conducive to walking, bicycling, and other physical activity.

Land Use and Urban Design Strategies

Table 7.1 lists several planning and design elements that can make a city more walkable or bikeable for daily activities. These elements overlap with the concepts of smart growth, new urbanism, and transit-oriented development (TOD), which have gained recognition in the past 20 years and are often thought of as antitheses to sprawl.

The concepts in table 7.1 address both land use and urban design. Cities and counties generally control land use by adopting comprehensive land use plans that guide where different uses, such as houses, apartments, and offices, will be located. The plan is implemented through zoning ordinances and other regulations, as well as infrastructure investments. A growing number of cities are adopting a variety of land use strategies that can encourage more walking and bicycling, including the following:

- Mixed-use zoning that requires or allows residential and commercial land uses on the same site
- Zoning to increase housing density, including minimum densities (particularly near transit), reducing minimum lot sizes, zero lot line zoning (allowing homes to have one side on the lot line), and reducing setback (the distance from the house to the sidewalk) requirements
- Transit-oriented zoning that requires higher-density housing, mixed land uses, and reduced parking near transit stations

TABLE 7.1

Strategies to Promote Walking and Bicycling in Urban Areas

Strategy	Why it may promote walking and cycling
Mixed land uses, such as locating shops below apartments and offices near houses	Reduces walk or bike travel time by shortening the distance between origins and destinations
Increased street connectivity by having fewer dead-end streets or cul-de-sacs and smaller blocks	
Increased housing and employment density, e.g., more houses per acre	
Increased density near transit stops and stations	Reduces walk or bike travel time to transit, making walking or biking more attractive than park and ride
Sidewalks, bike lanes, bike boulevards, and trails	Increases perception of safety
Crosswalks, bike and pedestrian traffic signals	
Street lights, trees, benches, and other amenities	Increases perception of safety; enhances aesthetics
Signs designating safe bike or walk routes, including travel times and directions to destinations	Provides information

- Density bonuses that allow developers to build more housing or commercial space if they provide amenities, such as transit access improvements, public art, or low-income housing
- Zoning that allows accessory dwelling units ("granny flats") on existing single-family housing lots
- Prohibiting auto-oriented land uses (e.g., car dealerships) near rail transit stations
- Urban growth boundaries that help contain growth and increase density
- Eliminating or reducing minimum parking requirements so that more land is available for housing or commercial uses
- Street connectivity standards that reduce the length of blocks and the number of dead ends for pedestrians and bicyclists

But creating a mix of land uses or increasing density, particularly outside a downtown area, is usually not as simple as creating a plan and the zoning that allows or even requires it, as the strategies listed above do. Cities and counties make the plans and regulations, but private developers invest the capital and build the land uses. In some cases, cities, counties, and even transit agencies have used public funds to subsidize mixed-use, higher-density developments. This goal can be accomplished by buying the land and selling it to a developer at a much reduced cost, providing direct subsidies to a developer to cover the increased construction costs, or by developing the project directly, such as with public housing. Governments have also helped spur this type of development by locating public buildings, such as city halls or libraries, in newly developing mixed-use centers and near transit stations.

Urban design refers to the quality or character of a community's built environment. Urban design addresses elements such as the relationship of buildings to the street and sidewalk, the facade of buildings, landscaping, and street furnishings. The urban design of a city or neighborhood influences the aesthetic qualities of the street, which can either inhibit or promote walking and cycling for transportation, recreation, or pleasure. Urban design is implemented through guidelines and design standards that are adopted by cities to ensure that the public right-of-way provides an attractive and safe experience for nonmotorized travel. Urban design strategies can encourage more pedestrian and bicycle trips through the following actions:

- Require sidewalks with adequate width (at least 6 feet, or 1.8 m) and buffer areas between the sidewalk and moving vehicle lanes
- Provide bicycle parking on public streets and require on-site bicycle parking for new development or significant redevelopment
- Require or provide landscaping and street trees to create a buffer zone between pedestrians and moving vehicles, to narrow the street visually, slow traffic, and provide relief from the pavement
- Require buildings to be constructed adjacent to the back of the sidewalk (eliminating parking between the sidewalk and the building), to orient main entries to the sidewalk, and to provide visually permeable display windows

Portland's New Urbanist Neighborhoods

The Portland, Oregon, region is one area in the United States that has embraced the planning concept of trying to integrate land use and transportation to reduce reliance on the automobile. This effort is prompted, in part, by state land use planning laws requiring the establishment of urban growth boundaries and regulations requiring transportation plans that aim to reduce auto dependence. Implementation of these strategies is furthered by having a directly elected regional government (Metro) that has land use planning authority—the only one of its kind in the country. Metro requires cities and counties within the region to adopt plans and zoning regulations implementing many of the strategies described earlier to promote walking and bicycling. As the metropolitan planning organization (MPO), Metro is also responsible for regional transportation planning and funding decisions. Because of these policies and investments, several new transit-oriented developments (TOD) and new urbanist developments have been built in the past 10 years. New urbanism claims that mixed-use, pedestrian-friendly neighborhoods have higher rates of walking than do single-use, auto-oriented neighborhoods. In many ways, the region is serving as a living experiment for concepts such as smart growth, new urbanism, and TODs. Therefore, many people are asking, "Is it working in Portland?"

Several recent studies are finding that people living in these new neighborhoods do walk and bike more. One study compared a new urbanist neighborhood that had higher-density housing, a mix of uses (public, commercial, and residential), and attractive pedestrian infrastructure to two nearby standard subdivisions (Dill, 2006a). Surveys revealed that the new urbanist neighborhood residents made about three times as many walking trips per week (more than six, compared with two or fewer). The difference in walking was for both transportation (e.g., to the library or store) and recreation (e.g., strolling in the neighborhood). The research did not reveal, however, whether residents in the other neighborhoods were getting daily physical activity through other means, such as going to the gym or using a treadmill at home. Examining four new urbanist subdivisions in the region, Lund (2003) found that local access, especially to retail shops, increased the amount of walking in those neighborhoods. But attitudes were just as important, if not more important, than the physical environment. Attitudes included both personal attitudes toward walking in general as well as favorable perceptions of the comfort and safety of the walking environment. Another study of a new urbanist TOD (Orenco Station) found that residents walked more often for nonwork purposes, compared with TODs that did not have a mix of land uses and other new urbanist features (Dill, 2006b). Distance from the transit station was also an important factor at the TODs examined. People living more than 0.25 mile (0.4 km) but less than 1 mile (1.6 km) away from a station were just as likely to use transit to get to work but were more likely to drive or be dropped off rather than walk to the station.

Transportation System Strategies

The design of streets is governed by cities, counties, states, and the federal government. Recently, the concepts of complete streets and context sensitive design, which encourage designs for multiple modes and users, have become more popular. These approaches emphasize the integration of factors, including the surrounding environment, access to destinations, and the aesthetics of the route, to promote walking and bicycling on all roadways.

- Policies should require or encourage a well-connected street network to reduce out-of-direction travel for pedestrians and cyclists.
- Complete streets policies also should include strategies to reduce and manage motor vehicle speeds, such as narrower streets and traffic-calming measures. Slower vehicles make streets safer and more inviting for nonmotorized travel.
- Local and state agencies also should develop plans and funding strategies to provide more comprehensive and integrated pedestrian and bicycle networks.

Building new bike trails and adding bike lanes, sidewalks, and other safety features to existing streets requires public funding. In the United States the largest source of money for transportation infrastructure is federal and state gas taxes. Other sources include vehicle taxes and fees, and sales, income, and property taxes. At the federal level, funding for bicycle and pedestrian projects increased significantly after the passage of the Intermodal Surface Transportation Efficiency Act (ISTEA) in 1991 and the Transportation Equity Act for the 21st Century (TEA-21) in 1998 (figure 7.2). Even with this increase, federal funding for bicycle and pedestrian projects represents just about 2 percent of all federal surface transportation funding. The latest federal funding law (SAFETEA-LU), passed in 2005, also included a new program, the Nonmotorized Transportation Pilot Program, that targets extra funding to four communities to see whether bicycling and walking can provide a significant share of people's travel. The results from this program may provide models for other communities in the future.

Additional funds for pedestrian and bicycle projects come from states, counties, and cities. For example, the State of Oregon passed a law in 1971 that requires the

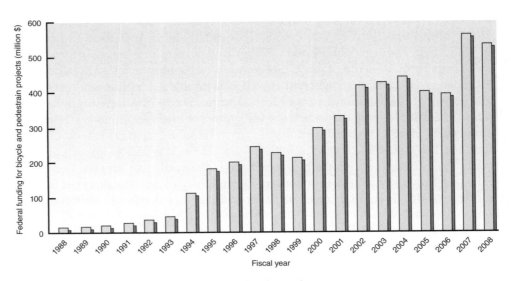

Figure 7.2 Federal funding for bicycle and pedestrian projects.

Data from http://www.fhwa.dot.gov/environment/bikeped/overview.htm

state, cities, and counties to spend reasonable amounts of their share of state highway money on bicycle and pedestrian facilities. The law also requires walkways and bikeways on any new or rebuilt road, street, or highway, unless it is unsafe or unnecessary, or if the costs are excessive in proportion to the potential use.

Trails in the United States

Separate paved paths or trails for pedestrians and bicyclists can provide a safe environment for people of all ages to be physically active. Several studies have found that people living closer to trails are more likely to use them (Saelens, Sallis, and Frank, 2003; Lindsey, Han, Wilson, and Yang, 2004). A national survey found that people who use trails once a week or more were more likely to meet physical activity recommendations (Librett, Yore, and Schmid, 2006).

The increase in federal funds available and the abandonment of many rail lines in urban areas have led many communities to build paved off-street trails, for both recreation and transportation. For example, when a rail line in the Seattle area was abandoned in the 1970s, the city, county, and other organizations joined to build the Burke-Gilman Trail. Originally just over 12 miles (19 km) in length, the trail connects key destinations along Lake Washington. Trail use has grown over the years, sometimes outpacing population growth. As the trail was extended and a key missing link was completed, more people began to use the trail for commuting or shopping, in addition to recreation (Puget Sound Regional Council, 2000).

The City of Indianapolis adopted a greenway plan in 1994 that called for building trails along seven corridors. By 2002 at least 30 miles (48 km) of multiuse trails were in use (Lindsey, Man, Payton, and Dickson, 2004). The most popular trail, the Monon Trail, connects downtown with suburban areas 10 miles (16 km) away and attracts from 10,000 to more than 80,000 people per month, depending on the time of year (Lindsey, Han, Wilson, and Yang, 2004). Well-designed trails may provide additional economic benefits. Evidence from Indianapolis, Austin, and Minneapolis has found that some (but not all) greenways and trails have a positive effect on nearby residential home values (Lindsey, Han, Wilson, and Yang, 2004; Nicholls and Crompton, 2005; National Cooperative Highway Research Program, 2006).

Park Planning and Design Strategies

Park characteristics, such as location, design, equipment, and facilities, can influence both whether people choose to go to a particular park and what they do there. Specifically, these characteristics can influence the frequency and duration of park visits, park choice, the type and intensity of physical activity, and the use of equipment and facilities. Park location, size, function, amenities, and design are driven by a combination of several factors: public agency regulations, private developers' goals and priorities, national park standards established by the National Recreation and Park Association (NRPA), and public input.

Just as they guide the development of housing and businesses, land use plans can direct the number, location, size, and type of park facilities that should be built or maintained in a community. Parks may be developed by public agencies themselves (cities, counties, and park districts), or the agency may oversee the development of parks by private developers. Regardless of who develops the parks, the park master plan should include the following strategies to promote active use by people of all ages.

- Require a neighborhood park to be located within a reasonable walking distance (0.5 mile, or 0.8 km) of all residences, although achieving this goal may be difficult because of funding and land acquisition constraints.
- Ensure that park and recreation facilities are distributed equitably and provide access to a variety of activities for people of all ages at both the neighborhood and community-wide levels.
- Locate parks where they are served by an interconnected street and sidewalk system to promote walking and bicycling to the park.

Most local park agencies follow the National Recreation and Park Association's (NRPA) guidelines for park acreage, type, and facilities. Although useful in providing general guidance for new park development, the NRPA standards are fairly narrow in scope and do not currently focus on promoting physical activity, especially among adults and seniors. For example, the NRPA guidelines for neighborhood parks focus primarily on parks as sites for children's play, and the standards for community parks recommend facilities for organized sports. The lack of guidelines that address a wider array of user groups and ages often results in new parks that lack facilities for physical activity, especially for adults and seniors. At the same time, demand is growing for new activities in parks, such as skateboarding, disc golf, off-leash dog facilities, and adult fitness. To ensure that parks maximize opportunities for physical activity, park policies and guidelines should:

- require facilities that promote active recreation for all ages, from toddlers to seniors;
- encourage special-interest facilities for underserved age groups such as teens and adults, including skateboard parks, disc golf, and fitness courses, where the public expresses a desire for them;
- provide dog facilities to encourage adult users to walk to the park; and
- include walking trails within the park.

Park plans and guidelines are even more important when parks are developed by private interests. When developers site and design parks, they often insert their own priorities into the decisions about the park location, function, and design. Because developers are in the business of selling homes and property, they often locate and design park spaces to enhance the visual appeal of their development rather than to promote active uses. This priority may result in park spaces that are not in convenient locations for users or that do not serve any active recreation functions.

Parks have great potential to increase regular physical activity, but need to be located and designed to promote active use. They can provide settings for various levels of informal sport and recreation for all ages, offer opportunities for children to play outdoors, and are accessible to large numbers of people.

Examples from Abroad

Rates of cycling and walking are far lower in the United States than they are in many other developed Western countries (figure 7.3). The differences can be explained largely by disparities in economic factors and public policy. All the other countries listed in figure 7.3 have higher gas taxes and other taxes and fees related to vehicle ownership, which raise the cost of driving. Some of these countries have invested significantly in improving infrastructure for bicycling and walking. The urban areas in these countries are also higher in density than most cities in the United States, so destinations are closer.

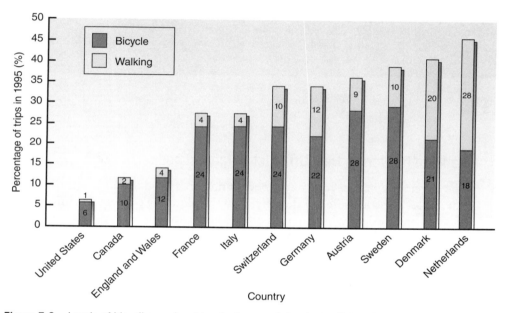

Figure 7.3   Levels of bicycling and walking for transportation in the United States and other countries.

Reprinted, by permission, from J. Pucher and L. Dijkstra, 2003, "Promoting safe walking and cycling to improve public health: Lessons from the Netherlands and Germany," *American Journal of Public Health* 92(9): 1509-1516.

Such policies explain the high rates of bicycling in Denmark and the Netherlands. Along with having more facilities, these countries have a bicycle infrastructure that looks far different from that in the United States. For example, Copenhagen, Denmark, has 332 kilometers of cycle tracks—paved pathways that are often located between the sidewalk and the motor vehicle lanes but separated from traffic by a curb, parking, or other means. Cycle tracks often have different pavement than the sidewalk or street to distinguish them even more (figure 7.4). Major intersections have separate traffic signals for bicyclists to minimize conflicts with cars. On one-way streets, bicycles can often travel in both directions. All these policies and investments increase the safety and convenience of cycling for people of all ages. Over one-third of commuters bicycle to work, and most people cycle for transportation, not recreation (City of Copenhagen, 2007). Cities in the Netherlands have similar infrastructure. In both countries, in contrast to the United States, cycling rates are high among all age groups. In the Netherlands, people age 65 and older make one-quarter of their trips by bicycle, a proportion slightly higher than that for adults aged 25 through 64 (Pucher and Dijkstra, 2003).

(continued)

Examples from Abroad *(continued)*

Figure 7.4 Cycle tracks in Copenhagen.
©Jennifer Dill

Parks in Portland's New Urbanist Neighborhoods

The development of several new urbanist neighborhoods in the Portland metropolitan region illustrate some of the ways that the planning process can influence park location and design, which in turn affects how people use, or do not use, the parks when they are built. First, the context is important. A recent study of Sunnyside Village, Fairview Village, and Orenco Station found that most park users live less than 0.5 mile (0.8 km) from parks, visit frequently, and walk to the park (Weigand, 2007). The basic design principles of new urbanism, such as pedestrian-friendly neighborhoods and nearby destinations, appear to support park use by locating the parks in neighborhoods where they are near homes and easy to walk to. In addition, the provision of sidewalks and an interconnected street network between home and park help encourage more walking trips to the park (Weigand, 2007).

Studies in these neighborhoods also found that most people visit their neighborhood parks with kids or dogs. Although some of the parks have play equipment for young children, many do not. In addition, none of the parks in these neighborhoods have recreational equipment for teens or adults (except ball courts), and none include any type of dog facilities (Weigand, 2007). Although new urbanism principles succeed in locating parks in the neighborhoods where people can get to them, they could do more to promote physical activity by encouraging park designs that support popular activities for adults, such as walking (with or without dogs).

Do These Strategies Work?

The question that researchers are trying to answer is, Does it work? If a city adopted all these strategies, would more residents walk and bike? And if they did, would they be healthier? Studies comparing neighborhoods that have many of these elements to neighborhoods that are more auto oriented have generally found that people living in more walkable neighborhoods do walk more, although questions remain about whether they drive less (Saelens, Sallis, and Frank, 2003; Transportation Research Board, 2005). The factors most important in determining walking rates seem to be higher accessibility to destinations through a mix of land uses, reduced distances created through a more connected, or gridlike, street pattern, and the presence of sidewalks. The influence of these factors on bicycling is less clear. In addition, most research shows that land use and infrastructure may be relatively small factors in decision making. Travel time and costs, along with attitudes, may play more significant roles.

Some recent studies trying to link land use and infrastructure to health outcomes have found small but statistically significant relationships between sprawl, weight, and health. One nationwide study found that even after controlling for demographics (such as age and income) and behavior (such as eating and smoking), residents living in more sprawling counties were less likely to walk for leisure, weighed more, and had a greater chance of suffering from hypertension (Ewing, Schmid, Killingsworth, and Raudenbush, 2003). Similarly, a study in the Atlanta area found that people living in areas without a mix of land uses were more likely to be obese (Frank, Andresen, and Schmid, 2004).

One issue that comes up in the debate about whether sprawl causes obesity is the question of self-selection. Do people who live in walkable and bikeable neighborhoods choose to live there because they want to walk and bike? The argument is that the neighborhood is not causing them to behave in a certain way (walking and biking more than people living elsewhere); rather, the neighborhood is attracting a concentration of people who would be doing those things anyway. Research does indicate that this is true to some extent but that it does not explain everything. People who value walking and biking are more likely to find a home that allows them to do so. But if people who do not already value those options moved to such a neighborhood—because the homes were desirable and the schools were of high quality, for example—would they change their behavior and walk and bike more? Some evidence indicates that they would. One problem is that researchers cannot assign people to a neighborhood and then test their behavior! Finally, recent research has found that many people are not able to match their neighborhood with their travel preferences because not enough walkable and bikeable neighborhoods are available to choose from (Levine, Inam, and Torng, 2005). In other words, more people would self-select into such areas if they existed. Those people often end up living in places where they do not walk or bike as much as they would like because the infrastructure or land use pattern makes the costs too high.

Research is also confirming what may seem intuitive: Parks that are nearby and easily accessible stimulate use and physical activity (Bedimo-Rung et al., 2005; Hoener et al., 2005; Moudon et al., 2005; Sallis et al., 2006). People use parks that are close to where they live, especially if they are less than 0.5 mile (0.8 km) away (Weigand, 2007). Not surprisingly, the proximity of parks also affects how people get there. People who live nearby tend to walk, whereas those who live farther away tend to drive (Weigand, 2007). Sidewalks in neighborhoods also encourage more walking and physical activity (Lee and Moudon, 2004). Children in particular are more active when they live close to playgrounds and parks where recreational facilities are available (Krahnstoever, et al., 2006). Within parks, children and youth tend to be more active than adults (Floyd et al., 2007, Sallis et al., 2006; Weigand, 2007), which is not surprising because most neighborhood parks are designed for children's use. Adults are most likely to walk in parks for physical activity (Sallis et al., 2006; Weigand, 2007). Parks with sport facilities also can increase levels of walking or vigorous physical activity (Floyd et al., 2007).

Future Trends

Changing land use, infrastructure, and parks to enable physical activity will not happen overnight. Developing and changing land use plans, zoning, and design regulations typically takes several months or years. Then developers need time to finance, plan, and build projects. Moreover, retrofitting existing neighborhoods can take longer than influencing new subdivisions or towns. But some of the strategies discussed in this chapter, such as building trails or bike lanes, improving the pedestrian environment with sidewalks, lighting, and amenities, and renovating parks, may be implemented more quickly.

Several indications point to the likelihood that urban areas will become more conducive to walking and bicycling. First, several national and global trends argue for or support such changes. These include increasing fuel prices, as well as concerns over sustainability, the environment, climate change, oil imports, and peak oil. The recent financial and housing crisis may lead to lessened demand for large homes on large lots. Second, some demographic trends appear to be increasing the market for higher-density, mixed-use, and transit-oriented developments. Our population is aging. In 2000, 12 percent of the U.S. population was age 65 or older. In 2050 the share is projected to be over 20 percent (He et al., 2005). Older adults are increasingly looking for places to live that are accessible, require less driving, and have fewer maintenance requirements. Younger households are becoming smaller; families have fewer children, and more adults live alone or with another adult, but with no children. Based on demographic and growth projections, one organization estimated that about a quarter of all new households (14.6 million) over the next 25 years could desire to live within a 0.5 mile (0.8 km) of a transit station (Reconnecting America, 2004). Third, private developers are gaining more experience in producing these new styles of development and are often finding them profitable. Increasing land prices will also drive these changes. A 2008 report on emerging trends in real estate identified infill development in urban cores as a market to watch, citing growing demand for less car-dependent lifestyles. The report predicted that "surviving homebuilders will refocus on infill concepts—denser communities with mixed uses and town center elements" (Urban Land Institute, 2008, p. 56). Finally, the number of local governments that have adopted policies like those discussed in this chapter has increased, and the trend is likely to continue. The amount of funding for bicycle and pedestrian infrastructure has also increased over the past 20 years, although whether that trend will continue in the future is less clear. State and local governments have been reluctant to raise fuel taxes, a major source of funding for transportation.

All these factors combined indicate that communities in the future may look more like those from the early 20th century, before our land use and transportation decisions created auto-oriented sprawl that prevents most of us from walking or bicycling for daily trips. Communities will increasingly mix residential, commercial, and civic uses to provide convenient access by foot and bicycle. Streetcars that once linked central cities and neighborhoods have made a comeback in recent years and may continue to expand in many cities. Larger, sprawling developments may be replaced or in-filled to create greater density in smaller living spaces. Whether all this leads to increased physical activity is perhaps a bigger question.

Conclusion

Americans and their cities have both been expanding their girth in recent years. We are less active and less healthy, living in communities that are designed for us to move less, not more. Although personal attitudes and perceptions certainly play a large role in individual activity and fitness levels, we know that how we plan and design the places where we live, work, and play can make a big difference in how much activity we get each day.

Because most Americans get little or no regular physical activity, regular walking and bicycling for transportation or recreation can go a long way toward increasing activity levels and improving individual health. Transportation systems, land use, and urban design characteristics can influence decisions to walk or bicycle. Mixing land uses and increasing density reduces the distance between destinations, such as home, shops, and school, which in turn shortens walking or biking travel time. Providing facilities such as sidewalks, bike lanes or boulevards, trails, crosswalks, and signals makes people feel safer when walking and bicycling. Improving roadways with lighting, street trees, landscaping, benches, and other amenities enhances the aesthetics and attractiveness of the route for walking and cycling. Parks located near homes and accessible by sidewalks can encourage people to participate in recreational activities and walk or bike to and from the park.

Changes to the physical environment of our communities will not necessarily persuade everyone to walk and bicycle for some or all of their daily travel or recreation. But places that have provided connected sidewalk, bikeway, and trail systems that link destinations and are convenient to use show increased walking and bicycling activity. Neighborhood parks that are built close to homes are used more. Decisions about community design can and do make a difference in helping Americans get their daily dose of activity, whether for transportation or recreation.

CHAPTER 8

MLB's Mixed Messages

African American Participation in Baseball

David C. Ogden

Since 1989, Major League Baseball has made a concerted effort to bring baseball to youth in urban areas where interest in the sport has shriveled or died altogether. That was the year when former major leaguer John Young convinced MLB to launch Reviving Baseball in the Inner Cities, or RBI. Young was concerned about what he viewed as a decreasing interest in baseball among African Americans and socioeconomically disadvantaged youth. When RBI began, about 17 percent of players on major-league rosters were African American. Almost 20 years later that figure had dwindled to 8 percent (Lapchick, Diaz-Calderon, and McMechan, 2009, p. 16).

This decrease has occurred amidst a barrage of communications and activities centered on African Americans and baseball. From commemorating Jackie Robinson's entrance into the majors (especially in 1997 and 2007, the 50th and 60th anniversaries respectively of Robinson's rookie year) to providing African American children with opportunities to play, Major League Baseball has publicly demonstrated its awareness of the history of baseball and African Americans. That awareness was manifested when MLB decided to help Young establish the first RBI program in Los Angeles and again in 1991 when the Boys & Girls Clubs of America became the official cosponsor and administrator of RBI.

This partnership has kept youth baseball viable in communities where municipal parks and recreation departments have had to curtail maintenance of ball fields and administration of leagues because of lack of finances or resources ("MLB refurbishes public ball fields nationwide," 2005). The joint venture of MLB and Boys & Girls Clubs presents a dichotomy in addressing the recreational needs of urban core areas. On one hand, the partnership gave several current major leaguers their first youth baseball experience, and it has been a model for aggregating resources to establish a baseball presence in areas where the game faded long ago. On the other hand, the situation demonstrates how a lack of public policy ensuring recreational opportunities for inner-city children can erode the relationship between a sport and neighborhoods in the urban core. In the case of baseball, public officials have been slow to recognize the recreational disparity between the suburbs and inner-city neighborhoods. Officials have also been slow to acknowledge that new facilities and millions of dollars alone will not turn the tide of African American interest in baseball. Infrastructure must include human resources, namely the support of key community members and organizations.

The issue has been clouded by promotional communiqués that tout the success of the RBI program and frame MLB as a pioneer of and standard-bearer for integration. Some critics charge that RBI promotions have thwarted the public's understanding of the demise of baseball among urban minorities, particularly Africa Americans, and have masked the dearth of publicly funded and administered youth baseball programs in the inner city.

Proponents of RBI, however, point to the number of children served by the program and the millions of dollars that have been spent to support it. Since its inception in 1989 RBI has

- provided baseball and softball leagues for approximately 120,000 youngsters (ages 13 to 18) in almost 200 cities worldwide,
- built a $10 million, 25-acre youth baseball academy in Compton, California, and is building similar academies in Atlanta and Houston,
- had 170 alumni drafted by major-league clubs, including 19 in 2007 and 7 in 2008,
- spent more than $30 million on programs and related efforts, and
- helped to raise more than $7 million for the Baseball Tomorrow Fund, which funnels the money to various youth baseball programs for field improvement and equipment (Major League Baseball, 2009, 2008a).

Besides using the RBI program to brand baseball as an attractive sport for African Americans, MLB has also made considerable efforts during the past two decades to brand itself as a pioneer in racial integration. Its primary focus has been Jackie Robinson. MLB's first major public demonstration of its recognition of Jackie Robinson and the desegregation of the major leagues was in 1987, the 40th anniversary of Robinson's rookie season. At that time the front offices of major-league teams contained few African Americans, and of the three African Americans who had managed a major-league team, all had been fired. Ten years later MLB's minority hiring practices had improved little; African Americans made up just 8 percent of senior administrators (Lapchick, 2004). MLB, however, launched a yearlong promotional campaign in 1997, which involved

- ceremonies and a video presentation on Robinson at all major-league ballparks,
- a national traveling exhibit on Robinson,
- a lecture series at the Smithsonian Institute about Robinson,
- the opening of a wing at the Baseball Hall of Fame and Museum to pay tribute to African American ballplayers, and
- the retirement of Robinson's uniform number in both leagues.

Through such festivities, MLB has glorified the influence of Robinson in opening doors for other African American major leaguers and has expressed the profundity of the leagues' recognition of the unfairness of Jim Crow. In his 1997 announcement of the retirement of Robinson's number, MLB Commissioner Bud Selig set the tone that would mark his organization's perspective for years to come: "The day Jackie Robinson stepped on a major-league field will forever be remembered as baseball's proudest moment" (Anderson, 2001). Selig echoed that sentiment in 2005 in proclaiming April 15 "Jackie Robinson Day."

> I have often stated that baseball's proudest moment and its most powerful social statement came on April 15, 1947, when Jackie Robinson first set foot on a major-league baseball field. On that day Jackie put an end to segregation in baseball and ushered in the era in which baseball became the true national pastime. (Hill, 2005)

MLB, however, can take no pride in the decades-long decline in the number of African Americans who play baseball. In 2007 the percentage of players on major-league rosters who were African American dipped to 8.2 percent, the lowest it had been since the 1950s after the first wave of Negro Leaguers entered major-league baseball (Lapchick, Little, and Lerner, 2008; Davis, 2007). In 2008 that figure increased to 10.2 percent, still about half what it was in 1995 (Lapchick, Diaz-Calderon, and McMechan, 2009) and much lower than in the NBA and NFL (see table 8.1). And although tributes to Jackie Robinson have been embraced by

TABLE 8.1

Representation of African Americans in Major-League Sports (Percent of Roster Spots)

	MLB[1]	NBA[2]	NFL[3]
2008	10	77	–*
2007	8	76	66
2006	8	75	67
2005	9	73	66
2004	9	73	–*
2003	–*	76	69
2002	10	–*	–*
2001	13	78	–*
2000	13	78	–*
1999	13	78	67
1998	15	78	66

*Information not available in *Racial and Gender Report Card.*

From [1]R. Lapchick, A. Diaz-Calderon and D. McMechan, 2009, *The 2009 racial and gender report card: Major league baseball* (Orlando, FL: University of Central Florida College of Business Administration), 16; [2]R. Lapchick et al., 2009, *The 2009 racial and gender report card: National basketball association* (Orlando, FL: University of Central Florida College of Business Administration), 17; [3]R. Lapchick, E. Little, and C. Lerner, 2008, *The 2008 racial and gender report card: National football league* (Orlando, FL: University of Central Florida College of Business Administration), 15.

African American former players, they have been chastised by some scholars and journalists as a thin veil to the leagues' failure to put more traffic on the inroads that MLB has supposedly built into minority communities.

That situation, coupled with MLB's past promotions of African Americans in baseball, produces communication quandaries for league officials: How does an organization celebrate the influence of a racial group on its game while recognizing the diminishing influence of the game on that group? How does MLB's public communication reflect or detract from public policy that targets inner-city youth recreation? MLB has yet to solve those quandaries, and the organization's public statements about the problem have been, at best, guarded. To understand the league's approach requires a careful examination of MLB's official communications surrounding the situation. Some scholars believe that such communications simply mask the widening gap between baseball and African American culture. Using the concepts of semiotic analysis, this chapter explores the disparity portrayed by MLB's pronouncements and the current relationship between baseball and African Americans. The chapter also discusses the influence of semiotics on quashing or developing public policy and on building community programs.

Myth and Semiotics

Applying the concept of "myth" from the science of semiotics can reveal much about MLB communiqués and the way in which the league is addressing the paucity of African Americans in baseball. "Myth," especially as it has to do with baseball, has been defined and described in different ways (see, for example, Blaisdell, 1992; Voight, 1978; Levy, 2002). This paper uses the concept of myth as described by the late French philosopher and sociologist Roland Barthes in his writings on semiotics. His approach is apt to this study for several reasons:

- In some of his more famous examples of semiotics, Barthes applies the science to pronouncements by institutions, from laundry detergent companies to the French government (Barthes, 1972, 1982).

- Barthes' approach to semiotics provides a way to deconstruct messages and to examine the institution's incentives for using myth and the roots of the myth (Fry and Fry, 1989).

- Barthes' approach provides flexibility in analyzing communication and language from a variety of sources and in a variety of situations.

Barthes and other semioticians believe that all forms of communication, even those that are seemingly innocuous, carry underlying and socially based meanings and messages. According to Barthes, language or objects are "signifiers" and embody or represent some concept or idea. The intended meaning of that concept or idea he calls the "signified." Together, the signifier and signified constitute a third entity, called the "sign," in which the object and meaning are fused and cannot be stripped from each other. But the sign can come to represent a deeper and socially accepted ideology that becomes unchallenged, taken for granted, or considered "nature." The sign takes on a second-order "meaning" when it is embodied with a social or cultural permanence, that is, "That's the way it is and will continue to be." Barthes calls the second-order meaning "myth."

> Barthes believed that the significant semiotic systems of a culture lock in the status quo. The mythology that surrounds a society's crucial signs displays the world as it is today—however chaotic and unjust—as natural, inevitable, and eternal. The function of myth is to bless the mess. (Griffin, 2003, pp. 357–358)

But it is only when language or communication is used to freeze reality and not change it that communication becomes myth. Myth can often evolve from communication that is meant to bring about change, which Barthes labeled "political speech." Language or communication remains political speech when it serves as "the language of man as a producer: wherever man speaks in order to transform reality and no longer preserve it as an image . . ." (Barthes, 1972, p. 146). Myth, on the other hand, "deflects action which could bring about change; by freezing situations, events, and persons, mythic speech functions to make them immune to human action" (Fry and Fry, 1989, p. 187). Fry and Fry (1989) argue that mythical speech is accepted and becomes part of a social or cultural lexicon only "because certain signs become so engrained in a culture that they are no longer questioned (i.e., they are naturalized); thus they forfeit their capacity to alter the world. This is the process through which political speech is transformed into mythic speech" (p. 187). Myth, then, appropriates political speech and changes its meaning and, in doing so, puts such language to "a use for which it was not initially intended" (Fry and Fry, 1989, p. 187).

According to Barthes, part of the process of depolitization, or the transformation from political to mythic speech, is the exclusion of the "Other"—anyone or anything that is foreign, different, or not explainable. From the perspective molded by myth, the "Other" threatens the stability or existence of that which myth conveys. Myth, therefore, ignores or transforms the "Other."

Fry and Fry (1989) claim that it is possible to challenge the "unified world" that myth presents and "draw attention to the gaps within the unity, the genuine human problems which cannot be solved by a prevailing system" (p. 195). They contend that mythic speech can be deconstructed by tracing it back to the political speech from which it grew. Audiences who are obstinate to the myth can serve to point out the gaps and problems. To some extent, the media served as an obstinate audience in noting MLB's failure to recognize the paucity of African Americans in baseball, while the organization trumpeted the legacy of Robinson and its supposedly lasting influence on baseball and society, and they could play the same role in questioning whether RBI and other programs have had the intended effect of bringing African Americans back to baseball.

Analyzing MLB's Messages

The relationship between political speech and myth, and the role of the obstinate audience can be better understood when applying some of Barthes' concepts to MLB's language surrounding RBI and its other urban youth initiatives and the tributes to Jackie Robinson. Such an analysis can show how myth serves to (1) freeze a situation or a point of time to deflect action or attention to the status quo, (2) appropriate history in making a situation or event seem natural, giving it a "natural and eternal justification," and (3) portray a "world without contradictions" and one of homogeneity (Barthes, 1972, p. 143).

The remainder of this chapter explores these elements of myth as they pertain to MLB's communication. The possible political language from which these functions feed will be identified, as will language from alternate semiotic systems and its effect and implications for public policy. The sections that follow will examine the potential for communications to challenge the myth and to develop local programs and policies for youth sports.

Freezing the Situation

MLB's snapshot of itself, as portrayed through Commissioner Selig's statements and league pronouncements regarding the Jackie Robinson anniversary celebration, reflects an egalitarian system and a game embraced by all cultures. In a story on the MLB Web site, Selig was quoted as saying that Jackie Robinson "changed the color, the feel and the texture of America's game," (Hill, 2005). The same story noted how African American players "benefited" from Robinson's actions of "breaking the color barrier and forever changing the game of baseball and society as a whole" (Hill, 2005; Major League Baseball, *White Sox celebrate*, 2005).

MLB uses Robinson as what Fry and Fry would refer to as an ingrained cultural sign, not for the purpose of action (to understand or explain the paucity of African Americans at all levels of baseball), but for the purpose of freezing Robinson's image as a representation of African American presence in the game today.

On the other hand, MLB has acknowledged the low African American representation on baseball fields when communicating about its initiatives for inner-city youth. Those initiatives, however, are often wrapped in mythic speech. Although MLB has touted the number of RBI participants who have been drafted by major-league clubs, MLB has also focused attention on the amount of money spent on the program; that focus serves as the core of MLB's mythic speech about the program. Through such promotion and language, money or economics become isolated as the major solution to the problem of developing interest in baseball among African American youngsters. (As will be discussed later, social and cognitive development theory and experiences by some youth leagues would indicate otherwise.)

Appropriating History

Barthes (1972) said that myth "bears on objects already prepared" and "must overlay [a world] which is already made" (p. 175). MLB uses a historic signifier in Robinson, one whose image as the representative of Blackness in the major leagues has already been forged. But MLB drains that history and uses its shell as a current representation of the state of baseball.

Robinson's image was not the only history appropriated in the celebration. Former fellow players of Robinson remembered the heydays during and after his inaugural year when throngs flocked to ballparks to watch the first African Americans to play at the major-league level. Longtime Dodgers manager Tommy Lasorda is among several former baseball players quoted by MLB to resurrect images of enthusiastic support from African Americans. "Our spring games over-flowed with fans," Lasorda recalled. "In fact, so many African American fans came out to watch Jackie they would have to rope off sections of the outfield for crowd control" (Lasorda, 2005).

When African American interest in baseball peaked in the 1930s and 1940s, baseball was connected to the urban core and its stadiums were part of the fabric of the inner city. MLB invokes the historical connection between ballparks and the inner city by spotlighting RBI's contributions to building and improving urban baseball facilities, but it distorts the connection and recasts it, ignoring the decline in the significance and cultural relevance of baseball to the urban core and the disappearance of routines that once made baseball an important part of the inner city. MLB summons a vision of baseball as the one that sprang from the crowded neighborhoods in New York and other east coast cities at the turn of the century. But history becomes the basis for an assumption, or "natural" in Barthes' terms, and is thrust on the public by proponents of RBI. In the case of RBI, history becomes nature when it is taken for granted, or it "goes without saying," that interest and routines surrounding baseball will spring naturally from the building of facilities (Barthes, 1972).

World Without Contradictions

In mythic speech, the "Other" is often ignored or disregarded. Fry and Fry (1989) define Barthes' term "Other" as "anything which is alien, novel, previously unex-plained: i.e., an anomaly" (p. 191). Using the Robinson celebration to stamp base-ball "as the democratic, all-inclusive national pastime" (Anderson, 2001, p. 220), MLB downplays the anomaly, which is the potential gulf between baseball and African Americans (and perhaps other minorities) and the feeling by some in those minority groups that baseball has become increasingly exclusive (Ogden, 2002).

MLB's speech surrounding the RBI program also reflects an assumption about the "Other." That assumption is that baseball can be "sold" to all children at the age of 13 or older, despite their different cultures or the possibility that they have spent their previous childhood years playing other sports or in an environment with little or no baseball. In MLB's approach, "any otherness is reduced to same-ness" (Barthes, 1972, p. 151).

Moving From Political Speech to Myth

If MLB's mythic speech in 1997 and afterward about Jackie Robinson was aimed to freeze Robinson's image as that of one still representing the major leagues, the political speech from which MLB's rhetoric grew is not difficult to trace. In the first half of the 20th century, several proponents of desegregation were outspoken about the injustice of segregated leagues. Those proponents included journalists Sam Lacy of the *Baltimore Afro-American* newspaper and Wendell Smith of the *Pittsburgh Courier*, who used their columns to challenge major-league clubs to give Negro League players a chance. The most prominent proponent historically is Branch Rickey, who paved the way for Robinson to enter the major leagues.

Rickey's plan and language called for wholesale change in the major leagues.

Biographer John Chalberg said Rickey's actions to desegregate the major leagues were based on an ideal. "At the heart of that ideal was a color blind America, an America of genuine equality of opportunity, an America in which character counted for everything and achievement was possible for everyone" (Chalberg, 2000, p. 2). Rickey's communication was intended to beget action, whereas Selig's pronouncements and consistent references to "baseball's proudest moment" have aimed to capture a historical moment and use it to ossify MLB's image as it pertains to minorities. Selig made such a pronouncement when he said, "By celebrating Jackie Robinson Day every April 15, we have ensured that the incredible contributions and sacrifices he made—for baseball and society—will not be forgotten" (Hill, 2005).

In appropriating Rickey's political speech, Selig and MLB do not deny any facets of Robinson's career and influence on baseball. But they use them for a different purpose than Rickey did.

> Myth does not deny things, on the contrary, its function is to talk about them; simply it purifies them, it makes them innocent, it gives them a natural and eternal justification, it gives them a clarity which is not that of an explanation but that of a statement of fact. (Barthes, 1972, p. 143)

MLB's mythic speech about RBI and its other urban youth initiatives stems from the situation that John Young observed: too few African American youths playing ball, reflected in a decreasing number of African American players at the major-league level. Although the political language that surrounded the establishment of RBI called for change, subsequent communications, especially those in the last few years, have served as myth in oversimplifying or glossing over the effect that RBI has had.

MLB states as a fact that RBI is changing the face of baseball, and league officials often remind the public of their commitment to use RBI to develop in urban youth "a lifelong relationship with the game of baseball" (Florida Marlins, 2008). Young expressed the same commitment in 1989 and used that commitment as the basis for action: starting the first RBI league in south central Los Angeles (Major League Baseball, 2008a). In 2003 Young expressed dismay that the number of African Americans in major-league uniforms was dropping 14 years after he began RBI. Young's response was political speech, calling for change in the program (Verducci, 2003, pp. 56–66). When Tom Brasuell, MLB's vice president for community affairs, was reminded in 2005 of the decreasing number of African Americans (at that time reported as 10 percent of major-league players), his response was that of mythic speech in reminding the public of MLB's awareness of the situation and the amount of money and work that has been put into the program. "I think the number of African Americans playing the game should reflect the population," said Brasuell. "If the 10 percent we have holds, we'll be OK. If it drops below that, there'll be real concern" (Svrluga and Pierre, 2005, p. 8). According to the latest *Racial and Gender Report Card* issued by the University of Central Florida, that figure dropped to 8.2 percent in 2007 (Lapchick et al., 2008, p. 16). It rose to 10 percent in 2008, "(a)midst the debates of why African Americans are abandoning the field of baseball" (Lapchick, Diaz-Calderon, and McMechan, 2009, p. 3).

Challenging Myth

As described earlier, obstinate audiences can play a role in challenging myth by using political speech to build alternative semiotic systems. Statistics, such as the number of African Americans currently playing in the major leagues, can serve as political speech, especially those statistics that run contrary to the myth of baseball as representative of all cultures. Whether those statistics could be classified as revolutionary language, which Barthes says "abolishes myth" (Barthes, 1972, p. 151), is a question, but sportswriters have certainly used such statistics to defy MLB's mythic language surrounding the Jackie Robinson celebration.

Anderson (2001) quoted an *Atlanta Journal-Constitution* columnist who called the celebration an "absolute joke" and noted that the "biggest joke is baseball's contention that it has repented most of its sins in regards to blacks during the 50 years since Robinson ended apartheid in the majors" (p. 221). A *Kansas City Star* reporter said that the celebration was "insulting" in light of the decreasing number of African Americans on major-league player rosters. A writer for the *New Yorker* asserted that MLB used the 50th anniversary as an opportunity to "touch up its own imperfect image in contemporary racial awareness" (Anderson 2001, p. 220).

> A number of sportswriters maintained that no one in MLB seemed to have the prescience to ensure the image that the tribute was designed to inspire (the administration works to ensure baseball is a democratic, American game) matched reality (the small number of minority executives cast aspersions on the democratic nature of baseball). In sum, the industry could not effectively promote itself as leaders in minority hiring when it had so few minority executives in visible positions. (Anderson 2001, p. 221)

The sportswriters' reactions should serve as a reminder to MLB officials that they should "ensure that the image they attempt to create or maintain for their organization meshes with the perception the desired target audiences have of the organization" (Anderson, 2001, p. 223).

At the least, statistics and other information may serve as part of the language of alternate semiotic systems whose purpose is to challenge "the unified world view mythically presented by the dominant system" (Fry and Fry, 1989, p. 195). RBI founder John Young's concerns that RBI has failed to increase the numbers of African Americans playing in college and the major leagues challenges the existing structure of the program. One of the RBI alumni, who did make it to the major leagues and who is touted by MLB in its RBI promotions, echoed Young's sentiments. Tampa Bay outfielder Carl Crawford, who played his youth baseball in inner-city Houston, has challenged the mythic speech surrounding the RBI program. RBI programs have been established in Houston, but Crawford said MLB does not follow up on the talent by sending major-league scouts to inner-city areas. "There's a lot of inner-city kids who aren't getting scouted," he said. "I don't know if they [the scouts] are intimidated. I can't really put my finger on what the problem is. They're just not there" (Chastain, 2005). A National League scout claims that RBI leagues do not field players who would draw interest from professional teams. "The RBI program is nice," the scout was quoted as saying, "but they're not getting the best athletes. Those athletes are going into other sports" (Verducci, 2003, p. 66).

Social science theories may be another form of political speech that can unmask myth, especially as it pertains to MLB's pronouncements about RBI. (The assumption is that myth is absent from scientific theory, but theory may be used to expose myth.) For example, cognitive development theories, most notably gender constancy, show that children begin developing sport interests well before the age of 13, which is the youngest age bracket served by the RBI program. In her research on gender constancy, psychologist Sandra Bem (1981) found that children realize by age 7 that their gender will not change and they begin emulating gender-specific activities, including sports. Although MLB defends targeting the RBI program to 13- to 16-year-olds, because that is the age range during which youngsters are more likely to quit playing sports, many coordinators of local RBI programs have added to the political language by claiming that enticing 13-year-olds to play baseball, when they have never played it before, is a difficult proposition. In the words of one RBI director, "It's difficult to get a kid who's never picked up a baseball to try something new. As kids get older they're not as likely to try something that they're going to fail at" (Ogden, 2002, p. 331). MLB did start an RBI-like program in 2002 for 5- to 12-year-olds, but the program (called Rookie League Baseball) has not gained the stature of the RBI program (Major League Baseball, 2008b).

Other theories and research focusing on cultural and peer influences on youth choices of recreational or leisure activities have also been ignored by MLB in promoting RBI. Some research has shown that numerous social and cultural factors have created a gulf between baseball and African Americans in the past few decades. For example, Ogden and Rose (2005) and Ogden (2004) consider the importance of socially and culturally accepted routines that serve as a foundation for youth interest in baseball. Without establishing such routines, not just the infrastructure that facilitates routines, spawning long-term interest in baseball is unlikely.

Other studies show that peer pressure is a potent force in a youth's decisions about which sports to play or watch. Among African Americans there is much greater peer pressure to attend to basketball rather than baseball (Wilson and Sparks, 1996). But the fact that 76 percent of players in the National Basketball Association (Lapchick, Hanson, Harless, and Johnson, 2009) are African American is not a reason for the paucity of African Americans in baseball. Rather, it is a result of African Americans' not having opportunities to receive extensive instruction in baseball and not living in an environment in which baseball is part of the cultural landscape.

Policy Implications for Myth Making

As mentioned previously, public policy regarding youth baseball must incorporate a recognition that children from the urban core and low-income families face a disadvantage in sport participation. As Wicks, Beedy, Spangler and Perkins (2007) noted,

> Public funding cuts, steep registration fees, and unsafe facilities have left many of these young people on the sidelines. The limited number of community programs that do focus on sports are all too often deficient in terms of staff, capacity and overall program quality. (p. 108)

Grassroots Baseball Initiatives:
Growing the Interest at Home

Numerous local initiatives have reached into neighborhoods where RBI has not. The two examples discussed here share basic philosophies about and approaches to involving inner-city youth in baseball. Those approaches include introducing factors to stabilize the participants' environments, providing instruction, making resources identifiable, using existing organizations and motivated people to provide infrastructure, and instructing youth at an early age.

■ *Elementary Baseball* (*Washington, DC*). Some youth baseball administrators have called John McCarthy's Elementary Baseball a national model for exposing inner-city grade school youth to baseball (Ogden, 2005). A former pitching prospect for the Baltimore Orioles, McCarthy began Elementary Baseball in 1994 not as a baseball instruction program, but as a literacy program. McCarthy used baseball as a reward for grade school students who agreed to participate in a one-on-one reading program (personal correspondence, May 24, 2005). McCarthy worked with third graders at Garrison Elementary School in Washington, DC, in an area that was predominantly African American. McCarthy recruited more than 80 court employees, including 15 judges, who were paired with the students for weekly reading sessions (McCarthy, 2008). Students who showed progress, or at least a desire to improve, were allowed to participate in McCarthy's after-school baseball clinics each weekday. Some students were also invited to participate at no cost in McCarthy's summer baseball clinics, called the Home Run Baseball Camp.

McCarthy eventually expanded his after-school program to all students at Garrison Elementary School. By 2008 approximately 600 students, most of them African American, participated in Elementary Baseball. McCarthy estimated that about 30 percent of the students at Garrison signed up for Elementary Baseball, and at one time he had a waiting list of 75 students (personal correspondence, May 24, 2005). Of those students who played at his baseball camp, 50 have gone on to play college baseball and three have signed major-league contracts (McCarthy, 2008).

■ *North High School* (*Omaha, NE*). When Scott Wulfing joined North High School as its varsity baseball coach, his mission was to build a baseball program of which the North Omaha community could be proud. North Omaha contains the largest concentration of African Americans in the city. His first step was to renovate North High's home field in the city's Fontenelle Park. The first time Wulfing saw the field, "There was trash everywhere. Nothing was really maintained, and the outfield was not mowed very often" (personal correspondence, May 13, 2005). With the support of the North High School administration and some assistance from a local travel agency, Wulfing replaced the all-dirt infield with a grass infield. He and community volunteers built brick dugouts with roofs, installed a sprinkler system, and developed a maintenance schedule for the field. Wulfing also gave the field a new moniker: The Ballpark at Fontenelle (Patterson, 2005, p. 3C). Wulfing is not sure about the effect of the renovated field on interest in baseball among North Omaha youngsters. But the project served to notify the public of Wulfing's role as a baseball resource. He was asked by the local Boys and Girls Clubs (which did not have enough players to receive an RBI grant) to present a baseball clinic for grade school children. In his first year at North High, Wulfing had 24 students, 2 of whom were African American, try out for his two teams—varsity and reserve. The next year that number grew to 45 students, 4 of whom were African American, and North High now fields three teams (varsity, reserve,

(continued)

and junior varsity), "a rarity at the school in recent years" (Patterson, 2005, p. 3C). By 2009 the North High School baseball program had 10 community sponsors and a board of directors consisting of parents and community leaders. That board coordinates leagues and maintains the field. The local chapter of the International Brotherhood of Electrical Workers erected the first electronic scoreboard at the ball field (Omaha North High School Grunwald Viking Baseball, 2009).

Youth baseball coordinators whose goal is to help African Americans advance to higher levels of competition (i.e., high school and college ball) must realize that those who play in city recreational leagues or RBI programs are at a disadvantage compared with those youngsters who play on "select," or travelling, teams. Players in recreational leagues seldom play more than 15 games each summer, whereas players on select teams play an average of at least 60 games per summer (Ogden, 2002). Research has shown that 90 percent of college players played select baseball as youngsters (Ogden, 2007). Introducing youth to baseball through a 6- to 8-week season will do little to prepare them to compete with counterparts on select teams for roster spots on high school teams and in NCAA baseball programs.

Recognition of such research and theories has remained outside the scope of MLB's mythic speech related to African Americans in baseball. That mythic speech has treated the RBI program as a panacea for enticing minorities to baseball and a national remedy for bolstering public policy to address the shortage of inner-city baseball facilities and mentors, but some youth baseball administrators have recognized that local initiatives can do more to give children opportunities to play ball (Ogden, 2002).

For example, in 1999 the RBI coordinators in Des Moines and Chicago balked at limiting participation in their programs to those between the ages of 13 and 18 (as mandated in RBI funding guidelines). These coordinators started their own leagues for youngsters between the ages of 7 and 12. In this case the coordinators became an obstinate audience, and their actions essentially served as political speech, revealing those issues that RBI did not address and calling attention to the lack of (and the importance of) baseball playing opportunities for grade-school-aged youngsters. Those actions demonstrate the necessity and advantages of homegrown youth baseball programs, which involve community leaders who have the knowledge and means to marshal community resources and to recognize local agencies that, through their partnerships, provide the greatest synergism in addressing youth baseball needs.

Future Trends

If myth comes from political speech, can it return to political speech and, if so, how? This question is central to the planning and development of local programs. If local youth baseball coordinators serve as an obstinate audience and address the shortcomings of RBI through their own initiatives to develop the interest of

African American and other minority youngsters in baseball, MLB's portrayal of a game that fulfills the legacy of Jackie Robinson may be justified. In other words, the actions of an obstinate audience as political speech can deconstruct and transform MLB's mythic speech into language that serves to further the causes of change. The importance of local initiatives in that change is exemplified by the fact that the majority of African American major league players are not RBI alumni. Of the 121 African American players on MLB rosters (Lapchick, Diaz-Calderon, and McMechan, 2009), 12 played in the RBI program (personal correspondence, MLB staff member Kevin Moss, June 3, 2009). The other 119 were exposed to the game through other means.

Organizations such as the National Recreation and Park Association have called for community parks and recreation departments to be aggressive in developing policies to address youth sport needs (Phillips, 2007). Doing so, however, requires community partnerships and grassroots efforts. Some of those efforts should include

- the identification of organizations (profit and nonprofit) willing to work together to invest time and resources into youth baseball facilities and operations,
- the development of coalitions of community leaders to advocate for the establishment and retention of youth programs, and
- the recruitment of people to serve as neighborhood baseball mentors who would use their knowledge and passion for baseball to attract children to the game through clinics, leagues, and individual instruction.

Public policies can serve as political speech in evoking changes that bring about opportunities for youngsters to play ball, but such policies cannot be implemented without the infrastructure and environment to support changes.

Although myth tends to support the dominant culture and to mask that which is contrary to the culture, its use by MLB to portray baseball as an egalitarian enterprise could be useful in attracting minority youth to the game. The development and communication of public policy should reflect an inclusiveness (even if there is not) in portraying baseball as a game that can be enjoyed by all. On the other hand, the myth of RBI as an avenue for inclusiveness should not overshadow or deter local efforts to establish baseball programs for inner-city or minority youth. Local efforts should reflect political speech in addressing issues that are unique to a community and that national programs like RBI do not address. Sustaining such initiatives requires a commitment of community organizations and individuals.

Conclusion

MLB's rhetoric about Jackie Robinson's contributions to baseball and about efforts to bring baseball to inner-city youngsters serves as an example of how myth drains political speech and recasts it as an object to be taken for granted or to be taken as nature. In promoting its RBI program, MLB notes the initial need for the program (few inner-city African American youth playing the game), but it does not acknowledge how such a situation came to be or how it is affecting the major leagues. MLB ignores or, at the very least, suppresses the history of the current condition between baseball and African Americans. MLB does not address what led to the cultural indifference that characterizes the relationship between baseball and African Americans. Seldom does MLB acknowledge that African Americans make up a smaller percentage of players on major-league rosters, compared with the 17 percent figure in 1989 when RBI began. Nor do such promotions cite the low percentage of African American players in college baseball and lower levels (see, for example, Lapchick, 2007; Ogden, 2007).

Former major league pitcher Jim "Mudcat" Grant is among several retired African American players who argue that MLB has not taken a African American cultural perspective in operating the RBI program. Grant said,

> As long as baseball promotes the word *RBI*, it would seem [in their minds] to be OK, but nothing is really happening in the inner-city communities when it comes to RBI. We have to get the cities involved where the ball fields are, where the RBI players play. (Bruce Markusen, personal communication, March 11, 2004)

Although mythic speech has not necessarily caused a decrease in the presence of African Americans in baseball, it downplays the magnitude of the problem and fails to encourage investigation of the history of that decrease. Understanding why fewer African Americans are participating in the game could foster new ideas for exposing African American youth to baseball and making the sport more culturally appealing. Those ideas can lead to better models and programs, and better public policy, for enhancing youth participation.

CHAPTER 9

Contradictions and Conflict

Ethical Dilemmas Inherent in Big-Time College Sports

Richard M. Southall, Mark S. Nagel, John Amis, and Crystal Southall

As president of the National Collegiate Athletic Association (NCAA) from 2002 until his death in 2009, Myles Brand was compelled to defend the business practices of an amateur endeavor. Not surprisingly, given his philosophy background, Brand's 2006 presidential message, which offered such a defense, reflected concepts of moral relativism and pragmatism, longstanding western philosophy traditions that can be traced from Protagoras (481–411 BC), one of the earliest Sophists, to William James (1842–1910), the most widely known American Pragmatist.

> Our mission is to ensure that intercollegiate athletics participation is an integral part of the higher-education experience. . . . Using "business" and "college sports" in the same sentence is not the same as labeling college sports *as* a business. It is not. College sports exhibits business aspects *only* when it comes to revenues—the enterprise is nonprofit on the expenditure side. . . . [W]e will be inflexible in our devotion to principles and in our commitment to higher education. (Brand, 2006, para. 2, 10, 16, emphasis in original)

Both Protagoras and James, if they were alive today, would recognize that Brand's statements define the "goodness" or "correctness" of any ethical position in reference to whether it furthers the NCAA's interests. As NCAA president, Brand's task was to defend the organization's truly "good" actions from unjustified criticism. Just as Protagoras and James, Brand's remarks suggest he accepted as true that which was expedient in the way of belief, and as good that which was expedient in the way of conduct.

Consistent with an a priori belief in NCAA customs and beliefs as true and good, Brand's discourse reflects a pragmatic institutional logic, which holds that engaging in big-time commercialized college sports is necessary for achieving unspecified but entirely "good" educational goals. Because it is a given that NCAA "principles," to which the organization is inflexibly committed, are good and correct, Brand argued that such desirable "nonprofit" ends justify involvement in a somewhat sordid commercial enterprise.

Brand's logic presupposes that because colleges are fundamentally involved in a "good" educational enterprise, its activities like organizing college sport competitions (in contrast to less savory professional sport contests) are innately good insomuch as they are also educational. By extension, because the business of big-time college sports generates revenue for non-revenue-generating educational or athletic programs, then it too is worth retaining, if not continually enhancing. Because the primary mechanism for generation of revenue for college sports is telecasts (specifically NCAA Division I men's basketball broadcasts), and revenue production is positive, such broadcasts are also innately good because they support a priori "good" NCAA principles (e.g., educational opportunities for athletes, athletic opportunities for athletes in sports that do not generate sufficient money to cover associated expenditures, and a sense of connectedness to college campuses of fans, alumni, and students).

Notwithstanding Dr. Brand's sophistry, college sports' alignment with educational institutions has long been problematic. Numerous researchers have identified a college sport system in conflict, to one degree or another, with universities' stated missions (Baxter and Lambert, 1991; Baxter, Margovio, and Lambert, 1996; Case, Greer, and Brown, 1987; DeBrock, Hendricks, and Koenker, 1996; DeVenzio, 1986; Eitzen, 1988; Frey, 1994; Lapchick, 1986; Padilla and Baumer, 1994; Sack, 1987; Sperber, 1998). Historically, such criticism of big-time college sports has involved examinations of the inherent contradictions between the institutional logics of commercialized big-time college sports and higher education. Noting the existence of various college sport models, Sack (1987) developed a corporate model to describe big-time college sports on the Division I-A, or Football Bowl Subdivision (FBS), level involving so-called revenue sports of football and men's basketball. Recently, women's basketball has begun to be viewed as the most big-time of women's college sports. Referring to Sack's corporate model, critics of college sports have argued that many Division I-A athletic departments are culturally and organizationally disconnected from the university to which they are ostensibly attached. The departments' actions often suggest that their primary institutional logic involves commercial goals of winning games and generating revenue.

As is the case with most policy discussions, disagreements over the existence or nature of a problem affect any examination regarding appropriate solutions. Fundamentally, such disputes often arise from individuals or organizations adhering to different, and often contradictory and conflicting, institutional logics. In this chapter the present state of college sports is discussed. We then define and elaborate on the concept of institutional logics, and examine the notion of competing and dominant institutional logics.

Using this framework, we pose this fundamental research question: Is there evidence to suggest the existence of a dominant commercial logic within the field of big-time college sports? Using discourse and content analysis research techniques, this chapter presents a case study involving 2006 NCAA Division I men's basketball tournament broadcasts to answer the posed research question. Faced with seeming contradictions and conflict within the college sport field, a moral question remains: Does the NCAA "do" as it "says"? In the specific context of the case study in this chapter, this question becomes: Do NCAA broadcasts of its marquee event (e.g., the NCAA Division I men's basketball tournament) represent an inflexible devotion to espoused NCAA principles and values and a commitment to higher education?

College Sports Today

To place in context this discussion of the contradictions and conflict in big-time college sports, the reader will find it helpful to have at least a cursory understanding of today's college sport environment. At the outset one thing is indisputable: Public interest in college sports is widespread. Such interest has been a long-standing phenomenon; approximately 37 percent of the American public says that they follow college sports (Harris Interactive, 2006). Since 2000, men's Division I college basketball has consistently generated strong attendance; approximately 24 to 25 million fans attend events each year (National Collegiate Athletic Association, 2000, 2006). The United States' largest intercollegiate athletic event, the 2006 NCAA Division I men's basketball tournament drew 670,254 on-site customers (an average of just over 19,150 per session), generated consistently high television ratings, and attracted higher levels of advertising spending than either the Super Bowl or the World Series (Bosman, 2006).

For several years, college sport marketers, including the NCAA itself, have used sport-marketing strategies designed to "help us as we move forward to develop strategies for increasing our fan base, from both television and arena attendance, and work to build lasting relationships with those fans" (National Collegiate Athletic Association, 1999, para. 2). Before the campaign began, the NCAA conducted research that "helped us [NCAA] better understand what types of consumers were most and least likely to be college basketball fans and why" (National Collegiate Athletic Association, 1999, para. 5). The multifaceted marketing campaign included a weekly 30-minute television program, public service announcements, and a new sport video game (National Collegiate Athletic Association, 1999).

Aware of possible contradictions and conflict between commercial and educational values that may arise from such popularity, however, the NCAA Division I Men's Basketball Committee officially recognizes a mandate to "exemplify the educational mission of intercollegiate athletics" and explicitly acknowledges the need to "balance the principle of student–athlete welfare with its attempt to maximize exposure and revenues from the championship" (National Collegiate Athletic Association, 2006, p. 7).

College sports have been viewed by some, including the NCAA, as an essential component of college education. Chu (1989) discussed the historical acceptance of the integration of the mental, physical, and spiritual development of individuals as a consistent rationale for the appropriateness of college sports as an educational enterprise in the United States. Baxter and Lambert (1991) discussed the many intercollegiate athletic administrators' contention that "the commercial success of intercollegiate athletics . . . [is] related to the belief in the educational purpose and high ethical standards of amateur competition" (p. 184). Some educators have praised intercollegiate athletics as an essential component of a collegiate experience that produces well-rounded people, capable of positively contributing to society (Chu, 1989; Coakley, 2001; Funk, 1992). College coaches invariably identify teamwork, discipline, and loyalty as benefits of sport participation (Maraniss, 1999).

According to a May 23, 2005, *NCAA News* article, "Intercollegiate athletics can and should be an integral part of the higher education experience" (Brown, 2005a, para. 8). Many reform organizations such as the Coalition for Intercollegiate Athletics (COIA) have articulated the desire for a close relationship between intercollegiate athletics and the academy:

> (a) For the athlete, the discipline and values of sports can contribute to personal development, reinforcing academic excellence; (b) For the campus, the ceremonies and competition of intercollegiate sports can contribute to community and institutional loyalty; and (c) For the college and university community, college sports can broaden positive interest in public support for higher education. The COIA believes college sports should be pursued in a way that supports those claims. "The strength of the COIA—and perhaps the difference between the COIA and other groups—is in our stating right up front that we feel athletics is an important part of the educational mission. . . . We are trying to find ways to protect that experience and make it the best possible for athletes." (Brown, 2005, para. 9)

Although few still argue that the sole purpose of college athletics is character development (Bailey and Littleton, 1991), athletic department mission statements often still contain language explicitly ascribing character-enhancing benefits to college athletics and expressing their department's preeminent concern for their athletes' educational well-being.

To many, college sports are the symbolic tie that binds alumni to current students. As Bailey and Littleton (1991) have noted, stadiums and coliseums, fixtures on major college campuses, "consecrate the identity and remembrance of past athletic triumphs in ways that classrooms and laboratories cannot hope to duplicate" (p. 14). College presidents, in the midst of their schools' trips to bowl games, cite the ability of collegiate athletics to attract people to the institution in a way that few things can today (Putler and Wolfe, 1999).

The potential of college sports, as the front porch of the university, to generate public interest and promote institutional messages has historically been cited as a rationale for the formal incorporation of athletics into the university structure. With colleges constantly searching for revenue sources, athletics has been viewed as a visible component of university life and an effective way of telling a university's story to the public and attracting resources. Many institutional messages communicated to the public come through vehicles directly related to the athletic program. Attempts to quantify the value of such messages have led researchers to examine the spillover effect for colleges and universities that have successful athletic programs. These studies have primarily focused on determining what variables have an effect on giving to a university's annual fund-raising program. The emphasis has been on determining the effect of various athletic success variables (Baade and Sundberg, 1996; Gaski and Etzel, 1984; Grimes and Chressanthis, 1984; Marts, 1934; Sack and Watkins, 1985; Sigelman and Carter, 1979). The researchers in three of these studies determined that athletic success, depending on the variable used to measure it, does have an effect on annual contributions to a university (Baade and Sundberg; Grimes and Chressanthis). But the researchers in the remaining four studies found no significant relationship between successful athletic programs and contributions to the university (Gaski and Etzel; Marts; Sack and Watkins; Sigelman and Carter). Recent research has suggested that increased athletic giving has a negative effect on overall university giving (Stinson and Howard, 2007).

According to a recent NCAA CEO Task Force report, "Intercollegiate athletics serves its highest purpose when it is fully aligned with the educational mission" (Brown, 2005b, para. 3). But as Gerdy (1997) stated,

> Organizations inevitably evolve to achieve that for which they are rewarded. Inasmuch as athletic departments have been rewarded principally for the purpose of winning games, they have evolved to emphasize achievement of this goal to the detriment of all others. (p. 7)

National Collegiate Athletic Association (NCAA)

Because the NCAA is the largest and most well known of four independent organizations that regulate intercollegiate athletics (Depken and Wilson, 2005), an examination of its expressed values and identified role in college sports is relevant within the context of college sports as an integral component of higher education. According to information posted on the NCAA Web site, the organization defines itself in the following way:

> The National Collegiate Athletic Association (NCAA) is a voluntary organization through which the nation's colleges and universities govern their athletics programs. It is comprised of institutions, conferences, organizations and individuals committed to the best interests, education and athletics participation of student–athletes. (NCAA, 2007a, para. 1)

The NCAA, as a membership organization, proposes, passes, and enforces its own set of rules and regulations governing topics ranging from academics to recruiting. As of 2007 the NCAA conducts 88 championships, in three divisions, for 23 sports and over 400,000 college athletes (NCAA, 2007c).

As is the case with many organizations, the NCAA has developed a mission statement. The NCAA's mission statement is broken down into a series of statements that articulate the organization's core ideology "consist[ing] of two notions: core purpose—the organization's reason for being—and core values, essential and enduring principles that guide an organization" (National Collegiate Athletic Association, 2007d, para. 1). The overriding purpose of the NCAA is to "govern competition in a fair, safe, equitable and sportsmanlike manner, and to integrate intercollegiate athletics into higher education so that the educational experience of the student-athlete is paramount" (National Collegiate Athletic Association, 2007d, para. 2). The core values elucidated by the NCAA include a belief in and a commitment to: (a) the collegiate model of athletics in which students participate as an avocation, balancing their academic, social and athletics experiences, (b) the highest levels of integrity and sportsmanship, (c) the pursuit of excellence in both academics and athletics, and (d) the supporting role that intercollegiate athletics plays in the higher education mission and in enhancing the sense of community and strengthening the identity of member institutions. (National Collegiate Athletic Association, 2007d, para. 3)

But reflecting the existence of a commercial logic within the organization, the NCAA also recognizes that college sports are a widely recognized and powerful sport brand (National Collegiate Athletic Association, 2007f). According to the NCAA, its NCAA brand has the following attributes: "Learning. Balance. Spirit. Community. Fair play. Character . . . that the NCAA promotes through its branding initiative. An important part of the NCAA brand is a consistent image that supports these attributes" (National Collegiate Athletic Association, 2007f, para. 1).

Corporatization in College Sports

Although they recognize possible contradictions and conflict, as well as identity dissonance (Elsbach and Kramer, 1996; Brand, 2006) within the college sport field, NCAA administrators are still comfortable with "the juxtaposition of the NCAA's educational mission with a commercial entity" (National Collegiate Athletic Association, 2002, para. 5) such as the Columbia Broadcasting System (CBS). Bob Lawless, NCAA Executive Committee chair, articulated the NCAA's position: "There's a realization that when you receive a certain amount of revenue from a network that they're going to generate revenue in order to meet the agreement of the contract" (National Collegiate Athletic Association, 2002, para. 6). According to the *NCAA News*, as recently as 2002, college presidents were unperturbed with "a corporate partner essentially 'sponsor[ing]' the NCAA's educational mission," as long as it is "done well and tastefully" (National Collegiate Athletic Association, 2002, para. 2, 6).

Responding to external events, including academic scandals, low graduation rates, and media criticism of the excessive commercialism in college sports, NCAA president Myles Brand, in his 2006 presidential message, rationalized the need to conduct the business of college sports well by referring to the NCAA's educational mission. Brand dismissed any apparent ethical contradictions arising from such commercialization, contending that NCAA members can remain true to the organization's identity and values while pursuing additional revenue opportunities associated with the NCAA's most valuable commodity—the Division I men's basketball tournament:

Our mission is to ensure that intercollegiate athletics participation is an integral part of the higher-education experience. . . That message seems pragmatic enough, but one piece might be perceived as anomalous. While we profess the integration of athletics within the educational mission and the moderation of athletics spending locally, the Association nonetheless must conduct the business of college sports well. That means the Association must pursue additional revenue options, as long as it is done within the mission and values of higher education. (Brand, 2006, para. 2, 9)

Without fail, Dr. Brand and other NCAA spokespeople have imbued the NCAA brand with nostalgic, and therefore "good," ideals of amateurism. Consistent with such branding efforts, NCAA advertising policies state, "The NCAA strives to be associated with entities and messages that . . . champion the STUDENT–athlete reflecting the integration and balance that student–athletes achieve every day between academics and athletics" (National Collegiate Athletic Association, 2005, para. 5, emphasis in original).

Such advertising policies reflect the existence of an educational institutional logic within the NCAA. However, policy development is not the same as policy implementation or standard operating procedures, and it may not reflect an organization's dominant institutional logic. To evaluate the consistency of NCAA policies with its stated mission, it is important first to understand the concept of institutional logics and then to use this concept to evaluate the organization's actions. The next section provides such an analysis.

Institutional Logics

Institutions, as Friedland and Alford (1991) pointed out, "have a central logic—a set of material practices and symbolic construction—which constitutes its organizing principles and which is available to organizations and individuals to elaborate" (p. 248). An institution's logics determine what are considered acceptable or unacceptable operational means, guide the evaluation and implementation of strategies, establish routines, and create precedent for further innovation (Duncan and Brummett, 1991; Friedland and Alford, 1991; Nelson and Winter, 1982; Washington and Ventresca, 2004). These logics become manifest in a particular organization or industry as shared, generalized expectations that allow institutions, or individuals within institutions, to engage in coherent, well understood, and acceptable activities that influence how people and institutions communicate, enact power, and determine what behaviors to sanction and reward (Barley and Tolbert, 1997). Eventually, the values that constitute these institutional logics become unquestioned, taken-for-granted "facts" that support and are supported by "correct" courses of action.

Over time, because of contradictions and conflicts within the field, contestation among different institutional logics usually results in the emergence of a dominant logic. This process works to establish local-meaning frameworks that guide strategy and structure by focusing the attention of decision makers toward the issues and values that are most consistent with the dominant logic and away from the issues that are not (Thornton, 2002). The values inherent in the dominant commercial logic that underpins "March Madness" are the culminations of many negotiated decisions and actions among prominent stakeholders or actors (e.g., the sanctioning body [NCAA], athletic conferences [Big Ten, Big XII, Pac 10], individual university athletic departments, the broadcast entity [CBS], and corporate sponsors and advertisers). Influential actors in other settings have been able to exert pressures that affect the broadcast of sport events (Duncan and Brummett, 1991; Silk and Amis, 2000). These pressures are exerted explicitly in formal or legal regulations, or they may take the form of taken-for-granted or institutionally prescribed codes and values (Silk and Amis). Note that such institutional pressures exerted on a broadcast organization involved in televising college athletics may come not only from the sponsors and advertisers specifically doing business with the network but also from the sanctioning body (NCAA) and its members, as well as sponsors or licensees aligned with it.

Although institutionally based forces are important, also relevant are the cognitive, or micro-level, processes that emanate from the ways in which individuals associated with any institution interpret accepted ethical rules to make sense of the world around them (Berger and Luckman, 1967; Scott, 2001). Day-to-day activities often become institutionalized or accepted without question (Berger and Luckman). As a result, routines are created—taken-for-granted, repetitive, and recognizable patterns of interdependent actions involving multiple actors (Feldman, 2000; Feldman and Pentland, 2003; Nelson and Winter, 1982). Similar to other habits, ethical routines become established conduits through which acceptable courses of action are promulgated. In Myles Brand's 2006 presidential message the unquestioned acceptance of a commercial institutional logic sanctified seeking new and expanded revenue streams in college sports and the appropriateness of big-time, commercialized college sports.

Adoption of the dominant commercial logic constrains the array of options perceived as available to decision makers in college sports and shapes not only a particular broadcast but also all good college sport decisions. This logic results in a repackaging or re-presentation of a mediated college sport event and involves not only the decision to broadcast some college sports and not others but also the decision to accentuate particular aspects of the chosen sport event for listeners and viewers (Sage, 1998; Silk and Amis, 2000).

Although the NCAA sport field seems to offer some support for the existence of two such logics—educational and commercial—strong evidence suggests that the commercial logic has been dominant for almost as long as the NCAA has been in existence. Indeed, Washington and Ventresca (2004) have proposed that the rationale for the development of sport programs by American universities and colleges was a desire to enhance resources and increase visibility. Such a motivation is reflective of the aggressive pursuit of television rights fees by the NCAA and its members since the early 1950s and the organization's willingness to position intercollegiate athletic competitions to maximize commercial revenue opportunities (see Washington, 2004). As others have found in various contexts (publishing, financial services, and so on), the existence of a dominant logic has pronounced implications for the direction of strategic decision making (Thornton, 2002) and provides a context for seeking to answer the following research question "Do NCAA broadcasts of its marquee event (e.g., the NCAA Division I men's basketball tournament) represent an inflexible devotion to espoused NCAA principles and values and a commitment to higher education?"

Case Study:
2006 NCAA Men's Basketball Tournament Broadcasts

Consistently, a primary justification for university sponsorship of athletics at the highly visible NCAA Division I level relates to the potential of an athletic contest to tell the institution's educational story to the public (Gerdy, 2006). For many big-time college athletics departments, television has become a prominent marketing and advertising vehicle. That being the case, it would follow that the content of televised college sport events—the images portrayed and messages conveyed during the course of such telecasts—would reflect the stated values of intercollegiate athletics and communicate the expressed purposes of higher education.

Methodology

To answer the posed research question, a mixed-methods approach including content and semiotic analyses was used. Semiotics is the science of signs and symbols, which "provides a set of assumptions and concepts that permit systematic analysis of symbolic systems" (Manning and Cullum-Swann, 1994, p. 466). Such a mixed-methods approach is most often based on language analysis but can include any sign system. Such analysis allows all human action to be interpreted as text and thus "read." Within this context a "sign" represents something in the mind of someone and is composed of (a) an expression (word, symbol, sound)—the signifier, and (b) content (the concept that it represents, meaning)—the signified. Using such a methodological approach allowed both quantitative and qualitative data collection.

The 2006 edition of *March Madness*, CBS' exclusive coverage of the 2006 NCAA Men's Division I Basketball Championship (n = 63 games [the play-in game held on Tuesday, March 14, 2006, was broadcast by ESPN and not included in study population]), began on Thursday, March 16, 2006, and culminated with the national championship game between the University of California at Los Angeles (UCLA) and the University of Florida. The case study sample consisted of (n = 31, 49.2%) randomly selected 2006 tournament game broadcasts. Games from all four tournament regions (Atlanta, Oakland, Washington, DC, and Minneapolis) were obtained from local CBS and *DirecTV Mega March Madness* telecasts of the 2006 NCAA Division I men's basketball tournament. The 31 sampled broadcasts included 20 randomly selected first-round games, five randomly selected second-round games, three randomly selected third-round games, both national semifinal games, and the national championship game.

The primary sources for the analysis included documents (e.g., *2004–2005 NCAA Broadcast Manual Championship Guidelines* and *2006 Division I Men's Basketball Championship Handbook*) that outlined contractual-based advertising and promotional standards, and broadcast policies and procedures. Secondary sources included periodicals such as *NCAA News*, newspapers, sports magazines, and sport business trade publications.

The coding schema for the study was consistent with a protocol outlined by Madden and Grube (1994) and involved analysis of nonprogram broadcast content from pregame, in-game, and postgame segments. Nonprogram content included traditional commercial advertisements (including network commercial time, local advertising spots, promotions, and public service announcements [PSAs]), as well as "nonstandard" in-game advertisements, graphics, promotional announcements and game announcer commentary (Gough, 2006). Nonprogram messages were also categorized as commercial or educational in nature.

The broadcast analysis units developed for nonprogram content included the following categories: (a) standard commercial advertisements (ADV), (b) NCAA public service announcement (NCAA), (c) corporate sponsor public service announcements (CORP), (d) nonstandard sponsorship graphics without verbal commentary (GR), (e) nonstandard sponsorship graphics with verbal commentary

(GR/VER), (f) academically related player information graphics (GR/ACA), and (g) positive or negative educational commentary (ED).

Educational messages were not limited to those that detailed a university's academic mission; they included any discussions of an athlete's major or course of study, classroom performance, or grade point average. In addition, identified educational messages were categorized as either positive or negative in nature (e.g., a negative educational message might detail a previous academic scandal or a player having been academically ineligible, whereas a positive educational message would involve any nonnegative message, such as a player's major being designated, or a positive discussions, such as a player being described as an Academic All-American).

Besides the quantitative content analysis, we also used qualitative methods to uncover possible underlying messages not only represented during NCAA Division I men's basketball tournament game broadcasts but also promoted in organizational documents, operational handbooks, and public statements (Bignell, 1997; Cresswell, 1998; Neuendorf, 2002; Patton, 2002). Such analysis allowed our data to be critically examined for both linguistic and visual signs to determine "what [was] portrayed and symbolized . . . and what [was] absent or silenced" (Rossman and Rallis, 1998, p. 146). In examining the data in this fashion, various levels of analysis were established, ranging from individual words and images to overall concepts—words and visual images grouped in concept clusters—contained in the broadcasts and documents (Bignell; Strauss and Corbin, 1990).

During this analysis, represented broadcast content was examined for consistency with stated NCAA goals, rules, policies, and guidelines, as well as organizational parameters outlined in primary and secondary sources, including official NCAA documents found on the NCAA.org Web site. Besides game-specific content and standard advertisements, nonstandard advertising and non-basketball-specific in-game messages were evaluated (Bignell, 1997; Madden and Grube, 1994).

Results

A critical component of CBS's NCAA men's basketball tournament broadcasts is nonprogram commercial advertisement content. Consistent with broadcast industry practices, the commercial format of NCAA men's basketball games is painstakingly designated by the NCAA in its *NCAA Division I Men's Basketball Championship Handbook*. According to that document's guidelines,

> The television commercial format during the NCAA Division I Men's Basketball Championship allows a maximum of 27 minutes of commercial time per game. In addition to that time, the network [CBS] may also air commercials during 60-second team-called time-outs in each overtime period. (National Collegiate Athletic Association, 2006, p. 107)

Within this 27-minute block (1,620 seconds) "10 'full television time-outs' shall be permitted per game" (National Collegiate Athletic Association, 2006, p. 107). The NCAA specifies that "each 'full television time-out' shall last 2 minutes, 15 seconds from the time the teams arrive at their benches to the 'second horn'" (National Collegiate Athletic Association, 2006, p. 107). In addition, the prescribed length of the full television time-out is relaxed during "the regionals and the Final Four, [when] the network may extend any two time-outs by 10 seconds" (National

Collegiate Athletic Association, 2006, p. 107). Explicitly, however, these extensions must not be used for commercial or promotional purposes (National Collegiate Athletic Association, 2006). Note that in the sampled broadcasts the average over-the-air standard commercial advertisement (ADV) full television time-out was nearly 2 minutes and 30 seconds, in excess of even the extended full television time-out length prescribed in NCAA documents.

Although the handbook clearly designates the maximum commercial time per game as 27 minutes, it contains several inconsistencies, including a detailed "permissible commercial format" in which the length of a full television timeout is decreased to "two minutes of commercials" (National Collegiate Athletic Association, 2006, p. 107). In addition, the handbook presents an exemplar detailing the permissible commercial content in an NCAA Division I men's basketball broadcast that exceeds the 27-minute maximum commercial time limit. Using the various NCAA definitions and guidelines, table 9.1 summarizes the range of possible standard commercial nonprogram totals.

Reflecting the nonprogram content categories listed earlier, the sampled broadcasts contained a total of 74,157 seconds of standard commercial advertisements (ADV), or an average of 39 minutes and 52 seconds of commercial advertisements per broadcast (table 9.2), strikingly longer than the NCAA-prescribed 27 minutes. The lowest ADV total was 29 minutes and 20 seconds (1,760 seconds) in the UCLA versus Belmont game, and the highest ADV total was 59 minutes and 30 seconds (3,570 seconds) in the Ohio State versus Davidson game.

Note that the NCAA's maximum allowable commercial time per game did not specifically exclude public service announcements from the total allowable nonprogram commercial time. This study, however, separated commercial advertisements (ADV) from public service announcements (NCAA and CORP). As a result, the ADV cumulative total and per game averages detailed earlier do not

TABLE 9.1

NCAA Men's Division I Basketball Championship Commercial Format

Category	Total time
Maximum commercial time per game[a]	27 minutes (1,620 seconds)[a]
Full television time-out[a] length	2 minutes, 15 seconds (135 seconds)[a]
Permissible commercial format[a] full television time-out length	2 minutes (120 seconds)[a]
Amount of standard commercial advertisement (ADV)[b] per game (using permissible commercial format)	46 minutes (2,760 seconds)
Standard commercial advertisement (ADV) per game (using full television time-out and permissible commercial format)	48 minutes, 30 seconds (2,910 seconds)

[a]Note. All terms are from *NCAA 2006 Division I Men's Basketball Championship Handbook.*
[b]A standard commercial advertisement is an advertisement broadcast during a full television time-out.
From *NCAA 2006 division I men's basketball championship handbook.*

TABLE 9.2

Nonprogram Content Summary

Category	Total seconds	Average time per broadcast
Standard commercial advertisements (ADV)	74,157	39 min, 52 seconds
NCAA public service announcements (NCAA)	1,620	52 seconds
Corporate sponsor public service announcements (CORP)	956	31 seconds
Nonstandard sponsorship graphics without verbal commentary (GR)	6,584	3 min, 32 seconds
Nonstandard sponsorship graphics with verbal commentary (GR/VER)	4,773	2 min, 34 seconds
Academically related player information graphics (GR/ACA)	58	1.8 seconds
Educational commentary (ED)	197	6.36 seconds

include PSAs or other in-game nonprogram content such as promotional or sponsor graphics, or verbal comments. Adding PSA totals to the ADV figures for the sampled broadcasts results in a cumulative total of 76,733 seconds, a per-game average of 41 minutes and 15 seconds of traditional nonprogram advertisements.

As marketers are well aware, technological advances such as digital video recorders (e.g., Tivo) allow television viewers the option of fast-forwarding through standard commercial breaks. This innovation has had the dual effect of (a) increasing the propensity of advertisers to look to sport properties because of their ability to draw live rather than delayed viewers and (b) increasing the use of within-game graphics and verbal references to decrease the likelihood of audiences being able to skip standard commercial advertisements and PSAs. In the sampled basketball broadcasts such graphics and verbal messages made up a substantial amount of nonprogram content: GR total (6,584 seconds cumulative total, a per-game average of 3 minutes and 31 seconds), and GR/VER total (4,773 seconds cumulative total, a per-game average of 2 minutes and 32 seconds). Such content, however, was not included in NCAA guidelines regarding maximum allowable commercial time (National Collegiate Athletic Association, 2006).

The educational message categories developed included academically related player information graphics (GR/ACA) and educational commentary by game announcers (ED). In the 31 sampled broadcasts, there was an aggregate of 58 seconds (a per-game average of 1.8 seconds) of academically related player information graphics ($n = 11$ player academic major graphics), and 197 seconds (a per-game average of 6.36 seconds) of educational commentary. Note that 21 percent (42 seconds of the 197 seconds total) of the educational commentary was categorized by the research team as negative in nature, detailing player ineligibility because of poor grades or other negative academic issues.

Case Study Discussion

An NCAA men's basketball tournament game, like any represented sport event, is produced "in accordance with its own codes, which highlight and thereby naturalize selected aspects" (Gruneau, Whitson, and Cantelon, 1988, p. 267). Decisions regarding the amount and type of advertising and sponsor graphics, as well as in-game announcer commentaries during an NCAA tournament broadcast, are the result of negotiations, both contractual and cultural, between various tournament constituencies and are fundamentally driven by each institution's logics.

The 2006 NCAA Division I men's basketball tournament did little to promote educational themes or images. Although the primary messages conveyed during any sport event are going to be related to the athletic contest itself, significant nonprogram messages are also conveyed during any sport broadcast. In 2006 NCAA Division I men's basketball tournament broadcasts, which were typically 2.5 to 3 hours in length, educational messages (both verbal and visual) were rare (on average 8.2 seconds per game). Within the game broadcasts, discussions of higher education, academics, or broader university missions of teaching, research, and service did not occur. Although CBS placed an average of nearly two NCAA PSAs per broadcast, in no instance did university-specific public service announcements occur in the sample. This lack of ad buys by universities participating in the NCAA tournament may be attributable to the high cost of a 30-second commercial spot (e.g., in 2005 a 30-second Final Four spot sold for $650,000, and a 30-second spot during the national championship game cost $1 million [Vasquez, 2005]). Besides having no standard advertising presence within broadcasts, rarely were universities specifically mentioned. Instead, athletic monikers, nicknames, and quasi-franchise or "program" references were the norm when referring to athletic teams. In fact, in the national championship game neither coach mentioned his university by name. Instead, the coaches referred to "their program and their fans" when thanking their constituencies. In addition, neither coach referred to his players as student–athletes in postgame CBS interviews. The only time that the titles "the University of California at Los Angeles" or "the University of Florida" were mentioned during the game broadcast was during Mr. Craig Littlepage's (director of athletics, University of Virginia) awards ceremony remarks.

As far back as 2001 college athletic administrators recognized that

> television networks are trying to do everything they can to add value and increase advertising sales to be able to pay the ever-increasing rights fees we ask for. . . . We are the ones driving their needs to do these types of things. (Weiberg, 2001, para. 3)

Contrary to then-president Cedric Dempsey's claim that "in actuality what we've done is provide more money without increasing ad time during event" (Brown, 2002, para. 44), documentary analysis revealed that the NCAA has increased the length of full television timeouts in its television commercial format. Whether this change was made unilaterally by the NCAA or whether CBS exerted pressure on the NCAA to increase advertisement time during events is not public knowledge. Note, however, that CBS' rights fees will escalate over the terms of the contract, from $420 million in 2005, to $453 million in 2006, and to $764 million by 2013 (Brown, 2002).

In discussing its 11-year, $6 billion television rights and marketing agreement with CBS, the NCAA stated that as an association "[it] wanted to be 'fairly compensated' for its wares . . . the NCAA didn't go looking for $6 billion—that was the market value of the package when it was put out to bid" (Brown, 2002, p. 2). In 2002 Brown noted, "To be sure, the NCAA isn't yet guilty of having sold its soul . . . the very act of selling that event [Division I men's basketball tournament] doesn't render the NCAA a commercial opportunist" (pp. 1–2). In addition, in 2002 NCAA senior vice-president Tom Jernstedt stressed the importance of "telling the truth—over and over again—through promotional platforms gained in the agreement . . . [about] the partnership between intercollegiate athletics and higher education" (Brown, 2002, p. 3).

Although the NCAA may tell its truth through other promotional platforms, NCAA Division I men's basketball tournament broadcasts offer few educational messages or messages consistent with the NCAA's stated core ideology, purpose, and values. David Goldfield (faculty athletic representative at the University of North Carolina) said, "There's nothing wrong with money and making it, especially if you can use it to further your mission" (Brown, 2002, p. 4). He warned, however, "It's easy for the NCAA's credibility to be compromised when the public is bombarded with mixed messages" (Brown, 2002, p. 4). Mr. Goldfield noted that the NCAA and its member institutions' academic credibility may be compromised by a dominant commercial logic: "The problem comes when the money diverts you from what you're supposed to be doing" (Brown, p.4). The results of this study suggest that such a dominant commercial logic exists within the NCAA. The 2006 NCAA Division I men's basketball tournament broadcasts did not bombard the viewing public with mixed messages. Overwhelmingly, more than 99 percent of the time, nonprogram broadcast messages are commercial in nature. Although the NCAA clearly promotes its commercial brand, education is rarely if ever represented.

Consistent with previous analyses (Rascher and Schwarz, 2000; Rascher, 2003a, 2003b) this case study offers clear evidence to suggest that the NCAA has evolved into a monopsonistic trade association designed to enhance visibility and resources for member schools, in which a dominant commercial institutional logic exists and is reflected in the NCAA's business decisions. Strong evidence suggests that NCAA actions reflect decision making that is continually focused toward those issues that are consistent with this dominant commercial logic and away from those that are not (Thornton, 2002).

Although college sports, reflected in the various NCAA divisions and other intercollegiate athletic associations (National Association of Intercollegiate Athletics [NAIA], National Junior College Athletic Association [NJCAA], and National Christian College Athletic Association [NCCAA]), includes multiple, competing logics, the NCAA, in particular NCAA Division I, is so dominant that it, together with its commercial partners, inevitably shapes the logic of college sports.

In addition, evidence exists of competing logics within the NCAA itself and the dominance of a commercial logic within the organization. Evidence for such a conflict is reflected in differences between membership divisions found on the NCAA Web site. NCAA Division I athletic departments, most notably those in the Football Bowl Subdivision (FBS) classification, are described as "usually fairly elaborate programs," and the foci of the D-I summary are requirements involving attendance and location of contests (National Collegiate Athletic Association, 2007g, para. 1). Perhaps coincidentally the term *student–athlete* never appears. In contrast, the Division III summary notes the following:

> Division III athletics features student–athletes who receive no financial aid related to their athletic ability and athletic departments are staffed and funded like any other department in the university. Division III athletics departments place special importance on the impact of athletics on the participants rather than on the spectators. The student–athlete's experience is of paramount concern. (National Collegiate Athletic Association, 2007g, para. 3)

Cognizant of such contradictions and conflict, the NCAA has developed a governance structure that allows each division to self-govern, thus preventing the majority of members (Division III) from interfering with the commercial activities of Division I big-time college sport programs. The NCAA's 1973 reorganization into three distinct and autonomous divisions, each with a separate independent management council, and the abolition of the necessity for association-wide approval for policies specific to each division (National Collegiate Athletic Association, 2007b, 2007e) lends credence to the organization's long-standing recognition of the dominance of a commercial logic in Division I and the efficacy of a governance structure that allows Division I athletic departments to conduct the business of college sports "well," free from less commercialized, educationally motivated constraints of Division III.

Future Trends

Recent judicial and congressional actions related to the commercial institutional logic and cartel behavior of the NCAA will likely create some degree of financial burden for the association and could potentially have significant influence on the future of college athletics.

In 2008 the NCAA settled a federal antitrust lawsuit (*White v. NCAA*) that argued that limiting scholarships to tuition, books, and housing amounted to a restraint of trade. As part of the settlement, the NCAA agreed to augment funding pools set aside to assist students with demonstrated financial need and to allow easier access to such funds. This change amounts to a minor, perhaps symbolic, victory for student–athletes seeking a balance of power in the relationship with the institutions that they represent. (This chapter's sidebar highlights the outcomes of several other important antitrust challenges that the NCAA has faced.)

Congress has recently taken issue with the NCAA's commercial interests, questioning whether those interests should affect the tax-exempt status that is offered to colleges and universities as institutions with a public mission. A 2009 report, *Tax Preferences for Collegiate Sports*, prepared by the Congressional Budget Office notes the following concern:

> The large sums generated through advertising and media rights by schools with highly competitive sports programs raise the questions of whether those sports programs have become side businesses for schools and, if they have, whether the same tax preferences should apply to them as to schools in general. (p. vii)

NCAA and Antitrust Challenges

As far back as *Justice v. NCAA* (1983) the courts have expressed the belief that the NCAA is, in many ways, a trade association involved in the business of corporate college sports. Although the factual situation in *Justice* involved questions of athletic eligibility and rule making, the court recognized the NCAA's metamorphosis from an organization involved solely in amateur eligibility issues to a monopoly also concerned with protecting its commercial and business interests:

> [I]n sum, it is clear that the NCAA is now engaged in two distinct kinds of rule-making activity. One type . . . is rooted in the NCAA's concern for the protection of amateurism; the other type is increasingly accompanied by a discernible economic purpose. (*Justice v. NCAA*, 1983, p. 28)

The courts' recognition of the NCAA's dual nature, and the ascension of a commercial institutional logic, can be seen in concurrent and subsequent antitrust cases. *NCAA v. the Board of Regents of the University of Oklahoma* (1984) involved a dispute between the NCAA, which had adopted a television plan for 1982–1985 college football games, and NCAA-member universities who were also College Football Association (CFA) members. The CFA was organized to promote big-time football schools' interests and increase its members' revenue. Accordingly, the CFA negotiated a contract with the National Broadcasting Company (NBC) that would have increased the revenues of CFA members and expanded the members' television appearances. After the signing of the CFA's contract with NBC, the NCAA announced that it would discipline any CFA member that participated in the agreement.

In *Board of Regents*, CFA member universities claimed that the NCAA's actions violated § 1 of the Sherman Act. Using a Rule of Reason analysis, the Court agreed and noted that the NCAA's actions clearly dealt with economic issues:

> The NCAA television plan on its face constitutes a restraint upon the operation of a free market, and the District Court's findings establish that the plan has operated to raise price and reduce output, both of which are unresponsive to consumer preference. (p. 2)

The court's recognition of the NCAA's commercial institutional logic and its involvement in a commercial enterprise was central to the court's rulings in *Law v. NCAA* (1998), in which U.S. district judge Kathryn H. Vratil determined that there was sufficient evidence for a jury to decide whether the NCAA was guilty of price fixing in violation of federal antitrust laws. The court's ruling was based on an examination of a 1991 NCAA rule that restricted the earnings of the lowest-ranking assistant coaches at Division I universities. A jury eventually awarded $22.28 million in damages, which was trebled under antitrust law.

When the NCAA again faced an antitrust challenge in 2001, the association opted to find an alternative means of settling the dispute. Although the NCAA men's tournament is the most popular college basketball event in the country, the National Invitational Tournament (NIT) has a longer history. Five New York City colleges (New York University, Manhattan, St. John's, Fordham, and Wagner) made up the Metropolitan Intercollegiate Basketball Association (MIBA) that had operated the NIT since 1938. In 2001 the MIBA sued the NCAA, alleging that NCAA bylaws pertaining to the NCAA men's basketball tournament violated federal antitrust laws *(MIBA v. NCAA*, 2005).

Although the NCAA denied the allegations and committed to fighting the lawsuit in court, it eventually decided simply to buy and operate the NIT rather than risk losing an additional antitrust lawsuit. The MIBA received $40.5 for the tournament and an additional $16 million to end the litigation (Moran, 2005).

Although the MIBA case did not result in any dramatic changes in the NCAA's business practices, it seemed to signal an attitude on the part of the NCAA that it may be more efficient to invest in potential buyouts rather than risk losing a case that could result in hundreds of millions of dollars in losses. The MIBA case suggests that the NCAA does not wish to tangle with antitrust laws, especially if less expensive business alternatives exist.

The congressional report suggests three potential policy options for changing the tax preference associated with college athletic programs: limiting the deduction of charitable contributions, limiting the use of tax-exempt bonds, and limiting the exemption from income taxation. The report acknowledges, however, that such policies are unlikely to cause a significant change in the nature of NCAA programs as long as such programs remain part of larger nonprofit or public universities because "schools would have considerable opportunity to shift revenue, costs, or both between their taxed and untaxed sectors, rendering efforts to tax that unrelated income largely ineffective" (p. vii). Although removing tax-exempt status from colleges and universities and their big-time football and basketball programs would be difficult, congressional action would be justified in attaching special limitations to athletics programs, such as restricting expenditures or mandating disclosures, if programs are to continue to receive preferential tax status.

Although these challenges hint at the potential for significant government intervention to change the status quo, their effect so far has been relatively minor. And it has become clear that the efforts of reform-minded organizations like the Knight Commission on Intercollegiate Athletics, the Coalition on Intercollegiate Athletics, and the Drake Group have had no direct effect on policy development or implementation in college sports. Unless the federal government is willing to go further than it has in regulating the NCAA, the trade association of the college sport cartel, big-time college sports will continue to be dominated by its institutionalized commercial logic, and most of us—as we cheer on our favorite teams—will ignore, as much as possible, the contradictions, conflicts, and ethical dilemmas inherent in big-time college sports.

Conclusion

Although the NCAA president officially espouses educational values, such rhetoric is largely ceremonial conformity to what is perceived to be a requirement for institutional legitimacy and does not reflect the NCAA's organizational behavior (Meyer and Rowan, 1977). In essence, the use of collegiate nomenclature becomes a point of competitive brand differentiation designed to distinguish the NCAA in an increasingly crowded sport marketplace. Although some NCAA officials, industry analysts, and members of the public may proclaim the preeminence of educational values, this assertion is, depending on one's viewpoint, either a naive interpretation or a deliberate attempt to mislead.

Specific to the NCAA Men's Division I Basketball Tournament, it is true that after CBS purchases the broadcast rights, it controls the commercials and, in fact, all nonprogram content associated with tournament broadcasts. But the NCAA asserts that it controls its championship events and that all decisions regarding NCAA championships are made based on the welfare of student–athletes (National Collegiate Athletic Association, 2006). In official documents the NCAA noted that even though CBS has purchased rights to NCAA Division I men's basketball game broadcasts, "All television rights (over the air and cable), both live and delayed, will be under the jurisdiction of the Division I Men's Basketball Committee" (National Collegiate Athletic Association, 2006, p. 33). If the NCAA's assertion that it maintains control over the game broadcasts is false, the NCAA has ceded control of the broadcasts to CBS, and as a result, CBS' dominant commercial logic permeates the analyzed broadcasts. But if the NCAA has in fact retained jurisdiction over the broadcasts, there is strong evidence that a commercial logic has come to dominate the NCAA Division I field.

In this context, the overwhelming commercialized nature of the nonprogram content of *March Madness* broadcasts has been justified as necessary to support the NCAA's mission. Some have proposed that just as churches, synagogues, and mosques must take up collections, require tithes, or solicit offerings to support their religious missions, the NCAA must conduct the business of college sports wisely and maximize revenue opportunities whenever possible in support of its educational mission. For this analogy to be valid, however, such religious collections must occur at the margin and constitute a small fraction of such religious events. To be legitimately defined as a religious service, the activity must retain its essential religious content and characteristics.

Conversely, if a religious organization's annual March religious celebrations (for the sake of argument, let us suppose that these services are the only time when most congregants attend services and that 90 percent of all organizational revenues are collected during these celebrations) consist almost entirely of nonreligious entertainment, paid commercial advertisements projected onto a supersized video display (including a specified number of beer commercials per service), and solicitations for other nonreligious events to be held in the community, an observer would correctly conclude that a dominant commercial logic has informed the religious organization's strategic decision making surrounding these services. This scenario illustrates how institutionally based forms of rationality can shape a field's structuration (Lounsbury, 2007).

The consequences of the inability of U.S. higher education to utilize this potentially powerful resource effectively have far-reaching public policy implications for American colleges and universities. One of the most pressing issues facing higher education today is declining public trust (Gerdy, 2006). A major contributing factor to that decline relates to the inability of higher education to tell its story to the public effectively. Specifically, much of the public does not seem to understand or believe that colleges and universities positively affect lives in real ways by providing resources potentially available to everyone (Gerdy). Inasmuch as athletics is the front porch of the higher education community, the way in which it is used to tell its story is critical. In short, although the college sport viewing audience may be enthralled with college athletics, with millions of potential students, donors, and community leaders tuning in weekly, when higher education has an opportunity to communicate its core mission through these broadcasts, the messages conveyed have little to do with education.

CHAPTER 10

Sport, Doping, and Public Policy

Bryan E. Denham

Scientists developed a synthetic version of testosterone, the male sex hormone, in 1935. Shortly thereafter, derivatives that included anabolic-androgenic steroids (AAS) became available for medicinal use (Hoberman, 2005). Designed to help people rebuild their bodies after suffering significant tissue loss, AAS functioned by synthesizing protein into muscle at an accelerated rate (Yesalis, 2000). To little surprise, the muscle-building capacities of AAS attracted the attention of athletes and their trainers, and throughout the latter half of the 20th century, use of the drugs proliferated in both amateur and professional sports, especially among those competing in football, track and field, weightlifting, and bodybuilding (Yesalis, Courson, and Wright, 2000).

Besides using AAS, athletes experimented with human growth hormone (HGH), the blood oxidizer erythropoietin (EPO), insulin, diuretics, strychnine, and other substances thought to enhance performance (see Armstrong, 2002; Ekblom, 2002; George, 2003; Kammerer, 2001; Karch, 2002; Mottram, 2003; Reents, 2000; Verroken, 2003; Yesalis and Bahrke, 2002). For the most part, people who used those substances did so in privacy, without counsel from medical professionals, following the "prescriptions" of self-declared experts. Sport journalists and audiences alike concerned themselves primarily with athletes in competition, as opposed to athletes *preparing* for competition, and rarely did behind-the-scenes stories about drug use reach the sporting masses. That changed following the 1988 Olympics in Seoul, South Korea (see Houlihan, 1997, p. 179; Voy and Deeter, 1991, p. 15).

At the Seoul Games, Canadian sprinter Ben Johnson tested positive for the anabolic steroid stanozolol after winning the 100 meters (Johnson and Moore, 1988), and his forced relinquishment of an Olympic gold medal subsequently became the quintessential example of an athlete who cheated to get ahead and then fell from grace. Johnson had defeated the favorite, U.S. track star Carl Lewis, in convincing fashion, and his victory was portrayed as a symbolic reminder that more than one nation existed in North America. When Johnson tested positive for AAS, Canadian national pride related to his accomplishments quickly dissipated. Lewis, who had tested positive for small amounts of stimulants before the 1988 U.S. Olympics trials (Denham, 2004a), received the gold, and Johnson departed Seoul persona non grata (see Jackson, 1998a, 1998b; Pound, 2006).

Highly publicized events, such as the athletic demise of Ben Johnson, have helped to precipitate the formation of public policy regarding performance-enhancing substances (Houlihan, 2002). Policy makers have upheld the need for regulation to protect at-risk populations and preserve fair competition (Denham, 2006, 2008). As a class of drugs, AAS, in particular, have been associated with health problems in both men and women (Elliot and Goldberg, 2000; Friedl, 2000), and scholars of sport ethics have outlined philosophical problems related to performance-enhancing drugs of all kinds (Brown, 2001; Simon, 2001). But to understand the formation of public policy, we must move beyond scientific and philosophical arguments and consider the pragmatic interests of multiple stakeholders, especially those who stand to profit from the athletic feats that performance-enhancing substances facilitate (see Hoberman, 2001). To succeed, athletes must keep pace with their peers, many of whom do not hesitate to use performance-enhancing substances. Team owners and league officials have observed a steady progression of athletic accomplishments and realize the difficulties associated with performances that do not meet or eclipse those already recorded. Media companies also profit from the spectacular, and although they may encourage fair play and air well-crafted public service announcements, their success depends largely on the extent to which they can produce dramatic imagery of ever-evolving athletic successes. On a national level, the United States and other countries have a stake in producing top-tier athletes, because Olympic and international sporting success can affect perceptions of nationhood, systems of governance, and overall quality of life.

Thus, as Elder and Cobb (1984) posited in their agenda-building research—an area of scholarship that focuses on reciprocity and interchange among the mass media, public policy makers, and mass publics—"Policy problems are not a priori givens but rather are matters of definition" (p. 115; see also, Cobb and Elder, 1971; Lang and Lang, 1983), and in the context of performance-enhancing substances, representatives from differing constituencies have helped define the issue. This list identifies some of the constituencies that have a stake in the regulation of AAS and other substances.

Constituencies With an Interest in the Regulation of Performance-Enhancing Substances

- Advertisers and corporate sponsors
- Athletes
- Drug-testing agencies and regulatory bodies
- Law-enforcement personnel
- League officials
- National and international athletic organizations
- News media

- Pharmaceutical companies
- Players unions
- Public policy makers
- Sport consumers
- Team owners

Both in the press and in government hearings, stakeholders have sought to protect their interests. This chapter examines those interests through a chronology of public policy initiatives related to doping, emphasizing media representations and the problems that those representations can cause. Because reports steeped in dramatic anecdotes and assumptions of causality have helped precipitate policy formation, some of the laws enacted have proved shortsighted and ineffective. Their enactments are more indicative of subjective social constructions than of objective assessments.

Mediated Doping Representations and the Formation of Public Policy

Writing about the intersection of sport and public policy, Wilson (1994) observed the following:

> There is nothing inherent in sports that would propel it onto the public stage, nor is there necessarily a set of organizational actors in society who claim responsibility for such matters. Indeed, there is considerable opposition to the idea that sport belongs on the public stage at all. (p. 388)

Chalip and Johnson (1996) noted as well that

> Although government intervention does occur occasionally, it generally is in reaction to demands from specific interests embroiled in a dispute or in response to public demand for protection from an industry practice deemed to be injurious to the public interest. (pp. 426–427)

Before the 1988 Olympics, the use of performance-enhancing drugs in amateur and professional sports had received modest attention in the popular press and almost no attention among public policy makers in the United States. *Sports Illustrated* had published reports about drug use in the National Football League during the 1980s (Johnson, 1985; Todd, 1983), and other media outlets had occasionally published news articles about AAS (see Todd and Todd, 2001), but the issue of performance-enhancing substances appeared to gain public policy momentum only when a series of real-world events and dramatic media reports occurred in a relatively short period (see Eitzen, 2006, pp. 80–83). As discussed later, in the United States these events and reports contributed to the formation and ultimate passage of the Anabolic Steroid Control Act of 1990, which classified AAS as a Schedule III controlled substance to be regulated by the federal government under the Omnibus Controlled Substances Act (Denham, 1997). Although the real-world event of Ben Johnson's losing his gold medal contributed to the policy momentum, dramatic narratives from the mass media added to the perceived need for government intervention.

As an example of how media reports assisted in defining steroid use as a policy issue, shortly after the 1988 Summer Olympics, *Sports Illustrated* published a dramatic first-hand account of AAS abuse, written by Tommy Chaikin, a football player at the University of South Carolina, and *Sports Illustrated* author Rick Telander (Chaikin and Telander, 1988). In "The Nightmare of Steroids," Chaikin described how he had experienced the adverse effects of AAS both physically and psychologically. The most dramatic parts of his story focused on a state termed *steroid psychosis*. Although scientists have debated the existence of this short-term rage, the Chaikin article included admissions of throwing a pizza delivery boy to the ground and holding him there at gunpoint and of going out for a drive with teammates and shooting cattle in nearby pastures, among other actions. As Denham (1997) noted, the Chaikin article "sent shockwaves through the National Collegiate Athletic Association" (p. 263), and from the standpoint of policy formation, a copy of the *Sports Illustrated* article appeared in the appendices of hearings held toward passage of the Anabolic Steroid Control Act of 1990. Indeed, had policy makers sought to manufacture a story that would have supported the introduction of legislation, they likely could not have constructed a tale as harrowing as that offered by Tommy Chaikin.

Four months after the Chaikin article appeared, Telander (1989) wrote a second article for *Sports Illustrated* focusing on the dangers of AAS among adolescents. In this case, the adolescent steroid user, Benji Ramirez, a 17-year-old high school football player, did not survive the use of AAS. The *Sports Illustrated* article included a photograph of Ramirez in his coffin. Although scientific evidence did not establish a causal relationship between the use of AAS and the enlarged heart that killed Ramirez, Ashtabula County (Ohio) coroner Robert A. Malinowski called AAS a contributing factor. This type of story has been a mainstay in the introduction of public policies related to performance-enhancing drugs. Pritchard (1994) explained that dramatic media reports can sometimes influence perceptions among lawmakers:

> The search for the link between public opinion and public policy often focuses on the press. After all, elected public officials and whatever nonelected policy makers they may appoint do not always (or even often) have direct measures of public opinion about issues that must be addressed. In the absence of direct measures of public opinion, policy makers may tend to use indirect indicators such as how much attention the news media devote to a given issue. (p. 107)

Like Pritchard, Kennamer (1994) described how media content sometimes serves as a surrogate measure of public opinion, and in the case of AAS, dramatic media reports indeed helped to demonstrate a perceived need for policy formation.

In the abstract, protecting at-risk populations from harm is an unassailable policy rationale, and as such, presents an excellent opportunity for policy makers to demonstrate initiative before constituents. But it also must be noted that new policies do not necessarily associate with the alleviation of social problems, and in the context of performance-enhancing drugs, the classification of AAS as a Schedule III controlled substance helped to expand black-market sales. With the expansion of black-market sales came an increase in bogus, and potentially toxic, substances being sold to unsuspecting youths (Denham, 2006; George, 2003), and the Internet has only exacerbated the problem. In certain respects, then, the fight against drugs in sports has served as a microcosm of the larger war on drugs in U.S. society. Both efforts tend to discount demand and systemic processes in favor of moral appeals and relatively futile attempts at enforcement (Denham, 1997; see also Waddington, 2000, pp. 89–95).

Before passage of the Anabolic Steroid Control Act of 1990, one of the most dramatic stories involving illicit drugs occurred in 1986, when basketball star Len Bias, a first-round draft choice of the Boston Celtics, died because of cocaine use (Daniellian and Reese, 1989; Merriam, 1989). His death helped the mass media construct compelling narratives about the perils of drug use (Voy and Deeter, 1991, pp. 7–8), and as Merriam (1989) explained, the Bias story "posed an almost media-perfect example of the dangers of drug overdose to a successful role model for youth. Concern for his death matched closely with the concerns national media and government were seeking to present" (p. 21). At the time, the sale of crack cocaine had escalated the violence of inner cities, and network news broadcasts routinely showed footage of young people caught in the drug crossfire. With the war on drugs as a backdrop, legislation involving AAS passed Congress with relative ease, although adolescent steroid use still managed to increase throughout the 1990s and into the 21st century (Denham, 2006). As Young (1981) summarized, "By fanning up moral panics over drug use, [media coverage] contributes enormously to public hostility to the drug taker and precludes any rational approach to the problem" (p. 334). To some extent, that assertion has applied to both narcotics and performance-enhancing substances.

Continuing the mass-communicated story of steroid use, after U.S. president George H.W. Bush signed the Anabolic Steroid Control Act of 1990 into law, Lyle Alzado, who played professional football for the Denver Broncos, Cleveland Browns, and Los Angeles Raiders, appeared on the cover of *Sports Illustrated* looking haggard and gaunt (see Alzado and Smith, 1991). Alzado had developed an inoperable brain lymphoma that he attributed to prolonged use of AAS, and like the Tommy Chaikin story from 1988, the 1991 Alzado account offered sport followers a harrowing report on which to base assumptions about the dangers of steroids (see Denham, 1999). Alzado had epitomized the aggressive and intimidating presence of NFL linemen, and his demise had left athletes and their fans in a state of disbelief. Was his condition really the result of steroid abuse?

Scientific evidence did not demonstrate a relationship between AAS and the lymphoma, but the image of an emaciated Alzado, who died in 1992, would nevertheless serve as a warning signal for adolescent athletes: "Attempt to cheat and this is what will happen." His story illustrates how mere assumptions of causal relationships can supersede evidence gathered scientifically and, in some cases, influence the formation of future policy. And although the mass media could undoubtedly report on medicine and science with greater rigor, the institutions of medicine (e.g., the American Medical Association) have contributed to some of the difficulties associated with the regulation of AAS and other performance-enhancing substances.

Only in recent years has the AMA acknowledged the capacity of AAS to enhance athletic performance, and one consequence of this reservation is that athletes tend to rely more on drug gurus than they do medical professionals. Recent studies demonstrate that AAS users continue to place little faith in physicians when it comes to advice on AAS (Monaghan, 1999; Pope et al., 2004). In looking back, had members of the AMA not testified at the hearings conducted in reference to the Anabolic Steroid Control Act of 1990, lawmakers may have classified AAS as a Schedule I controlled substance (as opposed to Schedule III), reserved for drugs with no medicinal value whatsoever (Denham, 1997). Public officials had been afforded a series of dramatic media reports on which to base policy actions, and had they overreacted in scheduling AAS, the substances might not be available at present to treat conditions such as anemia, muscle atrophy, and delayed puberty.

Although U.S. policy makers clamped down on AAS in 1990, highlighting threats to American youth, they appeared to move in the opposite direction in 1994, passing the Dietary Supplement Health and Education Act (DSHEA). This legislation exempted dietary supplements from the safety standards imposed on normal foods, meaning, in effect, that supplement manufacturers did not have to demonstrate the safety of a product before marketing it but that the Food and Drug Administration (FDA) and other agencies, if so inclined, had to show that a product was unsafe and therefore not ready for the marketplace (see Bass and Marden, 2005; Cohen, 2005; Mason, 1998). Industry lobbyists had campaigned for this type of legislation, contending that people should have access to supplements that might help them maintain good health and that the producers of these supplements should not have to spend large sums of money demonstrating product safety, especially given that DSHEA applied to "naturally occurring" vitamins and minerals.

As a political construction, DSHEA obscured key differences between food supplements and actual drugs. One example of the latter is androstenedione, the steroid precursor once used by former professional baseball player Mark McGwire, among others. Although the Anabolic Steroid Control Act of 2004 would later require androstenedione to be removed from the marketplace, it remained available to consumers for a full decade before public officials took action, and to little surprise, that action, when it came, was largely the result of media reports. Additionally, because language ambiguities in DSHEA lent the policy to political arguments instead of scientific reasoning (Mason, 1998), a substance similar to androstenedione, dehydroepiandrosterone (DHEA), remained available in the marketplace as an anti-aging product after androstenedione had been removed (Denham, 2006). In arguing for DSHEA to be repealed, Cohen (2005) summarized problems with the legislation:

> Although many dietary supplements share the physiologic and pharmacologic characteristics of pharmaceuticals, classification by statute rather than biology allows them to escape the far more stringent regulation required for pharmaceuticals. Rather than having separate regulatory schemes, the safety and efficacy of both dietary supplements and pharmaceuticals should be regulated identically. Although the FDA has not always fulfilled these ideals, permitting decisions regarding the marketing and advertising of supplements to be made by popular referenda is unsatisfactory. (p. 213)

In the United States, the nutrition supplement business is a billion-dollar industry, and with significant financial profits have come powerful lobbyists. As Denham (2006) explained, organizations such as the Council for Responsible Nutrition (CRN) had kept DHEA available as a nutrition supplement even though it converts to androstenedione and then to testosterone after it is inside the body. Lobbyists continue to mount efforts for product availability, proceeding from the standpoint of politics, not pharmacology.

Performance-Enhancing Substance or Antiaging Supplement?

The Politics of Dehydroepiandrosterone

When Congress passed the Anabolic Steroid Control Act of 2004, a piece of legislation that added steroid precursors such as androstenedione to the list of Schedule III controlled substances in the United States, they exempted dehydroepiandrosterone (DHEA), a hormone secreted by the adrenal gland (Denham, 2006). DHEA converts to androstenedione after it is inside the body, functioning as a steroid precursor, and in 2001 the U.S. Government Accountability Office (GAO) reported that studies had associated DHEA with increased risk of breast, prostate, and endometrial cancer, in addition to other health problems associated with AAS. Additionally, the GAO stated that although an acceptable range for active ingredients is 90 to 110 percent of that indicated, research had shown that just 44 percent of DHEA products met that standard. One product, the GAO noted, contained 150 percent of the level of the active ingredient indicated. Another study cited by the GAO found that one-fifth of DHEA products contained trace amounts or no active ingredient at all.

Nevertheless, lobbies such as the Council for Responsible Nutrition cited DSHEA in characterizing DHEA as a naturally occurring hormone that contained antiaging properties, and Orrin Hatch, a senator from Utah, appeared receptive to their messages. Major companies in the supplement industry had established their headquarters in Utah, and Hatch had threatened to scuttle the Anabolic Steroid Control Act of 2004, which he had helped to construct, if it did not exempt DHEA (Dembner, 2004; Kornblut and Wilson, 2005). Complicating matters further was the fact that Scott Hatch, son of the Utah senator, worked as a lobbyist for the National Nutritional Foods Association, and as Kornblut and Wilson (2005) reported, he had represented Twin Laboratories, which sold DHEA. Although Orrin Hatch maintained that his son did not influence his judgment, a conflict of interest seemed apparent. With DHEA generating sales of $47 million in 2003 (Dembner, 2004), political and economic interests appeared to rule the day.

Sporting Competition and the Formation of Regulatory Bodies

In professional sports, the year 1998 proved memorable. In Major League Baseball (MLB), Mark McGwire of the St. Louis Cardinals and Sammy Sosa of the Chicago Cubs engaged in an epic quest to break the single-season record for most home runs. McGwire eventually hit 70 to break the long-standing record of Roger Maris, who hit 61 in 1961. It was also the year in which a major doping scandal occurred at the Tour de France. French police and customs officials exposed widespread use of EPO and related performance-enhancing substances (Hanstad, Smith, and Waddington, 2008; Mignon, 2003; Schneider, 2006).

Where policy making is concerned, the Tour de France scandal in 1998 prompted the International Olympic Committee (IOC) to hold a 1999 conference addressing doping in sports. Out of the Lausanne, Switzerland, meeting came the formation of the World Anti-Doping Agency (WADA), now headquartered in Montreal, Quebec. As the organization notes on its Web site (wada.ama.org), "The Tour de

France scandal highlighted the need for an independent international agency, which would set unified standards for anti-doping work and coordinate the efforts of sports organizations and public authorities."

Like all agencies that have participated in the drug testing of athletes, WADA faces many challenges, not the least of which involves the continued production of substances that cannot be traced in the bloodstream. Human growth hormone is one such substance, and although it is quite expensive, professional athletes continue to use it as a performance enhancer. Additionally, as the 2003 investigation of Bay Area Laboratories Co-Operative (BALCO) in the United States revealed, supplement entrepreneurs, such as BALCO founder Victor Conte, Jr., may show little concern for the anti-doping rules of sports, developing undetectable steroids such as tetrahydrogestrinone (THG, known as "the clear"). In point of fact, apart from WADA, the United States Anti-Doping Agency (USADA) likely received its most significant press coverage in 2003, when a syringe containing the "designer steroid" THG arrived at its offices from an anonymous source. "The clear," which had been produced by BALCO and had been used by numerous high-profile athletes, would appear at the heart of a major doping scandal.

USADA had been established in October 2000 as the official drug-testing agency of U.S. Olympics athletes (see usantidoping.org). As Koller (2006) pointed out (and as U.S. officials learned in Lausanne in 1999), sporting bodies in other nations did not respect the methods through which the United States screened its athletes for performance-enhancing substances. With the Salt Lake City Olympics of 2002 on the athletic horizon, U.S. officials realized that they needed to enhance drug-testing efforts. Politically, although the Select Task Force on Drug Externalization of the United States Olympic Committee (USOC) received credit for establishing USADA, Koller (2006) explained that, in reality, the Office of National Drug Control Policy (ONDCP), headed by General Barry McCaffrey, as well as the U.S. Congress, played significant roles in the formation of USADA. For legal reasons, USADA needed to be recognized as a private entity, because if the agency could be considered an arm of the state, then Constitutional rights to privacy and due process would make drug testing significantly more complicated. In fact, when Congress turned up the proverbial heat on Major League Baseball in 2005, Donald Fehr, head of the Major League Baseball Players Association (MLBPA), grounded his objections to rigorous drug-testing procedures in Constitutional protections against search and seizure (Denham, 2007). Had Congress not become involved, Fehr may have experienced greater difficulty with the Constitutional arguments that he advanced in government hearings.

In the case of USADA, the agency has the power to test athletes randomly, in an unannounced fashion, and can also determine whether athletes should be disqualified for "non-analytical positives," when sport participants do not fail drug tests but are considered to have tested positive based on other evidence (e.g., a cancelled check to a known drug supplier, written correspondence with a supplier about dosages, testimony in a court of law, and so forth). Perhaps the most prominent track athlete to have been confronted with a non-analytical positive by USADA is Olympian Marion Jones. At the 2000 Games, held in Sydney, Australia, Jones won five medals, three of them gold, but in doing so, she used performance-enhancing substances supplied by BALCO (see Longman, 2008; Thompson and Vinton, 2008). When representatives of USADA confronted Jones in 2004, she threatened a lawsuit if she was not allowed to compete for a position on the 2004 U.S. Olympic squad. By October 2007, however, Jones had pled guilty to lying to federal investigators in the BALCO case, besides lying about her role in a check-fraud case involving fellow sprinter Tim Montgomery, father to her first child (Longman, 2008). She ultimately served six months in prison.

Although Jones may indeed have lied about using performance-enhancing drugs and about her involvement in the check-fraud case, the price she paid for her dishonesty—having to return her Olympic medals, declare bankruptcy, and serve time in federal prison—far exceeded the nearly clean slate that many juiced athletes have been afforded. Her story is indicative of the problems encountered when considering the overall fairness of doping policy in sports. Jones may not have been innocent, but treating her as a fallen hero who took actions that clean athletes did not shows tremendous naivety—and in some cases, deliberate castigation of the athlete—on the part of journalists and sporting officials. When Jones left prison in August 2008, newspapers described her as "disgraced" (Longman, 2008). Doug Logan, then a recently appointed chief executive of USA Track & Field, encouraged U.S. president George W. Bush to refrain from commuting Jones' sentence:

> To reduce Ms. Jones's sentence or pardon her would send a horrible message to young people who idolized her, reinforcing the notion that you can cheat and be entitled to get away with it. A pardon would also send the wrong message to the international community. Few things are more globally respected than the Olympic Games, and to pardon one of the biggest frauds perpetuated on the Olympic movement would be nothing less than thumbing our collective noses at the world. (Longman 2008, p. D1)

To some extent, athletic officials are expected to make such statements, given that part of their charge is to maintain the perceived sanctity of sports. Such characterizations keep advertisers and casual observers relatively content, removed from the realities of elite competition. Tens of millions have witnessed the extraordinary accomplishments of world-class athletes, whether those achievements refer to winning the Tour de France multiple times in succession, hitting more than 70 home runs in one baseball season, or throwing a discus farther than anyone would have thought possible. Spectators have been conditioned to expect the spectacular, and in some cases, spectacular athletic feats can be performed only with chemical assistance. But rather than acknowledge this basic truth, those associated with sports, especially at elite levels, experience an institutional pressure to attribute success to hard work and dedication. Such a practice invariably leads to scapegoating, as select individuals find themselves characterized as moral failures and cheaters. In truth, morality does not vary to the degree that sport officials and the media would have audiences believe.

Media Representations, Government Hearings, and Public Policy in the 21st Century

In June 2002 a former MLB Most Valuable Player named Ken Caminiti (now deceased) told *Sports Illustrated* as part of a drug expose that approximately half of all professional baseball players used AAS to enhance performance (see Verducci, 2002). As Denham (2004b) explained, the Caminiti allegations proved significant in that they helped to trigger a collective demand among sport journalists that Major League Baseball clean up the national pastime; to that end, just three months following the *Sports Illustrated* exposé and the media coverage that it prompted, professional baseball instituted a drug-testing procedure.

As history has shown, however, the drug-testing program implemented in 2002 lacked rigor and substance. MLB commissioner Bud Selig has said that he agreed to the limited drug-testing program, implemented as part of a larger labor agreement in August 2002, to avert a strike that had been threatened by the MLBPA (Denham, 2007). Unfortunately for Selig and fellow executives, although play did continue that season, the BALCO scandal in 2003 kept the issue of drugs in sports in the news, and when U.S. president George W. Bush in his January 2004 State of the Union Address urged sport officials to conduct a more vigilant fight against performance-enhancing drug use, U.S. policy makers seized the moment. Congressional hearings took place seemingly as quickly as they could be scheduled.

On March 10, 2004, John McCain, then chairman of the U.S. Senate Committee on Commerce, Science, and Transportation, presided over an initial set of hearings titled "Steroid Use in Amateur and Professional Sports." McCain reiterated what Bush had said during the 2004 State of the Union Address, chastising baseball, in particular, for not instituting a rigorous drug-testing program. Donald Fehr,

---

U.S. President George W. Bush Discusses the Use of Performance-Enhancing Substances in Athletics during the 2004 State of the Union Address

In January 2004, in his annual address to the nation, U.S. president George W. Bush encouraged athletes and their coaches to begin setting a positive example for impressionable adolescents by halting the use of steroids and other performance-enhancing drugs. Media reports of steroid use in baseball had helped bring the issue to the forefront, and Bush reiterated the concerns expressed by many sport columnists. "To help children make right choices," he said, "they need good examples. Athletics play such an important role in our society, but, unfortunately, some in professional sports are not setting much of an example." The president continued:

> The use of performance-enhancing drugs like steroids in baseball, football, and other sports is dangerous, and it sends the wrong message—that there are shortcuts to accomplishment, and that performance is more important than character. So tonight I call on team owners, union representatives, coaches, and players to take the lead, to send the right signal, to get tough, and to get rid of steroids now.

From a political standpoint, protecting the welfare of young people has long been used as a policy rationale, and in the weeks following the 2004 address, U.S. policy makers began holding hearings addressing the use of steroids in sports and society. Political scientists have observed the power of U.S. presidents to build policy agendas (see Graber, 2006), and when a controversial subject is addressed during a prime-time address to the nation, the issue tends to move up on the agenda.

representing the MLBPA, testified along with MLB commissioner Selig, National Football League (NFL) commissioner Paul Tagliabue, and NFL player representative Gene Upshaw. Tagliabue and Upshaw spoke of how the NFL had allocated $10 million annually to antidrug programs, and how the league had cooperated with USADA to develop a drug-testing research center in Utah.

Although the testimony of Tagliabue and Upshaw appeared factually accurate, it told a story quite different from that related by retired NFL player Steve Courson, who in 2005 characterized NFL officials as being "a prisoner to their own public relations myth" (Barker, 2008, p. D12). Continuing, Courson lamented, "The level of deception and exploitation that the NFL requires to do business still amazes me." Courson had been a source for the 1985 *Sports Illustrated* report on drug use in professional football (Johnson, 1985), and he had written about his own steroid use in his autobiography *False Glory* (Courson and Schreiber, 1991). He explained in his autobiography how coming clean about drug use had alienated him from coaches and other players, who appeared incredulous when Courson broke the code of silence expected among all who played and coached in the NFL.

To an extent, the type of posturing to which Courson referred took place one day after the March 10 hearings that McCain had conducted on Capitol Hill. U.S. senator Joseph Biden introduced legislation that would become the Anabolic Steroid Control Act of 2004—an act that added steroid precursors such as androstenedione to the list of Schedule III controlled substances. Biden had sponsored the Anabolic Steroid Control Act of 1990 as well, and his presence symbolized the lack of progress that had been made with the earlier legislation. Illicit use of AAS by adolescents had increased during the 1990s, especially among young women (Denham, 2006), and the addition of new substances to an ineffective law made the 2004 legislation appear somewhat dubious. The legislation also illustrated a common practice in policy-making arenas, namely that of discounting the failures of existing laws in favor of introducing *more* legislation—and seeking news coverage for having done so.

As with hearings held toward passage of the Anabolic Steroid Control Act of 1990, those related to the Anabolic Steroid Control Act of 2004 included testimony from individuals who had experienced the adverse consequences of steroid use. Testifying in 2004 was the father of a young man who had committed suicide as a possible consequence of steroid use, a convicted steroid dealer, and a former boxer and double-amputee named Bob Hazelton. The retired boxer, Hazelton, revealed that he had once injected himself with Armor All upholstery protectant, believing it to be a steroid that he had purchased (Denham, 2006). Besides those who had experienced adversity because of AAS use, a series of public policy makers as well as individuals with the Drug Enforcement Administration (DEA) and USADA testified before the House and the Senate, supporting the addition of steroid precursors to existing legislation.

After the Anabolic Steroid Control Act of 2004 had become law, public policy makers continued to hold hearings addressing the use of performance-enhancing substances in Major League Baseball. In 2005 retired player Jose Canseco published *Juiced*, a tell-all book about drug use in professional baseball, and legislators capitalized on the buzz that the book had generated. As Denham (2007) reported, U.S. senators and representatives introduced several prospective policy measures in 2005, including the Drug Free Sports Act (H.R.1862), the Professional Sports Integrity Act (H.R.2516), the Clean Sports Act (S.1114, H.R.2565), and the Professional Sports Integrity and Accountability Act (S.1334). As introduced, each of those measures served as a politically constructed lever to force Major League Baseball to implement more rigorous drug-testing procedures; some of the levers appeared after a nationally televised hearing involving Canseco and some of his contemporaries.

Televised live by ESPN, the March 17, 2005, hearing on Capitol Hill included testimony from Canseco, Mark McGwire, Raphael Palmeiro, Curt Schilling, Sammy Sosa, and Frank Thomas. McGwire and Palmeiro fared poorly at this hearing. McGwire refused to give direct answers, and Palmeiro adamantly stated that he had not used steroids; he was later suspended by MLB for testing positive for AAS. Again proceeding from the notion that public policy makers tend to use events such as the March 17 hearing to demonstrate political initiative before constituents, lawmakers criticized the players for setting a poor example for American adolescents, supporting their comments with testimony from the parents of two young men who committed suicide while using AAS. Because few would consider questioning the bereaved, especially in a public forum, the need to protect impressionable adolescents again proved unassailable as a policy rationale. Still, Denham (2007) identified the problems associated with government hearings and the politically expedient concerns of policy makers:

> Unfortunately, even if altruistic, these concerns will not be alleviated by punishing athletes in the professional ranks, for teenagers who choose to take steroids may do so for cosmetic reasons. Additionally, the fact that young women constitute the fastest growing population of steroid users undercuts the emulation rationale, as females generally do not seek to become professional baseball players. Both males and females may harm their health with bogus steroids obtained in bodybuilding gyms and via the Internet, and if lawmakers truly sought to protect young people from harmful substances, they would investigate why legislation such as the Anabolic Steroid Control Act of 1990 had not only failed to effect positive change, but may even have precipitated an increase in steroid use among at-risk populations. Alas, the analysis of existing legislation does not generate the kind of political capital that new legislation does and therefore the problems with adolescent steroid use will likely continue. (p. 390)

Although the acts proposed in the Senate and the House of Representatives accomplished what they had sought to do—to convince MLB players to agree to more rigorous drug-testing measures in 2005—the BALCO case in northern California again kept the drugs-in-sport issue salient to public policy makers and mass audiences. This time, a top-selling book, *Game of Shadows*, written by investigative reporters Mark Fainaru-Wada and Lance Williams (2006), chronicled the BALCO case and the alleged performance-enhancing drug use of star player Barry Bonds, among others. Following the March 2006 release of the book, MLB commissioner Bud Selig asked former U.S. senator George Mitchell to conduct a large-scale investigation of steroid use in professional baseball.

In December 2007 Mitchell released the findings of his investigation into performance-enhancing drug use in Major League Baseball. In assembling their final report, Mitchell and his investigators conducted more than 700 interviews, although it should be noted that the retired senator lacked subpoena power to question players whom the MLBPA had counseled to remain quiet. Mitchell (2007) summarized the roadblocks that he and his investigators encountered:

> The Players Association was largely uncooperative. (1) It rejected totally my requests for relevant documents. (2) It permitted one interview with its executive director, Donald Fehr; my request for an interview with its chief operating officer, Gene Orza, was refused. (3) It refused my request to interview the director of the Montreal laboratory that analyzes drug tests under baseball's drug program but permitted her to provide me with a letter addressing a limited number of issues. (4) I sent a memorandum to every active player in Major League Baseball encouraging each player to contact me or my staff if he had any relevant information. The Players Association sent out a companion memorandum that effectively discouraged players from cooperating. Not one player contacted me in response to my memorandum. (5) I received allegations of the illegal possession or use of performance enhancing substances by a number of current players. Through their representative, the Players Association, I asked each of them to meet with me so that I could provide them with information about the allegations and give them a chance to respond. Almost without exception they declined to meet or talk with me. (p. SR-7)

That passage is highly instructive for understanding the nature of doping in professional sports. Because Mitchell lacked subpoena power, his investigation could be only as complete as his interviewees would allow. Although he and his investigators collected thousands of primary and secondary documents pertaining to drug use, the documents generally required inferences to be drawn about what likely had transpired.

Kirk Radomski, a former clubhouse employee of the New York Mets, emerged as the most important source in the investigation, and through four interviews with Mitchell and law-enforcement officials, Radomski offered a lengthy list of players who he claimed had purchased AAS and human growth hormone from him. To the extent that Mitchell identified accused users of performance-enhancing drugs by name, his investigation eclipsed most of the public relations exercises that preceded it. Since December 2007 players named in the report have chosen both denial (e.g., pitcher Roger Clemens) and admission (e.g., pitcher Andy Pettitte) as strategies for restoring their images, and the identification of suspected AAS users has continued beyond *The Mitchell Report*.

In February 2009 *Sports Illustrated* reported that baseball superstar Alex Rodriguez had used AAS from 2001 through 2003 while playing for the Texas Rangers. Initially, Rodriguez said only, "You'll have to talk to the union" (Shaikin, 2009, p. D1), thus counting on the MLBPA to assist with damage control. Within days of the initial report, however, Rodriguez admitted to using AAS, stating that he had experimented with performance-enhancing drugs because of intense pressure to perform at an elite level. As Kepner (2009) reported in the *New York Times*,

> The admission also makes Rodriguez, who joined the Yankees in 2004 and has 553 career home runs, the most prominent baseball player to admit that he has knowingly used illegal substances. Three other equally famous players—Barry Bonds, Roger Clemens, and Mark McGwire—are widely suspected of having used performance enhancers, and have become infamous for their denials. (p. A1)

Attempting to preserve the integrity of Major League Baseball, Commissioner Bud Selig said that Rodriguez and others had "shamed the game" (Feinsand, 2009, p. 74) by using performance-enhancing substances, characterizing drug use as a moral failure instead of the systemic problem that it is. Additionally, while select members of the New York Yankees offered support for Rodriguez in the days following initial news reports, executives with the organization sought to distance themselves from their marquee player. Curry (2009) explained, "By not having individuals respond to Rodriguez's steroid admission, the Yankees were letting Rodriguez tell his own story and letting him absorb whatever criticism follows" (p. B13). The long-term consequences of that criticism will likely depend on the number of other MLB players who find themselves accused of using performance-enhancing drugs and whether sport fans, media companies, and advertisers of goods and services come to realize their indirect involvement.

Finally, in terms of high-profile players caught using performance-enhancing drugs, Manny Ramirez of the Los Angeles Dodgers received a 50-game suspension in 2009 after testing positive for a banned substance. Few players had been suspended for 50 games, and although drug use undoubtedly continues at some level, the Ramirez suspension did add a degree of credibility to the MLB drug-testing program. When athletes as prominent as Ramirez must watch games instead of participate in them, fans who buy tickets to see star players may choose to spend their money elsewhere.

The following list shows a timeline of significant events discussed in this chapter, beginning with the 1988 Olympic story involving Ben Johnson and concluding with the 2009 suspension of Ramirez. Taken both individually and as a whole, these events shed light on the directions in which doping policy may travel in future.

Significant Events Related to Doping Regulation and the Formation of Public Policy

- **1988**: Canadian sprinter Ben Johnson tests positive for the anabolic steroid stanozolol at the Seoul Olympics and forfeits a gold medal in the 100 meters. U.S. sprinter Carl Lewis, who had tested positive for small amounts of banned stimulants before the 1988 U.S. Olympic trials, receives the gold medal originally awarded to Johnson.

- **1988**: *Sports Illustrated* publishes dramatic article about the use of anabolic steroids in college football. Written by Tommy Chaikin, a former player at the University of South Carolina, and Rick Telander, a *Sports Illustrated* writer, "The Nightmare of Steroids" proves powerful enough to be included in the appendixes of subsequent congressional hearings about the use of steroids in sports and society.

- **1989**: U.S. policy makers hold hearings in reference to the Anabolic Steroid Restriction Act of 1989, partially the result of media reports and the Ben Johnson situation at the 1988 Seoul Olympics.

- **1990**: U.S. policy makers hold hearings in reference to the Anabolic Steroid Control Act of 1990, which, when signed into law, classifies steroids as a Schedule III controlled substance, to be regulated under the Omnibus Controlled Substances Act.

- **1991**: Ailing football player Lyle Alzado appears on the cover of *Sports Illustrated* and inside attributes his inoperable brain lymphoma to years of steroid abuse. Alzado dies in 1992.

■ **1994**: Congress passes the Dietary Supplement Health and Education Act. The act benefits the nutrition supplement industry, requiring the Food and Drug Administration to prove a product unsafe, as opposed to requiring supplement manufacturers to prove a product safe.

■ **1998**: Professional baseball players Mark McGwire and Sammy Sosa engage in a dramatic battle to break Roger Maris' longstanding record for most home runs in a season. McGwire breaks the record, with 70, but a reporter also spots the steroid precursor androstenedione in McGwire's locker.

■ **1998**: A major doping scandal occurs at the Tour de France when customs officials discover large quantities of substances such as erythropoietin in the luggage of cyclists.

■ **1999**: The World Anti-Doping Agency is created in response to the 1998 cycling scandal.

■ **2000**: Based on a recommendation from the U.S. Olympic Committee, the U.S. Anti-Doping Agency is created and given responsibility for drug-testing U.S. athletes in Olympic-related sports.

■ **2000**: U.S. sprinter Marion Jones wins three gold medals at the Sydney Olympics. She will later return the medals after she admits to using performance-enhancing substances.

■ **2002**: Retired baseball player Ken Caminiti (now deceased) tells *Sports Illustrated* that approximately half of all players in Major League Baseball use anabolic steroids to enhance performance. MLB institutes a drug-testing program as part of a larger labor agreement approximately three months later, in August 2002.

■ **2003**: The U.S. government investigates Bay Area Laboratories Co-Operative for distribution of performance-enhancing substances, implicating several professional athletes.

■ **2004**: In his State of the Union address, U.S. president George W. Bush discusses the use of performance-enhancing substances in sports.

■ **2004**: U.S. policy makers pass the Anabolic Steroid Control Act of 2004, adding steroid precursors such as androstenedione to the list of Schedule III controlled substances. Dehydroepiandrosterone is exempt.

■ **2005**: ESPN offers live coverage of a congressional hearing involving steroid use in professional baseball. U.S. policy makers subsequently "encourage" MLB to institute a more rigorous drug-testing program by introducing numerous legislative bills.

■ **2006**: Reporters Mark Fainaru-Wada and Lance Williams publish *Game of Shadows*, which links Barry Bonds with Bay Area Laboratories Co-Operative.

■ **2006**: Major League Baseball commissioner Bud Selig calls on former U.S. senator George Mitchell to lead an investigation into drug use in professional baseball.

■ **2007**: *The Mitchell Report* is released, implicating players such as Roger Clemens and Andy Pettitte in the use of performance-enhancing substances.

■ **2009**: *Sports Illustrated* reports that baseball superstar Alex Rodriguez had used steroids to enhance performance. Rodriguez ultimately confirms the allegations.

■ **2009**: MLB suspends Manny Ramirez of the Los Angeles Dodgers for 50 games after a positive drug test. Suspension lends a degree of credibility to the MLB drug-testing program.

Future Trends

As indicated at the beginning of this chapter, the regulation of performance-enhancing substances involves multiple stakeholders, some of whom stand to benefit from the accomplishments that drugs like steroids facilitate. In the coming years, negotiations among key stakeholders will likely involve the continued incorporation of Olympic-style drug-testing procedures into professional sports. At present, labor unions have been able to restrict certain types of testing, relying on one of the most powerful levers available to organized labor—going on strike. Because athletics play a prominent role in American society and billions of dollars are at stake, league leaders and public officials are cautious in challenging unions. Compromise and negotiation are essential, and they are likely to result, at best, in a tapering of use of performance-enhancing drugs rather than the categorical elimination of chemical substances. Additionally, because many professional athletes earn millions of dollars each year, they can afford to obtain substances that drug testers cannot identify.

If public policy makers are to succeed in reducing steroid use in amateur and professional sports, they will need to examine why existing legislation has failed instead of simply enacting more policy. As an example, in 2005 the United States Government Accountability Office (GAO) sent a report to U.S. congressmen Tom Davis and Henry Waxman, who had conducted hearings about steroid use in sports and society. GAO investigators indicated that they were able to obtain AAS easily without a prescription through the Internet. The GAO also reported on the countries from which it had obtained AAS and identified some of the obstacles faced by law-enforcement agencies in attempts at interdiction. At JFK airport in New York, the GAO noted, international mail facilities process approximately 1.3 million pieces of mail per day, making it difficult to identify drug shipments. Additionally, at the time, sentencing guidelines for AAS differed from those of other Schedule III controlled substances; steroid dealers received considerably less time in prison. The GAO report gave Davis and Waxman the political justification that they sought (i.e., a rationale for spending taxpayer dollars on drug programs), but to actually affect change, policy makers will need to address these kinds of practical considerations ahead of holding perfunctory hearings about the dangers of drug use.

Conclusion

Athletes have used performance-enhancing substances for centuries, but only in recent decades have sport and public officials established policies that regulate drug use. And although those policies have been enacted to help curb the use of chemical substances, they often appear to cause as many problems as they solve. This result is not the fault of those who institute regulations; it is symptomatic of a society that moves in one, and only one, direction where athletic achievements are concerned—forward. Because certain achievements in sports (e.g., hitting more than 70 home runs in a single baseball season) appear to require the use of performance-enhancing substances, those who participate in sports and those who attempt to regulate drug use engage in a perpetual cat-and-mouse game that does not offer systemic remedies but instead singles out athletes who happen to get caught using drugs. Those individuals stand to be vilified by sport journalists and officials alike. Such portrayals help to preserve the perceived sanctity and integrity of sporting competition, even though the athletes may have acted in a manner consistent with the majority, not the minority, of their peers.

In proposing legislation such as the Anabolic Steroid Control Act of 1990, as well as its 2004 extension, public policy makers responded to dramatic media reports of alleged crises (Denham, 1997; Houlihan, 2002). Such crises appear to threaten the well-being of at-risk populations and the fairness of competition, and by stepping in at opportune times, officials seek to demonstrate initiative before their constituents. Absent in legislation grounded in dominant conceptions of morality is a thorough consideration of the problems that prospective laws may introduce. Although the dramatic anecdotes that help to precipitate the formation of public policy should not be ignored, they do need to be considered as comparably independent events that are sometimes strung together for legislative convenience. Prudent policy is seldom achieved through moral panic, as the case of performance-enhancing drugs has demonstrated.

PART IV

Sport and Globalization

The title of the Thomas Freidman's 2005 best seller, *The World is Flat*, invokes the sport metaphor of a level playing field to describe the effects of globalization. Advances in technology have made the worldwide exchange of ideas, information, and goods easier, breaking down barriers to participation, fostering increased integration of national economies, and expanding both the size of markets and the diversity of players involved in those markets.

Throughout this book, we have illustrated that professional sports are big business and that the influences of globalization are as apparent in the sport industry as they are in any other. American sport leagues have developed an explicit agenda of global expansion—staging exhibitions, broadcasting events, and scouting for talent across the world. The factors behind this agenda are similar to those that have driven the global expansion of many other American industries: maturing or stagnating demand in home markets, the related desire to create overseas markets for consumption, and the allure of less expensive labor.

As a global endeavor, sports also reflect and become entangled in international relations, sometimes entering the realm of foreign policy as a means of exerting influence on or isolating unfriendly regimes. During the Cold War era, politically motivated boycotts disrupted the 1980 Moscow Winter Olympics and the 1984 Los Angeles Summer Games. Throughout much of the 1960s, '70s, and '80s, South Africa was barred from international competition in rugby, soccer, cricket, and the Olympic Games as part of a wider cultural boycott that many believe played an important role in ending the nation's segregationist apartheid policy.

Part IV of this book includes perspectives on sport and globalization. Chapters focus on how sport affects and is affected by international relations and the phenomenon of globalization.

In chapter 11, Gregory Andranovich, Matthew Burbank, and Charles Heying consider the relationship of globalization and a changing world economy to the Olympic Games. The chapter contrasts the varied experiences of Los Angeles, Atlanta, and Mexico City as host cities to explore the changing political economy of this international event and illustrate the shifting role of the state, the market, and civil society in resource allocation.

Chapters 12 and 13 examine Major League Baseball's efforts at global expansion, which mirror the business agenda of traditional American industries and reflect the state of American international relations.

In chapter 12, Charles Santo discusses Major League Baseball's global search for labor, with a focus on contrasting results and reactions in two Caribbean nations: the Dominican Republic and Cuba. The chapter explores how American baseball's interactions in those nations reflect their broader political and economic relations with the United States.

In chapter 13, Mark Nagel, Matt Brown, Dan Rascher, and Chad McEvoy provide a parallel look at baseball and globalization, examining Major League Baseball's expanding search for consumer markets. The chapter focuses on the league's efforts to organize the inaugural World Baseball Classic tournament in 2006, highlighting the associated economic, political, marketing, and legal conflicts. This story illustrates some of the growing pains and policy implications associated with globalization through the lens of sport.

CHAPTER 11

Political Economy of the Olympic Games

Greg Andranovich,* Matthew J. Burbank,
and Charles H. Heying

I n a new economy that actively seeks leisure and consumption investment and spending, sport is no longer just about athletic competition. Sport is transnational big business. And in an era of globalization, sports that command an international audience, such as soccer, are near the top of an entertainment hierarchy that includes economic, political, and cultural underpinnings that shape and are reflected in the global political economy. At the pinnacle of the international sport entertainment hierarchy sit the Olympic Games.

This chapter examines the political economy of the Olympic Games. The key features of this topic include globalization, a new economy built on leisure and consumption spending, and the politics of urban regeneration playing out in a shifting arena of local, national, and international decision makers. The chapter begins with a discussion of the changing world economy and its relationship to the political economy of the Olympic Games. We then examine the experiences of three cities that have hosted the Olympic Games: Los Angeles, Atlanta, and Mexico City. The chapter concludes with a discussion of how these cities' experiences highlight important lessons in the political economy of the Olympic Games.

Globalization, the New Economy, and Political Economy

Globalization, as we use the concept, refers to the increased interdependence and interpenetration among nations. The foundations of globalization rest on several

---

*Dedicated to the memory of Neslihan Girginkoc, basketballer, runner, and discus thrower back in the day, 1956–2007.

developments that occurred in previous decades, most notably the technological advances in telecommunications and electronics that became prominent in the 1970s, the economic changes resulting from President Nixon's decision to abandon the gold standard and effectively end the Bretton Woods agreement, and the political crisis that led to the rise of a variety of antisystemic movements—including human rights, feminism, and environmentalism—in the aftermath of the "world revolutions" of 1968 (Wallerstein, 2005). The result was a breakdown in the extant patterns of interstate and economic relations that had provided a period of economic growth since the end of World War II. The more than 20 years of sustained economic growth benefited many people in the industrialized world, although often at the expense of the remainder of the world's people. The ways that all nations facilitated, mediated, or blocked the penetration of Western economic values, cultural mores, and political demands depended on the particular historical relations that existed between and among nations. After 1968, however, the world became more turbulent and the waves of change became global. The global economic restructuring that occurred, and continues seemingly unabated for the moment, ushered in a new economy whose underlying features are privatization, the rising importance of financial speculation, and the attempt to roll back the state's role in redistribution as reliance on the individual has become a central tenet of economic policy. In the industrialized nations, this change was marked by the economic shift from manufacturing toward leisure and consumption services. These economic changes have influenced the domestic political economies of nations, and governments have attempted to mitigate the effect of the global economy on income distributions and patterns of uneven development. One attempted solution has been for national and local governments to seek new sources of investment, including the shifting of public funds, for the growing segments of the new economy.

One key to understanding the effects of globalization is to consider how the changing nature of physical space affects the new economy and how various actors—individuals, firms, and states—"imagine" these changes. For Appadurai (1990), the cultural aspects of mobility in the new economy provide a new wrinkle that must be addressed. How governments deal with the consequences of cultural mobility (including words, images, ideas, money, and people) is the public policy challenge for decision makers. This brief statement about the dynamic nature of the capitalist world system suggests that globalization, and the rise of the new economy, is a complex process and needs to be analyzed in historical context, not simply taken as natural and inevitable, or even as desirable.

Political economy is about resource allocation. As such, political economy examines various organizational approaches to resource allocation and asks whether civil society, the state, or the market provides the "best" mode of allocation. "Best" here refers to matching the process of allocation to its consequences under the normative proposition of transforming society toward more democratic, just, and egalitarian relations. The ascendance of the market system undermined the state and civil society as alternate modes of resources allocation. Still, as Polyani (1957) pointed out, this rise of the market economy resulted in a double movement of social transformation. First, the market penetrated all areas of human activity, and the resulting uneven development led to disruptive and destabilizing consequences. The second part of the movement was the demand for social protection from those negative consequences, and this demand required a renewed role for the state (Hettne, 1995). But what role should the state play? Scott's (2006) nuanced discussion of the key variables that policy makers must address in the new economy suggested that a formulaic approach might not simply ameliorate the inequities of a market economy. Indeed, the bifurcated nature of the jobs in the new economy suggests that inequality, a hallmark of the uneven development of the capitalist economy, will remain with us. Scott's argument was that in the new economy, the relations between networks of producers, the local labor markets that coalesce around them, and the organization of creativity that must develop between and among producers and creative labor, requires "a wider concern for conviviality and camaraderie (which need to be distinguished from the mechanical concept of 'diversity') [or] the urban community as a whole is doomed to remain radically unfinished" (2006, p. 15). Although this is easier said than done, city governments everywhere are supporting urban regeneration that includes culture and amenities in part as a response to fierce interurban competition (Clark et al., 2002; Smith, 2007). Thus, we return to the fundamental question of political economy: In the new economy is the market the "best" mode of allocation for resources, or is there a need for a greater role for the state or for civil society?

Political Economy and the Olympic Games

Are the Olympics Games merely a sporting event, or do the Games carry additional economic, cultural, political, and spatial import? The Olympics have since their inception been closely associated with an ideology of social and technical progress. In particular, these international sporting competitions have been used as a tool for expressing national goals and political agendas (Espy, 1979; Hill, 1996; Lenskyj, 2000). In addition, the economic value of the Olympics has increased dramatically over time, largely because of the telecommunications revolution and the increased amounts paid for national and international broadcast rights (Barney, Wenn, and Martyn, 2002; Larson and Park, 1993). Table 11.1 shows the increased revenues from television broadcast rights from 1960 to the 2008 Summer Games. With these increased revenues came greater commercialization of the Games (Magdalinski, Schimmel, and Chandler, 2005; Tomlinson, 2005), and with greater resources and the need to control their brand, the International Olympic Committee adapted as a transnational organization (Guttmann, 1994; Houlihan, 2005). Cities, too, began to respond to the greater prominence of the Olympics, and the competition to host the Games intensified (Andranovich, Burbank, and Heying, 2001; Shoval, 2002). In turn, the increased visibility of the Olympics and its close association with product marketing meant that various movements, both social and sport-related, have been co-opted into the Olympic family or have become a source of resistance (Burbank, Heying, and Andranovich, 2000; Kidd, 2005; Lenskyj, 2000; Schaffer and Smith, 2000).

Among assessments of the political economy of the Olympic Games, one topic that deserves particular scrutiny is the economic impact of the Games on their host cities. Kasimati (2003), for example, examined studies of the economic impact of hosting the Olympics and found that before the 1984 Games, no impact studies had been conducted. Since then, a variety of cities have conducted impact analyses

TABLE 11.1

Olympic Global Broadcast Revenues

Olympic Games	Host city	Broadcast revenue, US$ (millions)
1960	Rome	1.2
1964	Tokyo	1.6
1968	Mexico City	9.8
1972	Munich	17.8
1976	Montreal	34.9
1980	Moscow	88.0
1984	Los Angeles	287.0
1988	Seoul	402.6
1992	Barcelona	636.0
1996	Atlanta	898.2
2000	Sydney	1,331.5
2004	Athens	1,496.0
2008	Beijing	1,737.0

Data from IOC Factsheet, Revenue Generation and Distribution, update, Dec. 2005; IOC Marketing Media Guide; Beijing 2008, p. 5.

during the bidding phase and after the Games ended. Kasimati concluded that the rosy picture painted by studies produced during the bidding phase was "not confirmed by ex-post analyses and this therefore prompts the need for improved theory" (Kasimati, 2003, p. 442). Preuss (2000, 2002), who has conducted extensive analysis of the economics of the Games, suggested that since the 1980s, two things can almost be guaranteed about hosting the Games: First, the local organizing committees can be almost certain that there will be a financial surplus after the Games, largely because of the IOC's negotiation of international sponsorship and television contracts. Second, the Games have expanded to the point where huge sport facilities and new infrastructure for athletes, tourists, and the media are required. This gigantism is evidenced in the number of ticket sales and the fact that media representatives outnumber athletes at the Olympic Games (Preuss, 2002, p. 15). The size of the Olympics also increases the opportunity that cities have to use the Games as a basis for wide-scale redevelopment as Barcelona did for the 1992 Games and as Beijing did for the 2008 Games (Broudehoux, 2007; Essex and Chalkley, 1998). Such extensive redevelopment of cities, however, raises the question of whose interests are being served by the redevelopment because the new sport infrastructure is often at odds with the needs of residents.

The growth of the Olympics has resulted in another challenge for policy makers: the opportunity costs of hosting the Games. Essex and Chalkley (2003) identify crucial questions that local policy makers need to address: (1) Are local funds being diverted from service and education needs to support Olympic infrastructure? (2) Are local taxes being increased to pay for the new infrastructure? (3) Will the Olympics displace poor people or disrupt their neighborhoods? (4) If the costs of staging the Games continues to grow, will cities in developing nations ever be able to host the Games? Essex and Chalkley (2003, p. 14) noted that the IOC's Olympic Games Study Commission examined the issue of gigantism and concluded that it was time to manage the growth of the Games to preserve their attractiveness. All of this is part of the broader context for understanding the political economy of the Olympics.

Cities pursue the Olympic Games for three important reasons: tourism, image, and regeneration (Heying, Burbank, and Andranovich, 2007). The rise of tourism, and the response to it by nations, is a clear indication that the international economy has changed. The pursuit of leisure, both for its own reward and as part of business travel, is a growth sector of the new economy, and the development of an "infrastructure of play" is often the result (Judd, 2003). In 2005, for example, the Travel Industry Association of America (2006) reported that domestic and international travel added $650 billion to the U.S. economy, generating 8 million jobs, $171 billion in payroll income, and $105 billion in federal, state, and local tax revenues. It is no wonder that cities, states, and the federal government encourage tourism development. At the city level, policy makers attempt to attract travelers through the branding of places and by focusing regeneration strategies to attract investment funds and human capital (Smith, 2007).

Although discussion of the Olympics is often couched solely in terms of potential economic benefit, any analysis of the political economy of the Olympic Games, we argue, needs to be situated in the context of the broader issues of the politics and cultural imagination, as well as the economics, of these events. The Olympic Games are not just another one-off event; the bid period, the organizing period for the host city, and the open-ended legacy period following the Closing Ceremonies provide cities with a decade-long planning period and an infinite legacy horizon that can be oriented toward the values of the Olympic Games. The Olympics are a critical opportunity either for development or for exploitation, and the choice is made in policy decisions. Next, we briefly present three cities' host experiences to illustrate the political economy of the Olympics, characterizing each city according to the three modes of allocating resources: the market, the state, and civil society. Each mode illustrates different pressures and contextual influences, and we believe that this exercise demonstrates the importance of using political economy as an analytical frame and not just accepting the idea of hosting the Games as an inevitable, or even a desirable, policy outcome.

Los Angeles: The Market Matters Most

The Olympic Games are tightly controlled by the International Olympic Committee (IOC). The IOC sets the criteria for applicants to bid to host the Games, and by IOC rules the hosts must be cities. Bidding to host the Summer or Winter Olympic Games is a decade-long, two-phase process. The first phase requires winning the support of the national Olympic committee (for example, the United States Olympic Committee for American cities). These national candidates then compete on the international level in a second phase of the competition to host the Games. Only one city, Los Angeles, wanted to host the 1984 Olympics. The violence that marred the pre-Olympic activities in Mexico City in 1968 and the Games in Munich in 1972, coupled with the high costs absorbed by the residents of Montreal to host the 1976 Games had taken the luster off the Olympics. Some critics even said that the Olympic ideals of amateurism, athleticism, sportsmanship, and international understanding had been lost and replaced by the nationalism, commercialism, and professionalism (Nixon, 1988). It was in this atmosphere that Los Angeles made its bid to host the 1984 Games.

The negotiations were difficult. The IOC was leery of the local bid committee's description of the Games as spartan and needed to be assured that this cost-cutting language was intended only to address the fears of locals and not to challenge the authority of the IOC. Furthermore, the IOC needed to be convinced that a referendum on the Olympics would not be held after the Games were awarded (as had occurred in Denver after the city had been awarded the 1976 Winter Games). Another point of contention was the IOC's rule 4, which stipulated that the host city and the national Olympic committee take complete financial responsibility for the Games. Because the City of Los Angeles did not intend to be directly involved in financing or organizing the Games, these activities were to be handled by a private organization. As the negotiations continued, other issues arose including the sale of television rights, providing new facilities for the athletes, and demands by international sport federations. When it appeared as if Los Angeles would withdraw its bid, the IOC dropped the rule 4 stipulation and awarded the Games to the city. The U.S. Olympic Committee agreed to the Los Angeles plan and received a promise of a 40 percent share from any surplus (profit) from the Games.

The Los Angeles Olympic Organizing Committee (LAOOC) developed a new model for host cities—use existing venues whenever possible, build new facilities only when necessary and when paid for by a sponsor, and organize to facilitate the conduct of the Games. Almost every bid city since has claimed to follow the Los Angeles approach, although none has achieved the same result. The Los Angeles Olympics have been called the Capitalist Games because of the organizational strategy that focused on harnessing the power of the market (Nixon, 1988). Senn (1999) showed the interrelationships between the developers and financiers in the directorship of the IOC, which sets policy. At the level of practice, the Los Angeles Games reset the organization of the economics of the Olympics. The LAOOC was the first organizing committee in the history of the Games to be run entirely as a private organization. The LAOOC also sought new sources of revenue aggressively. This approach was so successful that the IOC adopted it after the 1984 Games, and today it is known as the Olympics Program (TOP). As table 11.2 shows, the IOC has seen sizable growth in its revenues since the initiation of TOP, which has increased its control of the Games.

To raise revenues, the LAOOC identified four potential sources: corporate sponsor, television rights, investment income, and tickets (Wilson, 2004). Corporate sponsorships were limited to make them more expensive. Three levels of sponsorship participation were offered—official sponsor, official supplier, and official licensee. This scheme resulted in 164 companies paying the LAOOC $127 million in cash, services, and products to participate in the Games. Television broadcast rights were sold to ABC and foreign broadcasters, raising $287 million, far surpassing the amount paid by NBC to broadcast the 1980 Moscow Games. Because most of this money was received up front, additional income resulted from investment. Finally, the more traditional revenue sources of ticket sales and commemorative coins brought in $156 million and $36 million, respectively.

In its approach to the sport venues themselves, the LAOOC made it clear that it was producing a sporting event, not doing community development work. The experience of the community can be illustrated in one of the most important locations for the 1984 Games, the Los Angeles Coliseum, where the Opening and Closing Ceremonies and track and field events were held. Although the LAOOC opened a field office in the community, provided a new gym floor, and supported youth activity programs in the South Los Angeles area, the bulk of the nearly $1.8 million in improvements that went into the Exposition Park area were exclusively for Olympic venue needs—new irrigation and lighting, new restrooms, roadway and parking lot repairs, landscaping, recreational equipment, and new signs. The Coliseum also received some repairs, but these were done as part of a proposed package to entice the NFL Oakland Raiders to Los Angeles and were to be repaid to the LAOOC. A new swim stadium was built at the University of Southern California, but the $4 million cost was funded entirely by McDonald's franchises. As the Exposition Park experience showed, the desire to conduct the Summer Games in a businesslike manner was reflected in LAOOC planning and practice, which supported business and institutional interests first. When the LAOOC closed its books in 1988, the tally showed a surplus of $230 million (Wilson, 2004, p. 209). A new era had dawned for the Olympics, one in which the market provided the key incentive, gain, to lure potential hosts into the competition to host the Games. The pursuit of Olympic revenue became an end in itself, and the pursuit of social progress was relegated to a background position.

TABLE 11.2

Olympic Sponsorship Program

Program	Olympiad	No. of partners	National Olympic committees	US$ (millions)
TOP I	1985–88	9	159	95
TOP II	1989–92	12	169	175
TOP III	1993–96	10	197	279
TOP IV	1997–2000	11	199	579
TOP V	2001–04	11	202	603
TOP VI	2005–08	12	202	866

Data from IOC Factsheet, Revenue Generation and Distribution, update, Dec. 2005; IOC Marketing Media Guide; Beijing 2008, pgs. 4,11.

Atlanta: The State Matters Most

In contrast to organizers in Los Angeles, city leaders in Atlanta wanted the city government directly involved with the Games so that city residents would benefit. The role of the local government entity in this process featured a redistributive vision that sought the transformation of Atlanta into a more democratic, just, and egalitarian place. The city's mayor, Maynard Jackson, described his vision using a metaphor of "the twin peaks of Atlanta's Mount Olympus." The first peak was to "stage the best Olympic Games ever," and the second peak was to "simultaneously uplift the people of Atlanta and fight poverty in the process" (Roughton, 1991, p. F3). The mayor's vision was not his alone; it reflected the expectations that many Atlanta residents had as they saw a future with better transportation, better housing, and better jobs paid at least in part through the bounty generated by hosting the Olympics. Given the history of Atlanta politics, a distinct racial undertone marked the relationship between city government, which tended to reflect the concerns of the predominantly African American residents and voters, and the local organizing committee, which tended to reflect the concerns of the largely white business community. The tension between the goals of the local organizing committee, to host the Games in a competent and appealing fashion, and the city, to address social inequities, became a substantial part of the story of the 1996 Atlanta Olympics.

As part of its efforts to address the concerns of residents, city officials established a new city department to address the ring neighborhoods—the Corporation for Olympic Development (CODA). CODA was born two years after Atlanta was named the host city, but it was late getting up and running and suffered from the lack of a dedicated source of funds. The so-called Olympic ring neighborhoods that were intended to be the focus of CODA's efforts included many of the city's poorest residents, and estimates for the cost of redeveloping those neighborhoods were between $500 million and $1 billion. One key problem was the differences in outlook between political, neighborhood, and business leaders (Burbank, Andranovich, and Heying, 2001, pp. 88–93). Mayor Jackson saw CODA as a way to generate public and private funds for bricks-and-mortar projects like sewers, bridges, and streets. Neighborhood activists focused on the immediate need for housing and jobs, whereas business leaders articulated neighborhood development in terms of urban landscaping, city parks, and pedestrian corridors. The local press described the mission of CODA as "making the city presentable" for the Games, whereas Olympic ring neighborhoods were regarded by Olympic organizers are being "outside the fences"—meaning that those areas were not considered part of an official venue and therefore would not receive Olympic funds.

The leaders of CODA blundered into unnecessary confrontations with the neighborhood activists by seeking city council approval to have some neighborhoods declared slum areas. The designation was supposed to give CODA special city powers to act on code violations and expedite condemnation procedures, but neighborhood activists who remembered the urban renewal displacements of the 1960s protested both the symbolism of the designation and its potential to hurt existing residents who had little ability to comply with the orders. In the end, CODA focused its efforts on what it termed "immediate opportunity areas," where matching funds from government, business, or foundations could be found. These areas were closely matched to the business and the local organizing committee agenda favoring downtown urban landscaping and high-visibility tourist and Olympic corridors.

Less than two years before the Olympics were to begin, the political tide in Atlanta shifted dramatically. A new business-friendly mayor, Bill Campbell, took office. When a major water main broke in downtown Atlanta, Campbell was forced to impose mandatory water rationing for two days and coverage in the local media raised the possibility of an Olympic embarrassment. Mayor Campbell pushed for new city bonds to pay for repairs, and his support among business leaders paid off when Coca-Cola chairman Robert Goizueta called on business leaders to take a leadership role in supporting public initiatives to help the city prepare for the Olympics or risk being embarrassed in front of the world. After 25 years of failed ballot measures, the bonds required to repair the city's water infrastructure passed. But the $225 million bond to upgrade the water system would double water rates over a three-year period, and a $150 million general obligation bond would, over the 20 years of repayment, be redeemed by tax revenues that might have gone to other city needs. Still, the Olympics provided political cover to displace these financial impacts.

The passage of the $150 million bond issue meant that CODA had a funding stream. But by this time, CODA had a new agenda that was favorable to downtown interests and focused on visible Olympic corridors. This agenda represented CODA's pragmatic response to federal dollars, the selective interests of private funders, and wording of the bond issue. Of the $76 million in CODA funds, roughly 46 percent was spent to improve streets and parks in the downtown business area, 31 percent went to pedestrian corridors leading to Olympic venues, and 14 percent was spent on other markets, parks, and art. Only nine percent of the total was expended specifically for neighborhood streets. No money was spent on housing. CODA closed its doors in June 1997.

Under Mayor Campbell, the city also attempted to capture a share of the lucrative Olympic marketing efforts. In the post–Los Angeles era, the sale of corporate sponsorships has been carefully controlled by the IOC, which has the intent of maintaining long-term relationships with major international corporations. The benefits of these sponsorships thus flow to the IOC and local organizing committees to support their common goal of putting on the Games. Governments of the host cities, however, are largely left out of these arrangements. In the run up to the Atlanta Games, the city attempted to find a way to benefit from these revenues.

The city's plan, managed by an entrepreneur with political ties to Mayor Campbell, projected $80 to $90 million in revenues from leasing public areas in the city to vendors and selling advertising space. The deal guaranteed the city an initial $2.5 million for the marketing contract and sliding scale returns on any money over that. The implementation of the marketing plan drew immediate resistance. The proposal to lease up to 1,000 vendor carts and tents at prices up to $20,000 per site was challenged in court by existing vendors. The IOC and the local organizing committee objected to the implied threat to international Olympic sponsors such as Kodak and Coca-Cola that the city's plan might open bidding to their competitors.

Although controversial, the plan helped to strengthen the mayor's hand in negotiations with the local organizing committee for reimbursement for city services, such as police overtime. In the end, the local organizing committee agreed to pay $8 million of the city's costs for providing additional services and the city agreed to protect the marketing rights of IOC sponsors and to reduce the number of vendor sites. Coca-Cola, Kodak, and others signed contracts for carts and the right to be official *city* sponsors. Even the local organizing committee paid $500,000 to lease street pole banners in the city. Although the city was able to generate some revenue, this plan drew unusual public complaints from members of the IOC and resulted in lawsuits against the city from vendors who claimed that the city had not delivered on its promises.

After the Games, it was clear that neither the expectations of city residents for improvements in their neighborhoods nor the desires of local entrepreneurs to cash in on the Games had been met. The city's attempts to leverage the Olympics for its benefit were largely frustrated by a lack of resources and an inability to alter the relationship between the IOC, the local organizing committee, and corporate sponsors. In the end, the high expectations set by Mayor Jackson were not realized and the redistributive goals of hosting the Olympics were dashed.

Mexico City: Civil Society Matters Most

The late 1960s were an auspicious time for Mexican officials. Mexico City was hosting the 1968 Olympic Games, and the country was slated to host the 1970 World Cup as well. To government officials, these events provided the opportunity to raise Mexico's global prestige, especially as a destination for foreign tourism and investment (Arbena, 2004). The Mexico City Games were indeed filled with symbolism. These Games were the first Olympics to be held in a developing nation, and for the first time a woman lit the Olympic flame at the Opening Ceremony. Yet the most memorable symbolic display at the 1968 Games was the protest by two American sprinters, Tommie Smith and John Carlos, who raised their gloved fists and bowed their heads during the medals ceremony to call attention to the problems faced by African Americans in the United States. In contrast to the Los Angeles and Atlanta Games, the Mexico City Olympics help to illustrate the influence of global social events on local politics.

In planning for the Games, the emphasis was to put the "Mexican Miracle" on display. This approach highlighted the role of culture and Mexico's cultural heritage as an important component of resource allocation. Architect Pedro Ramirez Vasquez led the local organizing committee as it sought to present its message about Mexico to the world in the realization that Mexico would be judged against the image of an underdeveloped nation (Zolov, 2004). In the year-long Cultural Olympiad that preceded the athletic competition, Mexico staged a variety of activities and events in 20 separate areas that promoted Mexico as a harmonizing nation that overcame internal divisions and as a "land of tomorrow" ready to handle whatever the future held. The Cultural Olympiad contained five central elements that were designed to meet these challenges: a peace dove to highlight Mexico's role in international affairs, a modern logo to present Mexico as forward looking, the presence of women to illustrate Mexico's modern values, elaborately staged folkloric activities to emphasize authenticity and the history of racial and ethnic harmony, and the use of bright colors to play on Mexico's image as festive land. The success of the Cultural Olympiad, staged at locations throughout Mexico, left a mood of anticipation about the start of the Games on October 12.

Six months of protest led up to the 1968 Olympic Games, focused on the expenditure of US$175 million on the Games in the face of pressing social issues in the country. Although this was a fraction of what Japan spent to stage the 1964 Games, it was an enormous sum. IOC President Avery Brundage objected to regarding the Olympics as a spending competition and encouraged Mexico City to "stage the Games in a Mexican manner" (Zolov, 2004, p. 167). Ten days before the opening ceremony, what had been a series of peaceful student protests became the site of a massacre. With the support of the government, the Mexican army cleared out the Plaza de las Tres Culturas in the Tlatelolco area of Mexico City, resulting in numerous deaths and the arrests of thousands of people (Atkinson and Young, 2005, p. 273; Witherspoon, 2008, pp. 104–122). The media did not cover the military action, in part because of the ruling party's concerns about internal political stability (Arbena, 2004).

The Games themselves featured a number of global storylines such as the fierce competition between Czech and Soviet athletes following the Soviet Union's brutal suppression of the Prague Spring some six months earlier, protests against apartheid in South Africa and Rhodesia, and the slow progress of civil rights in the United States, punctuated by the symbolic protest of Tommie Smith and John Carlos. Clearly, geopolitical events in the most tumultuous year of the 1960s took center stage. Still, when the Games ended, the final numbers showed that of the US$175 million spent, $54 million went into sport facilities, $16.5 million for city works, $16 million for the Olympic village, $13 million for accommodations for cultural delegations, and $77 million for the local organizing committee's direct expenditures (Arbena, 2004, p. 181). The Mexican government spent $57 million, and the local organizing committee brought in $20 million including ticket sales and $6.7 million for broadcast rights. Mexico received an enhanced television and communications system as a result of hosting the Games, built new sport facilities, garnered a number of cultural and artistic works, and discovered two new archeological sites in the process of Olympic development. Yet internal political challenges remained, most notably the problems posed by a monolithic ruling party. Zolov (2004, p. 188) concluded that "through the protests and ensuing repression, Mexicans and foreigners alike were reminded that beneath the psychedelic, Op Art twists of MEXICO68 lurked a grittier reality of economic inequalities and political authoritarianism which discourse and spectacle alone could not make disappear."

Future Trends

The claims made by supporters of the free market as the best mechanism for resource allocation suggest that sustained economic growth is the best path for human development and that free markets are the best mechanism for achieving

The Beijing Olympics

The 1984 Los Angeles Olympics are still the model for cities looking to host a successful market-based Olympic Games. But, what would the Olympic Games look like if they were held in a country with an extremely strong, indeed authoritarian, central government? Although the 1980 Moscow Olympics or the 1984 Winter Olympics in Sarajevo could be used to answer that question for the Cold War era, the recently concluded 2008 Beijing Olympics best illustrate the political economy of the Olympics Games in the contemporary era. In many ways, the Beijing Games showed both the prominence of the Chinese economy and the nature of politics in a county dominated by a single party with a tight grip on political power.

Since 1978, when the leadership of the People's Republic of China adopted a policy of economic liberalization that moved away from a centrally planned economy to a more capitalist economy, China has experienced economic growth that has made its economy the third largest in the world. Although China's political system is still firmly under the control of the Chinese Communist Party, the size and importance of China's economy has made it a major player in the capitalist world. The extent of China's integration into the capitalist global economy was evident in the 2008 Beijing Olympics, which were sponsored by such major international corporations as McDonald's, Coca-Cola, Samsung, Panasonic, General Electric, and Visa (IOC 2008, p. 9). In opening itself to the world, China has in recent years become a major international tourist destination. In 2006 China surpassed Italy to become the fourth-leading destination in international tourist arrivals behind only France, Spain, and the United States, according to the United Nations World Tourism Organization (2007, p. 8). Chinese officials who pursued Beijing's bid for the Olympics certainly intended to use the Games to showcase China's economic achievements. As one scholar put it,

> the symbolic significance of hosting the Olympics is what has driven the central government to support Beijing's bid. Similar to the Tokyo and Seoul Olympics for Japan and Korea, the Beijing Olympics is a coming-of-age event for China. It will represent to the world China's rise as a great global power backed by a dynamic national economy and consolidated under the rule of the Communist Party. (Ren, 2008, pp. 178–179)

For the organizers of the Beijing Olympics to have used the Games to attract tourists and show off national achievements was largely in keeping with how other host cities used the Olympics. Still, holding the Games in an authoritarian nation resulted in some clear differences from Olympics held in liberal democratic nations. Most notably, the Chinese national government was clearly in charge of preparations for the Games and used its authority to prepare for the Games according to its needs with little regard for the concerns of the residents of Beijing, local businesses, or opposition either internally or externally. The Chinese government used the Olympic Games to expand the Beijing airport and subway system and to build numerous new venues, most notably the National Stadium, dubbed the bird's nest because of its architectural design. In doing so, however, "millions of urban homes were demolished in order to make space for Olympics-related construction" and numerous residents of Beijing "were relocated to remote suburbs with poor infrastructure facilities" (Ren, 2008, p. 179). Similarly, to deal with Beijing's notoriously dirty air, the government relocated factories in advance of the Games and during the Games ordered some factories to close and ordered half the city's cars to stay off the roads (Strauss, 2008; Yardley, 2007). Unlike the citizens of democratic nations that hosted Olympics Games, Chinese citizens had few opportunities to protest if they were inclined to do so. In response to pressure from a number of foreign governments and the International Olympic Committee, the Chinese government provided for three protest zones in Beijing where people would be allowed to protest if they had a police permit to do so. During the Games, however, the government announced that no protest permits had been issued, although 77 permits had been requested. "Of the 77 applications, Chinese citizens had submitted 74—all withdrawn after 'consultations' with government authorities, police said" (Schiller, 2008).

this. Some suggest that the combination of economic globalization, privatization, and deregulation should be the objectives of public policy. The global economic crisis that began in 2007, however, has thrown the uncritical acceptance of free markets into question.

This crisis is likely to have several effects on the relationship between sport, economics, and public policy. One area where this will play out over the next few years is in how support for the Olympic Games is claimed. Although the 2008 Beijing Olympics were said to have resulted in a $176 million surplus, Vancouver (2010 Winter Games), London (2012 Summer Games), and Sochi (2014 Winter Games) are reportedly facing new financial issues in the run up to the Games. The IOC's corporate sponsorships are running at about the same rate as they did in the four years before the Beijing Games (around $900 million), indicating some of the problems facing the 2010 Vancouver Games. The latest (June 2009) travel industry data project continued declines in 2010.

If financial woes are part of the Olympic legacy of one or more of these Games, support for hosting the Games will erode. The question of public support for sport in the face of a down or recovering economy will prompt questions regarding the allocation of scarce public resources. Although each of these cities and the candidates for hosting future Olympic Games has a distinct local history, all face the same quandary over the next decade: Who has the power to decide their future? Is this power local, is it global, or is it found in the interaction of local engagement with global forces? And if it is the latter, how will this play out?

Research into the relationship between sport, economics, and public policy concerning the justifications for hosting the Olympics should include the following questions:

- What is the political process that makes decisions on an Olympic future in a given city?
- Who sets the priorities for local decision making, particularly regarding funding?
- What is the role of government at its various levels? What is the role of citizens and residents?
- What is the result of these governmental processes, particularly regarding taxing and spending, over time?
- How is the role of localities (regarding neighborhoods and the Olympics) changing over time?

Conclusion

Public policy makers are most often supportive of the claims of Olympics supporters and proponents, although the empirical evidence supporting public investment
does not match the rhetoric. In addition, the role of culture, more specifically the
role of social and technical progress highlighted in the mythology of the Olympics
and by the IOC, can be seen as a way to capture the popular imaginations—of
individuals, firms, and states. The results, as we have illustrated, have exacerbated
the uneven development of global capitalism and have not generally addressed
the needs of local residents.

Los Angeles showed that the Olympics could be a profitable marriage between
sport and entertainment. The Los Angeles Games illustrate the broader trends
evident in global economy in the late 1970s and early 1980s; they were as close to
a privatized Games as they could be. In Los Angeles the local Olympic organizing
committee emphasized the financial aspects of the Games, and in the aftermath of
the problems in the preceding Montreal and Munich Games, this strategy made
sense to local government officials. The resulting surplus established a model for
leaders in entrepreneurial cities. The Los Angeles Olympics were largely financed
by corporate sponsors, and there was no expectation that the Games would play
any role in redistributing anything in the city. In the post–Los Angeles era, as
Kasimati (2003) found, the use of economic analysis to buttress the claims of economic elites and sport boosters has become an important, and often uncritically
accepted, adjunct to sport and tourism development and policy making.

In Atlanta the failure of the state as an alternative mode of resource allocation
showed just how much the market approach has penetrated the imagination of
local government managers and just how difficult the task of redistribution is. The
responses by the city to try to capture a share of Olympic development for redistribution to meet the needs of local residents fell far short of stated expectations.
The city's attempt to set up a parallel sponsorship program showed the power of
the economic relationship between the IOC, the local organizing committee, and
corporate sponsors. At the same time, although the city government established
an office to handle local needs and demands, the organization was unable to establish an independent agenda and ultimately became a street beautification adjunct
for the local Olympic organizing committee. The role of the state as a mode of
resource allocation in the hosting of the Olympic Games is fraught with difficulty
because the economic development policy agenda is easily manipulated. Table
11.3 shows a list of corporate sponsors to illustrate that transnational corporations
are providing many of the resources for the Olympics. Under the IOC's rules for
conducting the Games, the economic concerns of these transnational corporate
sponsors, not the needs of localities, most heavily influence policy choices.

Mexico City's experience crystallizes the role of civil society as an alternative
mode of resource allocation, and the result was to show the tight relationship
between the political power of the state and the economic power of transnational
corporations. Mexico's use of cultural symbols to highlight its emergence into the
world system provides evidence for the possibility of a cultural basis for allocation,
but the unleashing of military power on student protesters and the killing of a

TABLE 11.3

Major Corporate Sponsors (TOP VI), 2008

Sponsors and Suppliers	Product or service category
Coca-Cola	Nonalcoholic beverages
Atos Origin	Information technology
Manulife	Life insurance and annuities
GE	Select GE products and services
Johnson & Johnson	Health care products
Kodak	Film, photography, imaging
Panasonic	Audio, TV, video equipment
McDonald's	Retail food services
Samsung	Communications equipment
Omega	Timing and scoring
VISA International	Consume payment systems
Lenovo	Computing technology equipment
Daimler Chrysler	Transport
Mizuno	Clothing
Schenker	Freight forwarding and customs services
UBS	Banking services, Olympic Museum supplier

Data from IOC Factsheet, Revenue Generation and Distribution, update, Dec. 2005; IOC Marketing Media Guide; Beijing 2008, pgs. 8-34.

number of the students showed the reality that a fresh coating of cultural symbols could not hide; the brutality of an authoritarian regime and the inequalities evident in even a model of development cannot be overcome by symbols alone. Yet the symbolism of the Cultural Olympiad and the lack of media coverage of the violence preceding the Games served to locate the Games in well-known narratives of competition and conflict, such as the rivalry between the Soviet and Czech athletes and the problem of racism in the United States and South Africa. In spite of these events, then, the entertainment value of the Olympics was evident in the Mexico City Games.

And this is our final point. As the Olympics have grown into an economic entertainment powerhouse (Zimmerman, 2005), the IOC has taken more control over the economics of the Games. Now, control over the cultural values that the Games purport to uphold and the politics of selecting host cities and organizing the Games has become a greater concern for the IOC. In its report after the Winter Games at Turin, the IOC's Coordination Committee called for greater IOC involvement in all aspects of the staging of the Games to control the value of the brand by providing as much consistency as possible to the mega-event, including the legacy period. Scott's conclusion, noted earlier, that the Olympics needs to embrace a "wider concern for conviviality and camaraderie" may seem to be a new concern for the IOC, but the result is not an interest in overcoming inequality, but rather in supporting the value of the Olympic brand.

CHAPTER 12

American Baseball and the Global Labor Market

Resistance and Hegemony in the Caribbean

Charles A. Santo

Although professional baseball is inherently tied to nostalgic conceptions of American culture, two points must be made clear about our national pastime: It has long been a business as well as a pastime, and it is a transnational endeavor in both respects. In the late 19th century Americans introduced the pastime of baseball to foreign lands, many of which adopted the game as their own and incorporated it into local culture. In recent decades the business of Major League Baseball, like many American industries, has set its sights on overseas markets in search of both new consumers and new talent. At the start of the 2009 season about 28 percent of major-league players were born outside the United States. The majority of these foreign-born players are from the Caribbean (Major League Baseball, 2009).

The nature of baseball in the context of contemporary globalization presents a set of challenging and sometimes paradoxical issues. In one sense baseball, among other sports, has served as an instrumental tool in developing national identity for many countries (Houlihan, 1994), but the efforts of American Major League Baseball to market its product worldwide and import the best players from foreign systems sends a message of American cultural imperialism. This chapter explores the influence of the globalization of American baseball on foreign cultures and examines the nature of the relationships that exist between the United States and the nations with which it interacts through baseball.

Cuba and the Dominican Republic, two Caribbean nations in which baseball balances between local culture and American influence, serve as contrasting case studies. Although baseball in these two nations has a common history rooted in late 19th-century colonialism, the paths of Cuban and Dominican baseball diverged following Word War II. In response to the growing influence and globalization of American baseball business interests, the two nations have taken essentially opposing stances, each closely associated with its political and economic relationships with the United States. Castro's Cuba, diplomatically isolated from the United States and strategically closed to any form of imperial influence, has no formal relationship with American baseball. On the other hand, the Dominican Republic, which remains heavily dependant economically on the United States, regularly supplies baseball talent to major-league franchises.

In examining the nature of the relationship of American baseball with these two nations, one would expect that the divergent nature of their political and economic relations with the United States would put Dominican and Cuban baseball on opposite sides of a dichotomy characterized by hegemony and exploitation versus resistance and nationalism. This chapter begins with an examination of the influences behind the globalization of American baseball. This section is followed by an exploration of the parallel roots of the game in Cuba and the Dominican Republic and the divergent reactions to the expanding influence of American baseball. Further analysis reveals that the distinction between Dominican and Cuban baseball and their relationship with the American game is more complex than a clear-cut dichotomy.

Globalization of American Professional Baseball

American baseball involved foreign players and had foreign fans long before the post-Fordist era of industrial globalization. Only within the last two decades, however, has Major League Baseball (MLB) developed an explicit business agenda of global expansion. The factors behind this agenda are similar to those that have driven the global expansion of many other American industries: maturing or stagnating demand in home markets, the related desire to create overseas markets for consumption, and the allure of less expensive labor (Guevera and Fidler, 2002).

To stimulate increased demand for its product, MLB has increasingly scheduled exhibitions and regular-season games in foreign countries. In 1999 MLB began a tradition of opening its season outside the United States, playing games in Mexico, Japan, and Puerto Rico. The league has also increased the international sale of licensed merchandise, expanded international broadcasting of games, and developed programs to teach baseball in European countries (Guevera and Fidler, 2002). Nagel, Brown, Rascher, and McEvoy address MLB's global consumer marketing efforts in greater depth in the following chapter, whereas this chapter focuses on MLB's global search for labor.

Although marketing efforts have concentrated on wealthier nations like those of Western Europe and Japan, MLB's international talent search has focused almost exclusively on the less developed Latin and Caribbean countries. Some cite a decline in North American talent and the expanded number of teams in the league (Wilkinson, 2000), but the low cost of those players relative to American talent has clearly been a key factor in increasing MLB's reliance on foreign players, as shown in table 12.1. Recruitment of international talent has been the

TABLE 12.1

Increase in Foreign-Born Players in Major League Baseball

Percentage of players foreign born	
2008	27.7
2000	23.8
1990	13.3
1980	11.7
1970	12.3
1960	9.6
1950	3.4
1940	1.5

Data from http://www.baseball-almanac.com.

most prominent aspect of MLB's global expansion and the one that has had the greatest effect on Caribbean baseball culture.

The willingness of Dominican and other Latin players to sign for a fraction of the costs of top American amateur draft picks has contributed to what some call a "boatload mentality"—the strategy of investing in dozens of Dominican prospects with the hope that one or two of them will advance to the major leagues (Breton and Villegas, 1999). Although the increased attention and activity of American player agents in the Dominican will surely alter this approach, the magnitude of MLB's dealings with Dominican talent is staggering. In 2002 there were an average of 51 Dominican minor-league players per major-league team (Guevera and Fidler, 2002). Despite the lack of any formal or sanctioned relationship with MLB, Cuban baseball has not been immune to the American talent drain. Since 1991 a steady stream of high-profile ballplayers have turned their backs on their homeland to play ball in the United States. The implications of this talent drain and the global strategies of MLB on Cuban and Dominican baseball will be discussed in detail in the following sections.

Shared History and Parallel Development of Caribbean Baseball

The game of baseball was exported to the Caribbean long before the business of baseball was carried to Cuba and the Dominican Republic by American scouts and player agents. Although various accounts exist, it is commonly accepted that baseball was first introduced to the Caribbean by Cuban students returning home from studies in the United States in 1864 (Van Bottenburg, 2001). Baseball's rapid rise in popularity in Cuba was in part a reflection of Cuban rejection of Spanish rule and colonial influence. Cubans quickly embraced the modernity of baseball and renounced the archaic brutality of Spanish pastimes like cockfighting and bullfighting (Guttman, 1994; Jamail, 2000).

Cubans who fled their homeland after the failure of their first war for independence brought baseball to the Dominican Republic, where the first organized games were played in 1891 (Guttman, 1994). Although baseball was an early symbol of resistance and nationalism in Cuba, in the Dominican it represented acceptance of foreign influence from the start.

> It was easy for the Dominicans to adopt the game in part because they were culturally close to the Cubans, and in part because baseball was the game invented and played by the Americans, the symbols of power who were increasingly present. (Klein, 1991, p. 16)

But baseball later provided the Dominicans with a representation of resistance when they beat an American military team during a period of U.S. occupation of the country.

By the 1920s both Cuba and the Dominican Republic had developed successful amateur and professional systems. Because the Dominican professional leagues played in the summer and Cuban leagues played in the winter, many talented Caribbean players earned extra money by participating in both leagues. As early as 1911, light-skinned Cuban players were playing in the American major leagues (Guttman, 1994). American MLB players and Negro League stars regularly played winter ball in Cuba, and the Dominican summer league competed with the Negro Leagues for American talent. In fact, in 1937 the success of the Dominican summer league put several Negro League teams out business (Klein, 1991). The Havana Sugar Kings operated as an American minor-league affiliate in the International League throughout the 1950s (Guttman, 1994).

Although Cuban and Dominican baseball experienced a period of parallel growth before World War II, their paths eventually diverged following a series of changes after the war: the racial integration of the American major leagues, the communist revolution in Cuba, and later the advent of free agency in American baseball. These divergent paths would appear to have placed the Dominican Republic and Cuba on opposite sides of a dichotomy of hegemony and resistance.

Dominican Dependency, Underdevelopment, and Exploitation

The racial integration of American major-league baseball began in 1947 when Jackie Robinson took the field for the Brooklyn Dodgers. The end of the color barrier meant the beginning of new opportunities for Dominican players. As shown in figure 12.1, what began as a trickle of players moving from the Dominican to the United States in the 1950s would grow to a flood by the 1990s because of systemic changes in both Dominican and American baseball and a formalization of the relationship between the two.

In 1955, following the success of several Dominican stars in the major leagues, American franchises developed formal working arrangements with Dominican teams. At the same time, the Dominican professional league changed its season from the summer to the winter months, making the league a complement to

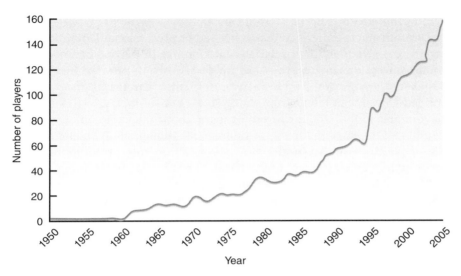

Figure 12.1 Influx of Dominican players in Major League Baseball.

Data from http://www.baseball-almanac.com.

MLB rather than a competitor. These changes helped institutionalize the flow of Dominican players to the United States throughout the 1960s. During this period, the Dominican winter leagues continued to operate successfully, with teams of both American and Dominican players, but dramatic changes would occur in the 1970s.

As the salaries of American players rose with the advent of free agency in 1976, the relative cheapness of Dominican talent grew in importance. Major-league teams not only increased the number of Dominican players signed but also established baseball academies to institutionalize the process further.

> The academy is the baseball counterpart of the colonial outpost, the physical embodiment overseas of the parent franchise. It operates more or less like the subsidiary of any other foreign company: It finds raw materials (talented athletes), refines them (trains the athletes), and ships abroad finished products (baseball players). (Klein, 1991)

Currently all 30 American major-league teams have baseball academies in the Dominican Republic.

In his analysis of Dominican baseball, sport anthropologist Alan Klein argues that the system that has developed under the influence of the American major leagues has contributed to a state of increased dependency and underdevelopment in Dominican baseball. American baseball offers a sort of false hope for most Dominican boys seeking an escape from poverty.

> The prospects for improving the lot of the Dominicans seems . . . bleaker when one realizes how few children attend school: At just about any time of the day one can find school-age children playing baseball instead. . . . Many Dominican boys see baseball as their only escape, and the inordinate pull of the sport over them is strengthened by the astounding success that the best Dominican players have achieved in North American professional baseball. (Klein, 1991, p. 58)

Dominican dependency on American baseball contributes to the underdevelopment of the nation's economy but more significantly to the underdevelopment of Dominican baseball itself. The American baseball academies have undermined the role of Dominican amateur leagues and direct talented young Dominicans to American teams instead of professional Dominican teams. Because of the relatively high salaries that Dominican players can command in the American major leagues, they are far less likely to play in the Dominican winter leagues any longer. And in many cases, American teams discourage their high-priced Dominican talent from doing so for fear of injury.

Guevera and Fidler (2002) express concern about the exploitation of Dominican youth at the hands of American interests. Although MLB rules prohibit the signing of players who are under the age of 17, no rule prohibits teams from inviting much younger players to the baseball academies for training and evaluation. "This practice is widespread and serves an important purpose: It keeps potential prospects away from the scouts of other major-league teams" (Guevera and Fidler, 2002, p. 33).

Dominican accommodation of American influence has clearly diminished the autonomy and quality of Dominican baseball. On the surface, the current system of baseball in the Dominic Republic is one of apparent hegemonic control and exploitation.

Cuban Nationalism and Resistance

Between 1947 and 1961, 135 Cubans played in the American major leagues (Jamail, 2000), but the success of the Cuban Revolution and Fidel Castro's rise to power brought drastic change to the Caribbean sporting landscape. In 1961 Castro eliminated professional sports in Cuba. Cuban athletes who played on professional teams outside the country faced exile. (See the sidebar, Baseball Diplomacy and the Generation Gap, for an example.) This decree coincided with the American embargo, which further prohibited the interaction of Cuban players and American teams. These changes played a role in the increasing reliance of American teams on Dominican players as described earlier.

In contrast to the Dominican accommodation of American influence that clearly diminished the autonomy and development of Dominican baseball, the changes wrought by the Castro's revolution were designed to ensure the opposite effect in Cuba.

> Cuba's national sports program . . . was aimed at two mutually reinforcing goals. International sports triumphs would spotlight the Cuban Revolution and symbolize its success. This would give Cubans pride in the Revolution and a sense of nationalism. . . . At the same time, the sports program would promote internal development. (Pettavino and Brenner, 1999, p. 523)

In his account of Cuban baseball, Jamail (2000) summarized the resistance ideals of Cuban policy under Castro's rule. "In 1959 Cuba became the first country in Latin America to define the interests of its own people ahead of the interests of foreign investors" (p. 8). The socialist ideals of Castro's regime equate professional baseball with a system of selling players, "a crude manifestation of the worst elements of capitalism" (Jamail, 2000, p. 29). The resistance of foreign influence has generally prevented the exploitation of Cuban players by American interests.

Baseball Diplomacy and the Generation Gap

Luis Tiant Sr. and Jr.

Cuban baseball star Luis Tiant Sr. saw his greatest success at the age of 40, when he pitched an undefeated season for the New York Cubans and led his team to a Negro League World Series title in 1947. Tiant Sr. split most of his professional career, which began in Cuba in 1926, between Cienfuegos in the Cuban league during the winter and the New York Cubans during the summer. He left the Negro League in 1937 to play two seasons with the Aguilas Cabaenas in the Dominican Republic before returning to the New York Cubans.

Tiant Sr. retired from baseball shortly after the 1947 Negro League series, his career running its course before Jackie Robinson broke the color barrier in American major-league baseball. (Although several light-skinned Cuban players participated in the major leagues before 1947, Tiant Sr. was considered too dark.)

Luis Tiant Jr. inherited his father's formidable pitching talent and began his professional career in a time that offered a world of opportunities that his father could never have, but those opportunities would come at tremendous personal cost.

Tiant Jr. was honored as the rookie of the year in the Cuban professional league in 1960, and he spent the following summer playing in the Mexican league before he was signed by the Cleveland Indians in 1961. But unfortunate timing would strike the Tiants again. Tiant Jr., who had married around the time of his signing with the Indians, was planning a trip to Cuba to celebrate and take a honeymoon when he received a letter from his father urging him not to come home. Tiant Sr. explained that the Cuban Revolution and Castro's ascendance to power meant the end of professional baseball in Cuba and that Castro was not allowing athletes to leave the island to pursue professional careers elsewhere. Tiant Jr. was ultimately faced with a choice: Pursuing his dream of pitching in the major leagues would mean that he could never go home again.

Luis Tiant Jr. went on to win 229 games in the major leagues, his most notable success coming with the Boston Red Sox in the 1970s, and he gained wide adoration for his charisma and unique pitching windup. But his success meant a 46-year separation from his home, which ended in 2008 when arrangements were made for him to travel as a coach with an amateur baseball team on a goodwill trip to Cuba.

The 2009 film *Lost Son of Havana* documents the trip and explores the emotional impact of Luis' exile. Filmmaker Jonathan Hoch described the paradox of Luis' success as follows: "Luis, in a way, becomes his own antagonist. The more he succeeds, the greater his guilt, the greater the sense of loss, the greater the emptiness of how much he's not been able to share it with his family" (Siegel, 2009).

Cuba's universal sport program identifies young talent and develops player through a series of state-run schools and academies, shepherding the best players through multiple levels of amateur competition (Pettavino and Brenner, 1999). These policies have developed what is arguably the best amateur baseball program in the world. The basis of this success is a fusion of the strong baseball tradition that existed before the Revolution and state-sponsored development of talent after the revolution (Svirsky, 2000).

Cuba's system serves to foster an apparent relationship of resistance to U.S. influence, resulting in an autonomous, stable, and fully developed form of baseball unlike that of the Dominican Republic. Recently, however, a series of cracks have begun to appear in Cuba's system of nationalism and resistance to foreign influence.

Movement Along the Spectrum

Evidence of waning nationalism and elements of increasing American influence have infiltrated Cuban baseball since the early 1990s. This development suggests that perhaps the apparent distinction between Cuban and Dominican baseball—the distinction between resistance and hegemonic influence—is not as simple as a clear-cut dichotomy. The state of Cuban baseball and that of the Dominican game in relation to expanding American influence would be more appropriately characterized by a spectrum of varying levels of resistance and hegemony. Although the two exist at opposite ends of this spectrum, some evidence suggests that their current states are closer together, and farther from the extremes, than they would first appear.

Waning Cuban Nationalism and Increasing American Influence

Since the 1990s Cuban baseball has suffered from a series of interrelated problems, including a spate of defections of its star players, decreasing quality of play, growing fan and player dissatisfaction, and a set of policies that have comprised the socialist ideals of the system. Cuba's ability to run a sustainable and autonomous baseball program based on nationalist ideals and free of foreign influence seems to be slipping.

Cuba did not lose any of its national team players to the United States until the 1991 defection of Rene Arocha opened a floodgate through which more than 50 Cuban players have passed (Beaton, 2003). Because of their superb talent, limited supply, and additional mystique, Cuban players have commanded large salaries and signing bonuses in the United States—further incentive for additional defectors.

Although the loss of many top players contributed to a decline in the quality of Cuban play, policies designed to stem defections have exacerbated the problem. The selection of the Cuban national team is now based not only on talent but also on political allegiance. Several top players have been banned for communicating with Cuban defectors.

In 1997 the Cuban national team saw their first defeat in international competition in 10 years, losing to a Japanese team in the International Cup in Barcelona (Jamail, 2000). The level of play in Cuba's domestic leagues diminished as well, and by the mid-1990s fans were becoming both disenchanted and too concerned about meeting their economic needs to concern themselves with attending baseball games (Jamail, 2000). This trend illustrates the importance of Cuba's economic circumstances on the state of the national game.

Already isolated from trade with the United States, the collapse of the Soviet Union decimated the Cuban economy in the early 1990s. The country entered a stage of austerity that it refers to as the *periodo especial* (special period) (Pettavino and Brenner, 1999). Most who have studied Cuban baseball agree that the country's economic crisis is the major factor influencing player defections and the declining quality of Cuban baseball. Cuban baseball historian Roberto Gonzalez Echevarria (1999) noted,

> It is no accident that the spate of defections has taken place after the collapse of the Soviet Union, with catastrophic results in a Cuba subsidized by the Communist bloc. The system of rewards to players has necessarily shrunken and has made their future look bleaker than before. (p. 387)

Cuba is no longer able to concentrate the quantity of resources in sport development that it once could, domestic leagues have been curtailed to conserve resources, and Cuban fans are now less concerned with baseball than they are with the necessities of life. American influence has contributed to this decline in Cuban baseball both directly and indirectly. American scouts and teams hungry for Cuban prospects give Cuban players an opportunity to escape the economic crisis imposed on their system in part by the U.S. embargo.

But the policies of Castro's regime have also contributed to the Cuban baseball crisis and have, in some cases, separated the game from its prior socialist and nationalist ideals. As discussed earlier, state-imposed bans have kept some of Cuba's top players off the field and pushed others to defect (Carter, 1999; Price, 2000). Jamail (2000) cited the lack of advancement opportunity afforded by the Cuban system as another internal contributor the increasing number of defections.

In determining the depth of the Cuban baseball crisis, perhaps nothing is more telling than the series of policies that Castro's regime has advocated that move the game away from its nationalist symbology. To counter the effects of Cuba's economic hardships, attempts have been made to make the sport support itself financially. In 1992 the Cuban government started a program that allowed Cuban coaches to work overseas and bring home part of their pay. In 1996 the government allowed players over the age of 30 to retire from Cuban amateur baseball and play in Japanese, Italian, and other Latin American professional leagues. In both cases, 80 percent of the income earned overseas would be collected by the government and reinvested in sport development programs (Jamail, 2000). Paired with increased defections, these policies contributed to the further decline in the quality of baseball played in Cuba, but more important they indicated an emerging division between doctrine and practice.

> On the one hand, the government can (as in other realms) negotiate professional contracts for some athletes, including ballplayers in professional leagues outside organized baseball, but individuals are not allowed to strike their own deals. (Echeverria, 1999)

Echeverria further questioned whether the concept of saving ballplayers from exploitation by eliminating professional sports was ever a reality to begin with. "The idea is of course that professional baseball is exploitation of man by man . . . but one wonders if the ballplayers in Cuba are not also being exploited for propaganda purposes" (quoted in Svirsky, 2000).

The nature of Cuban baseball has clearly changed in the past decade. This change has been the result of a combination of economic decline, American direct and indirect influence, and a set of Cuban policies that have separated the game from its nationalist idealism. As Klein observed,

It's not a system that we can go back to but . . . Cuban baseball in the 1980s was probably the best expression of playing for the right reasons in a state-controlled environment and building on a traditional indigenous system. (quoted in Svirsky, 2000)

Since the 1990s Cuban baseball has moved closer to the nature of baseball in the Dominican on the spectrum of resistance and hegemony.

Signs of Resistance and Empowerment in the Dominican Republic

The nature of Dominican baseball in response to expanding American influence may not be as clear as it first appears either. Although Dominican accommodation of American interests seems to illustrate a clear instance of cultural hegemony, this view might be oversimplistic. Evidence suggests that elements of resistance do exist in Dominican baseball culture and that opportunities for the empowerment of Dominican natives in Dominican baseball are expanding.

In his sociological analysis of the diffusion of sport, Guttman (1994) noted that Gramsci's concept of cultural hegemony is a more appropriate framework than that of cultural imperialism, in that imperialism assumes "that non-Western audiences simply accept, without selection or interpretation, whatever explicit or implicit messages the Western media transmit" (p. 178). But Guttman further noted that the framework of hegemony is flawed as well because it implies intentionality on the part of the donors and dismisses the role of emulation on the part of recipients: "While it is certainly true that cultures can be annihilated, it is also true that cultures can be resilient, adaptive, and transformative—in sports as in every other domain" (p. 185).

In the Dominican it may be impossible to separate the hegemonic influence of American interest from the true love of baseball that Dominicans adopted on their own. Consider the comments of a Dominican journalist in an interview with American writer Rob Ruck:

> You must understand that baseball is not thought of as the sport of the Yankee imperialists. That is a stupid way of thinking. Baseball is the national sport of the United States, and it is the greatest thing that the United States has given us and the other counties of the Caribbean. They have not given us anything else that, in my opinion, is of any value but baseball! And here, baseball is the king! (quoted in Ruck, 1999, p. 28)

How much of this love for baseball is of genuine origin, and how much is the result of self-interested American influence?

Klein's analysis further established the oversimplification of the cultural hegemony label:

> In assessing the impact of the United States on Dominican baseball, it is essential to distinguish the various levels: individual, institutional, and cultural. A failure to do so causes a good deal of confusion over whether Dominican players are exploited and whether the presence and growing interference of the United States in Dominican baseball and culture helps or hinders the game and society as a whole. (Klein, 1991, p. 57)

For the individual, American baseball represents hope, and even for those who never leave the island, it can bring major improvements in their quality of life. "Those who remain in the baseball academies for two years and do not play in the North America at all still earn more money that they would in a decade on the streets or in the cane fields" (Klein, 1991, p. 59). Although the influence of American baseball might be beneficial for individuals, it has had a detrimental effect on Dominican society as a whole.

Klein concluded that American hegemony in the Dominican Republic is not complete and that subtle forms of resistance exist in Dominican baseball culture in dynamic tension with hegemonic influence. He pointed to historical instances of resistance through baseball when Dominican teams beat American military teams during periods of U.S. occupation. Evidence of current cultural existence is present in the Dominican press, who focus almost exclusively on Dominican league play and the success of Dominican players in the United States while ignoring other important stories from the American major leagues. "Baseball journalists have become the gatekeepers of Dominican nationalism, for they carefully direct criticism away from criollos—native players—and toward the North Americans who control them" (p. 152). Klein also observed that the overwhelming majority of fans who attend Dominican games assert their national pride by wearing caps that represent Dominican teams rather than those of American teams, which are readily available.

Although these signs of resistance are restrained and understated, evidence of increasing Dominican empowerment within Dominican baseball culture is more palpable. Dominican and former major leaguer Junior Noboa is responsible for the first baseball academy in his home country *not* built by an American team. Dominicans, now more aware of the business aspects of major-league baseball, are also more commonly signing with player agents, who serve to protect them from exploitive deals with American teams. An increasing number of these agents are Dominican born. "These developments reflect a new level of Dominican participation in the game. No longer simply raw material or supervisors for the baseball industry, some Domincans are becoming stakeholders, if at a lower level of involvement" (Ruck, 1999, p. 200).

Although Dominican baseball is not autonomous, it does not reflect a complete submission of the Dominican people to American influence. Recent changes in the game are empowering Dominicans and limiting exploitation by American interests. Just as Cuban baseball does not represent clear-cut resistance and nationalism, the state of the Dominican game is not one of total hegemony and dependence. Both games exist somewhat closer to the middle of the spectrum of hegemony and resistance than would first appear—and somewhat close to one another.

Future Trends

The allure of less expensive labor fueled a massive surge of foreign-born players in major-league baseball, especially evident in the 1990s. This global influx cannot be expected to continue at the pace shown in table 12.1, but it is not clear whether it has yet reached its peak.

MLB experienced its highest percentage of opening day foreign-born players to date in 2005 (29.2 percent) (Major League Baseball, 2006). Since then, the figure has been relatively stagnant, dropping slightly to about 28 percent for the 2009 season, but nearly half of all current minor leaguers are foreign born (Major League Baseball, 2009). Between 2005 and 2009 the percentage of minor-league players under contract who were born outside the United States increased from 45 percent to 48 percent.

A recent change in immigration policy has allowed for continued growth in the number of foreign-born minor leaguers in the United States. Before 2006, foreign minor leaguers were required to obtain an H-2B visa—the same type used by most other industries recruiting foreign born labor—to play in the United States. The federal government issues a limited number of H-2B visas each year, and each MLB team was allocated only 26 per season. But after heavy lobbying by MLB, Congress passed the Creating Opportunities for Minor League Professionals, Entertainers and Teams through Legal Entry Act of 2006 (or the COMPETE Act of 2006), which allows foreign-born minor leaguers to obtain P-1 visas, previously restricted to players in the major leagues. There are no quotas on P-1 visas, which means that teams can now bring an unlimited number of minor-league players into the United States.

American baseball's global search for inexpensive labor is also expanding in scope as teams search for the next Dominican Republic. Although current major leaguers hail from 15 foreign countries and territories, 41 countries and territories are represented in the minors. MLB has recently sent delegations to establish relationships in Africa and China. The New York Yankees signed two Chinese players to minor-league contracts in 2007 after developing a formal working agreement with the China Baseball Association that could eventually lead to the development of a baseball academy (Olney, 2007). In 2008 the Pittsburgh Pirates signed two players from India, winners of a reality TV game show in that country called *The Million Dollar Arm*. In announcing the signing, Pirates senior vice president and general manager Neal Huntington explained the team's motivation:

> The Pirates are committed to creatively adding talent to our organization. By adding these two young men, we are pleased to not only add two prospects to our system but also hope to open a pathway to an untapped market. (Major League Baseball, 2008)

The change in immigration policy that allows American baseball teams to import more foreign talent occurred without much notice in popular media, but it has drawn criticism, especially among those concerned about the dwindling participation of African Americans in professional baseball (as discussed by David Ogden in chapter 8). Although the percentage of major leaguers born outside the United States has climbed to 28 percent, the percentage of major-league players who are African American has fallen to just 8 percent (Lapchick, 2008). Grassi (2007) questioned whether policy makers have considered this relationship, and whether they have chosen to interpret their own rules selectively to the benefit of baseball business interests:

> There is a proviso in the immigration law which both the U.S. Congress and MLB conveniently overlooked. The policy developed in 1998 . . . granted MLB its visa program contingent upon foreign-born players only occupying positions on a team that could not be filled by U.S. citizens.

Conclusion

Dominican and Cuban baseball are not positioned on opposite sides of a spectrum of hegemony and resistance with regard to American baseball, but they do illustrate the opposing ends of a spectrum of free trade and the difficulties posed by either extreme. Although a lack of any trade with the United States has crippled the Cuban economy, an unbalanced relationship with the United States has contributed to a loss of autonomy in the Dominican Republic.

It is unclear whether a relationship that is mutually beneficial at the societal level can be forged between American baseball interests and those in Cuba and the Dominican Republic. Similar to the trade relations between the United States and Japan, the relationship between MLB and Japanese baseball is much closer to the middle of the spectrum and could provide a benchmark for Cuban and Dominican interests. The free-agency relationships that dictate American interaction with Caribbean players are the exception rather than the rule in MLB signings of Japanese players. Through a formal arrangement established between MLB and Japanese professional baseball, American teams must bid for the services of Japanese players who are under contract with Japanese teams. This bidding process compensates Japanese teams for the talent extricated from their system. Winning bids for top Japanese players regularly top $10 million (Guevera and Fidler, 2002).

Such an arrangement is unlikely to arise in the Dominican Republic, where years of American intervention have turned the country's amateur baseball program into a direct feeder system for American teams. A system similar to the Japanese arrangement could be a better fit in Cuba, where the amateur leagues are of at least comparable quality to Japanese professional leagues. This type of agreement is not likely to occur given the current state of U.S.–Cuban diplomacy, but it is not clear what the future holds, especially in light of Fidel Castro's resignation from official political power in 2008.

CHAPTER 13

Expanding Global Consumer Market for American Sports

The World Baseball Classic

Mark S. Nagel, Matt T. Brown, Dan A. Rascher,
and Chad D. McEvoy

When Japan defeated Cuba 10-6 in the finals of the inaugural World Baseball Classic (WBC), the game not only completed a competitive baseball tournament but also symbolized a new era of globalization for Major League Baseball (MLB). The WBC was created to increase worldwide baseball participation, and more importantly, to increase consumption of baseball and baseball-related products. The tournament was designed to mirror soccer's World Cup—with one major structural difference. Although the World Cup is governed by an independent agency called the International Federation of Association Football (FIFA), the World Baseball Classic is administered by Major League Baseball and the Major League Baseball Players Association (MLBPA) (Schwarz, 2005). In addition, although soccer is played extensively in almost every nation on earth, baseball, though firmly established in some countries, has only recently been introduced in many others and in some countries remains relatively unknown (Foer, 2004; Szymanski and Zimbalist, 2005).

The effort by MLB to expand into untapped international markets mimics the actions of other sport and nonsport organizations. Globalization has been a prominent topic in the recent academic and practitioner literature (Friedman, 2000, 2005). The modern global economy permits greater flow of information as well as easier exchange of human and financial capital. Operating in diverse markets, however, is not without challenges. Cultural barriers and customs can negatively affect production, and different levels of government intervention may affect operations. Despite these obstacles, the sport industry has noticed global trends and has begun to attract employees from various continents and to develop new markets and delivery channels (Foster, Greyser, and Walsh, 2006).

Designing and implementing the first WBC required MLB to interact extensively within this changing global market place. This chapter details some of obstacles encountered during the creation and development of the WBC. It begins with a brief history of international baseball and then explores some of the economic, political, marketing, and legal factors regarding the first World Baseball Classic. It concludes with a discussion of future World Baseball Classics as well as the effect of other MLB globalization initiatives.

Baseball's Worldwide Development

Although the sport of baseball has long been considered the American national pastime (Guevara and Fidler, 2002), it has enjoyed mixed success when introduced in foreign countries. In 1889 Albert Spalding organized a baseball tour to Hawaii and Australia (Szymanski and Zimbalist, 2005). While in Australia, he decided to continue the tour back to the United States via Egypt and Europe. Although the tour generated some curious observers, for the most part the sport did not become popular. But American Horace Wilson, a history teacher working in Tokyo, had introduced baseball to Japan in 1873 with much greater success (Whiting, 1990). Shortly after its introduction, the game grew throughout the country. In 1908 the first of many American baseball tours brought major- and minor-league stars to Japan for an extended visit (Whiting, 2004). Later visits by star players such as Lou Gehrig and Lefty O'Doul enhanced interest in the sport. In 1934 Babe Ruth led a contingent of prominent American players who toured Japan and sparked interest in creating a professional league (Rains, 2001).

As described in the previous chapter, baseball was introduced to Cuba in the 1860s, where it quickly grew in popularity and eventually emerged as the sport of choice for Cubans seeking a national identity and independence from colonial ruler Spain. In 1880 brothers Ignacio and Ubaldo Alorma emigrated from Cuba to the Dominican Republic and brought baseball to the island, where it quickly proliferated (Klein, 2006). From its roots in Cuba and the Dominican Republic, the game of baseball rapidly spread throughout the Caribbean and into South American countries such as Venezuela.

The growth of baseball's popularity resulted in the formation of professional teams and leagues. In 1869 the Cincinnati Reds became the first professional baseball team in the world ("Cincinnati Reds," n.d.). In 1876 the National League was established as the highest-caliber baseball league in the world, both in on-field talent and financial backing. Baseball's popularity was so prevalent throughout the United States that most cities of significant size had semiprofessional or professional teams (Seymour, 1971). Baseball was clearly America's game of choice, for both participation and consumption. Among the rival professional leagues to emerge in the late 19th and early 20th century, the American League, established in 1901, was by far the most successful. The two leagues formed Major League

Baseball and participated in the first World Series in 1903. Major League Baseball has since reshaped and organized many of the minor professional leagues in the United States (Miller, 1990; Seymour).

The creation of Nippon Professional Baseball (NPB) in 1936 rapidly increased the popularity of the sport in Japan (Rains, 2001). The NPB has clearly established itself as the second-best professional baseball league in the world, with a rich tradition, successful players, and substantial financial support from the league's owners (Whiting, 2004). Numerous American players have played in the NPB since, beginning soon after its inception (Whiting). Although Masanori Murakami played for the San Francisco Giants in 1964, it was not until the last 12 years that considerable numbers of Japanese players signed contracts to play in MLB (Edes, 2007). Many more Japanese players are likely to come to America in the next decade (Edes).

Other countries have established professional and semiprofessional leagues. The Mexican League is perhaps best known for producing pitching sensation Fernando Valenzuela, but it also has a long, rich tradition. Although not in the American spotlight, countries such as the Dominican Republic, Cuba, South Korea, and Taiwan also developed professional leagues soon after the sport began to be played in those areas. Each of those countries' leagues has had various levels of success (Klein, 2006). Baseball has only recently been introduced in the Netherlands, Italy, and South Africa, and amateur and semiprofessional leagues have been established (Klein).

Consumption of MLB in the United States

The popularity of Major League Baseball grew rapidly after the first World Series in 1903. Although the 1919 Chicago Black Sox scandal caused concerns, the sport rebounded and increased its influence, primarily because of the emergence of Babe Ruth. Later stars such as Joe DiMaggio, Ted Williams, and Stan Musial helped MLB dominate the American sport consumption landscape until the late 1950s when the National Football League (NFL) and other leagues began to erode its market share. By the 1970s the NFL had surpassed baseball as the most-watched American sport and had likely passed baseball as the national pastime (Harris, 1986).

The success of the NFL was partly due to Commissioner Pete Rozell's lobbying of Congress to pass the Sports Broadcasting Act of 1961. Although MLB already enjoyed an antitrust exemption from the *Federal Baseball Club v. National League* (1922) case as discussed in chapter 1, other leagues did not enjoy antitrust immunity. The Sports Broadcasting Act granted limited antitrust exemptions to sport leagues, which permitted the NFL and other leagues to negotiate television contracts collectively and to reduce availability to NFL broadcasts through mechanism such as blackouts. The NFL, more than any other league, embraced the potential power of television and used the Sports Broadcasting Act to achieve a rapid increase in popularity.

Despite the success of other sports and the growth of other entertainment options, MLB has continued to enjoy a strong following. Although recent polls indicate that fewer and fewer people identify MLB as their favorite sport, it still remains popular among Americans (Klein, 2006).

Major League Baseball has maintained a strong fan base despite recent crises. Numerous labor stoppages have certainly hurt the sport and its popularity, but even the cancellation of the 1994 World Series did not completely destroy its popularity (Wetzel, 2006). A few teams had difficulty retaining many of their previous customers after the work stoppage (Foster, Greyser, and Walsh, 2006), but as an industry, MLB quickly recovered. And despite recent steroid scandals that have generated considerable negative attention and some fan and media backlash, MLB realized record attendance in 2004, 2005, 2006, and 2007 (Newman, 2007). Despite a slight decline, the league's 2008 attendance was the second highest in MLB history (Fisher, 2008).

Although labor unrest and steroid scandals have not deterred fans from attending and watching MLB games in record numbers, MLB owners have cause for long-term concern. The number of American children playing and watching baseball has declined over the past few years ("What are today's youth playing and watching?" 2006). There is an overall apprehension that traditional American consumer sports, such as MLB, are no longer holding the attention of the next generation of consumers at the same rate as emerging sports such as the X-Games or nonsport activities such as video games. Major League Baseball (among some other leagues) has also scheduled prominent games at times too late in the evening for young children to watch (Deford, 1999). If young fans are not attracted to the sport as participants or consumers, the future purchasers of tickets, media, and licensed merchandise may spend their dollar elsewhere after they have develop disposable income streams.

Creation of the World Baseball Classic

Major League Baseball has certainly been aware of its attendance successes and failures as well as the potential issues regarding its current and future fan demographics. In addition, MLB has long recognized that the United States and Canada account for only about 330 million of the 6.5 billion people in the world and that a key component of future growth will be exploring opportunities in foreign markets (Guevara and Fidler, 2002). MLB president Bob DuPuy noted, "Our world has become increasingly smaller. As a result, entertainment product— our product—is going to be worldwide. You can't be parochial any more. It can't just be about the United States" (King, 2006, p. 1). Before contemplating a world baseball tournament, MLB had been implementing activities around the globe through MLB International, which was founded in 1989 (*Major League Baseball International*, n.d.). MLB International was designed to generate revenue for MLB franchise owners by selling broadcast rights, securing sponsorships, and staging events abroad (Guevara and Fidler). MLB International organized MLB exhibition games in Cuba in 1999, the Dominican Republic and Venezuela in 2000, and Puerto Rico and Mexico in 2001 (Guevara and Fidler). In 1999 MLB opened the regular season in Monterrey, Mexico, as the Colorado Rockies defeated the San Diego Padres 8-2 (Biertempfel, 2007). Other regular-season games were played in Tokyo, Japan, (2000, 2004, and 2008), and a planned set of games in Tokyo in 2003 was cancelled because of the Iraq War (Biertempfel). San Juan, Puerto Rico, hosted regular-season games in 2001, and that city was also the part-time home of the Montreal Expos during the 2003 and 2004 seasons (Guevara and Fidler; *Historical moments*, n.d.). Future exhibition and regular-season games will likely be played in various countries, perhaps on an annual basis.

Besides playing games, MLB has implemented international activities in a variety of countries. MLB has created an Envoy program that sends coaches to teach the game in emerging baseball countries (*Development initiatives*, n.d.). In 1991 the first set of coaches went to Holland, and since then instruction has been delivered in more than 60 countries. MLB has also developed the Pitch, Hit, and Run (PHR) curriculum to be administered in physical education classes in developing countries around the world. Over 3 million students in countries such as Australia, Germany, Italy, Korea, Mexico, Puerto Rico, South Africa and the United Kingdom have learned the intricacies of the game through the PHR program. In addition, MLB also sponsors baseball festivals and supports baseball academies.

Global Marketing in Other Leagues

Major League Baseball is not the only North American professional sport league attempting to expand into international markets. The National Basketball Association (NBA), National Football League (NFL), and National Hockey League (NHL) have already implemented globalization initiatives and have focused their efforts toward future endeavors. In 1990 the NBA became the first major North American professional sport league to play outside of North America when the Utah Jazz played two games against the Phoenix Suns in Japan (*NBA international historic timeline*, n.d.). NBA commissioner David Stern has long professed his desire to have teams based in Europe eventually. The NBA recently opened a permanent office in London, England, which may signal that expansion is likely to occur in the next 10 years (*NBA announces opening*, 2007). The NHL, based in Canada and the United States, has been successful in attracting players from numerous European countries since the early 1980s (Lapointe, 1992). In 2007 the Anaheim Ducks and Los Angeles Kings played the first games outside North American when the teams met for two games in London, England ("London calling," 2007).

The NFL initiated perhaps the most interesting international development involving North American professional sports. Although it is the dominant American consumer sport, American football has not generated nearly as strong an international audience, primarily because the sport is not played extensively in most countries. The NFL has played preseason games in foreign countries since 1986, and in 2005 the San Francisco Forty-Niners and Arizona Cardinals played a regular-season game in Mexico City in front of over 100,000 spectators (Wilner, 2006). NFL Europa (previously called the World League of American Football and NFL Europe) was established in 1991, but a fan base sufficient to support the league never developed. NFL owners voted to close NFL Europa in 2007. The league later announced that up to two NFL regular-season games would begin to be played each year in foreign countries ("NFL to play," 2006). Mexico, Canada, Britain, and Germany were among the countries likely to be included in the rotation. In 2007 the first overseas regular-season game was played in London between the New York Giants and Miami Dolphins.

Guevara and Fidler (2002) have noted that MLB international initiatives serve different purposes in various countries. MLB has analyzed every country and rated each one based on its recognition and understanding of the game, participation development, and ability to consume baseball and baseball-related products (Klein, 2006). MLB will seek different goals in specific areas. In some countries, such as most of those in Europe, baseball is not a popular participation sport, let alone one that customers would likely immediately consume. Most citizens of European countries, however, have some disposable income to buy MLB-related products, an expenditure that could occur in the future if the sport can increase its popularity. In countries throughout Latin America and parts of South America, playing and watching baseball are popular pastimes, but limited financial resources for most potential consumers constrict the ability of MLB to sell extension products (e.g., licensed merchandise, media rights). Baseball is popular in Japan and Korea, but MLB faces challenges to sell its products because both countries have extensive professional leagues as well as established baseball cultures (King, 2006). MLB's greatest but most difficult marketing opportunity may be in China. The understanding of baseball is limited there, and several generations deny the existence of the game as a suitable pastime because Mao Zedong had once declared it illegal (Posner, 2006).

In each potential country, MLB faces a variety of political factors as its works to grow baseball participation and consumption. Although sport development and management is an important political topic in the United States, in other countries it is not as important a priority. For instance, MLB vice president for Asia, Jim Small, noted, "Japanese cities are unlikely to devote any substantial public funds for the growth of professional baseball" (Personal communication, June 8, 2009). As MLB works within emerging markets, their understanding of established public policies and protocols will be as important as their ability to teach the game or develop the business of baseball.

Overcoming the Logistical Difficulties of a Global Event

Despite the challenges unique to international markets, by 2004 MLB desired to expand its global presence by attempting to build a baseball tournament that would bring the top world competitors together much as the Olympics and World Cup do every four years. MLB hoped that it could overcome political, social, and cultural barriers and begin to build an event that would not only generate short-term revenues during a two-week tournament but also create profits throughout the year from other critical sport revenue streams such as the sale of sponsorships, media rights, and licensed merchandise. MLB initially planned to stage the first World Baseball Classic in 2005, but officials from Japanese baseball would not commit to a format in which Major League Baseball would retain control of the tournament and the majority of the profits (Szymanski and Zimbalist, 2005).

Eventually, MLB and the MLBPA each took 25 percent of the potential profits from the tournament, and the other 50 percent of the profits was divided among the participating teams, with half of each participating country's share required to be given to the country's baseball governing body to grow the game (Fisher,

2006a). Japanese officials agreed to the established financial and structural terms, and in 2005 the World Baseball Classic was tentatively scheduled to be played in March 2006 (Schwarz, 2005).

Immediately upon announcing the March 2006 WBC schedule, critics began to note potential areas of concern. Sixteen countries representing the greatest baseball playing nations in the world were selected to compete (see "Countries participating in the 2006 World Baseball Classic"). Although MLB and the MLBPA had established guidelines regarding participation as well as rules to prevent injury, such as strict pitch counts (*World Baseball Classic FAQ*, 2006), pundits immediately noted that many of the best players in the world would not participate because the games would be played during MLB spring training (McGrath, 2006). Despite concerns from managers and owners such as the New York Yankees' George Steinbrenner, few significant injuries occurred. Besides the concerns about injuries, the WBC would be played during the same year as the Winter Olympic Games and the World Cup, two international events that could potentially siphon off some fan and media attention from the tournament. Despite those concerns, MLB enthusiastically implemented the plan to stage an international baseball tournament in the global marketplace.

Countries Participating in the 2006 World Baseball Classic

- Australia
- Canada
- China
- Cuba
- Dominican Republic
- Italy
- Japan*
- Mexico
- Netherlands
- Panama
- Puerto Rico**
- South Africa
- South Korea
- Taiwan
- United States***
- Venezuela

*Hosted first-round games
**Hosted first- and second-round games
***Hosted first- and second-round games as well as semifinals and finals

Despite some initial objections regarding the hosting of the various rounds, preliminary games were scheduled in Japan, Puerto Rico, and the United States. To permit Asian teams time to recuperate from travel, pool A games were completed five days before the completion of the other pools. To save time and costs, second-round games were played in Puerto Rico and the United States during the second week of March, and the final round was played in the United States during the third week of March. The schedule enabled players from Asian professional leagues ample time to travel back across the Pacific Ocean after the WBC ended. In addition, the contesting of the second-round and final-round games in North America enabled MLB players to return to their professional team almost immediately after their countries were eliminated from competition.

Overcoming the Political Difficulties of a Global Event

Despite extensive planning for logistics and attention to detail, political consid-erations nearly derailed the World Baseball Classic months before the first pitch. Globalization has made the world smaller and made people more aware of the cultural differences among various nations, but it has not assuaged all previous disputes. For over 40 years before the first World Baseball Classic, the United States had considered Cuba a rogue nation and had extended an economic embargo against Fidel Castro's island nation (Edelman, 2005). Although American citizens were not prohibited from travelling to Cuba before the first WBC, direct com-mercial flights were not available. In addition, Americans were prohibited from making direct investments on the island. Despite the creation of the WBC and the announcement of the playing schedule, on December 13, 2005, the United States Treasury Department denied a request by MLB for a waiver for the Cuban national team to participate in games on U.S. soil (Edelman). The refusal to grant the waiver placed MLB and Cuba in a precarious position. If Cuba were to advance past the second round, it would have to forfeit its position in the final round, creating a potentially chaotic situation.

The WBC was not the first attempt by MLB to involve Cuba in an international baseball competition. In 1999 the Baltimore Orioles petitioned and received an exemption from the embargo to play a not-for-profit home-and-home series against the Cuban national team with the proceeds going to Hurricane Mitch victims ("Political hardball," 1999). The two-game series elicited considerable criticism because of Castro's notorious human rights violations (Blum, 2005). MLB umpire Rich Garcia expressed the thoughts of many when he noted, "My God, you can't bring a Cuban cigar across the U.S. border yet we're going to take a baseball team over there and try to be nice to this man" ("Political hardball," para. 10). Despite the uproar regarding the Orioles' games, the U.S. government permitted the series, in part because it had previously allowed Cuba to compete in the 1996 Atlanta Olympics (Blum).

As the deliberations regarding Cuba's participation in the WBC continued, some critics noted that the United States could be jeopardizing its opportunity to host future international sporting events, including the Olympic Games (Blum, 2005). Hoping to avoid an embarrassing situation in which one of the top baseball teams was absent, MLB petitioned the United States Treasury Department for a WBC exemption while at the same time exerting political pressure through a variety of channels. After over a month of negotiations, on January 23, 2006, the U.S. govern-ment issued a special license for Cuba to participate. As part of the license, Cuba agreed to forgo any financial gain from the tournament by donating any profits that it received to victims of Hurricane Katrina (*Treasury Department allows*, 2006).

Despite the initial concerns, after the tournament Cuban manager Higinio Velez noted that Cuba had such a positive experience that it would like to bid to host games in future World Baseball Classics (Rojas, 2006). Although the U.S. govern-ment has gradually scaled back its overall Cuban embargo and has sought closer relations, MLB is unlikely to pursue Cuba as a potential host in the near future. Regardless of the political relationship between the two countries, Cubans have limited disposable income to purchase licensed merchandise and other MLB-related products.

World Baseball Classic Revenue Sources

The organizers of any sporting event ultimately judge their level of success by achieving financial objectives. Major League Baseball envisioned that the WBC would generate income through traditional revenue sources such as ticketing, media, sponsorships, and licensed merchandise. These revenue streams could be evaluated as soon as the tournament ended. In addition, MLB hoped that the WBC would instigate short- and long-term increases in consumption patterns for all MLB-related products and services. Measuring success in these areas is certainly difficult but could initially be evaluated by the reaction and attitudes of fans and by the desire of participants and participating teams to compete in future World Baseball Classics.

Ticketing

After resolving the dispute regarding Cuba's participation, the greatest concern for the WBC was potential live attendance. During the first games held in Japan, it appeared that on-site attendance would fall woefully short of the projected 800,000 (Fisher, 2006b). For the three opening games in Japan that did not involve the home team (South Korea, China, Taiwan), total attendance was only 13,695 (Fisher). The situation in Japan convinced many observers that few customers at any site would bother to attend games if the home team was not playing (McGrath, 2006). But after games began in Puerto Rico and the United States, attendance increased, particularly in the United States. For the entire tournament, 737,112 customers attended. The final in San Diego between Japan and Cuba drew 42,696 (Fisher).

One of the reasons that games in the United States were able to attract fans for non-U.S. competitions was that many recent immigrants of Hispanic descent attended games played by their home countries. In addition, many fans traveled to the United States with the intent to include attendance at WBC games as part of their vacations. The initial critics of WBC attendance did not recognize that Japan and the United States have vastly different demographics. The Hispanic population in the United States is growing rapidly, and 25 percent of all Hispanics in the United States attended at least one MLB game in 2004, more than the number who attended professional soccer games (Eros, 2005). The 41.4 million Hispanics living in the United States have demonstrated a passion for "American" sports that has resulted in their having higher consumption rates for major professional sports like football than do Caucasians and African Americans (Eros). A high level of energy and excitement was present at most games in Puerto Rico and the United States (Fisher, 2006a). This enthusiasm bolstered MLB hopes for future tournaments and additional global-marketing and revenue-generating initiatives.

Media Coverage

Although the success of any live sporting event is initially judged by in-person attendance, media attention indicates the potential for short- and long-term growth. In the case of a worldwide event like the WBC, television ratings may be even more important than on-site attendance because many potential viewers may not have the ability to travel to see a game in person. In the United States, the

MLB's Previous Caribbean Experiments

Major League Baseball has had mixed success in its previous attempts to market its product in Central America. Recognizing the growing numbers of Latin American players in the major and minor leagues and hoping to establish new marketing opportunities, in 2000 MLB sponsored preseason games between the Boston Red Sox and Houston Astros in the Dominican Republic. Despite the strong passion for baseball and the presence of prominent Dominicans in the games, thousands of the seats were empty, primarily because many of the tickets were priced at roughly $60. Although those prices were common in the United States, few Dominicans could afford to attend. Red Sox pitcher Pedro Martínez strongly criticized MLB for not recognizing the differences between the countries, and he called the ticket prices "extremely abusive" (Enders, 2000, para. 38).

Major League Baseball later attempted to market regular-season games in Central America. In the late 1990s the Montreal Expos began to experience difficulties retaining paying customers as the quality of their on-field product diminished. As interest and attendance began to wane, MLB purchased the team and began to investigate opportunities to generate additional revenue. During the 2003 and 2004 seasons, the team played some regular-season games in San Juan, Puerto Rico. The announcement that the Expos and prominent players such as Vladimir Guerrero would be playing regular-season games in San Juan's Hiram Bithorn Stadium generated tremendous local interest and enthusiasm. But pricing was again an issue. Winter league games in Puerto Rico typically cost $5, but the Expos' regular-season games were priced at about $30 per ticket, similar to the price of MLB games in the United States (Paese, 2002). Average attendance for 2004 Expos' Puerto Rico games was only 10,333, a significant decline from an average of 14,222 per game in 2003 (*No plans*, 2004). Despite the initial excitement, the low attendance prompted Major League Baseball to forgo future regular-season games in the Caribbean, primarily because the economics of the countries cannot yet provide the revenues necessary to justify MLB investment.

Besides failing to attract sufficient attendance, the games in Puerto Rico demonstrated that government officials often make policy decisions that have selected benefits. Although the ticket prices for the Puerto Rico games were much higher than the average citizen could afford, the government elected to pass a special tax package just a few days before the first games were played. The special tax on player compensation mimicked similar tax plans implemented by many U.S. cities. But the Puerto Rican government also elected to include a special provision in its tax code that absolved Major League Baseball, the participating teams, and the promoter of any tax liability on their profits (Rovell, 2003).

12 WBC telecasts on ESPN had a 1.1 rating (1,205,600 households), and the 20 telecasts on ESPN2 had a .6 rating (657,600 households) (Fisher, 2006a). (*Rating* represents the number of households watching a television program, whereas *share* measures the percentage of televisions that are in use and are tuned to the selected show. Each rating point is roughly 1 percent of the total 109,600,000 households in the United States [Neilson Media Research, n.d.]). Of particular

interest for the future growth of the WBC in the United States was the 1.8 rating (1,972,800 households) for the WBC final because the American team had been eliminated in the second round. Although the U.S. ratings were not spectacular compared with playoff or World Series games, they greatly exceeded projections. When considering the Americans' on-field performance and the fact that the WBC was scheduled during the heart of the NCAA March basketball tournament, the ratings and overall interest bode well for the future of the WBC.

Besides the solid television viewership figures in the United States, strong ratings were achieved in Japan for the semifinal game between South Korea and Japan, despite its being shown at a less-than-desirable time of day (Bloom, 2006). The Japanese victory over Cuba in the finals also attracted strong ratings. Certainly, Japanese fans were primarily focused on their team, but such strong ratings for an event played in the middle of the night in Japan signals the long-term interest in continuing the event. Paul Archey, MLB vice president for international business operations, noted MLB's reaction to the television ratings: "It's important, and I don't want to diminish its importance. ESPN is very happy with how they've done, and so are we, but it's foremost about growing the game globally, and we can't lose sight of that" (Fisher, 2006a, p. 1).

The strong media numbers generated by the WBC continued an overall increasing worldwide ratings trend for MLB. In 1990 MLB generated $10 million total from all revenue sources outside North America, whereas in 2005 those sources generated $120 million (King, 2006). ESPN recently launched a version of ESPN Classic in Europe, which now reaches 8 million homes in Great Britain and an additional 8 million homes on the European continent (Bernstein, 2006). ESPN's European presence likely helped to double MLB's European rights fees to $20 million over five years (Bernstein). Interestingly, ESPN was outbid for those rights by Ireland-based North American Sports Network (NASN), a company that was initially formed to service expatriated North Americans. NASN recently discovered, however, that 70 percent of their subscribers were native Britons (Bernstein).

Although television is currently the dominant media forum, in 2000 MLB established a subsidiary, Major League Baseball Advanced Media (MLBAM), to extend the presence of MLB operations across the rapidly growing Internet (Brown, 2005). Within two years of its creation, MLBAM began to generate a profit, and revenues and profits continue to increase rapidly (Moag & Company, 2006). MLBAM has not only advanced baseball-related content but also has positioned MLB as an investor in the global sport environment. MLBAM recently purchased a 10 percent stake in World Championship Sports Network (WCSN), which broadcasts sports such as track and field, rowing, and wrestling (Brown, 2005). In addition, MLBAM has begun to sign agreements with numerous international companies to license baseball-related content for games in countries such as Japan and South Korea (*MLB Advanced Media and Reakosys*, 2006; *MLB Advanced Media and Tasuke*, 2006). A significant component of MLB's continued foray into international markets involves MLBAM's delivering baseball-related content in combination with MLB's staging of a world tournament. Currently, MLBAM broadcasts more live events than any other Web site in the world, and it continues to add content (Ortiz, 2007).

Sponsorship

The development of on-site customers and media consumers was only part of MLB's revenue plan for the WBC. Major League Baseball also hoped to attract numerous international corporations as sponsors of the World Baseball Classic. Soon after the WBC was scheduled, Mastercard signed on as a sponsor. Tom Murphy, vice president of sponsorships for Mastercard, noted his company's interest in the potential of the WBC: "The Classic is a great way to extend our established ties to baseball, and it's one of the very few global sports properties" (Lefton, 2006, p. 3). Konami joined Mastercard as the other WBC global sponsor. In total, 26 companies sponsored the WBC at the national or regional level. Among the American companies were Anheuser-Busch, Gatorade, and MBNA (*Sponsorship roster announced*, 2006). In addition, other companies who were not official sponsors, such as Taco Bell, bought considerable advertisement time on ESPN and ESPN Deportes in an effort to target emerging demographics in the global marketplace (Lefton). Although only two global sponsors participated in the initial WBC, MLB hopes to increase that number significantly for future tournaments. Other national and regional sponsors will also be solicited.

Besides the activities centered on the WBC, MLB has diligently been building its other sponsorship relationships outside North America. Since it opened a permanent office in Asia, MLB has been able to negotiate multiyear agreements for 60 percent of its sponsorships in that region, up from a recent figure of only 20 percent (King, 2006). In Latin America, despite the limited disposable income of most potential consumers, total sponsorship dollars have increased 140 percent to $3 million a year over the last two years (King). MLB overseas offices are an indication that they understand the value, both financial and symbolic, that a daily presence in the marketplace provides for future marketing penetration.

MLB's international sponsorship effort has occasionally encountered unique challenges. Historically, teams and leagues in the United States have discouraged or prohibited sponsor logos on uniforms, but they have typically displayed logos throughout sport facilities. In professional sport leagues in Asia and Europe, however, uniform sponsorships are a common practice (Lefton, 2006). MLB has learned that sponsorships need to be tailored to the unique aspects of each country rather than to an area of the world. MLB vice president for Asia Jim Small noted, "The thing we've learned is that you can't just say were going to do something across a region. Strategies have to be customized, country by country" (King, 2006, para. 16). Paul Archey echoed Small's comments when he specifically discussed MLB's Asian sponsorship initiatives:

> Japan and Korea are as different as two cultures can get, they just happen to be in close proximity. But they speak different languages and they have different cultures and food. Certainly we shouldn't expect to be able to put the same strategy in Japan and take it to Korea or China and have it work just because it's Asia. (Fisher, 2006b, p. 62)

MLB has also had to educate some of its overseas sponsors regarding the combination of marketing activities beyond the simple sponsorship investment ("WBC silences its critics," 2006). Although American-based companies such as Mastercard have focused on sponsorship activation for years, companies overseas have often not moved beyond viewing sponsorship simply as signage or isolated advertisements. Jim Small commented on this sponsorship aspect:

They want to pay you for the marks and run an ad and that's it. If they decide they want to run another ad next year, they do another deal. What we're trying to do is get them to realize that it's not just an advertising vehicle, but also a sales tool. We're trying to change the way sports marketing is conducted here. It's difficult, but we're making progress. (King, 2006, para. 39)

The development of viable sponsorships will certainly be a vital component of MLB's globalization activities. As more American-based businesses expand their operations away from North America, MLB hopes to become a viable marketing outlet for those companies to reach potential customers. In addition, companies in foreign countries can utilize MLB-related events and content to grow their businesses. Ultimately, the sale of sponsorships will be driven by in-person attendance and media consumption of the WBC and other MLB events.

Licensed Merchandise

Perhaps the most important area of revenue growth for MLB and the WBC is the sale of licensed merchandise, particularly sales beyond the traditional American and Canadian markets. Although MLB trails the NFL in licensed merchandise sales (Weisman, 2004), it still realized over $3.5 billion in total sales of licensed merchandise in 2005 (Horrow, 2005). Because more people throughout the world play and watch baseball than play and watch American football, MLB believes that tremendous growth opportunities are available in various international markets.

MLB viewed licensed merchandise sales as a key component of the WBC. The sale of licensed merchandise in Mexico and throughout Latin America was brisk during the tournament. Vendors often ran out of product before games ended. Paul Archey was asked to assess the television ratings and the sale of licensed products south of the U.S. border. He said, "Our business partners in Mexico . . . think this may be the biggest thing to happen for baseball down there since Fernando (Valenzuela)" (King, 2006, para. 45). Despite the failure of the U.S. team to make the WBC finals, merchandise sales at the championship game in San Diego generated $10 per attendee for the 42,696 attendees, which compares favorably with a typical World Series game (Fisher, 2006a). For a regular-season San Diego Padres' game, the licensed merchandise per attendee was $2 during the 2006 season (Fisher).

The tremendous sales during WBC games signal a potential area of revenue growth, but conducting business in foreign markets presents potential challenges. Many countries, particularly those in Asia and in Central and South America, do not have the same strict intellectual property protections that businesses in the United States enjoy. On a recent trip to Venezuela, Longley and McKelvey (2006) noted the vast number of counterfeiters who were brazenly selling pirated merchandise outside a baseball stadium. Even in countries where trademarks are protected, consumers prefer different methods of purchasing merchandise. For instance, in South Korea about 50 "team" stores account for the majority of sales of all licensed sport merchandise. Japan, however, has few team stores, and licensees simply produce and distribute merchandise through a myriad of channels such as traditional department stores (King, 2006). If MLB hopes to maximize revenues from the vast numbers of potential consumers around the world, they will need to study the unique marketing and legal aspects of the different areas of the global marketplace.

Future Trends

Despite initial concerns regarding participants, logistics, and attendance, the initial World Baseball Classic was a financial success, particularly because interest remained high despite the elimination of the U.S. team before the finals. Before the start of the championship game between Cuba and Japan, MLB commissioner Bud Selig noted, "Anything you do for the first time is not going to be perfect. But by any stretch of the imagination, this tournament exceeded my expectations in a myriad of ways" (Bloom, 2006, para. 2). After initially worrying that the event might lose money, a $10 million profit was realized, even though attendance fell short of the projected 800,000 (Fisher, 2006a). MLB and the MLB Players Association were certainly pleased to split $5 million, and the remaining money distributed to the participating countries increased the likelihood that the next tournament would be expanded to include more countries and additional preliminary rounds.

Rather than play in 2010, MLB decided to stage the subsequent World Baseball Classic in 2009 and to schedule succeeding tournaments every four years thereafter. This format avoids any competition for the world's attention from the Olympics or World Cup. The International Olympic Committee recently announced that 2008 was the last time that baseball would be contested (Goldman, 2005), leaving MLB in a position to develop the sport and prosper from its future growth. The World Baseball Classic succeeded by attracting MLB-caliber players, something the Olympics was unable to accomplish since its reintroduction as a medal sport in 1992.

As MLB attempts to build its brand through future World Baseball Classics, a variety of issues will need to be overcome. One of the most important aspects will be the expansion of the tournament from 16 teams. To do this, MLB may need to lobby numerous countries to provide greater financial support to increase baseball participation and consumption. Although most MLB teams have been successful in lobbying local communities to assist or even take the lead in building new state-of-the-art facilities, simply developing minimal government support in other countries may be a tough proposition. Numerous American companies have encountered difficulties when they have conducted business in foreign countries. Because many of the additional WBC teams will likely come from emerging economies, lobbying regarding local policies will likely need to be conducted.

An expanded tournament will also present potential scheduling concerns. Many baseball federations are already concerned that the World Baseball Classic is scheduled to accommodate Major League Baseball rather than to determine which country fields the best baseball team. As the tournament expands, additional preliminary rounds will need to be played. Where and when those rounds will be played will be important decisions for MLB and the various constituents involved.

The success of the Netherlands in the 2009 tournament potentially will spur other emerging baseball countries to contemplate enhancing their baseball focus. The Netherlands was able to defeat the favored Dominican Republic twice in a four-day span. Such monumental upsets in soccer's World Cup Finals would have likely shut down an underdog nation for many days, if not an entire week of celebration. Although the Dutch defeat of the Dominican Republic did not capture the country's full attention, it did elicit strong responses from sport fans. As more upsets occur in future World Baseball Classics, the momentum to develop the sport will likely increase in many countries.

One major hurdle that needs to be overcome before the World Baseball Classic becomes a truly worldwide event is the staging of later rounds outside the United States. Numerous countries have the baseball infrastructure to support a tournament, but concerns exist that other countries would not attract significant in-game attendance if the host nation was eliminated from competition. Japan has discussed its desire to host the 2013 semifinals and finals, but given the attendance at the 2006 WBC, Japan is unlikely to be able to support those games unless the home team is playing. "Japan has to establish they can draw a non-Japanese audience," noted MLBPA chief operating officer Gene Orza when asked about moving the later rounds from the United States (Fisher, 2006b, p. 62).

Although the United States is likely to host the later rounds in the 2013 tournament, by 2017 the globalization of baseball through the WBC might create a worldwide event that several countries could support regardless of the participating teams. Until that time, however, only the United States, with its large population and diverse demographics, is likely to draw significant numbers of fans to games if the home team is not participating. Future tournament games held outside the United States might spur new young participants to embrace the sport. Ultimately, MLB would love to see a new generation of fans in Europe or a Yao Ming of baseball from China who could galvanize the most populous nation on earth.

Conclusion

The initial World Baseball Classic was a successful venture because a variety of stakeholders worked together to host the event. Despite some initial political and cultural difficulties, the event nearly hit its attendance projections and it had strong television viewership. In addition, the event generated sufficient revenues from sponsorship and licensed merchandise sales to build on for the future.

Besides generating initial profits, the WBC has positioned MLB to be the leader in growing the game of baseball and the commercial aspects of the sport throughout the world. As baseball grows, and more important, as the American brand of baseball grows, watching the worldwide reaction will be interesting, particularly if MLB begins to generate large profits overseas. Other prominent American brands such as Coke, Nike, Disney, and McDonald's have been both embraced and scorned as they have ventured beyond the 50 U.S. states. MLB will have unique challenges as well as tremendous opportunities as it attempts to expand its potential marketplace from the 330 million North American consumers to the entire world. Ultimately, the long-term effect of the initial World Baseball Classic will not be known for many years, but it appears that the initial tournament met, and in some cases, exceeded expectations.

References

Chapter 1

DiMeo, N. (2007, October 5). *My plan to save hockey*. www.slate.com/id/2175024/ [June 10, 2008].

Duquette, Jerold J. (1999). *Regulating the national pastime: Baseball and antitrust*. Westport, CT: Praeger.

Federal Baseball Club of Baltimore, Inc. v. National League of Professional Baseball Clubs.. 259 U.S. 200 (1922).

Freyer, Tony. (1989). Economic liberty, antitrust, and the Constitution, 1880–1925, in *Liberty, property, and government: Constitutional interpretation before the New Deal*, ed. Ellen Frankel Paul and Harold Dickman. Albany: State University of New York Press.

Horn, Dan. (2004, March 12). NFL denies acting as monopoly. *Cincinnati Enquirer*. www.enquirer.com/editions/2004/03/12/loc_nflsuit12.html [June 5, 2008].

Los Angeles Memorial Coliseum Commission v. National Football League. 726 F. 2d 1381 (9th Cir. 1984).

Leuchtenburg, William. (1995). *The Supreme Court reborn: The Constitutional revolution in the age of Roosevelt*. New York: Oxford University Press.

Letwin, W. (1965). *Law and economic policy in America: The evolution of the Sherman Antitrust Act*. New York: Random House.

Lowe, Stephen R. (1995). *The kid on the sandlot: Congress and professional sports, 1910-1992*. Bowling Green, OH: Popular Press.

Mackey v. National Football League. 543 F. 2d 606 (8th Cir. 1976).

Quirk, James, and Fort, Rodney D. (1992). *Pay dirt: The business of professional team sports* Princeton, NJ: Princeton University Press.

Rader, Benjamin. (2002). *Baseball: A history of America's game* (2d ed.) Urbana: University of Illinois Press.

Radovich v. National Football League, et al. 352 U.S. 445 (1957).

Reiss, Steven (1995). *Sport in industrial America, 1850–1920*, The American History Series, John Hope Franklin and A.S. Eisenstadt (Eds). Wheeling, IL: Harlan Davidson.

Roberts, Gary R. (1991). Professional sports and antitrust law. In Paul D. Straudohar and James A. Mangan (Eds.), *The business of professional sports* (pp. 135–151). Urbana: University of Illinois Press.

Ross, Stephen F. (1991). Break up the sports league monopolies. In Paul D. Straudohar and James A. Mangan (Eds.), *The business of professional sports* (pp. 152–174). Urbana: University of Illinois Press.

Rossi, John. (2001). *The national game: Baseball and American culture*. Chicago: Ivan R. Dee.

Schlosser, Jason. (2007, June 21). 6th Circuit says final gun sounded in Bengals stadium suit. *Findlaw for Legal Professionals*. http://news.lp.findlaw.com/andrews/bt/sel/20070621/20070621_bengals.html [June 5, 2008].

Seymour, Harold. (1960). *Baseball, vol. I*. New York: Oxford University Press.

Sherman Antitrust Act. (1980). Reprinted in Hans B. Thorelli (1954), *The federal antitrust policy: Organization of an American tradition*, pp. 610–611. Baltimore: The Johns Hopkins Press.

Smith v. Pro Football, Inc. 420 Supp. 738 D.D.C. (1976).

Spink, J.G. Taylor. (1974). *Judge Landis and 25 years of baseball*. St. Louis: The Sporting News.

Szymanski, S., and Zimbalist, Andrew. (2005). *National pastime: How Americans play baseball and the rest of the world plays soccer*. Washington, DC: Brookings Institution Press.

Toolson v. New York Yankees. 346 U.S. 356 (1953).

United States v. International Boxing Club of New York, Inc. 348 U.S. 236 (1955).

U.S. Congress. House of Representatives. Subcommittee on the Study of Monopoly Power. (1951). *Part 6, Organized Baseball, hearings*. Washington, DC: G.P.O.

U.S. Congress. House of Representatives. Subcommittee on the Study of Monopoly Power. (1952). *Organized Baseball, report*. Washington, DC: G.P.O.

Voight, David Quentin. (1983). *American baseball, vol. I: From gentleman's sport to the commissioner system*. University Park, PA: Pennsylvania State University Press.

Voigt, David Q. (1991). Serfs versus magnates: A century of labor strife in major league baseball, in Paul D. Straudohar and James A. Mangan (Eds.), *The business of professional sports* (pp. 95–114). Urbana: University of Illinois Press.

Yasser, Ray, et. al. (2000). *Sports law: Cases and materials* (4th ed). Cincinnati: Anderson.

Chapter 2

David, Ruth. (2007). Broadcaster launches rebel Indian cricket league. *Forbes Magazine*, April 3.

Disney, Richard. (2006). The remuneration of sports stars: Implications for regulation. Modern Law Review Seminar, University of Leicester, England, May 11.

Dunning, Eric, and Sheard, Kenneth. (1976). The bifurcation of rugby union and rugby league: A case study of organizational conflict and change. *International Review for the Sociology of Sport, 11*, 31–72.

Economic Times. (2007, August 21). Indian cricket is in a league of its own.

Hope, Wayne. (2002). Whose All Blacks? *Media, Culture and Society, 24*, 235–253.

Indian Cricket League, Wikipedia, http://en.wikipedia.org/wiki/Indian_Cricket_League [June 1, 2008].

Morgan, Michael. (2002). Optimizing the structure of elite competitions in professional sport: Lessons from rugby union. *Managing Leisure, 7*, 41–60.

Noll, Roger B. (2002). The economics of promotion and relegation in sports leagues: The case of English football. *Journal of Sports Economics, 3*(2), 169–203.

Ross, Stephen F. (2001). Antitrust options to redress anticompetitive restraints and monopolistic practices by professional sports leagues. *Case Western Law Review, 52*, 133–171.

Southall, Richard M., Nagel, Mark S., and LeGrande, Deborah J. (2005). Build it and they will come? The Women's United Soccer Association: A collision of exchange theory and strategic philanthropy. *Sports Marketing Quarterly, 14*.

World Series Cricket. Wikipedia, http://en.wikipedia.org/wiki/World_Series_Cricket [June 1, 2008].

Chapter 3

Berri, David J., and Krautmann, Anthony C. (2006),Shirking on the court: Testing for the incentive effects of guaranteed pay. *Economic Inquiry, 44*, 536–546.

Berri, David J., Schmidt, Martin B., and Brook, Stacey L. (2006). *The wages of wins: Taking measure of the many myths in modern sport*. Stanford, CA: Stanford University Press.

Bradbury, John Charles. (2007). *The baseball economist: The real game exposed*. New York: Dutton.

Bureau of Labor Statistics, U.S. Department of Labor. Work stoppages involving 1,000 or more workers, 1947–2003. http://stats.bls.gov/cba/hwstable.pdf [June 25, 2007].

Burger, John D., and Walters, Stephen J.K. (2003). Market size, pay, and performance: a general model and application to Major League Baseball. *Journal of Sports Economics, 4*, 108–25.

Burger, John D., and Walters, Stephen J.K. (2008). The existence and persistence of a winner's curse: New evidence from the (baseball) field. *Southern Economic Journal, 75*(1), 232–246.

Cassing, James, and Douglas, Richard W. (1980). Implications of the auction mechanism in baseball's free agent draft. *Southern Economic Journal, 47*,110–121.

Coates, Dennis, and Humphreys, Brad R. (2001). The economic consequences of professional sports strikes and lockouts. *Southern Economic Journal, 67*, 737–747.

Edge, Marc. (2004). *Red line, blue line, bottom line: How push came to shove between the National Hockey League and its players.* Vancouver, BC: New Star Books.

Gustafson, Elizabeth, and Hadley, Lawrence. (2007). Revenue, population, and competitive balance in major league baseball. *Contemporary Economic Policy, 25*, 250–261.

Hakes, Jahn K., and Sauer, Raymond D. (2006). An economic evaluation of the *Moneyball* hypothesis. *Journal of Economic Perspectives, 20*, 172–185.

Hausman, Jerry A., and Leonard, Gregory K. (1997). Superstars in the National Basketball Association: Economic value and policy. *Journal of Labor Economics, 15*, 586–624.

Idson, Todd L., and Kahane, Leo H. (2000) Team effects on compensation: An application to salary determination in the National Hockey League. *Economic Inquiry, 38*, 345–357.

Kahn, Lawrence M. (1991). Discrimination in professional sports: A survey of the literature. *Industrial and Labor Relations Review, 44*, 395–418.

Kahn, Lawrence M. (2000). The sports business as a labor market laboratory. *Journal of Economic Perspectives, 14*, 75–94.

Krautmann, Anthony C. (1999).What's wrong with Scully estimates of a player's marginal revenue product? *Economic Inquiry, 47*, 369–381.

Lehn, Kenneth. (1990). Property rights, risk sharing and player disability in Major League Baseball. In Brian Goff and Robert D. Tollison (Eds.), *Sportometrics* (pp. 35–58) College Station, TX: Texas A&M Press.

Lewis, Michael. (2003). *Moneyball: The art of winning an unfair game.* New York: Norton.

MacDonald, Don N., and Reynolds, Morgan O. (1994). Are baseball players paid their marginal products? *Managerial and Decision Economics, 15*, 443–457.

Marburger, Daniel R. (2004). Arbitrator compromise in final offer arbitration: Evidence from Major League Baseball. *Economic Inquiry, 42*, 60–68.

Maxcy, Joel, and Mondello, Michael. (2006). The impact of free agency on competitive balance in North American professional team sports leagues. *Journal of Sport Management, 20*, 345–365.

Merron, Jeff. (n.d.) Taking your Wonderlics. *ESPN.com Page Two.* http://espn.go.com/page2/s/closer/020228.html [June 30, 2007].

Navin, John C., and Sullivan, Timothy S. (2004). The relationship between bargaining power and salary: Evidence from the National Hockey League. *Southern Business and Economic Journal, 27*, 200–213.

Richardson, David H. (2000). Pay, performance, and competitive balance in the National Hockey League. *Eastern Economic Journal, 26*, 393–417.

Rosen, Sherwin. (1981). The economics of superstars. *American Economic Review, 71*, 845–58.

Scully, Gerald W. (1974). Pay and performance in Major League Baseball. *American Economic Review, 64*, 915–930.

Scully, Gerald W. (1989). *The business of Major League Baseball.* Chicago: University of Chicago Press.

Staudohar, Paul. (1996). *Playing for dollars; labor relations and the sports business.* Ithaca, NY: ILR Press.

Stevens, Carl M. (1966). Is compulsory arbitration compatible with bargaining? *Industrial Relations, 5*, 38–50.

Stiroh, Kevin J. (2007). Playing for keeps: Pay and performance in the NBA. *Economic Inquiry, 45*, 145–161.

Taylor, Beck A., and Trogdon, Justin G. (2002). Losing to win: Tournament incentives in the National Basketball Association. *Journal of Labor Economics, 20,* 23–41.

Yost, Mark. (2006). *Tailgating, sacks, and salary caps.* Chicago: Kaplan.

Zimbalist, Andrew. (1992). *Baseball and billions: A probing look inside the big business of our national pastime.* New York: Basic Books.

Chapter 4

Archer, B.H. (1982). The value of multipliers and their policy implications. *Tourism Management, 3*(4), 236–241.

Arthur Andersen, Hospitality and Leisure Services. (2000). *The Sydney Olympic Performance Survey: The Sydney Olympic Games on the Australian hotel industry.*

Austrian, Z., and Rosentraub, M.S. (1997). Cleveland's gateway to the future. In R. Noll and A. Zimbalist (Eds.), *Sports, jobs and taxes: The economic impacts of sports teams and stadiums* (pp. 355–384). Washington, DC: Brookings Institution Press.

Baade, R.A. (1996). Professional sports as catalysts for metropolitan economic development. *Journal of Urban Affairs, 18*(1), 1–17.

Baade, R.A., and Dye, R. (1990). The impact of stadiums and professional sports on metropolitan area development. *Growth and Change,* Spring, 1–14.

Baade, R.A., and Sanderson, A.R. (1997). The employment effect of teams and sports facilities. In R. Noll and A. Zimbalist (Eds.), *Sports, jobs, and taxes: The economic impact of sports teams and stadiums* (pp. 92–118). Washington, DC: Brookings Institution Press.

Burbank, M., Andranovich, G.D., and Heying, C.H. (2001). *Olympic dreams: The impact of mega-events on local politics.* Boulder, CO: Lynne Rienner.

Coates, D., and Humphreys, B.R. (1999). The growth effects of sport franchises, stadia, and arenas. *Journal of Policy Analysis and Management, 18*(4), 601–624.

Community impact of the 1984 Olympic Games in Los Angeles. (1986). Los Angeles: Economic Research Associates.

Crompton, J.L. (1995). Economic impact analysis of sports facilities and events: Eleven sources of misapplication. *Journal of Sports Management, 9,* 14–35.

Crompton, J.L. (1999). *Measuring the economic impact of visitors to sports tournaments and special events.* Ashburn, VA: National Recreation and Park Association.

Deloitte & Touche. (1993). *Economic impact study of a Major League Baseball stadium and franchise.* Phoenix.

Demick, B. (2009, February 22). Beijing's Olympic building boom becomes a bust: Many buildings in the city's impressive skyline are empty. *Los Angeles Times.* http://articles.latimes.com/2009/feb/22/world/fg-beijing-bust22?pg=1 [June 15, 2009].

Depken, C.A. (2004, January 2). Economic impact of Super Bowl hard to figure. *Houston Business Journal.*

Epstein, E. (1997, April 10). Key questions on stadium deal: Here are some answers, but 49ers scramble for specifics. *San Francisco Chronicle,* p. A1.

Fuller, S.S. (2003). *Economic and fiscal impacts of a Major League Baseball franchise and stadium on the Commonwealth of Virginia.* Fairfax, VA: George Mason University.

Grose, T. (2008, August 22). London admits it can't top lavish Beijing Olympics when it hosts 2012 Games: Facing an economic downturn, British officials are trying to keep costs down. *U.S. News and World Report.* www.usnews.com/articles/news/world/2008/08/22/london-admits-it-cant-top-lavish-beijing-olympics-when-it-hosts-2012-games.html [June 15, 2009].

Heylar, J. (2003, November 24). The only company Wal-Mart fears. *Fortune,* 148.

Hopkins, N. (2001, July 13). *Business eyes Olympic gold in Beijing.* www.cnn.com/2001/WORLD/asiapcf/east/07/12/olympics.business/ [July 21, 2004].

Hudson, I. (2001). The use and misuse of economic impact analysis. *Journal of Sport and Social Issues, 25*(1), 20–39.

InterVISTAS. (2002). *The economic impact of the 2010 Winter Olympic and Paralympic Games: An update*. Vancouver, BC.

Keynes, J.M. (1933). The multiplier. *The New Statesman and Nation*, 405–407.

Laris, M., and Montgomery, L. (2004, July 11). Washington's major league divide: Competing bids for baseball team show split between city, suburbs. *Washington Post*, p. A1.

Noll, R., and Zimbalist, A. (1997). The economic impact of sports teams and facilities. In R. Noll and A. Zimbalist (Eds.), *Sports, jobs and taxes: The economic impact of sports teams and facilities* (pp. 55–91). Washington, DC: Brookings Institution Press.

Porter, P.K. (1999). Mega-sports events as municipal investments: A critique of impact analysis. In J. Fizel, E. Gustafson, and L. Hadley (Eds.), *Sports economics: Current research* (pp. 61–73). New York: Praeger.

Quinn, P. (2004, June 11). A weekly look at Athens' preparations for the Olympics. *Associated Press*, p. 1.

Rosentraub, M.S. (1997). *Major league losers: The real cost of sports and who's paying for it*. New York: Basic Books.

Rosentraub, M.S. (1999). *Major league losers: The Real cost of sports and who's paying for it* (Revised ed.). New York: Basic Books.

St. Louis Regional Chamber and Growth Association. (2004). *Cardinals ballpark and ballpark village is substantial economic boost to St. Louis region, RCGA economic impact analysis concludes* (Press release). St. Louis.

Shaffer, M., Greer, A., and Mauboules, C. (2003). *Olympic costs and benefits: A cost–benefit analysis of the proposed Vancouver 2010 Winter Olympic and Paralympic Games*. Vancouver, BC: Canadian Centre for Policy Alternatives—BC Office.

Shook, Dennis (2004, January 14). Team Parked:Foti, Busalacchi say lease will keep Brewers in city. *Waukesha Freeman*.

Siegfried, J., and Zimbalist, A. (2000). The economics of sports facilities and their communities. *Journal of Economic Perspectives, 14*(3), 95–114.

Siegfried, J., and Zimbalist, A. (2002). A note on the local economic impact of sports expenditures. *Journal of Sports Economics, 3*(4), 361–366.

Smale, W. (2004, June 2). Is Euro 2004 worth it for Portugal? http://news.bbc.co.uk/go/pr/fr/-/1/hi/business/3765529.stm? [July 21, 2004].

Spiros, D. (2004, January 18). Business of the NHL: League heading toward lockout. *Star Tribune*.

Standeven, J., and Knop, P.D. (1999). *Sport tourism*. Champaign, IL: Human Kinetics.

Struck, D. (2002, June 29). Hosts left to foot World Cup bill: Promises of payoff go largely unmet for S. Korea, Japan. *Washington Post*, p. A1.

Zimbalist, Andrew. (2003). *May the best team win: Baseball economics and public policy*. Washington, DC: Brookings Institution Press.

Chapter 5

Adams, B., and Engel, M. (2002). *Fodor's baseball vacation: Great family trips to minor league and classic major league ballparks across America*. New York: Fodor's Travel Publications.

Andrews, C., and Horn, D. (2004, March 11). County joins lawsuit: NFL, Bengals accused of squeezing taxpayers. *Cincinnati Enquirer*.

Austrian, Z., and Rosentraub, M.S. (2002). Cities, sports and economic Change: A retrospective assessment. *Journal of Urban Affairs, 24*(5), 549–563.

Bartimole, R. (2003). *Why Cleveland remains a Little League city*. www.citynewsohio.com/News/article/article.asp?NewsID = 31913&sID = 4 [August 21, 2004].

Brooks, D. (2004). Couple's 55,650-mile tour takes in nation's ballparks. *Seattle Times*.

Carlino, G., and Coulson, N.E. (2002). *Compensating differentials and the social benefits of the NFL* (Working paper No. 02-12). Philadelphia: Federal Reserve Bank of Philadelphia.

Coates, D., and Humphreys, B.R. (1999). The growth effects of sport franchises, stadia, and arenas. *Journal of Policy Analysis and Management, 18*(4), 601–624.

Crowell, C. (2005, July 27). Big project agreements yield big community benefits. Michigan Land Use Institute. www.mlui.org/growthmanagement/fullarticle.asp?fileid = 16902 [June 10, 2009].

Crowley, J. (2004, May 7). Selig: A's need new park. *San Francisco Examiner*.

Danielson, M.N. (1997). *Home team: Professional sports and the American metropolis*. Princeton, NJ: Princeton University Press.

Elkin, S.L. (1987). *City and regime in the American republic*. Chicago: University of Chicago Press.

Euchner, C. (1993). *Playing the field: Why sports teams move and cities fight to keep them*. Baltimore: Johns Hopkins Press.

Fainaru, S. (2004, June 28). Expos for sale: Team becomes pawn of Selig. *Washington Post*, p. A1.

Hanemann, W.M. (1994). Valuing the environment through contingent valuation. *Journal of Economic Perspectives, 8*(4), 19–44.

Heath, T. (2004, February 27). Phoenix has become valley of the subsidy; taxpayers give $700 million to sports venues. *Washington Post*, p. D1. http://rockpile.buffalonet.org/home.html [August 1, 2004].

Irani, D. (1997). Public subsidies to stadiums: Do the costs outweigh the benefits? *Public Finance Review, 25*(2), 238–253.

Johnson, B.K., and Whitehead, J.C. (2000). Value of public goods from sports stadiums: The CVM approach. *Contemporary Economic Policy, 18*(1), 48–58.

Keating, D.W. (1997). Cleveland and the "comeback" city: The politics of redevelopment amidst urban decline. In M. Lauria (Ed.), *Reconstructing urban regime theory: Regulating urban politics in a global economy* (pp. 189–205). New York: McGraw-Hill.

Keating, R. (1999). Sports pork: The costly relationship between major league sports and government. *Cato Policy Analysis, 339*.

Kenny, W. (2004, February 12). Going once? Twice? SOLD! *Northeast Times*.

Leventhal, J. (2000). *Take me out to the ballpark: An illustrated tour of baseball parks past and present*. New York: Black Dog & Leventhal.

Logan, J.R., and Molotch, H. (1987). *Urban fortunes: The political economy of place*. Los Angeles: University of California Press.

Michener, J.A. (1976). *Sports in America*. New York: Random House.

Mitchell, R.C., and Carson, R.T. (1989). *Using surveys to value public goods: The contingent valuation methodology*. Washington, DC: Resources for the Future.

Molotch, H. (1976). The city as a growth machine: Toward a political economy of place. *American Journal of Sociology, 82*, 309–332.

Munsey, and Suppes. (n.d.) *Ballparks*. www.ballparks.com [August 1, 2004].

Noll, R. (1974). *Government and the sports business*. Washington, DC: Brookings Institution Press.

Noll, R., and Zimbalist, A. (1997a). Build the stadium—create the jobs! In R. Noll and A. Zimbalist (Eds.), *Sports, jobs and taxes: The economic impact of sports teams and facilities* (pp. 1–54). Washington, DC: Brookings Institution Press.

Noll, R., and Zimbalist, A. (1997b). The economic impact of sports teams and facilities. In R. Noll and A. Zimbalist (Eds.), *Sports, jobs and taxes: The economic impact of sports teams and facilities* (pp. 55–91). Washington, DC: Brookings Institution Press.

Okner, B. (1974). Subsidies of stadiums and arenas. In R. Noll (Ed.), *Government and the sports business*. Washington, DC: Brookings Institution.

Ozanian, M.K. (2003, September 15). *Showing you the money*. www.forbes.com/free_forbes/2003/0915/081tab.html [August 20, 2004].

Portney, P.R. (1994). The contingent valuation debate: Why economists should care. *Journal of Economic Perspectives, 8*(4), 3–17.

Quirk, J., and Fort, R.D. (1992). *Pay dirt: The business of professional team sports.* Princeton, NJ: Princeton University Press.

Rafool, M. (1997). *Playing the Stadium Game: Financing Professional Sports Facilities in the 90s.* Denver: National Conference of State Legislatures

Rappaport, J., and Wilkerson, C. (2001). What are the benefits of hosting a major league sports franchise? *Economic Review, Federal Reserve Bank of Kansas City,* (First Quarter), 55–86.

Reichard, K. *Ballpark Digest.* www.ballparkdigest.com/ [August 1, 2004].

Rosentraub, M.S. (1997). *Major league losers: The real cost of sports and who's paying for it.* New York: Basic Books.

Rosentraub, M.S. (1999). *Major league losers: The real cost of sports and who's paying for it* (Revised ed.). New York: Basic Books.

Rosentraub, M.S., and Swindell, D. (1998). Who benefits from the presence of professional sports teams? *Public Administration Review, 58*(1), 10–21.

Santo, C. (2007). Beyond the economic catalyst debate: Can public consumption benefits justify a municipal stadium investment? *Journal of Urban Affairs 29* (5), 455-479.

Schuerman, M. (2006, April 9). The Yankees's $700,000 play: 'It is not a shakedown.' *New York Observer,* www.observer.com/node/38670 [June 10, 2009].

Siegfried, J., and Zimbalist, A. (2000). The economics of sports facilities and their communities. *Journal of Economic Perspectives, 14*(3), 95–114.

Sports facility reports. (2003). Milwaukee: National Sports Law Institute of Marquette University Law School.

Sports facility reports. (2007). Milwaukee: National Sports Law Institute of Marquette University Law School.

Sports facility reports. (2009). Milwaukee: National Sports Law Institute of Marquette University Law School.

Stone, C. (1989). *Regime politics governing Atlanta, 1946–1988.* Lawrence: University of Kansas Press.

Sullivan, N.J. (2001). *The diamond in the Bronx: Yankee Stadium and the politics of New York.* New York: Oxford University Press.

Williams, T. (2006, March 22). $28 Million for the Bronx in the Yankees' stadium plan. *New York Times.*

Williams, T. (2008, January 7). Stadium goes up, but Bronx still seeks benefits. *New York Times.*

Zimbalist, A. (2003). *May the best team win: Baseball economic and public policy.* Washington, DC: The Brookings Institution.

Zimmerman, D. (1997). Subsidizing stadiums: Who benefits, who pays? In R. Noll and A. Zimbalist (Eds.), *Sports jobs and taxes: The economic impact of sports teams and stadiums.* Washington, DC: Brookings Institution Press.

Chapter 6

Agranoff, R., and McGuire, M. (2003). *Collaborative public management.* Washington, DC: Georgetown University Press.

Bornstein, D. (1998). Changing the world on a shoestring. *Atlantic Monthly, 281*(1): 34–39.

Clubb, Deborah. (1999, August 13, Final Edition). Plan is about more than baseball. *Commercial Appeal,* p. A1.

Clubb, D., and Johnson, R. (1999, June 12, Final Edition). Behind-scenes backing for AutoZone Park is emerging in contracts. *Commercial Appeal,* p. A1.

Danielson, M. (1997). *Home team, professional sports and the American metropolis.* Princeton University Press.

Dees, J. (1998). *The meaning of "social entrepreneurship."* Draft report for the Kauffman Center for Entrepreneurial Leadership. 6 pp.

Dees, J., and Anderson, B. (2006). Framing a theory of social entrepreneurship: Building on two schools of practice and thought. *ARNOVA Occasional Paper Series, 1*(3):39–66.

Eikenberry, A., and Kluver, J. (2004). The marketization of the nonprofit sector: Civil society at risk. *Public Administration Review, 64*(2), 132–140.

Guo, K. (2006). Entrepreneurship management in health services: An integrative model. *Journal of Health and Human Services Administration, 28*(4): 504–530.

Kennedy, S., and Rosentraub, M. (2000). Public private partnerships, professional sports teams and the protection of the public's interest. *American Review of Public Administration, 30*(4), 436–459.

Kerlin, J. (2006). Social enterprise in the United States and abroad: Learning from our differences. *ARNOVA Occasional Paper Series, 1*(3), 105–125.

Kinnander, O. (2001, March 30). The end of an audit: IRS, Redbirds Foundation reach agreement. *Bond Buyer,* 335 (31108), p. 1, 2p, Item 4340208.

Korosec, R., and Berman, E. (2006). Municipal support for social entrepreneurship. *Public Administration Review, 66*(3), 448–462.

Kraker, D. (2000, Winter). Keeping the minors home. *New Rules, 2,* 13–15.

Kraker, D., and Morris, D. (1998). Roots, roots, roots for the home team. The Institute for Local Self-Reliance. www.newrules.org/resources/rootsroots.pdf.

Kramer, M., and Kania, J. (2006). Changing the game: Leading corporations switch from defense to offense in solving global problems. *Stanford Social Innovation Review, 4*(1), 20–27.

Light, P. (2006). Searching for social entrepreneurs: Who they might be, where they might be found, what they do. *ARNOVA Occasional Paper Series, 1*(3), 13–37.

Massarsky, C. (2006). Coming of age: Social enterprise reaches its tipping point. *ARNOVA Occasional Paper Series, 1*(3), 67–87.

Meder, J.W., and Leckrone, J.W. (2002). HARDBALL: Local government's foray into sports franchise ownership. *Journal of Urban Affairs,* 24 (3), 353–368.

Memphis Redbirds Foundation. (2004). *Memphis Redbirds 2004 souvenir yearbook.* [Brochure].

Peredo, A.M., and McLean, M. (2006). Social entrepreneurship: A critical review of the concept. *Journal of World Business, 41*(1), 56–65.

McClearly, K., Rivers, P., and Schneller, E. (2006). A diagnostic approach to understanding entrepreneurship in healthcare. *Journal of Health and Human Services Administration, 28*(4), 550–577.

Schwab Foundation for Social Entrepreneurship. (n.d.). www.schwabfound.org [March 30, 2006].

Sharir, M., and Lerner, M. (2006). Gauging the success of social ventures initiated by individual social entrepreneurs. *Journal of World Business, 41*(1), 6–20.

Sheffield, M. (2003, October 10). Redbirds personnel, park busy in off season. *Memphis Business Journal.* www.bizjournals.com/memphis/stories/2003/10/13/ newscolumn1.html. [October 26, 2006].

Weerawardena, J., and Mort, G. (2006). Investigating social entrepreneurship: A multidimensional model. *Journal of World Business,* 41 (1), 21–35.

Winer, Michael, and Ray, Karen. (1994). *Collaboration handbook.* Saint Paul, MN: Amhurst H. Wilder Foundation.

Chapter 7

Bedimo-Rung, A., Mowen, A.J., & Cohen, D.A. (2005). The significance of parks to physical activity and public health: A conceptual model. *The American Journal of Preventive Medicine,* 28 (2S2), 159-168.

Centers for Disease Control. (2005, December 2). *MMWR Weekly, 54*(47), 1208–1212.

Centers for Disease Control. (2005, July). *Preventing chronic diseases: Investing wisely in health.*

Centers for Disease Control. (2007). *Physical activity for everyone.* www.cdc.gov/nccdphp/dnpa/ physical/recommendations/index.htm [October 22, 2007].

City of Copenhagen (2007). *Copenhagen city of cyclists bicycle account 2006.* www.vejpark2.kk.dk/ publikationer/pdf/464_Cykelregnskab_UK.%202006.pdf.

Cohen, D.A., McKenzie, T.L., Sehgal, A., Williamson, S., Golinelli, D., and Lurie, N. (2007). Contribution of parks to physical activity. *American Journal of Public Health, 97*(3), 509–514.

Cranz, G. (1989). *The politics of park design: A history of urban parks in America.* Cambridge. MA: MIT Press.

Dill, J. (2006a). Evaluating a new urbanist neighborhood. *Berkeley Planning Journal, 19,* 59–78.

Dill, J. (2006b). *Travel and transit use at Portland area transit-oriented developments (TODs).* Final Technical Report TNW2006-03. Seattle: University of Washington, TransNow.

Ewing, R., Schmid T., Killingsworth, R. and Raudenbush, S. (2003). Relationship between urban sprawl and physical activity, obesity, and morbidity. *American Journal of Health Promotion, 18*(1), 47–57.

Finkelstein, E.A., Fiebelkorn, I.C., and Wang, G. (2003). National medical spending attributable to overweight and obesity: How much, and who's paying? *Health Affairs,* W3, 219–225.

Floyd, M.F., Spengler, J.O., Confer, J.J., Maddock, J.E., and Gobster, P.H. (2007, February). *Exploring the relationship between neighborhood factors and physical activity in public parks in diverse communities.* Paper presented at the Active Living Research Conference, Coronado, CA.

Frank, L.D., Andresen, M.A., and Schmid, T.L. (2004). Obesity relationships with community design, physical activity, and time spent in cars. *American Journal of Preventive Medicine,* 27 (2), 87–96.

Frank, L.D., Engelke, P.O., and Schmid, T. (2003). Health and community design: The impact of the built environment on physical activity. Washington, DC: Island Press.

Frumkin, H., Heiling, A., Mumford, K., Dempsey, S., French, S.P., and Waller, L. (2004, February). *Neighborhood parks and active living (NPAL).* Paper presented at the Active Living Research Conference, Coronado, CA.

Godbey, G.C., Caldwell, L.L., Floyd, M., and Payne, L.L. (2004). Contribution of leisure studies and recreation and park management research to the active living agenda. *American Journal of Preventive Medicine, 28*(2, 2S), 150–158.

Haskell, W.L., et al. (2007, August). Physical activity and public health: Updated recommendation for adults from the American College of Sports Medicine and the American Heart Association. *Medicine and Science in Sports and Exercise, 39*(8), 1423–1434.

He, Wan, Sengupta, Manisha, Velkoff, Victoria A., and DeBarros, Kimberly A. (2005). *65+ in the United States: 2005.* U.S. Census Bureau, Current Population Reports, P23-209. Washington, DC: U.S. Government Printing Office.

Hoehner, C. M., Brennan, L.K., Brownson, R. C., Handy, S. L., and Killingsworth, R. (2003). Opportunities for integrating public health and urban planning approaches to promote active community environments. *American Journal of Health Promotion,* 18, 14-20.

Kitamura, R., Mokhtarian, P.L., and Laidet, L. (1997). A micro-analysis of land use and travel in five neighborhoods in the San Francisco Bay Area. *Transportation, 24,* 125–158.

Krahnstoever, K., and Lawson, C. (2006, February). Associations between children's physical activity and the physical environment: A review and recommendations for future research. Presented at the Active Living Research Conference, Coronado, CA.

Lee, C., and Moudon, A.V. (2004) Physical activity and environment research in the health field: Implications for urban and transportation planning practice and research. *Journal of Planning Literature, 19*(2), 147–181.

Levine, J., Inam, A., and Torng, G. (2005). A choice-based rationale for land use and transportation alternatives. *Journal of Planning Education and Research, 24*(3), 317–330.

Librett, J.J., Yore, M.M., and Schmid, T.L. (2006). Characteristics of physical activity levels among trail users in a U.S. national sample. *American Journal of Preventive Medicine, 31*(5), 399–405.

Lindsey, G., Han, Y., Wilson, J., and Yang, J. (2006). Neighborhood correlates of urban trail use. *Journal of Physical Activity and Health, 3*, S139–S157.

Lindsey, G., Man, J., Payton, S., and Dickson, K. (2004). Property values, recreation values, and urban greenways. *Journal of Park and Recreation Administration, 22*(3), 69–90.

Lund, H. (2003). Testing the claims of new urbanism: Local access, pedestrian travel, and neighboring behaviors. *Journal of the American Planning Association, 69*(4), 414–429.

Moudon, A.V., Lee, C., Cheadle, A.D., Collier, C.W., Johnson, D., Schmid, T.L., and Weather, R.D. (2005). Cycling and the built environment, a US Perspective. *Transportation Research Part D: Transport and Environment, 10* (3), 245—261.

Ministry of Transport, Public Works and Water Management. (2007). *Cycling in the Netherlands.* www.minvenw.nl.

National Cooperative Highway Research Program. (2006). *Guidelines for analysis of investments in bicycle facilities.* Washington, DC: Transportation Research Board.

Nicholls, S., and Crompton, J.L. (2005). The impact of greenways on property values: Evidence from Austin, Texas. *Journal of Leisure Research, 37*(3), 321–341.

Pate, R.R., et al. (1995). Physical activity and public health. A recommendation from the Centers for Disease Control and Prevention and the American College of Sports Medicine. *Journal of the American Medical Association, 273*(5), 402–407.

Pucher, J., and Dijkstra, L. (2003). Promoting safe walking and cycling to improve public health: Lessons from the Netherlands and Germany. *American Journal of Public Health, 93*(9), 1509–1516.

Pucher, J., and Renne, J.L. (2003). Socioeconomics of urban travel: Evidence from the 2001 NHTS. *Transportation Quarterly, 57*(3), 49–77.

Puget Sound Regional Council. (2000, November). Burke-Gilman/Sammamish River Trail use. *Puget Sound Trends, 14.* www.psrc.org/publications/pubs/trends/t14nov00.pdf.

Reconnecting America, Center for Transit-Oriented Development. (2004, September). *Capturing the demand for housing near transit.*

Saelens, B.E., Sallis, J.F., and Frank, L.D. (2003). Environmental correlates of walking and cycling: Findings from the transportation, urban design, and planning literatures. *Annals of Behavioral Medicine, 25*(2), 80–91.

Sallis, J. F., Cervero, R. B., Ascher, W., Henderson, K. A., Kraft, M. K., & Kerr, J. (2006). An ecological approach to creating active living communities. *Annual Review of Public Health, 27*, 297-322.

Transportation Research Board, Institute of Medicine of the National Academies. (2005). *Does the built environment influence physical activity? Examining the evidence.* Special Report 282. National Research Council.

U.S. Department of Health and Human Services. (2003). *Healthy people 2010: Understanding and improving health* (2nd ed). Washington, DC: U.S. Government Printing Office.

Urban Land Institute, PriceWaterhouseCoopers. (2008, October). *Emerging trends in real estate 2009.*

Weigand, L.R. (2007). *Active recreation in parks: Can park design and facilities promote use and physical activity?* Unpublished doctoral dissertation, Portland, OR: Portland State University.

Chapter 8

Anderson, B. (2001). Celebrating Jackie Robinson? Major League Baseball sees the limitations of promotions. *Journal of Promotion Management, 7*, 215–224.

Barthes, R. (1972). *Mythologies.* New York: Hill and Wang.

Barthes, R. (1982). *A Barthes reader.* New York: Hill and Wang.

Bem, S.L. (1981). Gender schema theory: A cognitive account of sex-typing. *Psychological Review, 88*, 354–364.

Blaisdell, L.D. (1992). Legends as an expression of baseball memory. *Journal of Sport History, 19*, 227–243.

Chastain, B. (2005, September 1). *Notes: Crawford speaks up for inner city*. Tampa Bay Devil Rays Web site: http://tampabay.devilrays.mlb.com/NASApp/mlb/news/article.jsp?ymd = 10050901&cont. [January 16, 2006].

Chalberg, J. (2000). *Rickey and Robinson: The preacher, the player and America's game*. Wheeling, IL: Harlan Davidson.

Davis, Y. (2007, May). Where are the African-American baseball players? *Ebony, 62*, 172–174.

Florida Marlins (2008, May 22). *Marlins RBI season currently underway*. Florida Marlins Web site: http://florida.marlins.mlb.com/news/press_releases/press_release.jsp?ymd = 20080522&con [May 27, 2008].

Fry, D.L., and Fry, V.H. (1989). Continuing the conversation regarding myth and culture: An alternative reading of Barthes. *American Journal of Semiotics, 6*, 183–197.

Griffin, E. (2003). *A first look at communication theory*. Boston: McGraw-Hill.

Hill, J. (2005, April 15). *Notes: Crisp thankful for Robinson*. Major League Baseball Web site: http://mlb.mlb.com/NASApp/mlb/news/article.jsp?ymd = 20050415&content_id = 1016711 [January 16, 2006].

Lapchick, R. (2004). *2003 racial and gender report card*. Orlando: University of Central Florida College of Business Administration.

Lapchick, R. (2007). *2006–2007 racial and gender report card*. Orlando: University of Central Florida College of Business Administration.

Lapchick, R., Little, E., and Lerner, C. (2008). *The 2008 racial and gender report card: National Football League*. Orlando: University of Central Florida College of Business Administration.

Lapchick, R., Diaz-Calderon, A., and McMechan, D. (2009). *The 2009 racial and gender report card: Major League Baseball*. Orlando: University of Central Florida College of Business Administration).

Lapchick, R., Hanson, J., Harless, C., and Johnson, W. (2009). *The 2009 racial and gender report card: National Basketball Association*. Orlando: University of Central Florida College of Business Administration.

Lasorda, T. (2005, April 14). Robinson had the heart of a lion. Major League Baseball Web site: http://mlb.mlb.com/NASApp/mlb/nws/article_perspectives.jsp?ymd = 20050414 [January 16, 2006].

Levy, A. (2002). The right myths at the right time: Myth-making and hero worship in post- frontier American society—Rube Waddell vs. Christy Mathewson. In William H. Simons (Ed.), *The Cooperstown Symposium on Baseball and American Culture, 2001* (pp. 51–65). Jefferson, NC: McFarland.

McCarthy, J. (2008). *Home Run Baseball Camp: About the director*. Home Run Baseball Camp Web site: http://homerunbaseballcamp.com/html/director.html [June 10, 2009].

Major League Baseball. (2005, April 13). *White Sox celebrate Jackie Robinson Day*. Major League Baseball Web site: http://chicago.whitesox.mlb.com/NASApp/mlb/news/press_releases/press_release.jsp?ymd [January 16, 2006].

Major League Baseball. (2008a). 2007 RBI facts. Major League Baseball Web site: http://mlb.mlb.com/mlb/official_info/community/rbi.jsp?content = facts [May 27, 2008].

Major League Baseball. (2008b). 2007 Rookie League facts. Major League Baseball Web site: http://mlb.mlb.com/mlb/official_info/community/rbi_rookie.jsp [May 27, 2008].

Major League Baseball. (2009) 2009 RBI 20th anniversary fact sheet. Major League Baseball Web site: http://mlb.mlb.com/mlb/official_info/community/rbi_facts.jsp [June 9, 2009].

MLB refurbishes public ball fields nationwide (2005, July). *Parks and Recreation, 40*(7), 564.

Ogden, D.C. (2002). Youth select baseball in the Midwest. In W.M. Simons and A. Hall (Eds.), *The Cooperstown Symposium on Baseball and American Culture, 2001* (pp. 322–335). Jefferson, NC: McFarland.

Ogden, D.C. (2004) The welcome theory: An approach to studying African American youth interest and involvement in baseball. *Nine: A Journal of Baseball History and Culture, 12*, 114–122.

Ogden, D.C. (2005). *Reviving baseball interest among African-Americans: What theory and youth programs can teach us about bringing the game back to black communities?* Paper presented at the 17th Annual Cooperstown Symposium on Baseball and American Culture, June 8–10, 2005, Cooperstown, NY.

Ogden, D.C. (2007). *The pipeline of baseball: African Americans' interest in the game*. Paper presented at the Iowa Baseball Symposium at the Herbert Hoover Presidential Library and Museum, August 3–4, 2007, West Branch, IA.

Ogden, D., and Rose, R.A. (2005). Using Giddens's structuration theory to examine the waning participation of African Americans in baseball. *Journal of Black Studies, 35*, 225–245.

Omaha North High School Grunwald Viking Baseball. (2009). *Welcome*. Grunwald Viking Baseball Web site: http://leaguelineup.com/welcome.asp?cmenuid=1&url=onvb&sid=161308166.

Patterson, M. (2005, April 9). North molds its field of dreams. *Omaha World Herald*, p. 3C.

Phillips, M. (2007, June). Advocacy update: The importance of youth sport. *Parks and Recreation, 12*(6), 16–17.

Svrluga, B., and Pierre, R.E. (2005, April 4–10). It's more than just a game. *Washington Post, national weekly edition*, pp. 8–9.

Verducci, T. (2003, July 7). Blackout: The African-American baseball player is vanishing. Does he have a future? *Sports Illustrated, 99*, 56–62.

Voight, D.Q. (1978). Myths after baseball: Notes on myths in sports. *Quest, 30*, 46–57.

Wicks, A., Beedy, J., Spangler, K., and Perkins, D.F. (2007). Intermediaries supporting sports-based youth development programs. *Directions for Youth Development, 2007*(115), 107–118.

Wilson, B., and Sparks, R. (1996). "It's gotta be the shoes": Youth, race and sneaker commercials. *Sociology of Sport Journal, 13*, 398–427.

Chapter 9

Baade, R.A., and Sundberg, J.O. (1996, December). Fourth down and gold to go? Assessing the link between athletics and alumni giving. *Social Science Quarterly, 77*(4), 789–803.

Bailey, W.S., and Littleton, T.D. (1991). *Athletics and academe: An anatomy of abuses and a prescription for reform*. New York: Macmillan.

Barley, S.R., and Tolbert, P.S. (1997). Institutionalization and structuration: Studying the links between action and institution. *Organization Studies, 18*, 93–117.

Baxter, V., and Lambert, C. (1991). Competing rationalities and the politics of interorganizational regulation. *Sociological Perspectives, 34*(2), 183–203.

Baxter, V., Margovio, A.V., and Lambert, C. (1996). Competition, legitimation, and the regulation of intercollegiate athletics. *Sociology of Sport Journal, 13*(1), 51–64.

Berger, P., and Luckman, T. (1967). *The social construction of reality: A treatise in the sociology of knowledge*. Garden City, NY: Anchor Books Doubleday.

Bignell, J. (1997). *Media semiotics: An introduction*. Manchester, UK: Manchester University Press.

Bosman, J. (2006, March 16). The media business: Advertising: March Madness afflicts advertisers. [Electronic version]. *New York Times*. http://select.nytimes.com [January 10, 2007].

Brand, M. (2006, September 11). President's message—call for moderation is a complex message, not a mixed one. *The NCAA News*.

Brown, G.T. (2002, March 18). The $6 billion plan: NCAA wants TV contract to increase revenue, decrease tension between scholarly mission and commercial image. *The NCAA News*.

Brown, G.T. (2005a, May 23). Faculty group presents syllabus for reform: Coalition for Intercollegiate Athletics advocates curricular integrity. *The NCAA News*.

Brown, G.T. (2005b, June 20). Presidents lay groundwork for reform sequel. *The NCAA News*.

Case, B., Greer, H., and Brown, J. (1987). Academic clustering in athletics: Myth or reality. *Arena Review*, 11(2), 48–56.

Chu, D. (1989). *The character of American higher education and intercollegiate sport*. Albany: State University of New York Press.

Coakley, J.J. (2001). *Sport in society* (7th ed.). Boston: McGraw-Hill.

Congressional Budget Office. (2009). *Tax preferences for collegiate sports*. Congress of the United States.

Cresswell, J.W. (1998). *Qualitative inquiry and research design: Choosing among five traditions*. Thousand Oaks, CA: Sage.

DeBrock, L., Hendricks, W., and Koenker, R. (1996). The economics of persistence: Graduation rates of athletes as labor market choice. *Journal of Human Resources*, 31(3), 512–538.

Depken, C., and Wilson, D. (2005). Rules enforcement and competitive balance in college football. *Economics of Collegiate Sports*, 1–15.

DeVenzio, D. (1986). *Rip-off U: The annual theft and exploitation of revenue producing major college student–athletes*. Charlotte, NC: Fool Court Press.

Duncan, M.C., and Brummett, B. (1991). The mediation of spectator sport. In L.H. Vande Berg and L.A. Wenner (Eds.), *Television criticism: Approaches and applications* (pp. 367–387). New York: Longman.

Elsbach, K.D., and Kramer, R.M. (1996). Members' responses to organizational identity threats: Encountering and countering the business week rankings. *Administrative Science Quarterly*, 41, 442–476.

Eitzen, D.S. (1988). Ethical problems in American sport. *Journal of Sport and Social Issues*, 12(1), 17–30.

Feldman, M.S. (2000). Organizational routines as a source of continuous change. *Organization Science*, 11, 611–629.

Feldman, M.S., and Pentland, B.T. (2003). Reconceptualizing organizational routines as a source of flexibility and change. *Administrative Science Quarterly*, 48, 94–118.

Frey, J.H. (1994). Deviance in organizational subunits: The case of college athletic departments. *Journal of Sport and Social Issues*, 18, 110–122.

Friedland, R., and Alford, R.R. (1991). Bringing society back in: Symbols, practices, and institutional contradictions. In W.W. Powell and P.J. DiMaggio (Eds.), *The new institutionalism in organizational analysis* (pp. 232–262). Chicago: University of Chicago Press.

Funk, G.D. (1992). *Major violations: The unbalanced priorities in athletics and academics*. Champaign, IL: Leisure Press.

Gaski, J.F., and Etzel, M.J. (1984). Collegiate athletic success and alumni generosity: Dispelling the myth. *Social Behavior and Personality*, 12(1), 29–38.

Gerdy, J.R. (1997). *The successful college athletic program: The new standard*. Phoenix, AZ: American Council on Education and the Oryx Press.

Gerdy, J.R. (2006). *Air ball: American education's failed experiment with elite athletics*. Oxford: University Press of Mississippi.

Grimes, P.W., and Chressanthis, G.A. (1994, January). Alumni contributions to academics: The role of intercollegiate sports and NCAA sanctions. *American Journal Economics and Sociology*, 53(1), 27–40.

Gruneau, R., Whitson, D., and Cantelon, H. (1988). Methods and media: Studying the sports/television discourse. *Society and Leisure*, 11(2), 265–281.

Gough, P. (2006, May 5). Pardon the interruptions: Primetime ads increasing. *The Hollywood Reporter.com*. www.hollywoodreporter.com/thr/television [May 9, 2006].

Harris Interactive. (2006, March 29). *The Harris Poll #28, March 29, 2006: Duke may not be in the Final Four, but they continue to be the nation's favorite college basketball team*. www.harrisinteractive.com/harris_poll/index.asp?PID = 652 [November 9, 2007].

Justice v. NCAA, 577 F. Supp. 356, Dis. Ct. Ariz. (1983).

Lapchick, R.E. (1986). *Fractured focus*. Lexington, MA: Heath.

Law v. National Collegiate Athletic Association, 134 F.3d 1010 (10th Cir. 1998).

Lounsbury, M. (2007). A tale of two cities: Competing logics and practice variation in the professionalizing of mutual funds. *Academy of Management Journal, 50*(2), 289–307.

Madden, P.A., and Grube, J.W. (1994). The frequency and nature of alcohol and tobacco advertising in televised sports 1990 through 1992. *American Journal of Public Health, 84*, 297–299.

Manning, P., and Cullum-Swan, B. (1994). Narrative, content, and semiotic analysis. In N. Denzin and Y. Lincoln (Eds.), *Handbook of qualitative research*. Thousand Oaks, CA: Sage.

Maraniss, D. (1999). When *pride still mattered: A life of Vince Lombardi*. New York: Simon & Schuster.

Marts, A.C. (1934). College football and college endowment. *School and Society, 40*, 14–15.

Metropolitan Intercollegiate Basketball Association v. NCAA, 337 F. Supp. 2d 563, 571 (SDNY 2004).

Meyer, J., and Rowan, B. (1977). Institutional organizations: Formal structure as myth and ceremony. *American Journal of Sociology, 83*, 340–363.

Moran, M. (2005, August 17). NCAA buys NIT for $56.5 million. *USA Today*. www.usatoday.com/sports/college/mensbasketball/2005-08-17-ncaa-nit-purchase_x.htm [June 29, 2009].

National Collegiate Athletic Association. (1999, February 22). NCAA launches marketing campaign to promote college basketball. *The NCAA News*.

National Collegiate Athletic Association. (2000). *2000 national college basketball attendance*. http://www.ncaa.org/wps/wcm/connect/397e9e804e0ba3638315f31ad6fc8b25/2000_basketball_attend.pdf?MOD = AJPERES&CACHEID = 397e9e804e0ba3638315f31ad6fc8b25 [August 20, 2009].

National Collegiate Athletic Association. (2002, March 18). CEOs don't blink on corporate tag. *The NCAA News*.

National Collegiate Athletic Association. (2005). *The NCAA's advertising and promotional standards*. http://www.ncaa.org/wps/ncaa?ContentID = 635 [August 20, 2009].

National Collegiate Athletic Association. (2006). *2006 Division I men's basketball championship handbook*. http://www.ncaa.org/wps/ncaa?ContentID = 36602 [August 20, 2009].

National Collegiate Athletic Association. (2006). *2006 national college basketball attendance*. http://www.ncaa.org/wps/wcm/connect/372241804e0ba36f833df31ad6fc8b25/2006_basketball_attend.pdf?MOD = AJPERES&CACHEID = 372241804e0ba36f833df31ad6fc8b25 [August 20, 2009].

National Collegiate Athletic Association. (2007a). *About the NCAA*. http://www.ncaa.org/wps/ncaa?key = /ncaa/ncaa/about + the + ncaa [October 31, 2007].

National Collegiate Athletic Association. (2007b). *Historical outline of multidivision classification*. http://www.ncaa.org/wps/ncaa?key = /ncaa/NCAA/About%20The%20NCAA/Membership/The%20Divisions/historical_outline.html [July 28, 2007].

National Collegiate Athletic Association (2007c). *NCAA Sports and Championship Administration*. http://www.ncaa.org/wps/ncaa?key = /ncaa/ncaa/sports + and + championship/basketball/index.html [October 30, 2007].

National Collegiate Athletic Association (2007d). *Our mission*. http://www.ncaa.org/wps/ncaa?key = /ncaa/NCAA/About%20The%20NCAA/Overview/mission.html [October 31, 2007].

National Collegiate Athletic Association. (2007e). *Rules and bylaws*. http://www.ncaa.org/wps/ncaa?key = /ncaa/ncaa/legislation + and + governance/rules + and + bylaws [July 28, 2007].

National Collegiate Athletic Association. (2007f). *The NCAA brand.* http://www.ncaa.org/wps/ncaa?key=/ncaa/NCAA/About+The+NCAA/The+NCAA+Brand/ [April 15, 2007].

National Collegiate Athletic Association. (2007g). *What's the difference between Divisions I, II and III?* http://www.ncaa.org/wps/ncaa?ContentID=418 [July 28, 2007].

NCAA v. Board of Regents of Univ. of Okla., 468 U.S. 85 (1984).

Nelson, R.R., and Winter, S.G. (1982). *An evolutionary theory of economic change.* Cambridge, MA: The Belknap Press of Harvard University Press.

Neuendorf, K.A. (2002). *The content analysis guidebook.* Thousand Oaks, CA: Sage.

Patton, M.Q. (2002). *Qualitative research and evaluation methods* (3rd ed.). Thousand Oaks, CA: Sage.

Padilla, A., and Baumer, D. (1994). Big-time college sports: Management and economic issues. *Journal of Sport and Social Issues, 18,* 123-143.

Putler, D.S., aand Wolfe, R.A. (1999). Perceptions of intercollegiate athletic programs: Priorities and tradeoffs. *Sociology of Sport Journal, 16,* 301-325.

Rascher, D.A., and Schwarz, AD. (2000). Amateurism in big-time college sports, *Antitrust, 14,* 51-56.

Rascher, D. (2003a). *Issues and discussion of NCAA and athletes compensation.* Unpublished manuscript. University of San Francisco.

Rascher, D. (2003b). *Oral testimony regarding California State Senate Bill 193, student athletes' bill of rights.* Testimony to the California State Senate Subcommittee on Entertainment, Sacramento, CA.

Rossman, G.B., and Rallis, S.F. (1998). *Learning in the field: An introduction to qualitative research.* Thousand Oaks, CA: Sage.

Sack, A.L. (1987). College sport and the student–athlete. *Journal of Sport and Social Issues, 11*(1/2), 31-48.

Sack, A.L., and Watkins, C. (1985). Winning and giving. In D. Chu, J.O. Segrave, and B.J. Becker (Eds.), *Sport and higher education* (pp. 299-306). Champaign, IL: Human Kinetics.

Sage, G.H. (1998). *Power and ideology in American sport.* Champaign, IL: Human Kinetics.

Scott, W.R. (2001). *Institutions and organizations* (2nd ed.). London: Sage.

Sigelman, L., and Carter, R. (1979, September). Win one for the giver? Alumni giving and big-time college sports. *Social Science Quarterly, 60,* 284-293.

Silk, M.L., and Amis, J. (2000). Institutional pressures and the production of televised sport. *Journal of Sport Management, 14,* 267-292.

Sperber, M. (1998). *Onward to victory: The crises that shaped college sports.* New York: Henry Holt.

Stinson, J.L., and Howard, D.R. (2007). Athletic success and private giving to athletic and academic programs at NCAA institutions. *Journal of Sport Management, 21*(2), 235-264.

Strauss, A., and Corbin, J. (1990). *Basics of qualitative research: Grounded theory and techniques.* Newbury Park, CA: Sage.

Thornton, P.H. (2002). The rise of the corporation in a craft industry: Conflict and conformity in institutional logics. *Academy of Management Journal, 45,* 81-101.

Vasquez, D. (2005, March 17). Ad dollars and sense of March Madness. *MedialifeMagazine. com.* www.medialifemagazine.com/News2005/mar05/mar14/4_thurs/news4thursday.html [October 21, 2006]

Washington, M. (2004). Field approaches to institutional change: The evolution of the National Collegiate Athletic Association 1906-1995. *Organization Studies, 25,* 393-414.

Washington, M., and Ventresca, M.J. (2004). How organizations change: The role of institutional support mechanisms in the incorporation of higher education visibility strategies, 1874-1995. *Organization Science, 15,* 82-97.

Weiberg, K. (2001, October 22). Too much corporate fruit around to reduce the harvest. *The NCAA News.*

Chapter 10

Alzado, L., and, Smith, S. (1991, July 8). I'm sick and I'm scared. *Sports Illustrated*, pp. 21–27.

Armstrong, L.E. (2002). Diuretics. In M.S. Bahrke and C.E. Yesalis (Eds.), *Performance-enhancing substances in sport and exercise* (pp. 109–116). Champaign, IL: Human Kinetics.

Barker, J. (2008, 6 July). A letter "from the grave." *St. Louis Post Dispatch*, p. D12.

Bass, S., and Marden, E. (2005). The new dietary ingredient safety provision of DSHEA: A return to congressional intent. *American Journal of Law and Medicine, 31*, 285–304.

Brown, W.M. (2001). As American as Gatorade and apple pie: Performance drugs and sports. In W.J. Morgan, K.V. Meier, and A.J. Schneider (Eds.), *Ethics in sport* (pp. 142–168). Champaign, IL: Human Kinetics.

Canseco, J. (2005). *Juiced: Wild times, rampant 'roids, smash hits, and how baseball got big*. New York: Regan.

Chaikin, T., and Telander, R. (1988, October 24). The nightmare of steroids. *Sports Illustrated*, pp. 84–102.

Chalip, L., and Johnson, A. (1996). Sport policy in the United States. In L. Chalip, A. Johnson, and L. Stachura (Eds.), *National sports policies: An international handbook* (pp. 404–430). Westport, CT: Greenwood.

Cobb, R.W., and Elder, C.D. (1971). The politics of agenda-building: An alternative perspective for modern democratic theory. *Journal of Politics, 33*, 892–915.

Cohen, P.J. (2005). Science, politics, and the regulation of dietary supplements: It's time to repeal DSHEA. *American Journal of Law and Medicine*, 31, 175–214.

Courson, S., and Schreiber, L.R. (1991). *False glory: The Steve Courson story*. Stamford, CT: Longmeadow.

Curry, J. (2009, 10 February). As Rodriguez delivers his admission, the Yanks offer support. *New York Times*, p. B13.

Daniellian, L.H., and Reese S.D. (1989). A closer look at intermedia influences on agenda setting: The cocaine issue of 1986. In P J. Shoemaker (Ed.), *Communication campaigns about drugs* (pp. 47–56). Hillsdale, NJ: Erlbaum.

Dembner, A. (2004). Herbal industry fending off FDA. *Boston Globe*, 26 March, p. A1.

Denham, B.E. (1997). Sports Illustrated, "The War on Drugs," and the Anabolic Steroid Control Act of 1990: A study in agenda building and political timing. *Journal of Sport and Social Issues, 21*, 260–273.

Denham, B.E. (1999). Building the agenda and adjusting the frame: How the dramatic revelations of Lyle Alzado impacted mainstream press coverage of anabolic steroid use. *Sociology of Sport Journal*, 16, 1–15.

Denham, B.E. (2004a). Hero or hypocrite? United States and international media portrayals of Carl Lewis amid revelations of a positive drug test. *International Review for the Sociology of Sport* 39: 167–186.

Denham, B.E. (2004b). Sports Illustrated, the mainstream press, and the enactment of drug policy in Major League Baseball: A study in agenda building theory. *Journalism: Theory, Practice and Criticism*, 5, 51–68.

Denham, B.E. (2006). The Anabolic Steroid Control Act of 2004: A study in the political economy of drug policy. *Journal of Health and Social Policy*, 22, 51–78.

Denham, B.E. (2007). Government and the pursuit of rigorous drug testing in Major League Baseball: A study in political negotiation and reciprocity. *International Journal of Sport Management and Marketing*, 2, 379–395.

Denham, B.E. (2008). Calling out the heavy hitters: What performance-enhancing drug use in professional baseball reveals about the politics and mass communication of sport. *International Journal of Sport Communication*, 1, 3–16.

Eitzen, D.S. (2006). *Fair and foul: Beyond the myths and paradoxes of sport* (3rd ed.). Lanham, MD: Rowman & Littlefield.

Ekblom, B.T. (2002). Erythropoietin. In M.S. Bahrke and C.E. Yesalis (Eds.), *Performance-enhancing substances in sport and exercise* (pp. 101–108). Champaign, IL: Human Kinetics.

Elder, C.D., and Cobb, R.W. (1984). Agenda-building and the politics of aging. *Policy Studies Journal, 13*, 115–129.

Elliot, D.L., and Goldberg, L. (2000). Women and anabolic steroids. In C.E. Yesalis (Ed.), *Anabolic steroids in sport and exercise* (2nd ed.) (pp. 225–246). Champaign, IL: Human Kinetics.

Fainaru-Wada, M., and Williams, L. (2006). *Game of shadows: Barry Bonds, BALCO and the steroids scandal that rocked professional sports.* New York: Gotham.

Feinsand, M. (2009, 13 February). Alex heads to hall of shame. Selig backs off ban, rips into A-Rod as disgrace to game. *New York Daily News*, p. 74.

Friedl, K.E. (2000). Effects of anabolic steroids on physical health. In C.E. Yesalis (Ed.), *Anabolic steroids in sport and exercise* (2nd ed.) (pp. 175–223). Champaign, IL: Human Kinetics.

George, A.J. (2003). Peptide and glycoprotein hormones and sport. In D.R. Mottram (Ed.), *Drugs in sport* (3rd ed.) (pp. 138–188). London: Routledge.

Graber, D.A. (2006). *Mass media and American politics* (7th ed.). Washington, DC: CQ Press.

Hanstad, D.V., Smith, A., and Waddington, I. (2008). The establishment of the World Anti-Doping Agency: A study of the management and of organizational change and unplanned outcomes. *International Review for the Sociology of Sport, 43*, 227–249.

Hoberman, J. (2001). How drug testing fails: The politics of doping control. In W. Wilson and E. Derse (Eds.), *Doping in elite sport: The politics of drugs in the Olympic movement* (pp. 241–274). Champaign, IL: Human Kinetics.

Hoberman, J. (2005). *Testosterone dreams: Rejuvenation, aphrodisia, doping.* Berkeley: University of California Press.

Houlihan, B. (1997). *Sport, policy and politics: A comparative analysis.* London: Routledge.

Houlihan, B. (2002). *Dying to win* (2nd ed.). Strasbourg, France: Council of Europe.

Jackson, S.J. (1998a). Life in the (mediated) fast lane: Ben Johnson, national affect and the 1988 crisis of Canadian identity. *International Review for the Sociology of Sport, 33*, 227–238.

Jackson, S.J. (1998b). A twist of race: Ben Johnson and the Canadian crisis of racial and national identity. *Sociology of Sport Journal, 15*, 21–40.

Johnson, W.O. (1985, May 13). Steroids: A problem of huge dimensions. *Sports Illustrated*, pp. 38–61.

Johnson, W.O., and Moore, K. (1988, October 3). The loser. *Sports Illustrated*, pp. 20–26.

Kammerer, R.C. (2001). What is doping and how is it detected? In W. Wilson and E. Derse (Eds.) *Doping in elite sport: The politics of drugs in the Olympic movement* (pp. 3–28). Champaign, IL: Human Kinetics.

Karch, S.B. (2002). Amphetamines. In M.S. Bahrke and C.E. Yesalis (Ed.), *Performance-enhancing substances in sport and exercise* (pp. 257–265). Champaign, IL: Human Kinetics.

Kennamer, J.D. (1994). Public opinion, the press, and public policy: An introduction. In J.D. Kennamer (Ed.), *Public opinion, the press, and public policy* (pp. 1–17). Westport, CT: Praeger.

Kepner, T. (2009, February 10). Rodriguez, with an apology, says he used banned drugs. *New York Times*, p. A1.

Kochakian, C.D., and Yesalis, C.E. (2000). Anabolic-androgenic steroids: A historical perspective and definition. In C.E. Yesalis (Ed.), *Anabolic steroids in sport and exercise* (2nd ed.) (pp. 17–49). Champaign, IL: Human Kinetics.

Koller, D.L. (2006). Does the Constitution apply to the actions of the United States Anti-Doping Agency? *Saint Louis University Law Journal, 50*, 91–136.

Kornblut, A.E., and Wilson, D. (2005, April 17). Beyond BALCO—how one pill escaped the list of controlled substances. *New York Times*, p. 1.

Lang, G.E., and Lang, K. (1983). *The battle for public opinion: The president, the press, and the polls during Watergate*. New York: Columbia University Press.

Longman, J. (2008, July 23). Letter urges president not to give Jones pardon. *New York Times*, p. D1.

Mason, M.J. (1998). Drugs or dietary supplements: FDA's enforcement of DSHEA. *Journal of Public Policy and Marketing*, 17, 296–302.

Merriam, J.E. (1989). National media coverage of drug issues, 1983–1987. In P. Shoemaker (Ed.), *Communication campaigns about drugs* (pp. 21–28). Hillsdale, NJ: Erlbaum.

Mignon, P. (2003). The Tour de France and the doping issue. *International Journal of the History of Sport*, 20, 227–245.

Mitchell, G.J. (2007). Report to the commissioner of baseball of an independent investigation into the illegal use of steroids and other performance enhancing substances by players in Major League Baseball. Office of the Commissioner of Baseball, December 13.

Monaghan, L. (1999). Challenging medicine? Bodybuilding, drugs and risk. *Sociology of Health and Illness*, 21, 707–734.

Mottram, D.R. (2003). Prevalence of drug misuse in sport. In D.R. Mottram (Ed.), *Drugs in sport* (3rd ed.) (pp. 357–378). London: Routledge.

Pope, H.G. Jr., Kanayama, G., Ionescu-Pioggia, M., and Hudson, J. (2004). Anabolic steroid users' attitudes toward physicians. *Addiction*, 99, 1189–1194.

Pound, D. (2006). *Inside dope*. Mississauga, Canada: Wiley.

Pritchard, D. (1994). The news media and public policy agendas. In J.D. Kennamer (Ed.), *Public opinion, the press, and public policy* (pp. 103–112). Westport, CT: Praeger.

Reents, S. (2000). *Sport and exercise pharmacology*. Champaign, IL: Human Kinetics.

Sage, G.H. (1998). *Power and ideology in American sport*. Champaign, IL: Human Kinetics.

Schneider, A J. (2006). Cultural nuances: Doping, cycling and the Tour de France. *Sport in Society*, 9, 212–226.

Shaikin, B. (2009, February 8). A-Rod tied to steroids. *Los Angeles Times*, p. D1.

Simon, R.L. (2001). Good competition and drug-enhanced performance. In W.J. Morgan, K.V. Meier, and A.J. Schneider (Eds.), *Ethics in sport* (pp. 119–129). Champaign, IL: Human Kinetics.

Telander, R. (1989, February 20). The death of an athlete. *Sports Illustrated*, p. 68–78.

Thompson, T., and Vinton, N. (2008, October 30). Jones takes act to Oprah. *New York Daily News*, p. 79.

Todd, T. (1983, August 1). The steroid predicament. *Sports Illustrated*, pp. 62–77.

Todd, J., and Todd, T. (2001). Significant events in the history of drug testing and the Olympic Movement: 1960–1999. In W. Wilson and E. Derse (Eds.), *Doping in elite sport: The politics of drugs in the Olympic movement* (pp. 65–128). Champaign, IL: Human Kinetics.

United States General Accounting Office. (2001). *Health products for seniors: "Anti-aging" products pose potential for physical and economic harm*, GAO-01-1129, September. Washington, DC: United States General Accounting Office.

United States Government Accountability Office. (2005). *Anabolic steroids are easilypurchased without a prescription and present significant challenges to law enforcement officials*, GAO-06-243R, November. Washington, DC: United States Government Accountability Office.

Verducci, T. (2002, June 3). Totally juiced. *Sports Illustrated*, pp. 34–48.

Verroken, M. (2003). Drug use and abuse in sport. In D.R. Mottram (Ed.), *Drugs in sport* (3rd ed.) (pp. 29–62). London: Routledge.

Voy, R., and Deeter, K.D. (1991). *Drugs, sport, and politics*. Champaign, IL: Leisure Press.

Waddington, I. (2000). *Sport, health and drugs: A critical sociological perspective*. London: Taylor and Francis.

Wilson, J. (1994). *Playing by the rules: Sport, society, and the state*. Detroit: Wayne State University Press.

Yesalis, C.E. (2000). Introduction. In C.E. Yesalis (Ed.), *Anabolic steroids in sport and exercise* (2nd ed.) (pp. 1–13). Champaign, IL: Human Kinetics.

Yesalis, C.E., Courson, S.P., and Wright, J.E. (2000). History of anabolic steroid use in sport and exercise. In C.E. Yesalis (Ed.), *Anabolic steroids in sport and exercise* (2nd ed.) (pp. 51–71). Champaign, IL: Human Kinetics.

Yesalis, C.E., and Bahrke, M.S. (2002). History of doping in sport. In M.S. Bahrke and C.E. Yesalis (Eds.), *Performance-enhancing substances in sport and exercise* (pp. 1–20). Champaign, IL: Human Kinetics.

Young, J. (1981). The myth of drug takers in the mass media. In S. Cohen and J. Young (Eds.), *The manufacture of news* (pp. 326–334). Beverly Hills, CA: Sage.

Chapter 11

Andranovich, Greg, Burbank, Matthew J., and Heying, Charles H. (2001). Olympic cities: Lessons learned from mega-event politics. *Journal of Urban Affairs, 23*(2), 113–131.

Appadurai, Arjun. (1990). Disjuncture and difference in the global cultural economy. *Theory, Culture, and Society,* 7 (2), 295–310.Arbena, Joseph L. (2004). Mexico City 1968. In John H. Findling and Kimberly D. Pelle (Eds.) *Encyclopedia of the modern Olympic movement* (pp. 175–183). Westport, CT: Greenwood Press.

Atkinson, Michael, and Young, Kevin. (2004). Political violence, terrorism, and security at the Olympic Games. In Kevin Young and Kevin B. Wamsley (Eds.), *Research of the sociology of sport, Vol. 3, Global Olympics* (pp. 269–294). San Diego: Elsevier.

Baade, Robert A. (1996). Professional sports as catalysts for metropolitan economic development. *Journal of Urban Affairs,* 18 (1), 1–17.

Baim, Dean V. (1994). *The sports stadium as a municipal investment*. Westport, CT: Greenwood Press.

Barney, Robert K., Wenn, Stephen R., and Martyn, Scott G. (2002). *Selling the five rings: The International Olympic Committee and the rise of Olympic commercialism*. Salt Lake City: University of Utah Press.

Broudehoux, Anne-Marie. (2007). Delirious Beijing. In Mike Davis and Daniel Bertrand Monk (Eds.), *Evil paradises: Dreamworlds of neo-liberalism* (pp. 87–101). New York: New Press.

Burbank, Matthew J., Heying, Charles H., and Andranovich, Greg. (2000). Antigrowth politics or piecemeal resistance? Citizen opposition to Olympic-related economic growth. *Urban Affairs Review, 35*(3), 334–357.

Burbank, Matthew J., Andranovich, Greg, and Heying, Charles H. (2001). *Olympic dreams: The impact of mega-events on local politics*. Boulder, CO: Lynne Rienner.

Chu, Henry. (2008, October 18). Financial crisis dampens London's Olympic plans. *Los Angeles Times*. http://articles.latimes.com/2008/oct/18/world/fg-britolympics18.

Clark, Terry Nichols, Lloyd, Richard, Wong, Kenneth, and Jain, Pushpam. (2002). Amenities drive urban growth. *Journal of Urban Affairs, 24*(5), 493–515.

Dyreson, Mark. (1998). *Making the American team: Sport, culture, and the Olympic experience*. Urbana: University of Illinois Press.

Espy, Richard. (1979). *The politics of the Olympic Games*. Berkeley: University of California Press.

Essex, Stephen, and Chalkley, Brian. (1998). Olympic Games: Catalyst of urban change. *Leisure Studies, 17*(3), 17–26.

Essex, Stephen, and Chalkley, Brian. (2003). Urban transformation from hosting the Olympics (University lecture on the Olympics). Barcelona: Universitat Autonoma de Barcelona, Centre d'Estudis Olimpics. http://olympicstudies.uab.es/lectures/.

Guttmann, Allen. (1994). *Games and empires: Modern sports and cultural imperialism*. New York: Columbia University Press.

Hettne, Bjorn. (1995). Introduction: The international political economy of transformation. In Bjorn Hettne (Ed.), *International political economy: Understanding global disorder* (pp. 1–30). Atlantic Highlands, NJ: Zed Books.

Heying, Charles H., Burbank, Matthew J., and Andranovich, Greg. (2007). World class: Using the Olympics to shape and brand the American metropolis. In Melanie K. Smith (Ed.), *Tourism, culture and regeneration* (pp. 101–110). London: CAB International.

Hill, Christopher R. (1996). *Olympic politics* (2nd ed). Manchester, UK: Manchester University Press.

Houlihan, B. (2005). International politics and Olympic governance. In K.B. Wamsley and K. Young (Ed.) *Global Olympics: Historical and Sociological Studies of the Modern Games*. (pp. 127-142), Amsterdam: Elsevier.

IOC (International Olympic Committee). (2005). *Factsheet: Revenue generation and distribution. Update—December 2005*. Lausanne, Switzerland: IOC. http://multimedia.olympic.org/pdf/en_report_845.pdf.

IOC (International Olympic Committee). (2008). *IOC marketing media guide: Beijing 2008*. Lausanne, Switzerland: IOC. http://multimedia.olympic.org/pdf/en_report_1329.pdf.

Judd, Dennis, ed. (2003). *The infrastructure of play: Building the tourist city in North America*. Armonk, NY: Sharpe.

Kasimati, Evangelia. (2003). Economic aspects and the summer Olympics: A review of related research. *International Journal of Tourism Research*, 5 (6), 433–444.

Kidd, Bruce. (2005). "Another world is possible": Recapturing alternative Olympic histories, imagining different games. In Kevin Young and Kevin B. Wamsley (Eds.), *Research of the sociology of sport, Vol. 3, Global Olympics* (pp. 143–158). San Diego: Elsevier.

Larson, James F., and Park, Heung-soo. (1993). *Global television and the politics of the Seoul Olympics*. Boulder, CO: Westview.

Lenskyj, Helen Jefferson. (2000). *Inside the Olympic industry: Power, politics, and activism*. Albany: State University of New York Press.

Magdalinski, Tara, Schimmel, Kimberly S., and Chandler, Timothy J.L. (2005). Recapturing Olympic mystique: The corporate invasion of the classroom. In John Nauright and Kimberly S. Schimmel (Eds.), *The political economy of sport* (pp. 38–54). New York: Palgrave Macmillan.

Nixon, Howard L. (1988). The background, nature, and implications of the organization of the "capitalist Olympics." In Jeffrey O. Seagrave and Donald Chu (Eds.), *The Olympic Games in transition* (pp. 237–251). Champaign, IL: Human Kinetics.

Noll, Roger G., and Zimbalist, Andrew. (1997). The economic impact of sports teams and facilities. In Roger G. Noll and Andrew Zimbalist (Eds.), *Sports, jobs and taxes* (pp. 55–91). Washington, DC: Brookings Institution.

Polyani, Karl. (1957). *The great transformation*. New York: Penguin.

Pope, S.W. (1997). *Patriotic games: Sporting traditions in the American imagination, 1876–1926*. New York: Oxford University Press.

Preuss, Holger. (2000). *The economics of the Olympic games: Hosting the games 1972–2000*. Petersham, New South Wales, Australia: Walla Walla Press.

Preuss, Holger. (2002). Economic dimension of the Olympic Games (University lecture on the Olympics). Barcelona: Universitat Autonoma de Barcelona, Centre d'Estudis Olimpics. http://olympicstudies.uab.es/lectures/.

Ren, Xuefei. (2008). Architecture and nation building in the age of globalization: Construction of the national stadium of Beijing for the 2008 Olympics. *Journal of Urban Affairs*, 30 (2), 175–190.

Rosentraub, Mark S. (1999). *Major league losers: The real costs of sports and who's paying for it* (Rev. ed.) New York: Basic Books.

Roughton, Bert Jr. (1991, July 21). Atlanta Olympics update '91. *Atlanta Journal Constitution*, p. F3.

Schaffer, Kay, and Smith Sidonie (Eds.) (2000). *The Olympics at the millennium: Power, politics, and the Games*. New Brunswick, NJ: Rutgers University Press.

Schiller, Bill. (2008, August 19). China gets 77 protest applications, approves 0. *Toronto Star*, p. A3.

Scott, Allen J. (2006). Creative cities: Conceptual issues and policy questions. *Journal of Urban Affairs*, 28(1), 1-17.

Senn, Alfred E. (1999). *Power, politics, and the Olympic Games*. Champaign, IL: Human Kinetics.

Shoval, Noam. (2002). A new phase in the competition for the Olympic gold: The London and New York bids for the 2012 games. *Journal of Urban Affairs*, 24 (5), 583-599.

Smith, Melanie K. (2007). Towards a cultural planning approach to regeneration. In Melanie K. Smith (Ed.), *Tourism, culture and regeneration* (pp. 1-11). London: CAB International.

Strauss, Valerie. (2008, August 5). Preparing for the big show. *Washington Post*, p. C12.

Tomlinson, Alan. (2005). The commercialization of the Olympics: Cities, corporations, and the Olympic commodity. In Kevin Young and Kevin B. Wamsley (Eds.), *Research of the sociology of sport, Vol. 3, Global Olympics* (pp. 179-200). San Diego: Elsevier.

Travel Industry Association of America. (2006). *Travel and tourism works for America (the economic impact of travel on state and congressional districts)*. Washington, DC: Travel Industry Association of America.

Travel Industry Association of America. (2009). *U.S. Travel outlook research and trends from Dr. Suzanne Cook*, June. www.tia.org/pressmedia/Newsletters/Outlook.html.

United Nations World Tourism Organization. (2007). *World Tourism Barometer*, 5 (2), 1-48.www.unwto.org.

Wallerstein, Immanuel. (2005). *World-systems analysis: An introduction*. Durham, NC: Duke University Press.

Wilson, Wayne. (2004). Los Angeles 1984. In John H. Findling and Kimberly D. Pelle (Eds.), *Encyclopedia of the modern Olympic movement* (pp. 207-216). Westport, CT: Greenwood Press.

Witherspoon, Kevin B. (2008). *Before the eyes of the world: Mexico and the 1968 Olympic Games*. DeKalb: Northern Illinois University Press.

Yardley, Jim. (2007, December 29). Beijing's Olympic quest: Turn smoggy sky blue. *New York Times*, p. A1.

Zimmerman, Kevin. (2005, October 3). Global sports market to top $111 billion by 2009. *Hollywood Reporter*.

Zolov, Eric. (2004). Showcasing the "land of tomorrow": Mexico and the 1968 Olympics. *The Americas*, 61 (2), 159-188.

Chapter 12

Beaton, Rod. (2003, February 3). Cuban players cash in on mystique. *USA Today*, p. 8.

Breton, Marcos, and Villegas, Jose Luis. (1999). *Away games: The life and times of a Latin ball player*. New York: Simon and Schuster.

Carter, Thomas. (1999). The political fallacy of baseball diplomacy. *Peace Review*, 11(4).

Echeverria, Roberto Gonzalez. (1999). *The pride of Havana: A history of Cuban baseball*. New York: Oxford University Press.

Grassi, D. (2007, February 19). Major League Baseball profits from new change in immigration law. *California Chronicle*. www.californiachronicle.com/articles/view/20897 [May 26, 2009].

Guevera, Arturo J. Marcano, and Fidler, David P. (2002). *Stealing lives: The globalization of baseball and the tragic story of Alexi Quiroz*. Bloomington: Indiana University Press.

Guttman, Allen. (1994). *Games and empires: Modern sports and cultural imperialism*. New York: Columbia University Press.

Houlihan, Barrie. (1994). *Sport and international politics*. New York: Harvester Wheatsheaf.

Jamail, Milton H. (2000). *Full count: Inside Cuban baseball*. Carbondale: Southern Illinois University Press.

Klein, Alan M. (1991). *Sugarball: The American game, the Dominican dream*. New Haven, CT: Yale University Press.

Lapchick, R. (2008). *2008 gender and race report card: Major League Baseball*. University of Central Florida Web site: www.bus.ucf.edu/sport.

Major League Baseball (2006, April 5). *27.4 percent of Major League Baseball players born outside the U.S.* Press release.

Major League Baseball (2008, December 24). Pirates sign pair of Indian born players. Press release.

Major League Baseball (2009 April 6). *Opening day rosters feature 229 players born outside the U.S.* Press release.

Olney, B. (2007, January 25). Yankees seek working agreement with China baseball. *ESPN the Magazine*.

Pettavino, Paula, and Brenner, Philip. (1999). More than just a game. *Peace Review, 11*(4), 523–530.

Price, S.L. (2000). *Pitching around Fidel: A journey into the heart of Cuban sports*. New York: Harper Collins.

Ruck, Rob. (1999). *The tropic of baseball: Baseball in the Dominican Republic*. Lincoln: University of Nebraska Press.

Seigel, R. (2009, April 22). The long road home for a Cuban baseball legend. [Radio broadcast]. *All things considered*. Washington, DC: National Public Radio.

Svirsky, Salome Aguilera (Writer). (2000). Stealing home: The case of contemporary Cuban baseball [Video]. In R.A. Clift and S.A. Svirsky (Producers). New York: Dugout Productions.

Van Bottenburg, Maarten. (2001). *Global games*. Urbana: University of Illinois Press.

Wilkinson, Todd. (2000). America's favorite pastime goes global. *Christian Science Monitor, 92*(86), 1.

Chapter 13

Baseball in Latin America. (n.d.). *Encyclopedia Britannica*. www.britannica.com/eb/article-229950/baseball [July 29, 2007].

Bernstein, A. (2006, March 13). Competition pumps up MLB rights in Europe. *SportsBusiness Journal*, p. 5.

Biertempfel, R. (2007, July 15). Pirates keen to idea of taking games overseas. *Pittsburgh Tribune-Review*. www.pittsburghlive.com/x/pittsburghtrib/s_517378.html [July 22, 2007].

Bloom, B.M. (2006, March 21). *With Classic over, MLB looks ahead*. www.worldbaseballclassic.com/2006/news/article.jsp?ymd = 20060321&content_id = 1358067&vkey = wbc_news&fext = .jsp&sid = wbc [April 29, 2006].

Blum, R. (2005, December 16). Cuban decision gets discussion flowing. *USA Today*. www.usatoday.com/sports/baseball/2005-12-16-cuban-decision-reax_x.htm [July 29, 2007].

Brown, M. (2005, December 5). MBLAM: The stealthy money making machine. *Hardball Times*. www.hardballtimes.com/main/article/mlbam-the-stealthy-money-machine/ [April 30, 2006].

Cincinnati Reds. (n.d.). *Baseball almanac*. www.baseball-almanac.com/teams/reds.shtml [July 29, 2007].

Deford, F. (1999, April 7). It's never too late for wrestling. *Sports Illustrated*. http://sportsillustrated.cnn.com/inside_game/deford/990407/ [July 29, 2007].

Development initiatives. (n.d.). http://mlb.mlb.com/mlb/international/index.jsp?feature = development [July 27, 2007].

Echevarria, R.G. (1999). *The pride of Havana: A history of Cuban baseball*. New York: Oxford Press.

Edelman, M. (2005, December 26). A strike against diamond diplomacy. *SportBusiness Journal*, p. 30.

Edes, G. (2007, March 30). Rising influence. *Boston Globe*. www.boston.com/sports/baseball/articles/2007/03/30/rising_influence/?page = full [July 29, 2007].

Enders, E. (2000). *Timeline of international baseball, 1847–present*. www.ericenders.com/internationalbb.htm [October 20, 2007].

Eros, A. (2005, May 23). To reach Latinos, think beyond soccer. *SportsBusiness Journal*, p. 22.

Federal Baseball Club v. National League, 259 U.S. 200 (1922).

Fisher, E. (2006a, March 27). Classic produces comeback victory for commissioner. *SportsBusiness Journal*, p. 1.

Fisher, E. (2006b, March 27). Japan wants final, but doubts persist. *SportsBusiness Journal*, p. 62.

Fisher, E. (2008, October 6). MLB attendance ends strong, but no record. *SportsBusiness Journal*, p. 8.

Foer, F. (2004). *How soccer explains the world*. New York: Harper Collins.

Foster, G., Greyser, S.A., and Walsh, B. (2006). *The business of sports*. Mason, OH: Thompson Southwestern.

Friedman, T.L. (2000). *The Lexus and the olive tree*. New York: Anchor Books.

Friedman, T.L. (2005). *The world is flat*. New York: Farrar, Straus, and Giroux.

Goldman, T. (2005, July 8). *Olympics to cut baseball, softball from roster*. www.npr.org/templates/story/story.php?storyId = 4735891 [August 11, 2007].

Guevara, A.J., and Fidler, D.P. (2002). *Stealing lives: The Globalization of baseball and the tragic story of Alexis Quiroz*. Bloomington: Indiana University Press.

Harris, D. (1986). *The league*. New York: Bantam Books.

Historical moments. (n.d.). www.sportsecyclopedia.com/nl/mtlexpos/expos.html [August 3, 2007].

Horrow, R. (2005, July 8). *MLB business report: Halfway through 2005*. http://cbs.sportsline.com/general/story/8630563 [April 30, 2006].

King, B. (2006, March 13). Speaking their language. *SportsBusiness Journal*. www.sportsbusinessjournal.com/index.cfm?fuseaction = search.show_article&articleId = 49774&keyword = speaking,%20language [April 14, 2006].

Klein, A.M. (2006). *Growing the game: The globalization of baseball*. New Haven, CT: Yale University Press.

Lapointe, J. (1992, October 19). European influx challenges NHL's new world order *International Herald Tribune*. www.iht.com/articles/1992/10/19/hock_0.php [July 29, 2007].

Lefton, T. (2006, February 20). Classic rounding third toward a profit. *SportsBusiness Journal*, p. 3.

London calling. (2007, March 1). *Sports Illustrated*. http://sportsillustrated.cnn.com/2007/hockey/nhl/03/01/hkn.duck.kings/index.html [July 29, 2007].

Longley, N., and McKelvey, S. (2006, March 13). Venezuela holds lessons for MLB. *SportsBusiness Journal*, p. 24.

Major League Baseball International. (n.d.). http://mlb.mlb.com/mlb/international/index.jsp?feature = mlbi [July 26, 2007].

McGrath, J. (2006, March 5). World Baseball Classic? Not until it's in July. *News Tribune*. www.thenewstribune.com/sports/columnists/mcgrath/story/5567786p-5009783c.html [April 29, 2006].

Mickle, T. (2006, April 3). Finding the path to Hispanic fans. *SportsBusiness Journal*, p. 5.

Miller, J.E. (1990). *The baseball business*. Chapel Hill: University of North Carolina Press.

MLB Advanced Media and Reakosys sign wireless game publishing agreement in Korea. (2006, April 4). http://mlb.mlb.com/news/press_releases/press_release.jsp?ymd = 20060404&content_id = 1383276&vkey = pr_mlbcom&fext = .jsp&c_id = mlb [July 25, 2007].

MLB Advanced Media and Tasuke sign wireless game publishing agreement in Japan. (2006, July 31). http://mlb.mlb.com/news/press_releases/press_release.jsp?ymd = 20060731&content_id = 1585428&vkey = pr_mlbcom&fext = .jsp&c_id = mlb [August 7, 2007].

Moag & Company (2006, Fall). *Diamond note$.* www.moagandcompany.com/i_a/dn_2006_baseball.pdf [August 7, 2007].

NBA announces opening of office in London. (2007, July 10). www.nba.com/global/uk/nba_london_office_070516.html [July 29, 2007].

NBA international historic timeline. (n.d.). http://hoopedia.nba.com/index.php/NBA_International_Historic_Timeline [July 30, 2007].

Neilson Media Research (n.d.). *TV ratings.* www.nielsenmedia.com/nc/portal/site/Public/menuitem.55dc65b4a7d5adff3f65936147a062a0/?vgnextoid = 34953b318b906010VgnVCM100000880a260aRCRD [April 30, 2006].

Newman, M. (2007, July 29). *With records looming, baseball booming.* http://mlb.mlb.com/news/article.jsp?ymd = 20070729&content_id = 2116693&vkey = news_mlb&fext = .jsp&c_id = mlb [August 2, 2007].

NFL Europa closes. (n.d.). www.nfleurope.com/news/story/10243240 [July 29, 2007].

NFL to play regular season games outside the U.S. starting in 2007. (2006, October 24). *USA Today.* www.usatoday.com/sports/football/nfl/2006-10-24-international-games_x.htm [July 29, 2007].

No plans for Pirates to play in Puerto Rico in 2005. (2004, July 21). http://sports.espn.go.com/espn/wire?section = mlb&id = 1843575 [October 11, 2007].

Ortiz, J.L. (2007, December 5). MLB's advanced media arm pulls in profits. *USA Today.* www.usatoday.com/sports/baseball/2007-12-04-baseball-online_N.htm [April 22, 2009].

Paese, G. (2002, November 22). It's official: The Expos will play 20 games in San Juan in 2003. *Puerto Rico Herald.* www.puertorico-herald.org/issues/2002/vol6n47/PRSportsBeat0647-en.html [October 12, 2007].

Political hardball. (1999, March 26). *Sports Illustrated.* http://sportsillustrated.cnn.com/baseball/mlb/news/1999/03/25/cuba_package/ [August 12, 2007].

Posner, J. (2006, March 2). World Baseball Classic: Pool A. *San Diego Union Tribune.* www.signonsandiego.com/uniontrib/20060302/news_lz1s2poola.html [April 30, 2006].

Rains, R. (2001). *Baseball samurais.* New York: St. Martins.

Rojas, E. (2006, March 16). Cuba wants to host WBC, play more often. http://sports.espn.go.com/mlb/worldclassic2006/news/story?id = 2371083 [April 24, 2006].

Rovell, D. (2003, April 7). Baseball, not players, receive tax break from Puerto Rico. http://espn.go.com/mlb/s/2003/0407/1535207.html [July 27, 2008].

Schwarz, A. (2005, May 10). World Cup announcement made. *Baseball America Online.* http://sports.espn.go.com/mlb/news/story?id = 2057633 [July 29, 2007].

Seymour, H. (1971). *Baseball: The golden age.* New York: Oxford University Press.

Sponsorship roster announced for the inaugural World Baseball Classic. (2006, March 7) http://mlb.mlb.com/NASApp/mlb/news/press_releases/press_release.jsp?ymd = 20060307&content_id = 1338217&vkey = pr_mlb&fext = .jsp&c_id = mlb [April 29, 2006].

Szymanski, S., and Zimbalist, A. (2005). *National pastime: How Americans play baseball and the rest of the world plays soccer.* Washington, DC: Brookings Institute.

Treasury Department allows Cuba into WBC. (2006, January 23). http://sports.espn.go.com/mlb/worldclassic2006/news/story?id = 2299485 [August 12, 2007].

Turning the dream into reality. (n.d.). www.nfleurope.com/news/archive/15082000_histintro [July 29, 2007].

WBC silences its critics. (2006, March 27). *SportsBusiness Journal,* p. 58.

Weisman, L. (2004, July 21). Silver and black still tops in NFL merchandise sales. *USA Today.* www.usatoday.com/sports/football/nfl/2004-07-21-merchandising-sales_x.htm [July 28, 2007].

Wetzel, D. (2006, September 3). A question of mistrust. http://sports.yahoo.com/mlb/news?slug = dw-howard090306&prov = yhoo&type = lgns [August 11, 2007].

What are today's youth playing and watching? (2006, March 27). *SportsBusiness Journal*, p. 46.

Whiting, R. (1990). *You gotta have wa*. New York: Vintage Books.

Whiting, R. (2004). *The meaning of Ichiro*. New York: Warner Books.

Wilner, B. (2006, March 30). NFL may play preseason game in China. http://news.imagethief.com/blogs/china/archive/2006/03/30/6252.aspx [July 29, 2007].

World Baseball Classic FAQ. (2006). www.worldbaseballclassic.com/2006/about/index.jsp?sid = wbc [April 29, 2006].

Index

Note: The italicized *f* and *t* following page numbers refer to figures and tables, respectively.

About the Editors

Charles A. Santo, PhD, is assistant professor of city and regional planning at the University of Memphis in Tennessee. He also serves as coordinator of the Planning Innovations Technology Lab. In addition to having taught courses on sport and public policy, he has published many peer-reviewed articles on the relationship between sport, economic development, and urban public policy. He has been invited to share his research at regional, national, and international conferences. Dr. Santo is a member of the Urban Affairs Association. He earned a PhD in urban studies from Portland State University.

Gerard C. S. Mildner, PhD, has been at Portland State University since 1991. Currently he is associate professor of urban studies and planning and director of the Center for Real Estate. Dr. Mildner has written extensively about real estate and location within cities. He is the author of several book chapters, including one on baseball and basketball stadium ownership and franchise incentives to relocate. He is a member of the Urban Affairs Association. He earned his PhD in economics from New York University.

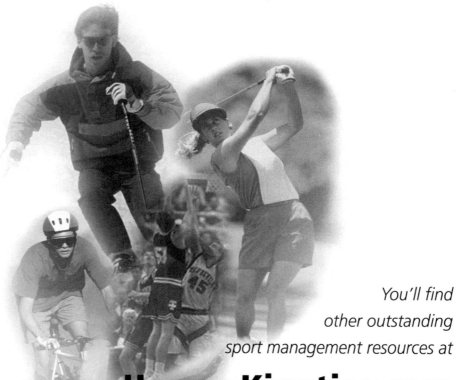